Protestant Identities

RELIGION, SOCIETY,
AND SELF-FASHIONING IN
POST-REFORMATION ENGLAND

EDITED BY
Muriel C. McClendon
Joseph P. Ward
Michael MacDonald

STANFORD UNIVERSITY PRESS
STANFORD, CALIFORNIA

Stanford University Press
Stanford, California
© 1999 by the Board of Trustees of the
Leland Stanford Junior University
Printed in the United States of America

CIP data appear at the end of the book

For Paul Seaver,
colleague, mentor, friend

Preface

The study of religious change in early modern England has undergone a significant transformation in the past quarter century. Thanks to "revisionist" historians, the ascent of Protestantism in Tudor England is no longer considered either broadly popular or inevitable, and the events of the 1640's are no longer viewed as signifying a "Puritan Revolution." Nonetheless, the generally declining status of what Eamon Duffy has called "traditional religion" had important implications for all facets of life in early modern England. This book contributes to our understanding of this development by looking at how early modern religious change provided English men and women with new challenges and new opportunities when constructing their identities and negotiating their relations with their society.

Paul Seaver's approaching retirement from full-time teaching at Stanford University provides an excellent opportunity for considerations of this topic, because his (to date) two monographs and many articles and book chapters have all contributed to our understanding of it. His first book, *The Puritan Lectureships: The Politics of Religious Dissent, 1560–1662*, offered the first full exploration of the motives and the ways of thinking of those lay Puritans who endowed lectureships to promote the preaching clergy during the century that followed the Elizabethan religious settlement. As institutions designed by laymen to make the Church of England better suited to meet their spiritual needs—as they defined them themselves—the lectureships inspired the enmity of leading churchmen, most notably of Archbishop Laud, who saw them as a direct challenge to their own authority. Seaver's second book, *Wallington's World: A Puritan Arti-*

san in Seventeenth-Century London, remains the most fully realized analysis of the work habits, domestic life, and personal religious experience of a godly layman from the lower ranks of early modern society. In turning from the collective body of the lecturers to this Eastcheap turner, he moved from the sermon-makers to their auditory, all the time succeeding in the biographer's most difficult task: to delineate the life history of a particular, unique individual without abstracting him from his social and historical ambience.

Like all those engaged in research into religion and society in early modern England, the contributors to this book owe Paul Seaver a great intellectual debt, among other things, and we hope that what follows will be some small payment toward it. The editors also wish to thank those who have eased their way in assembling this book. The contributors have been a joy to work with, as have Norris Pope, John Feneron, and Elaine Otto at Stanford University Press. Particular thanks go to Lori Anne Ferrell, Sue Grayzel, Michael Salman, Tom Tentler, Shauna Mulvihill, and Jan Fisk.

Joseph P. Ward with Wallace MacCaffrey

Contents

Contributors

ILANA KRAUSMAN BEN-AMOS is senior lecturer in the history department at Ben-Gurion University. She has published articles on apprenticeship in early modern England, and she is the author of *Adolescence and Youth in Early Modern England* (Yale University Press, 1994). She is currently engaged in research on informal support in early modern England.

DAVID R. COMO is a Schmidt instructor at the University of Chicago. He recently completed a Princeton University history dissertation entitled "Puritans and Heretics: The Emergence of an Antinomian Underground in Early Stuart England."

DAVID CRESSY is professor of history at Ohio State University. He was educated at Cambridge and made most of his career in California. He has published numerous books and articles on religion, culture, and society in early modern England, including *Birth, Marriage, and Death: Ritual, Religion, and the Life Cycle in Sixteenth- and Seventeenth-Century England* (Oxford University Press, 1997).

RICHARD L. GREAVES is the Robert O. Lawton Distinguished Professor of History at Florida State University. He has written or edited two dozen books, including *God's Other Children: Protestant Nonconformists and the Emergence of Denominational Churches in Ireland, 1660–1700* (Stanford University Press, 1997), and *Dublin's Merchant-Quaker: Anthony Sharp and the Community of Friends, 1643–1707* (Stanford University Press, 1998). A fellow of the Royal Historical Society, Dr. Greaves is past president of the American Society of Church History and the International John Bunyan Society.

BURKE W. GRIGGS is an assistant professor of history at Boston College. He is completing his first book, a study of how the memory of rebellion and civil war transformed British political argument and denominational conflict during the later seventeenth century.

FELICITY HEAL is fellow and tutor in modern history at Jesus College, Oxford. Her areas of research interest are the British Reformation, sixteenth-century social history, and the English gentry. She has published several books and numerous articles, including *Of Prelates and Princes* (Cambridge University Press, 1980), *Princes and Paupers in the English Church, 1500–1800* (Barnes and Noble Books, 1981), *Hospitality in Early Modern England* (Oxford University Press, 1990), and, with Clive Holmes, *The Gentry in England and Wales, 1500–1700* (Stanford University Press, 1994).

THOMAS R. HOLIEN was a fellow in the Lilly Fellows Program in the Humanities and the Arts at Valparaiso University from 1993 to 1995. From 1995 to 1998, he taught in Valaparaiso's history department and freshman seminar program.

CLIVE HOLMES taught at Cornell University for many years and is now fellow and tutor in modern history at Lady Margaret Hall, Oxford. His interests focus on the legal, administrative, and social history of early modern England. He is the author of many articles and three books: *The Eastern Association in the English Civil War* (Cambridge University Press, 1974), *Seventeenth-Century Lincolnshire* (Society for Lincolnshire History and Archaeology, 1980), and, with Felicity Heal, *The Gentry in England and Wales, 1500–1700* (Stanford University Press, 1994).

MURIEL C. MCCLENDON is assistant professor of history at the University of California, Los Angeles. She has published articles on urban culture and religion in early modern England and is the author of *The Quiet Reformation: Magistrates and the Emergence of Protestantism in Tudor Norwich* (Stanford University Press, 1999).

J. SEARS MCGEE is professor of history at the University of California, Santa Barbara. He edited volume 3 of the *Miscellaneous Works of John Bunyan* (Oxford University Press, 1987), and he is studying lay piety and politics in early Stuart Britain.

ROBERT B. SHOEMAKER is a senior lecturer in the history department at the University of Sheffield. He is the author of *Prosecution and Punish-*

ment: Petty Crime and the Law in London and Rural Middlesex, c. 1660–1725 (Cambridge University Press, 1991) and *Gender in English Society, 1650–1850: The Emergence of Separate Spheres?* (Longman, 1998). He is currently working on a study of public conflict in eighteenth-century London.

JOHN SMAIL is associate professor of history at the University of North Carolina, Charlotte. He is the author of *Merchants, Markets, and Manufacture: The English Wool Textile Industry in the Eighteenth Century* (St. Martin's Press, 1999). "The Sources of Innovation in the Eighteenth-Century Yorkshire Woolen Industry" appeared this year in *Business History*. He is currently working on an edition of eighteenth-century business letters for the Yorkshire Archaeological Society. His previous publications include *The Origins of Middle-Class Culture: Halifax, Yorkshire, 1660–1780* (Cornell University Press, 1994).

KATHARINE W. SWETT has taught British and European history at Santa Clara University and The Ohio State University, and she has published articles on widowhood and friendship for the north Welsh gentry. She is currently working on a book about gender, patriarchy, and family relations among the Wynns of Gwydir.

JOSEPH P. WARD teaches history at the University of Mississippi. He is the author of *Metropolitan Communities: Trade Guilds, Identity, and Change in Early Modern London* (Stanford University Press, 1997) and coeditor, with Gerald MacLean and Donna Landry, of *The Country and the City Revisited: England and the Politics of Culture, 1550–1850* (Cambridge University Press, 1999).

PROTESTANT IDENTITIES

MURIEL C. MCCLENDON

AND JOSEPH P. WARD

Introduction

RELIGION, SOCIETY, AND SELF-FASHIONING

IN POST-REFORMATION ENGLAND

... that to force men, against their mind and judgement, to believe what other men conclude to be true would prove such tyranny as the wicked Procrustes (mentioned by Plutarch) practised, who would fit all men to one bed by stretching them out that were too short, and by cutting them shorter that were too long.

—William Walwyn, *The Compassionate Samaritane* (1644)

A gross error it is to think that regal power ought to serve for the good of the body and not of the soul, for men's temporal peace and not their eternal safety; as if God had ordained kings for no other end and purpose but only to fat up men like hogs, and to see that they have their mash?

—Richard Hooker, *Of the Lawes of Ecclesiasticall Politie: The Sixth and Eighth Books* (1648)

The current direction of research on the English Reformation was set by the major works of Christopher Haigh and Eamon Duffy that appeared in the early 1990's. Duffy's *Stripping of the Altars* and Haigh's *English Reformations* together marked the culmination of a revisionist project begun nearly two decades earlier whose aim was first to challenge, and then to demolish utterly, the previously accepted notion that Protestantism was popularly embraced shortly after its appearance in England.[1] Now, thanks to Duffy, the vitality of late medieval English Christianity is understood as giving it considerable resistance to the theological and cultural objectives of the Reformation, a resistance plainly visible in the popular support for

Queen Mary's restoration of the Church of Rome to its former primacy. As a result, Protestantism achieved wide—but not necessarily enthusiastic—acceptance only during the reign of Queen Elizabeth and then almost entirely as the result of concerted efforts from the central government to remove from its subjects' view all remnants of their "traditional religion" and to wrench their gaze in a new direction. This model of religious change in sixteenth-century England is endorsed by Haigh, who stresses the plural "Reformations" to distinguish between a mainly successful legislative Reformation intended to dismantle Catholic practices and a largely unsuccessful Protestant Reformation aimed at converting the laity to a new faith. He ends his survey with this observation: "While politicians were having their hesitant Reformations, while Protestants were preaching their evangelical reform, parish congregations went to church: they prayed again to their God, learned again how to be good, and went off home once more. That was how it had been in 1530; that was how it was in 1590. Some Reformations."[2]

Having accomplished its goal of establishing a new understanding of the causes and consequences of the English Reformation, revisionism is now a spent force. Its chief legacy is a view of sixteenth-century England in which Protestants may be seen to have played a largely negative role. The present challenge for researchers in this field is to move beyond the characterization of the English Reformation to an assessment of its legacy of increasing religious diversification. This book approaches the subject of religious change in post-Reformation England from a postrevisionist perspective by observing that despite Mary's resolve to restore Catholicism in England, her father's break with Rome and the implementation of a Protestant agenda during her brother's reign had a lasting effect on the laity's beliefs and practices. If, as Duffy has shown, late medieval Christianity provided the laity with a wide array of means with which to internalize and individualize their religious experiences, then surely the events of the early 1530's to the early 1550's served only to expand vastly the field over which the religiosity of English men and women could range. This book addresses the unfolding consequences of this theological variegation—of the English Reformation—over the subsequent century and a half for the place of religion in the lives of individuals and localities. The purpose is to explore the complex ways in which the religious innovations of the mid-sixteenth century presented English men and women with new ways in which to fashion their own identities and to define their relationships with society.[3]

THE REFORMATION WAS the most disruptive development in European history since the Black Death. While late medieval religion had never been monolithic or static, the Reformation completely transformed the religious landscape by destroying whatever unity European Christians had shared. In permanently fragmenting Christendom, the Reformation also occasioned long periods, and a number of dramatic episodes, of religious violence and intolerance that remain well known. In the Holy Roman Empire, Luther's call for Christian freedom became entangled with social grievances that exploded in the bloody Peasants' War of 1525. Religious violence erupted there again in 1547 when Imperial armies routed the forces of the Schmalkaldic League, a Lutheran defensive alliance. France was also a scene of sectarian upheavals, particularly in the late sixteenth century. The most dramatic incident during those struggles, collectively remembered as the Wars of Religion, was undoubtedly the 1572 St. Bartholomew's Day massacre, when thousands of Protestants throughout France were slaughtered. France's Wars of Religion ended with the 1598 Edict of Nantes, which offered limited freedom of worship to the country's Protestant minority. In England, the Reformation was no less disruptive than it was on the Continent, especially as official religious policy fluctuated with the inclinations of the monarch. The Tudors and the early Stuarts pursued an ideal of doctrinal unity among their subjects, but religious homogeneity remained elusive.

Henry VIII's 1534 rejection of papal authority, his government's subsequent dissolution of the monasteries, abrogation of traditional holy days, and promulgation of the Lutheran-influenced Ten Articles of 1536 provoked hostility among those in England who preferred traditional forms of worship. But they also encouraged others to call for and engage in even more sweeping changes. Some of the officially sanctioned alterations to religion proved to have consequences that were both unexpected and unsettling. For example, the aim of the 1538 Injunction that placed a vernacular Bible in every parish church was to allow all Christians to read or hear "the very lively word of God," while avoiding "all contention and altercation therein" and referring "the explanation of obscure places to men of higher judgement in Scripture."[4]

Yet this was not always as simple a matter as it sounded. Reformation historians remember the tale of William Maldon, a young man from Chelmsford, Essex. Repeatedly prohibited by his father from hearing the Bible read in English in the local parish church, young Maldon resolved to learn to read in order to have access to Scripture on his own. In doing so, he came to reject the traditional reverence of the crucifix as idolatry. Maldon's mother was horrified, and his father became so enraged that he nearly killed his son (according to William's narrative written many years later), demanding, "Serra, who is your scholmaster? tell me." It was undoubtedly scenes such as this one that led to the passage of the 1543 Act for the Advancement of True Religion, which sought to restrict access to the Bible on the basis of social status.[5] Yet attempts to stem the course of religious reform and innovation, which were also represented by the draconian Six Articles of 1539, were not completely successful. The execution of Anne Askew for heretical views on the Sacrament and the arrest of hundreds of others demonstrated to all observers that the course of religious reform and innovation would be difficult to check.[6]

If the approval and later condemnation of particular doctrines and practices by Henry VIII's regime caused uncertainty and confusion about the theology of the Church of England, the government of his successor, Edward VI, opened the floodgates of Protestant reform. The young king's short-lived government replaced many traditional doctrines and practices with unmistakably Protestant ones. His first Parliament suppressed chantries, guilds, and other intercessory institutions at whose foundation lay the doctrine of purgatory. Edward's government also banned a number of practices in religious services, such as the use of ashes and holy water; it permitted the marriage of priests; and it passed two Acts of Uniformity in 1549 and 1552, which sanctioned and enjoined Protestant forms of worship.

Those innovations were enthusiastically embraced by some, such as the cleric Thomas Hancock, whose Protestant preaching tour of southwestern England in the late 1540's is well known.[7] A few Protestant enthusiasts also found places on the episcopal bench after resignations and ejections created vacancies. The most vigorous of the new bishops was undoubtedly John Hooper of Gloucester. Hooper energetically policed his diocese from his arrival in 1551 to root out opinions and practices among clergy and laity that were no longer considered orthodox, leaving behind perhaps the most detailed set of visitation articles composed in the sixteenth century.[8] Among England's laity, support for Edwardian Protestantism was greatest in some of the larger towns, including London, Norwich, Bristol, and Coventry.[9]

As familiar to historians as Hancock's sojourn and Hooper's visitation is the vehement distaste for the Edwardian changes dutifully recorded by the Yorkshire priest Robert Parkyn. Parkyn railed against, among other changes, the abrogation of customary ceremonies, the abolition of the Mass, and the marriage of priests. Nevertheless, he conformed sufficiently (though quite unhappily) to the Edwardian Settlement that he was able to retain his living long enough to welcome the restoration of Catholicism under Queen Mary and beyond.[10]

Parkyn's dislike of Edwardian Protestantism undoubtedly reflected the sentiments of the majority of the English population in the late 1540's and early 1550's. Efforts to reeducate the inhabitants of Gloucester diocese were not as successful as Bishop Hooper had wanted. Thomas Hancock was repeatedly subjected to harassment by the laity during his sermons.[11] And there were other more dramatic demonstrations around England against the new religion during Edward's reign, most notably the Western Rising of 1549. Opposition to the new Prayer Book in Devon and Cornwall developed into full-scale revolt during the summer of that year, with rebels laying siege to the city of Exeter. The uprising was eventually suppressed by a royal force, led by Lord Russell, which left an estimated 4,000 rebels dead. The Western Rising exposed a profound antagonism toward Protestantism in the west and also serious divisions in local society.[12]

Those who demonstrated against the Edwardian Prayer Book, as well as others who abused Hancock and rejected his Protestant message, and their like-minded traditionalists around England all rejoiced when the Catholic Mary Tudor ascended the throne in 1553. Even before her government had a chance to repeal the legislation of her two predecessors and restore the Roman Communion, the old liturgy was celebrated again in many parishes around the country from the first months of her reign.[13] Mary also married Philip II of Spain, believing that progeny of their alliance would secure England's future as a Catholic country.

Nevertheless, the queen's plans for a full and complete Catholic restoration were derailed, in part, by the dramatic refusal of nearly 300 men and women to conform and their subsequent executions. Although Protestants (whether they were among those executed for heresy or those who practiced their faith in secret conventicles) certainly did not form a majority in Marian England, the burnings revealed them to be a force not easily eradicated. If the Reformation was not complete in the 1550's, neither could it be easily or quickly checked. Thus, despite the best efforts of the queen, her councillors, and her Church, England remained a more theologically heterogeneous country than it had been prior to the break with Rome.

Confessional divisions were a source of concern to Mary's successor, Elizabeth, although the new queen sought to establish Protestant uniformity. In 1559, her government created a Protestant church for England, but one that was meant to encompass the broadest possible constituency. It has become a cliché to note that the Elizabethan Settlement actually settled very little and that the queen spent the rest of her reign defending the Church from numerous detractors. Religious traditionalists did not quickly embrace the Church and by the 1570's and 1580's, the government was increasingly worried about the influx of Catholic priests and about Catholic plots to depose the queen. However, Catholic opposition eventually dissipated, as there proved to be too little to sustain it in England. By the defeat of the Spanish Armada in 1588, the remaining Catholics (chiefly aristocrats and gentry) showed themselves to be politically loyal to the queen, even if they would not espouse her religion.

Religious diversity in the Elizabethan era was not solely a function of Catholic resistance to the Church of England. As the queen found, not all Protestants wished to conform to the Church's practices either. From the 1560's, there was pressure for further Protestant reform from those who were derided as "Puritans." Most made their calls for change from within the Church, but a few took the step of separating themselves from it completely. Under Archbishop Whitgift, the queen instigated a crackdown on Puritans in the 1590's, and some separatists were even executed in the fray. Nevertheless, by the end of the century it was clear that Puritans, like Catholics, would be a permanent feature of religious life in England. Upon Elizabeth's death in 1603, both groups looked forward to the arrival of the new king, James Stuart, from whom they hoped to receive warmer consideration and greater tolerance.[14]

Their hopes remained unfulfilled by James, who embraced the Elizabethan church structure with its emphasis on obedience to ecclesiastical law. At the Hampton Court conference of 1604, James indicated his un-willingness to implement Puritan plans for further Church reforms. He consented to only a single Puritan petition—the request for a new transla-tion of the Bible—and that took a further seven years to complete. During the remainder of James's reign, Puritans were troubled by his emphasis on his patriarchal authority in Church and state, his promotion of ceremoni-alist bishops, and his interest in maintaining diplomatic ties with conti-nental Catholic powers. These policies provoked increasing criticism from preachers like Richard Seldon, who offered his London audience in 1622 a thinly veiled warning about the drift of the Church of England toward a reunion with Rome.[15]

To Protestant observers, conformist and Puritan alike, the policies of James's son and successor, Charles I, seemed to make the reunion all the more likely. Charles's marriage to the French Catholic princess Henrietta Maria in 1625 raised doubts about his personal religious feelings, and these were soon exacerbated by the actions of the Arminian William Laud, whom Charles elevated to bishop of London in 1628 and to archbishop of Canterbury in 1633. Church policy during the 1630's, including the reis-suing of the Jacobean Book of Sports, which offended the Puritans' rever-ence for the Sabbath, the imposition of a new Prayer Book for Scotland, and the brutal repression of preachers who decried the growing Arminian direction of the church, reflected a hierarchy with no patience for criticism or dissent. Although some measures—such as the rejuvenation of cere-mony and the validation of Sunday recreations—enjoyed support from many of the clergy and laity, the controversies swirling around the church contributed to the mistrust that Charles faced when he sought Parlia-ment's assistance in 1640 in suppressing the rebellion that the new Prayer Book sparked in Scotland. Anxieties over supposed Catholic plots to overturn English Protestantism reached their zenith in the subsequent dis-pute over the appointment of officers to the army to repress the rebellion in Ireland in 1641. That was the atmosphere in which the nation drifted toward civil war.[16]

Although religious controversy contributed to the crisis of the early 1640's, many of the "godly" who had hoped Charles could be convinced to purify the Church of England also decried the violence and disregard for authority that resulted from the war and revolution. As the war progressed, Parliamentary leadership increasingly rested in the hands of those who sought sweeping reform of the church structure, notably Presbyterians who favored adherence to a strict national church and Independents who championed broad toleration for gathered congregations. With Parliament's military victory and the revolution that followed, religious uniformity was swiftly brushed aside, with the Church hierarchy abolished and attendance of established church services no longer required by law. Recent studies of local reactions to these national events in places as varied as London and Dorchester indicate that those who had been critical of Charles's religious policies often deplored the slide toward religious anarchy that became evident in the proliferation of sects such as Fifth Monarchists, Muggletonians, Ranters, Baptists, and Quakers during the Interregnum.[17]

The Church of England regained its prominent role upon the restoration of the Stuart monarchy in 1660, but this by no means signaled the end of theological diversity. The series of legislative acts that returned the Church of England to its central place in national religion and politics—the Corporation Act, the Quaker Act, the Act of Uniformity, the Conventicles Act, and the Five Mile Act—may have marginalized all Protestant Nonconformists, including the more moderately disposed, like the Presbyterians, but it hardly eliminated them. The crises of the 1640's and 1650's left an indelible mark upon the attitudes of many leading churchmen, encouraging prominent figures, including some bishops, to embrace the philosophy that has come to be known as "Latitudinarianism," an outlook that held it possible to include all but the most radical Protestants within the Church. Their broad-mindedness was tested, however, by Charles II's efforts to tolerate Nonconformists as part of his attempt to bolster Catholics. Once again, it appeared to a wide range of observers that the Church of England was threatened from within more powerfully than from without. The political divisions that began in the late 1670's with rumors of Catholic plots reminiscent of those of the early 1640's led to the attempt to exclude the Catholic duke of York from following his brother to the throne and culminated in the Glorious Revolution, which secured a Protestant succession.[18]

The subsequent Toleration Act offered Protestant Nonconformists limited relief from the more burdensome aspects of the Restoration legislation while securing a monopoly on political and ecclesiastical power for Anglicans. Four years after Louis XIV revoked the Edict of Nantes, thereby outlawing all forms of Protestantism in France, William and Mary moved England in the other direction by acknowledging the futility of pursuing rigid religious uniformity in an officially Protestant country. The number of Nonconformists would remain small—perhaps less than 6 percent of the population in the early eighteenth century—but their value as a continued bulwark against Catholicism revealed the ongoing anxiety that Catholicism could provoke among the English elite more than a century and a half after the Henrician Reformation.[19]

THE STUDY OF the English Reformation and its legacy have posed special problems for historians, as Christopher Haigh pointed out more than two decades ago. At a 1978 conference on the social history of the English and German Reformations, Haigh noted that historians of Germany could speak with a precision about specific changes, events, and social groups that was not possible for historians of the English Reformation. There were no Imperial free cities, no Martin Luther, and no Peasants' War in England. Even the role of the English monarchy in the Reformation was not straightforward. Haigh's book *Reformation and Resistance in Tudor Lancashire* had shown that there was considerable opposition to the government-imposed Reformation in that remote area of England from its earliest days under Henry VIII well into the reign of Elizabeth. For Haigh, then, the English Reformation "was not a single event but a long and complex process" that could be said to have been completed minimally between 1529 and 1559 but for which a good maximum case for completion "could be made for the years 1378 to 1660."[20]

Haigh has, of course, since gone on to become one of the leading voices of the "revisionist" historians of the English Reformation. The revisionists have challenged older interpretations of a speedy and fairly popular Reformation in England by exposing and highlighting the attachment that many men and women felt for the traditional Church and their reluctance to abandon its doctrine and worship. They have also shown the lengths to which ordinary people went to defend the worship and practices of the Catholic Church and their intransigence in accepting new Protestant doctrines and customs.[21]

While revisionists such as Haigh have enhanced our understanding of the Reformation by highlighting the lingering and substantial resistance to religious change, their interpretive scheme has left several questions unanswered. Virtually all early modern historians now accept a "slow" Reformation in England, yet periodization remains an issue. Little if any recent research claims the ascension of Elizabeth as the Reformation's end. Some scholars have concluded their studies in the 1580's, while Patrick Collinson has argued that the early Stuart years should be considered a part of the Reformation era. A recent collection of essays has suggested that the repercussions of religious change, "England's Long Reformation," were visible in English society well into the eighteenth century.[22] This lack of consensus about a terminal point for the English Reformation has rightly led one scholar to ask, "How slow is slow?" and when do inquiries into the Reformation's legacy become inextricably entangled in other issues such as the causes of the Civil War?[23] In addition to raising lingering questions about periodization, revisionist historians of the Reformation have proved less successful in differentiating among the groups and communities in English society who opposed religious innovation and those who embraced it. And their stress on continuity has caused them to devote less attention to the impact of Protestantism, let alone any variation in the meaning(s) of Catholic practice.

If questions about the beginning and the end of the Reformation cannot be answered with any certainty, it is clear that the fragmentation of Christian unity had significant consequences in England. The revisionists are surely right in their assertion that, in the words of Patrick Collinson, "it is only with the 1570's that the historically minded insomniac goes to sleep counting Catholics rather than Protestants," but it must also be said that the effects of the Reformation were manifest long before that time.[24] Even though it was Elizabeth's Protestant Church which finally gained broad support among the English people, the queen did not begin the process of Protestantization afresh upon her ascension to the throne. Mary attempted to quench the flames of Protestantism, but the embers still smoldered and reignited during the second half of her reign.

As unpopular as Protestantism and the Reformation may have been among the majority of English men and women before Elizabeth's ascension and even afterwards, they nevertheless had significant religious, social, cultural, and political effects that cannot be overlooked. In this vein, recent scholarly attention has focused on assessing the impact and legacy of the Reformation, keeping in mind the important contributions made by the revisionists while attending to other possible outcomes of religious change.

Several historians have shown that, despite the laity's reluctance to embrace Protestant reform fully, the result of the Reformation was not simply a confrontation between the mutually exclusive camps of Protestants and Catholics.

Judith Maltby's recent study has focused on one response to religious change—sincere conformity to the Elizabethan and early Stuart Church—that has received little recent notice from historians. Maltby has uncovered a significant portion of England's population for whom worship according to the Prayer Book was not the least of several evils or the path of least resistance but a matter of firm conviction. Many actively defended the Prayer Book, complaining to bishops in instances when local clergymen failed to use it properly. This was the course of action adopted by parishioners in Manchester who, in 1604, complained to the bishop of Chester that curate Ralph Kirk had declared that the Prayer Book "was no scripture."[25] Some parishioners had the wherewithal to take complaints about misuse of the Prayer Book to the consistory court. Genuine attachment to the Church of England was not to be found only in complaints lodged with ecclesiastical officials. Maltby has found lay demonstrations of support for conforming clergymen as well as petitions from laypeople expressly defending the worship and liturgy found in the Prayer Book.[26]

Of course, the appearance of conformity could provide a cover for a range of attitudes. Tessa Watt's study of "cheap print"—single-sheet broadsides—has identified and traced the formation of a hybrid religious culture in the century after the Reformation began. Broadside ballads set to popular tunes were given new godly lyrics, and they enjoyed a considerable commercial success in the later sixteenth and seventeenth centuries. Traditional images of Christ and of biblical texts resurfaced, now accompanied by Protestant texts. As Watt concludes, "old and new beliefs rubbed elbows without apparent sense of contradiction."[27] Similarly, Caroline Litzenberger's research has revealed complex and diverse responses to religious change among the laity of Gloucestershire. She has highlighted the different paths taken by two parishes—St. Mary, Tewkesbury, and St. Michael, Gloucester—which at first glance appear to share many features. With only a few exceptions, St. Michael's complied promptly with the dictates of successive Tudor religious regimes. By contrast, the parishioners of St. Mary's balked at conforming with Elizabethan religious policies until pressured to do so. Litzenberger argues that the nature of parish leadership accounts for this apparent dichotomy. At

St. Michael's, a unified parish elite presented a public image of conformity to the rest of the city and to diocesan authorities, thereby masking any heterodox opinions among the laity, while divisions among St. Mary's leaders interfered with the timely adoption of Elizabethan mandates.[28]

These and other studies reflect a growing recognition among scholars that the Reformation was not simply a platform tendered by England's political and religious elites to lay men and women who either accepted or rejected it out of hand.[29] The course of religious change was complex, uneven, and unpredictable, transforming even the face of traditional religion in the process. This book continues this broader examination of the results of the Reformation. While not denying the discord that accompanied religious change, the chapters that follow show that the disintegration of religious unity in England also created new opportunities for individuals from every stratum of English society to pick and choose, in new ways, the degree to which religion would influence their identities. The long, drawn-out process of religious change during the sixteenth and seventeenth centuries gave individuals new theological tools with which to forge identities for themselves. It offered them a broader range of choices in ordering their relationships not only with God but also with their neighbors, family, colleagues, and friends. Drawing on Stephen Greenblatt's observation that there was in sixteenth-century England "an increased self-consciousness about the fashioning of human identity as a manipulable, artful process," Margo Todd demonstrated how the Puritan Samuel Ward fashioned his own religious identity out of the choices available to him in the late sixteenth and early seventeenth centuries.[30] This volume utilizes Greenblatt's and Todd's insight in analyzing the ways in which the English people incorporated early modern religious change into their self-perceptions, a process that might usefully be considered "Reformation self-fashioning." At its most essential level, such self-fashioning was an individual phenomenon, but at all times the ability of individuals to adapt themselves to the religious changes and controversies of the period was influenced by their particular social circumstances. Therefore, the analysis of the consequences of the English Reformation requires the investigation of a broad array of individuals and localities over an extensive period, a task that is best suited to a collection of monographic studies such as this.

In seeking to capture the wide variety of responses to religious change in post-Reformation England, this book's argument proceeds in three stages. The first analyzes how some individuals interpreted Protestant messages in ways that led them to reject conformity to the dominant codes of behavior in society. David Cressy examines the passions that could be unleashed by "a deeply divided discourse" and channeled in the form of violent symbolic actions, such as the public burning by Chester city officials of five empty picture frames that had held portraits of William Prynne in 1637. Violent death was the consequence for Nicholas Sheterden, the subject of Thomas Holien's chapter, for his defiance of the Marian regime's demand that English subjects worship according to the rites of Rome. Even as Sheterden lingered in prison under sentence of execution for heresy, his fervent attachment to Protestantism compelled him to make one final attempt to persuade his mother to abandon the Roman Catholic Church. Finally, David Como's study of the radical Puritan John Traske explores the life and thought of an early Stuart cleric whose religious beliefs, like those of Nicholas Sheterden, stood outside the mainstream. In examining Traske's highly unconventional thought, Como shows how he serves as an important link between the sober, moderate Puritanism of the pre–Civil War era and the colorful radicalism of the 1640's and 1650's. In doing so, Como reminds us that "the genesis of Puritan radicalism should probably be viewed as a development that took place within the godly community itself."

The second stage of the argument turns to the limited appeal of such intense responses to Protestantism. J. Sears McGee examines the life of an individual whose access to various ideas allowed him to construct an elaborate and idiosyncratic religious self. Sir Richard Berkeley was a well-educated and politically ambitious Elizabethan country gentleman, knighted by the queen during a 1574 progress. Berkeley's writings, an "odd and interesting" book entitled *A Discourse on the Felicitie of Man, or His Summum Bonum*, reveal him to have been a tepid but orthodox Protestant whose beliefs were also laced with a popular pre-Reformation outlook that approached Manicheanism. Another unconventional figure is the subject of Felicity Heal and Clive Holmes's study of Lady Jane Bacon, a woman who inverted a number of cultural conventions during her lifetime and left permanent expression of her attitudes and beliefs in the shape of the elaborate and highly unusual tomb she designed for herself. Lady Bacon's proper Protestant pedigree and later close relationship to the godly minister Elnathan Parr did not prevent her from drawing upon Madonna-like images for her tomb.

The final three chapters in this section point to the limits to which godliness as social reform proved contagious. Ilana Krausman Ben-Amos explores the superficial impact of calls for godly reform by revealing that there was little popular regard given to the well-known Puritan attacks on the disorderly poor. Instead, she demonstrates the great lengths to which early modern men and women offered friendly encouragement to a wide range of people forced to wander the English countryside. Joseph Ward shows the restricted success that London-based benefactors had in bringing enlightenment to the "dark corners of the land." By analyzing the management of provincial schools entrusted to the care of London trade guilds during the sixteenth and seventeenth centuries, he demonstrates the many obstacles facing Londoners who hoped to reform provincial society and culture to fit their image of godliness. Burke Griggs focuses on the efforts of the early eighteenth-century Anglican minister John Walker to challenge a popular account of the sufferings of Dissenting clergymen ejected from their livings in 1662 compiled by the Presbyterian Edmund Calamy. Walker penned his own empirically based narrative of Anglican afflictions endured during the Civil War, which he hoped would challenge Calamy's martyrologically inspired history.

The book's final section argues for the importance of social dynamics within localities for understanding why the expanding range of religious identities in post-Reformation England did not lead to generalized upheaval. Although the English were by no means indifferent to religion, it was hardly all-compassing or totalizing for their lives. Muriel McClendon argues that, contrary to expectations, Norwich magistrates resisted the "culture of persecution" radiating from Marian London. Like McClendon, Richard Greaves is concerned to reveal the limited enthusiasm at the local level for religious persecution, but in his chapter the focus is on the de facto toleration of Quakers in Ireland, many of whom were either English or of English descent, in the period between the Stuart Restoration and the Glorious Revolution. John Smail's chapter argues that the ideas of Oliver Heywood, a Presbyterian minister in Halifax, Yorkshire, demonstrate how the fluidity of early modern religious identities impinged on the emerging political labels of "Whig" and "Tory." Katharine Swett then analyzes theological diversity in London by investigating the limited spiritual unity among Welsh migrants, something that set them apart from the other prominent ethnic subgroups in the metropolis. Robert Shoemaker displays the divergence between discourse and practice in London gender roles in the Restoration period, suggesting that it stemmed from efforts by the godly to restore religious unity that had little impact on daily practice.

Taken together, the chapters all contribute to the ongoing process of estimating the long-term consequences of the Reformation for the English people. From Mary's reign well into the eighteenth century—and, of course, beyond—the divisions that the Henrician break with Rome began, and the Edwardian theological reforms continued, stirred up controversy among those who would have preferred religious uniformity. At the same time, individual men and women seemed fully capable of developing their own unique stances regarding religion. Such religious self-fashioning at times set individuals at odds with their society, but it was a society that seemed prepared to accept a range of attitudes far wider than that in place prior to the Reformation.

PART I

Passion and Practice

Different Kinds of Speaking

SYMBOLIC VIOLENCE AND SECULAR
ICONOCLASM IN EARLY MODERN ENGLAND

An astute observation about early modern England was that people were governed more by the word than by the sword in time of peace. Lacking powers of effective policing or coercive force, the Elizabethan and Stuart regimes relied heavily on discursive authority to secure social and political control. The word of God in particular, mediated by the Church of England, taught people what to believe and how to behave. Catechism, prayer, and preaching supported the established order, while textual instruction, persuasion, and interpretation reinforced the magisterial chain of command. Writs and statutes, tracts and sermons, books and pamphlets, letters and libels, added to the welter of words that made language, whether written or spoken, and writing, whether scribal or printed, the principal means of socialization, education, and power. With its high regard for literacy, rationality, and conventionally ordered discourse, the mainstream culture of early modern England (like our own world) could be described as linear, logical, and logocentric. It was left-brain dominant, as ours is, guiding the activities of the right hand.

Yet the right brain hemisphere also had its domain, intuitive, sinister, and synoptic. Historians would be remiss if they neglected the didactic and persuasive power of this alternative analogic domain. Analysis of cultural cohesion, for example, would be limited if it omitted the force of spectacle, the significance of imagery, and the effects of symbolic action. Royal and aristocratic politics would remain opaque without apprehension of the theater of majesty and the manipulations of heraldic display. Cultural and religious conflict would be similarly incomprehensible without considera-

tion of the counter spectacles of resistance, the complex valences of gesture, and the theatrical exhibitions of iconoclasm. For what people *saw*
could be as persuasive as what they heard, what they *did* as eloquent as
what they said, their actions worth a thousand words. In myriad circumstances and settings, the visual announcements of banners, badges, portraits, statues, and the paraphernalia of religious devotion prompted surges
of awe and agitation, appealing to the literate and illiterate alike. Attacks
on these symbols, through mockery, desecration, or destruction, spoke of
anger, derision, and contempt. Gestures or actions in dumb show likewise
signaled a range of attitudes and responses, including reverence, solidarity,
and disapprobation. An expressive lexicon of movements, images, and
symbols stirred people's emotions or served as metonymic shorthand for
deeper sets of memories, values, or associations.

In a passage of remarkable semiotic sensitivity, the Restoration Catholic
John Gother insisted, "Words are nothing more than for their significa-
tion; and if we signify our thoughts by any other way, as by signs, by any
motion or gesture of our body, these actions being to express the same affection of our soul which we other ways do by words, they are as innocent
as our words." Controversial liturgical actions such as kissing, bowing, uncovering, and kneeling, which Puritans had long excoriated, Gother commended as harmless "exterior professions . . . of interior respect." In honoring the cross, as in honoring the king, he argued, "'Tis the same thing
before God and men whether we signify this outwardly by our tongues, or
by our lips, or by our hands, or by our heads, or by our knees; these being
only so many different kinds of speaking."[1]

This chapter sets out to examine some of the "different kinds of speaking" in the semiotic environment of early modern England. It argues that
utterance could be effective, eloquent, and persuasive, even if it was not
originally set forth in words. Symbolic action, sound and light, gesture,
spectacle, movement, and display carried powerful didactic messages that
were noisy, colorful, and even dangerous. But the "speaking" could be ambiguous as well as forceful, appealing to different viewpoints or traditions.
The actions and gestures that carried meanings within both religious and
political culture were at once more numinous and more nebulous than
formulae set forth in words.[2] The theatricality of kingship and the theatricality of worship both depended, to a large degree, on visual and visceral
appeals, and both, in times of crisis, became subject to theatrical assault.

By attending to a variety of such actions that punctuated the political and religious cultures of Tudor and Stuart England, we may better understand the power of imagery and the communicative *frisson* of iconoclastic violence.

Everyone knew that loyalties and animosities could be articulated through spectacle and action as well as through speech or text. When the duke of Newcastle advised Charles II that, "though ceremony is nothing in itself, yet it doth everything," he was invoking a venerable tradition.³ As early as the reign of Henry VIII, the propagandist Richard Moryson observed that "into the common people things sooner enter by the eyes, than by the ears, remembering more better that they see than that they hear." Stephen Gardiner also noted in the sixteenth century how royal authority was represented heraldically by "images of three lions and three fleurs de lis, and other beasts holding those arms. And he that cannot read the scripture written about the king's great seal, either because he cannot read at all or because the wax doth not express it, yet he can read Saint George on horseback on the one side and the king in his majesty on the other."⁴ The general ability to "read" the picture and to recognize the majesty it represented was an important asset for early modern regimes. To misread the image, or to give it ill treatment, was *lèse majesté*, a serious political offense. To disparage the royal portrait, whether printed or painted, sculpted or coined, was to attack the majesty of the monarch.

Depending on their presentation and context, and contingent on the political climate, dramatic actions involving visual materials provoked contradictory partisan reactions. Sometimes officially sponsored, at other times irregular and spontaneous, they signaled allegiance and involvement, conformity or challenge, mockery or approbation. Protestant iconoclasts destroyed and despoiled the symbolic apparatus of their religious opponents; Catholics did the same when they came back to power. When the northern rebels took Durham cathedral in 1569, they tore up the English Bible and overthrew the holy furniture in ways that anticipated the rebellion in Dublin in 1641.⁵ In Elizabethan England, the Jesuit Edward Oldcorne smashed a window, the design of which he thought offensive; under Charles I, the Puritan Henry Sherfield did much the same. The power of these episodes lay in action, and only later were words introduced to mitigate or to explain.⁶ Similarly, on anniversaries with contested meanings such as "Gunpowder Treason Day" through most of the seventeenth century, possession of the belfry, control of the bonfire, and command of the ritual in the street could be as important for political purposes as control of the pulpit and the press.[7] Lighting candles, ringing bells, setting bonfires, burning books, exhuming corpses, breaking windows, and parading and burning effigies belonged to an expressive political vocabulary that drew on the communicative lexicon of violence, fire, and destruction.

It was not enough, for example, for the regime of Mary Tudor to denounce the Protestant heresy and to bring back Roman Catholicism. The program of confessional restoration was promoted by *coups de théâtre*, of which the Smithfield fires were the most dramatic. Just as expressive was the ritual purgation of defiled sacred space, as the bodies of the Protestants Bucer and Fagius were exhumed from Great St. Mary's, Cambridge, and mockingly tried, executed, and burned.[8] Echoing this holy action, and following in the footsteps of earlier iconoclasts, the Irish Catholic rebels of 1641 pulled down Protestant pulpits and desecrated English Bibles, but their most shocking action was to disinter the corpses of Protestants that had been buried in Dublin's churches. This symbolic action spoke louder than any manifesto or sermon. Though violent and gruesome, the desecrations of Dublin were not simply the product of mindless fury, Irish barbarism, or popish malice. Rather, they were purposeful and expressive actions, with a communicative logic that contemporaries throughout Europe could understand. News of these outrages horrified Stuart Englishmen, and the stories grew in the telling, but the symbolic significance of the action would not have been lost on them. A generation later, the restored Stuart monarchy engaged in its own complex theater of the macabre when they exhumed and then executed the bodies of dead regicides.[9]

Parts of this semiotic outpouring can be readily decoded, but others remain problematic. What did it mean, for example, when a Jacobean courtier flung mud at the picture of the earl of Somerset or when parliamentary soldiers poked swords or knives into a portrait of Charles I? What was going on at Chester in 1637 when the city authorities gave solemn execution to five empty picture frames or at Chichester in 1646 when iconoclasts cut out the eyes from a picture of Edward VI? Why did some people react violently against Cheapside Cross in London while others bowed their heads toward it, and why did the waits sing and the wine flow when the Cross was solemnly destroyed in 1643? Each of these episodes involved ritualized attacks against symbolic targets which in some way represented a controversial person, position, or set of associations. Each incident involved the play of signs and symbols, memories and associations, prompts and cues, that built on previous or similar activities and that could be read, metaphorically, for meaning and response. Interpreting them involved tests of semiotic literacy for the participants and observers, which in turn create further tests for ourselves. The meanings are by no means clear, and it is well to be reminded that interpretation, both contemporary and modern, could fall short of all that was intended. For the actors and audience, perpetrators and protagonists, their performances made vividly expressive statements. Parading, stoning, burning, desecrating, cutting, and casting down were part of an outdoor political vocabulary that Tudor and Stuart historians have rarely paused to examine.[10]

I

In popular culture, as is well known, a set of horns implied cuckoldry or sexual incontinence, so setting up horns at a wedding or outside a married couple's house offered derisive commentary on domestic and gender relations. Displayed as an object or performed as a gesture (fingers on the forehead), the horns were a symbol that everyone could understand. When guests turned up to blow horns at a London wedding in 1579, when Edward Row "did fasten a pair of horns upon the churchyard gate" at an Essex wedding in 1605, and when Robert Broke wore "a great pair of horns upon his head . . . when Henry Hall and his wife were going to be married" in Sussex in 1639, the insulting mockery did not have to be translated into words.[11]

Similarly, a maypole symbolized springtime frolics and licentious games, and it may have had pagan or phallic associations. The maypole was a pivot of the old festive calendar, a symbol of village pride and good fellowship. It was the tree brought into the parish center, the woodland socialized and the community made forest. By Charles I's reign, maypoles carried the extra freight of Puritan animosity and the contested authority of the king's Book of Sports. The tree itself might be considered pagan or popish, and any delight in it a sign of godlessness. So cataloging the accidents that befell maypole dancers (as did Nehemiah Wallington, William Whiteway, and Henry Burton) was a way of witnessing and associating oneself with providential retribution against the symbol. And attacking a

maypole and cutting it down (as Londoners did in Edward VI's reign, as
John Endecott did at Merry-mount in New England, and as parliamentary
authorities did again in the 1640's) was an assertive and didactic action to
remove the abomination, not simply an exercise in woodcutting. Violence
against the symbol implied a casting down of the powers and traditions it
embodied. Down went Dagon, the defeated god of the Philistines.[12]

A similar logic seems to have served in the burning of images, effigies,
and books, a practice which became more common and more creative in
the course of the sixteenth and seventeenth centuries. The iconoclasm of
Edward VI's reign and at the beginning of Elizabeth's reign entailed widespread destruction of popish relics. Mass books, rood screens, holy images,
and the accoutrements of Catholic worship were pulled down, cast out,
and publicly burned. With ceremonial staging in churchyards, in market
squares, and on village greens, this state-supported iconoclasm blended
didactic, festive, and vindictive elements. The iconoclasts who burned pious pictures asserted the triumph of reformed religion and challenged the
previously venerated objects to display their power. Why else arrange for
their ritual debasement and annihilation if the images were not thought to
retain some residue of power? Margaret Aston has likened this symbolic
violence to the rites of passage of the new regime. Although Patrick Collinson has perceived a change from iconoclasm to iconophobia in the course
of Elizabeth's reign, the visual and dramatic aspects of religious and political conflict did not entirely disappear. Vice Chancellor Abbot's bonfire of
Romish pictures at Oxford around 1600 may be seen as iconophobia in
action, but the very act of destruction created a vivid instructional tab-
leau.[13]

By the seventeenth century, there were fewer offensive relics left to burn
and very few sponsored occasions for their destruction. Much of the fury
had faded from official Protestantism. But that did not prevent antipopish
zealots from targeting symbolically sensitive objects. A new round of iconoclasm accompanied the crisis of the 1640's, as Puritan militants attacked
altar rails, religious pictures, windows, and fonts.[14] Not content to break
glass, hammer statues, and deface offensive pictures, creative iconoclasts of
the Stuart era turned to effigies and replicas representing the pope and all
his works. The effigy became a stand-in for the image. Easily identifiable
figures were given public parade and symbolic execution. The anniversary
of the Gunpowder Plot, in particular, provided an annual occasion for

building and burning artificial figures, which seem to have made their first appearance in the course of the English Revolution. "Fine popish gods" were burnt on November 5 in the 1640's, and Whigs of the 1670's extended the treatment to effigies of the pope himself, the Whore of Babylon, and the perpetrators of the Popish Plot. (The mannequin of Guy Fawkes was a later addition to this tradition.) The effigies assumed lifelike properties and were made to suffer debasement and death.[15]

The forethought required in constructing these effigies and the theatricality of their parade and burning reminds us that these were studied rather than spontaneous actions, designed to elicit a partisan response. At the Whig pope burnings in the 1670's, for example, the colors, lights, music, images, location, and timing of the spectacle all carried symbolic references that enhanced their effect. The processions made effective use of the symbolic geography of London—through the memory-charged sites of Cheapside, Smithfield, Temple Bar, and the Monument—and ended with the effigies being strung up, shot, and burned. Tories retaliated with bonfires of their own, burning effigies of Jack Presbyter and Old Noll and representations of the Solemn League and Covenant. Indeed, as Tim Harris has shown, much of the extraparliamentary politics of the later seventeenth century can be followed through the flaunting or defacing of partisan symbols, including ribbons, statues, pictures, and the signs of inns like the King's Arms, the Duke's Head, or the Cardinal's Hat.[16]

II

Governments, too, used fire and destruction for dramatic and symbolic purposes, as part of their repertory of power. Offensive books as well as images could be consigned irretrievably to the flames. The spectacle entailed the triumph of action over words, the reduction of text to ashes. At their most elaborate, book burnings were staged as symbolic executions, sometimes with the author in attendance. Conducted by the state, they served as signals of authority, demonstrations of control, and assertions of orthodoxy over deviance and error. Destruction by fire hinted at the treatment of heretics and other enemies of God. The flames could be seen as a vilification, a vindication, and a public ceremonial purging. They also served as a rebuke to the Stationers, a loss to the printers, and a means of disposing of offensive books.[17]

Every stage of the Reformation and Counter Reformation was marked
by book burnings, as well as by iconoclasm, counter-iconoclasm, and public executions. Luther's works were burned in London in 1521, to be followed a generation later by bonfires of popish missals. Protestant books (as
well as real Protestants) were burned under Mary; popish and Separatist
works were burned under Elizabeth. So too were seditious books touching
on dynastic matters and libertine writings containing "matters unfit to be
published."[18]

Some early Tudor book burnings were elaborate punitive affairs, designed for maximum effect. The destruction of Luther's works by Henry
VIII involved Wolsey as master of ceremonies, with an international audience of dignitaries and crowds of Londoners to witness the flames at Paul's
Cross. Elizabethan and Jacobean book burnings, by contrast, were more
commonly conducted indoors, in the kitchen of Stationers' Hall or within
the house of the bishop of London.[19] The burning required official witnesses to certify its completion, but little attempt was made to convert the
occasion into a public spectacle. On special occasions, however, a book
burning would be staged to accompany other punishment—the humiliation, mutilation, or execution of an enemy of the state—and therefore demanded an audience. John Stubbe's *Discoverie of a Gaping Gulf,* which opposed Elizabeth's proposed French marriage, was condemned to be "destroyed in the open sight of some public officer" in 1579, while the author
was to lose the hand that wrote it. Stubbe himself turned his punishment
into a counter-spectacle of loyalty and courage by raising his severed arm
in salute before he fainted.[20] Fiery spectacles, like the burning of 40 volumes at the execution of religious radicals in 1583, were rare under Elizabeth and James, yet each incident helped to shape expectations for those
that followed. Cowell's *Interpreter* is said to have been "condemned to a
fire set by the hangman" in 1610, but the actual means of its suppression is
unclear. The proclamation called in all copies but did not say how they
should be destroyed.[21]

Book burnings became more flamboyant in the 1620's and 1630's. Instead of relying on office procedures before an episcopal notary, the Caroline regime preferred outdoor spectacles commanding maximum attention. If offensive books spoke, the government would speak louder by
staging their ultimate rebuttal. The change was signaled in February 1625,
the last month of James's reign, when more than 800 copies of Edward

Elton's book, *God's Holy Minde*, underwent "a *februation* or purging by fire." According to Daniel Featley, himself a former censor, their burning constituted "the greatest holocaust that hath been offered in this kind in our memory. . . . Before the burning of the books, the preacher at the cross declared divers erroneous assertions therein, condemned (as he said) by authority." Popular reaction, as usual, was mixed. Some spectators were seen "partly weeping and wiping their eyes to see a book so full (as they conceived) of heavenly zeal and holy fire, sacrificed in earthly and unhallowed flames."[22]

The government of Charles I still burned some books in private,[23] but devised innovative public punishments for the work of its most hated enemies. This is best illustrated by the case of William Prynne, whose mocking and critical writings called forth a fury of symbolic violence. Prynne's *Histrio-Mastix*, a treatise against stage plays published in 1633, was construed to be so offensive to established authority and so insulting to the queen that ordinary censorship and punishment would be insufficient. Among other things, it railed against playacting and costuming, an activity in which Henrietta Maria had recently taken part. Official retribution included not only physical mutilation of the author but also the public burning of his books and, eventually, after Prynne compounded his offense in 1637, the ritual obliteration of his image. This complex play of spectacle and action was orchestrated by the forces of order, not by an unruly mob, and it shows the importance of displaying and controlling the repertory of symbols. The Prynne episode drew creatively on past traditions and set new standards of outdoor political theater.

Chancellor of the Exchequer Cottington sentenced *Histrio-Mastix* to a self-consciously innovative destruction. "I condemn it to be burnt, in the most public manner that can be. The manner in other countries is . . . to be burnt by the hangman, though not used in England. Yet I wish it may, in respect of the strangeness and heinousness of the matter contained in it, to have a strange manner of burning; therefore I shall desire it may be so burnt by the hand of the hangman." The other judges endorsed this innovation. They further committed Prynne to "perpetual imprisonment," levied a fine of £5,000, expelled him from Lincoln's Inn and from the practice of law, and stripped him of his degrees from the University of Oxford.[24]

This was harsh, perhaps excessive, but only the beginning of Prynne's ordeal. Fining, imprisoning, disbarring, and degrading were indoor judgments—office procedures appropriate for a lawyer and gentleman—but Prynne was also to star in a more humiliating and painful outdoor spectacle that was staged to express the government's anger and contempt. The sentence continued, "that he be set in the pillory at Westminster, with a paper on his head declaring the nature of his offense, and have one of his ears there cut off; and at another time be set in the pillory in Cheapside, with a paper as aforesaid, and there have his other ear cut off; and that a fire shall be made before the said pillory, and the hangman being there ready for that purpose, shall publicly in disgraceful manner cast all the said books which could be produced into the fire to be burnt, as unfit to be seen by any hereafter."[25]

Justice (or vengeance) would be seen to be done. Prynne would be on view, displayed in the pillory and publicly mutilated in the streets of London and Westminster. His literary offense would be countered by a written declaration, and the offending books would be burnt before their author's eyes, in a fire fueled by the common hangman. The punishment was clearly theatrical in its staging, with set, script, actors, audience, and props, and it was particularly appropriate for one who had written against dramatic representation. Prynne was not a heretic to be burned, nor were his cropped ears (or other members) roasted in front of him; but the possibilities of greater violence hung over the occasion. The hangman's usual business was with ropes, not books, and Cheapside was the site of earlier bonfires, associated with the Marian martyrs and the commemoration of November 5.

Henceforth the hangman was de rigueur for the public burning of books. The parliamentary regime of the 1640's appointed the common hangman to burn such offensive items as the Book of Sports, and the restored regime of Charles II used the hangman to destroy the detested Solemn League and Covenant. London crowds became accustomed to viewing such spectacles in the standard venues: Cheapside, Cornhill, Smithfield, Paul's Cross, and Westminster Palace Yard.[26]

By 1637 Prynne was in trouble again and was condemned, along with Burton and Bastwick, for writing the pamphlet *News from Ipswich*. Again he was pilloried and humiliated, and the offending texts were ritually destroyed. The remains of Prynne's ears were hacked off, and his cheek was branded with the letters S. L. (for seditious libel or, as Prynne boasted, *stigmata Laudis*). Here again the sign was ambiguous, laden with contradictory meanings. The state showed its power by imposing pain and disfigurement, but the subject turned his punishment into a triumph of propaganda. As the chronicler Thomas Fuller recalled, "So various were men's fancies in reading the same letters, imprinted in his face, that some made them to spell the guiltiness of the sufferer, but others the cruelty of the imposer."[27]

The authorities then faced the further problem of quelling public sympathy for Prynne as he rode off to exile and imprisonment. Prynne's journey from London to North Wales in the summer of 1637 took on some of the attributes of a defiant progress attended by knots of supporters. When he paused at Chester at the end of July, he was rapturously received by Puritan well-wishers. Someone commissioned a local artist—Thomas Pulford, limner—to paint Prynne's portrait, and several copies of this likeness circulated as cherished tokens. What followed is further revealing of the power of the image and the elaborate pains taken by the authorities to counteract it. The government had not exhausted its repertoire of symbolic action, and it was prepared to do battle to extinguish unlicensed imagery and to reassert its own.

Bishop Bridgeman, who was absent from Chester at the time of Prynne's visit, declared the city "much defamed by having entertained notorious and factious schismatics."[28] A process of cleansing and purgation was initiated, which ended with a remarkable display of official iconoclasm. As the target of this attack later reported, the commissioners, "hearing that there were pictures of Mr. Prynne's portraiture in Chester, persecuted the poor painter . . . for drawing them, and then made two orders in court, first to deface and then to burn them publicly at the cross in Chester."[29]

Having "seized on five pictures of Prynne, drawn by the painter Pulford," Bridgeman wrote to the archbishop of York on November 10 seeking further instructions. Should they be sent to the High Commission at York or be "sacrificed here to Vulcan, either publicly in the market, or privately before some good witnesses"? (The bishop's flippant invocation of classical divinity and pagan sacrifice was just the sort of thing that serious Protestants like Prynne found so offensive.) Archbishop Neile, in response, ordered the Chester officials to "spoil and deface, or else cause to be spoiled and defaced, the aforesaid pictures" and to return their frames to the artist. On November 15, Bridgeman's vicar general, Mainwaring, re-

ported to the archbishop, "I caused the pictures . . . to be defaced before
my Lord of Chester, and in the presence of a public notary." The deed was
done in private, before solemn witnesses, using procedures similar to those
traditionally employed for the burning of books. But by this time the High
Commissioners had changed their minds, or had perhaps caught up with
London fashions, and now desired that the pictures, like Prynne's books at
Cheapside, should be publicly burned. Word reached Chester too late.
The vicar general wrote, "I am sorry that my zeal and duty to obedience
hath anticipated your late resolutions. But," he added helpfully, "I have the
frames still."[30]

The public retribution that was to be unleashed against the portrait (itself a substitution for the living Prynne) might now be visited on their
frames (which were contaminated by association or contagion). Whether
symbolic violence or sympathetic magic, the business of Prynne's pictures
and their frames would occupy the authorities in Chester for several more
weeks. To make up for their earlier slackness, the civic and episcopal
authorities put on a show of loyal diligence and dedication. On December
12, 1637, the mayor and aldermen of Chester, ecclesiastical dignitaries, and
"other citizens and persons to the number of a thousand" assembled at the
High Cross in Chester to witness the public burning. The crowd, no
doubt including some who had welcomed Prynne five months earlier, was
incited to call out to the contaminated picture frames, "Burn them, burn
them." According to Prynne, who published these documents in 1641 as
part of his attack on the bishops, "the pursuivant standing there in his coat
of arms bid them thus cry in the king's name, and commanded the mayor
and aldermen to be present at this bonfire." The frail sticks of the picture
frames that represented seditious libel and Puritan defiance were no match
for the costume of lions and fleurs de lis that stood for the king. Using an
intimidating display of royal emblems and the ritual vocabulary of fire, the
government orchestrated the occasion to exorcise Chester's previous support for the troublesome lawyer. The citizens were treated to a winter bonfire (itself a potent symbol), with costumed representatives of civic; episcopal, and royal authority to witness and complete the purgation. As
Prynne himself put it, "These High Commissioners not satisfied with the
defacing of the pictures, would needs proceed to burn them for heretics;
and since they could not burn Mr. Prynne in person as they desired, being
then on the sea sailing to Jersey, they would do it at least by effigy; and to

show the extravagance of their unlimited malice, not only the pictures but the very frames wherein they stood (poor innocents) must to the fire."[31] Thus was completed a metonymic chain, in which Prynne represented the enemies of Laudianism, the portrait stood for Prynne, and the paintings were represented by their frames. One finds little mention of this episode in the books about Prynne or in studies of Stuart Chester. But it is richly revealing of symbolic discourse within a contested political culture.

III

Disputes intensified in Charles I's reign over "different kinds of speaking." Two aesthetics, which might be construed as Baroque sensibility versus iconophobic plainstyle, jostled for cultural dominance in both secular and spiritual domains. Competing cultures, as well as rival strains of theology and patterns of preferment, contested for control of the church. With the Protestant Reformation behind them, a new generation of churchmen felt no need to downgrade ceremony or to oppose religious images, and some were intent on rebeautification. Ceremonialist clerics of the 1620's and 1630's, among them Prynne's enemies, were especially keen on reverent ornamentation and liturgical action that would resanctify religious practice and resacralize God's church. Laudians preferred "pompous spectacles of glittering pictures and histrionical gestures" to the austerities of Protestant preaching, so their enemies proclaimed. "Instead of defacing images," which should have been their duty, charged the Durham prebendary Peter Smart, "they have given them new faces, bravely painted and gilded; instead of abolishing them, they have multiplied them and renewed their memory in walls, windows, copes, etc."[32] The ceremonialist advocacy of the beauty of holiness spoke volumes about their stewardship of the Church of England and, not surprisingly, provoked a reaction among more radical Protestants. Responsible Puritans charged religious ornamentation as idolatrous and sinful, and they saw kneeling and crossing as signs of a resurgent Catholicism. Hotter bloods preferred action to words, and after 1640 they made their case against altars and images by pulling them down.

In a work that reached its fourth edition in 1633, the Jacobean divine George Hakewill argued against the dangerous "allurement of the eyes." Drawing on a tradition stretching back to St. Augustine, he wrote both to

comfort a gentlewoman who had been "bereaved of her sight" and to promote an iconophobic Protestant aesthetic. The eye, Hakewill asserted, "is
the instrument of wantonness, gluttony and covetousness" that leads to
idolatry and "spiritual fornication." Especially to be avoided was that popish "eye service" which beguiled weak worshipers "in the magnific and
pompous fabric and furniture of their churches and attiring their priests,
in gazing upon their dumb ceremonies . . . and lastly in fixing their eyes
upon pictures and images, giving them the titles of remembrances for the
learned and books for the laity."[33] Like many Jacobean treatises that were
not, at first, especially controversial, these iconophobic strictures gained a
new edge in the 1630's in light of the Caroline enthusiasm for church fur-
nishings, fabric, ceremonies, and pictures.

Reacting against the Laudian rebeautification of the church in the late
1630's, the East Anglian minister Edmund Gurnay felt "a palpable incensement and provocation" in the face of religious paintings and carvings.
Like other members of the godly iconophobic tradition, Gurnay had little
confidence in aesthetic discipline and warned of "an unreasonable proneness in the heart of man to sin by images, even to the bowing down with
them, and committing spiritual fornication with them." Like Hakewill, he
cautioned against the allurement of the eye and reserved particular scorn
for the Laudian decorative program. "The setting up of images or anything
else in churches, only to please the outward eye . . . is rather a profanation,
pollution and prostitution unto those kind of places, than any perfection
or beautification." It was a small step from "palpable incensement" to
iconoclastic action. Gurnay himself was not about to take up a hammer
against images, but in 1641 he warned of "the proneness of the times to advance them, making it rather an act of necessity than of idleness to oppose
them." Setting the earlier official homily on images against the recent
Laudian canons, he thought it "rather an act of authority than of rashness
utterly to deface them."[34] If the minister of Harpley, Norfolk, expressed
such sentiments, how might wilder subjects behave when such a steadying
influence was removed?

The campaign against images heated up in 1641, amid the collapse of
episcopal authority. Thomas Warmstry, a Worcestershire minister, dis-
tanced himself from his superiors when he wrote against the Laudian canons. His aim, he said, was to save the church from ceremonial innovators
as well as sectarian extremists. Religious ornaments and images should be

removed, he argued, because they were snares and distractions; they brought "scandal" on the church and raised "suspicion of inclination to Popery." Christ was to be viewed through "the eye of the soul" rather than through fleshly optical organs. "What next?" he asked. "Must we demolish these churches that are decked and adorned with images? There is no need of that, I hope. There are many things now to be reformed that I hope will not be pulled down. And yet if there were such need I dare say, better forty churches demolished than one soul ruined." Like many mainstream ministers, Warmstry wanted peace in the church, not violent destruction. Yet his words against images could be taken as incentives to iconoclasm.[35]

Also in 1641, George Salteren, a layman, rehearsed many of the traditional arguments against idolatry. Religious images, he claimed, were "abominable before God" as well as "stumbling blocks . . . to the weak, simple and blind common people." Parishioners who were deluded by their eyes could be considered metaphorically blind. The only way to save simple souls and to deflect the wrath of God was "the abolishing and destruction of images and pictures in temples and churches." Here, too, from a member of the Puritan gentry, was an apparent call for licensed iconoclasm.[36]

Even more militant in calling for the immediate elimination of images, by violence if necessary, was the London minister John Vicars. The time had come, he charged, "to fetch out the core or corrupt matter" like a surgeon attending to a wound, and "to pluck them up by the roots" like a gardener eradicating poisonous weeds. Pictures, in Vicars's view, were "fire to man's nature, which is like tinder, apt to set them afire." Secular pictures for "civil use" might escape these strictures, but all crucifixes and images of Christ should be destroyed wherever they were found. If Hezekiah, a godly king, had been commended for breaking the brazen serpent, he concluded, "How much more ought we, in holy zeal, to destroy and utterly ruinate all the pictures or images of the Lord?"[37] Like the Israelites expelling Dagon, or Joshua's army exposing the sin of Achan and eliminating "the accursed thing,"[38] God's people in England were called upon to remove the impurities from their midst, in particular the pollution of images.

IV

Religious radicals had no principled objection to royal ceremonial or to representations of the monarch, at least not before 1649, but secular images were never immune from symbolic attack. They too spoke of tradition and authority and could be spoken against by irreverent action. The royal arms, emblems, portraits, and statues that projected state power into noble houses, town squares, magistrates' parlors, and hundreds of parish churches were extensions of kingly authority, but they did not always enjoy the respect for which they were designed. Occasionally, and dramatically, the majestic icon felt a blow. Prints and sculptures of Charles I suffered especially violent abuse in the years of revolution, but these were not the first royal portraits to experience abuse. A review of some earlier episodes will lead us back to the 1640's.

Enemies of Queen Elizabeth attacked her picture when they could not overthrow her regime. According to Sir Roy Strong, "Throughout the reign efforts were made to dispose of the queen by stabbing, burning, or otherwise destroying her image. . . . In 1591 a religious maniac called Hacket expressed his hatred of Elizabeth by defacing the royal arms and stabbing a panel portrait of her through the breast. . . . O'Rourke, the Irish rebel, caused a wooden image of her to be trailed through the streets while boys hurled stones at it. In France under the Catholic League, Elizabeth's portrait was publicly consigned to the flames and even, it was reported in 1590 . . . hung up upon a gallows from which it was rescued by some patriotic Englishman."[39]

The Irish assault on the royal image was especially outrageous and theatrical. According to reports reaching London, Sir Brian O'Rourke obtained a wooden statue of a woman and "wrote upon the breast thereof QUEEN ELIZABETH, which done he presently fell with such spiteful and traitorous speeches to rail at it, and otherwise to filthily use it, as I protest unto your lordship I abhor to remember. . . . During which time his barbarous gallowglasses standing by played their parts as fast, who with their gallowglass axes striking the image one while on the head, another while on the face, and sometimes stabbing it in the body, never ceased until with hacking and mangling they had utterly defaced it. And being nevertheless not contented herewith they, the more to manifest the malice of their traitorous hearts, fastened a halter about the neck of the image, and tying it to a horse tail dragged it along the ground, and so beating it with their axes, and railing most despitefully at it they finished their traitorous pageant." The reporter's phrases "played their parts," "striking the image," and "traitorous pageant" are especially telling. In other versions of the story, the statue "was drawn at a garran's tail in derision of her majesty," hinting at sexual degradation as well as political despite. This outrage occurred in 1586, but the government was still trying to get to the bottom of it five years later.[40]

In cases like these, the royal image, venerated as an icon by loyal subjects, became a victim effigy for the queen's enemies. The visual representation was treated as animate, as if it could suffer the pains of stabbing, dragging, stoning, and burning, not unlike the wax figures employed in popular sorcery. The statue became a stand-in for the living queen. Fueled by frustration and venom, the disfigurement had a theatrical quality, requiring an audience to appreciate the degradation and symbolic downfall of the person on display. If the portrait was adopted as a fetish, against which might be practiced malicious sympathetic magic, it had this in common with the *pittura infamante* and *damnatio memoriae* of late medieval and Renaissance Italy. English political portraits were not the only ones to be gibbetted, slashed, or stoned.[41]

James I's image, portrait, arms, and symbols seem unfailingly to have attracted respect, but his favorites came in for their share of symbolic abuse. In 1615 there was held "a great but private entertainment at supper, at Baynard's Castle, by the family of Herberts, Hartford and Bedford" to decide whether to back George Villiers against Robert Carr, the earl of Somerset. On the way back, "in Fleet Street hung out Somerset's picture at a painters stall; which one of the lords envying, bad his footman fling dirt in the face, which he did." This apparently trivial action can be seen as a calculated degradation, a shaming and vilification. The mudslinging signaled a change in the pattern of ascendancy and patronage at court, and Somerset fell rapidly from favor after this assault on his image. The action is suggestive of the ritual besmirchment with mud or excrement and the *envoutement* or image magic found elsewhere in Renaissance Europe. Like the popular insult "a turd in your teeth," the assault on the picture was a "different kind of speaking."[42]

Charles I's loyal subjects knew as well as those of Henry VIII that the majesty of the monarch resided symbolically in his seal and his arms, his image and effigy, and even extended to his empty throne. The Laudian minister William Quelch recognized this when discussing the semiotics of "outward gesture, whether it be kneeling, standing, bowing, crossing, uncovering, or whatever else of the same alloy." Men bared their heads during religious services, he explained, in the same way as "we make it a sign of reverence in civil worship; for servants uncover to their masters, children to their parents, subjects to their prince, yea and to the chair of his state too, as a type and figure of his presence."[43] Bowing to the chair was a dutiful subjectlike action; but reversing the gesture, refusing to kneel before a king, to rise before a judge, to doff one's hat before superiors, or to show due respect for the emblems of hierarchical authority—these were defiant acts that challenged the established order. William Prynne wryly noted that "the trampling of the king's seal or writ under feet is an high contempt against his royal person, punishable severely by the law." Judge Robert Heath observed similarly in 1643 at the contested Assize of Sarum that "the king speaks by his broad seal," and to frustrate or void that image was undoubted treason.[44]

Representations of Charles I, which at first attracted conventional veneration, experienced ritual debasement as his rule disintegrated in violence, both real and symbolic. It was especially ironic that a king with an elevated sense of the importance of his visual image should have that image degraded and besmirched. Statues and portraits of the king that once were garlanded with flowers were later attacked and pulled down. In the 1630's, stimulated by classical and Renaissance examples as well as by local sycophancy, several cities erected statues of Charles I. Viscount Wimbledon's instructions to the mayor of Portsmouth in 1635 reveal how the government intended the royal statue to be honored. The same kind of deference that was due to the monarch himself, or to the empty chair of state, was required before the three-dimensional representation of the king. No officers or soldiers should be permitted to pass by the statue "without putting off their hats." Simple hat doffing was not enough, however, for the viscount further ordered the removal of all public inn signs in Portsmouth that "not only obscure his majesty's figure but out face it." No such encounters could be tolerated, he explained, "for any disgrace offered to his majesty's figure is as much as to himself." Pictures were not permitted to look upon pictures lest they diminish the royal honor.[45]

Although political leaders distinguished between the person of the king and the trappings of kingship, between the majesty of the Crown and the evil that could corrupt it, and between the king himself and mere artistic representations, these distinctions collapsed in the heat of action. Responsible parliamentarians sought to contain royal power, not ridicule it, but their war was sometimes fought by symbolic action as well as by military and political means. Parliamentary troopers occasionally behaved toward the royal icon in the same way that the Irish rebels dishonored Elizabeth I, venting their spleen against the image if they could not reach the person. Representations of the king, which in happier times betokened loyalty and affection, became targets of violent iconoclasm. Angry roundheads assaulted the royal statue at Winchester cathedral in 1642, pointedly damaging the sword, the orb, and the crown.[46] And after 1649, most public statues of the king were broken down or removed.

Outraged royalists shared stories of attacks against the portrait or effigy of his sacred majesty. In September 1642, for example, Anthony Wood reported, "Lord Seye went to New College [Oxford] and searched Dr. [Robert] Pink's study, taking out some papers from thence; and in the lodging one of my lord's men [a parliamentary trooper] brake down the king's picture that stood there, made of alabaster and gilt over, for which my lord was much displeased." As far as we can tell, the destruction was not accidental but rather a product of the trooper's anger or enthusiasm. Perhaps he thought he was advancing the parliamentary cause by damaging this statue of the king.[47]

In the same year, when soldiers ransacked the house of Sir Richard Mynshall in Buckinghamshire, "the first thing on which they express their rage is the King's picture, which with their swords they most traitorously pierce through in divers places; and not content to wound him in that representation . . . they whet their tongues against their sovereign, using traitorous and scornful language against him." Bruno Ryves, who tells this story, remarks, "What wonder is it, that these miscreants should offer such scornful indignities to the representation of his royal person and the emblems of his sacred power, when the heads of this damnable rebellion . . . offer worse affronts to his sacred person himself, and . . . daily strike at the substance of that power of which the crown, the sword, and scepter are but emblems and shadows."[48] Sophisticates and illiterates alike could be moved by "emblems and shadows," which constituted so much of their semiotic world.

In another extraordinary incident, a band of parliamentary soldiers is said to have captured one of their men who had switched to the royalist side. "Nothing will serve to hang him on, but the sign post of the King's Head in Thame." The story goes that one of the soldiers "turned the dying man's face towards the sign itself of the King's Head, and jeeringly said, 'Nay, Sir, you must speak one word with the king before you go; you are blindfold, and he cannot see, and by and by you shall both come down together.'"[49] This grotesque scene may remind us of the confrontation at Portsmouth, when the inn signs were denied their conversation with the image of the king.

When the king did come down finally in 1649, it was not enough just to execute him and abolish his office. The republican government also sought to purge the king's image from public places and his name from legal documents. In a process similar to what we have seen recently in Eastern Europe, royal statues were thrown down and royal arms were removed from churches. All public and legal business, all writs, grants, suits, and proceedings, were henceforth to be conducted in the name of the custodians of the liberties of England rather than in the name of the king. And instead of dating business by the regnal year, "the date shall be the year of the lord, and none other." Sessions of the Peace of the King were now to be "the sessions of the public peace." And "in all indictments and presentments where mention is to be made of highways, the same shall be called Common Highways, and not the King's highways."[50] The schoolboy Isaac Archer recalled his confusion at this time when his father defaced a print of King Charles, coated with isinglass and silk. "My father, I know not why, with a knife cut out his head in the picture; this I told in Colchester and it made some wonder, for I told them my father cut off the king's head; this at first was not understood but afterwards they knew the mistake. The Lord forgive me that I should be instrumental in defaming my father."[51]

V

One unlikely target of the iconoclasm of the 1640's was the portrait of King Edward VI, which became bound up with antagonism to the Book of Common Prayer. To an earlier generation of English Protestants, the boy king represented England's heroic and imperial stance against Rome. Godly activists of the early Stuart period held Edward VI in high regard, second only to Queen Elizabeth as the founding genius of their church. Edward was revered as the young Josiah, the scourge of idolatrous images, and the father of the Book of Common Prayer. During the 1630's, both Puritans and Laudians applauded the memory of Edward VI, for everyone wanted the founding Protestant monarch on their side. Parliamentary preachers in 1640 included historical tributes to Edward in sermons before the House of Commons, while Archbishop Laud himself in that same year invoked Edward's memory in support of ecclesiastical discipline. But in 1643 the champion of attacks on superstitious images was himself disturbed by a wave of sanctioned iconoclasm. The parliamentary committee appointed to deal with monuments of superstition and idolatry authorized desecration of the altar in Henry VII's chapel at Westminster, which happened to be where Edward VI was buried.[52]

More serious attacks were to follow, as reverence for the Book of Common Prayer declined. Strict adherence to the prayer book had long been a source of friction between Puritans and episcopal authorities, and the wave of troubles since 1637 could be traced to Laud's attempt to force an English prayer book on Scotland. But one is hardly prepared for the report from 1646, that in the course of ransacking Chichester cathedral, "One of those miscreants picked out the eyes of King Edward the sixth's picture, saying, That all this mischief came from him, when he established the book of common prayer." This comes from *Mercurius Rusticus,* which, though highly partisan, was not prone to invention. The story rings true and can be validated in part by inspection of the painted portraits at Chichester. But even if we doubt its full authenticity, the report is indicative of what royalist propagandists wanted their readers to believe.[53]

The attack on the royal portrait at Chichester seems to have been an isolated act, a rogue assault by an inventive parliamentary soldier, like his counterpart in Dr. Pink's study at Oxford. Perhaps it was an act of bravado, designed to annoy the cathedral authorities and to win cheers from fellow iconoclasts who were chipping away at religious targets. A context was provided by the parliamentary campaign against images of idolatry and by the tradition of Puritan distrust for visual allurements of any sort.

The royalist apologist Bruno Ryves found the assault on Edward's picture particularly shocking, a symptom of the collapse of order and the disintegration of traditional respect unleashed by the parliamentary rebellion. Here was a violation of sacred space, as troopers ransacked a cathedral. Here was contempt for the monarchy, represented by one of the present king's illustrious predecessors. Even more distressing was this calculated and self-justifying assault on the memory of the very king most associated with the establishment of English Protestantism. Could history be un-

made, could the late unhappy troubles have been avoided, if King Edward
had not established the Book of Common Prayer? The soldier seemed to
know exactly what he was doing when he precisely defaced the picture. But
was there a streak of madness in his blinding the image, cutting out the boy
king's eyes? Perhaps this soldier of the New Model Army was emulating
the blinding of Zedekiah, the king of Judea, who laid the way for the
Babylonian captivity. Or he may have recalled other incidents in folklore
and literature—from Oedipus to Sejanus[54] to Gloucester in *King Lear*—
where blinding brought about a horrific kind of justice. Henceforth the
patron of the prayer book would no longer gaze on the transformed liturgical scene.

Recent art-historical work on responses to images suggests that the iconoclast may have been guided by a hidden logic. Edward's portrait was not the
only one to lose its eyes. Other examples can be found from the fifteenth
century to the present day. An early critic of Andrea Mantegna's fresco of the
Martyrdom of St. James scratched out the executioner's eyes.[55] The eyes, it is
suggested, are the surest sign of life in a picture; take away the eyes and you
reduce its vitality. The eyes were the noblest of the senses and the windows of
the soul in Platonic and Renaissance medical literature, but they were also, so
some preachers alleged, the entry point for delusion, distraction, and vanity.
One is reminded of the messianic delusion of the man who attacked the
tomb effigy of the earl of Essex (also in 1646), or more recent attacks on
Rembrandt's "Night Watch" or Michelangelo's Pieta or David. The mutilation of the picture was yet another kind of speaking, but so incoherent that
this time it had to be put into words.

VI

One final episode illustrates the interplay of image and action and
official and unofficial iconoclasm. In 1643, one of London's best known
landmarks, Cheapside Cross, was systematically demolished. John Vicars,
who had written earlier against images, gave a gleeful and gloating account
of this action: "Upon Tuesday, May the Ninth, the gorgeously gilt leaden
coat of Cheapside Cross was plucked over its ears, and its accursed carcass
also piecemeal tumbled down to the ground; even on that day which the
popish asses glosses say was *Inventio crucis*, was now at London in Cheapside *destructio crucis*." With redirection of the festive energies of Maytide, a

symbol analogous to the maypole was ceremoniously pulled down. "Many thousands of people . . . came to see . . . the fatal fall of that whore; yea, and the work was both guarded and solemnized with brave bands of soldiers, sounding their trumpets and shooting of their pieces . . . as well as joyful acclamations at the happy downfall of Antichrist in England. Nor was this abominable idol . . . left without a funeral solemnity; for upon the Friday following at night . . . a great fire was made in Cheapside, just where the cross stood, whereinto the leaden gods, saints, and popes were cast, and there melted to make bullets yet further to bang and break down the living idols or idolators of Rome." With guns, bells, drums, trumpets, the singing of the waits, and "most jocund and joyful acclamations of men's voices," the last trappings of the monument were consumed by fire.[56]

The symbolic importance of the site was confirmed a week later when the king's Book of Sports was publicly burned by the hangman "in the very place where that Romish cross in Cheapside formerly stood." This was a central and sensitive location, where heretics and seditious books had been burned and where Prynne had so recently undergone his ordeal. The new authority extinguished the old, in a dramatic display of symbol against symbol.

Underlying this episode, and fueling the iconoclastic energy, was more than half a century of argument concerning Cheapside Cross. First erected in the thirteenth century by Edward I, and most recently restored by Elizabeth I, the cross dominated the western end of Cheapside, in the commercial heart of London, with representations of saints, bishops, and the divinity. Cheapside Cross was a secular public edifice of civic and national importance, but it was also, in Puritan eyes, "a monument of idolatry" and an icon of the old religion. Devout traditionalists bowed in reverence to Cheapside Cross, while radical sectarians approached it with scorn. It was said, during Charles's reign, that "sundry sorts of people have by three o'clock in the morning come barefoot to the Cross, and have kneeled down and said something to themselves, crossed their forehead and their breast, and so risen and making obeisance went away. . . . Likewise, that hundreds of people . . . in the midst of day bend their bodies to it, and put off their hats, and cross themselves . . . and do reverence to it." The Cross had become Dagon, with bestial personality. In 1641, some would-be iconoclasts made a night raid on the cross, defacing some of its figures and precipitating a spate of satiric prints and verses.[57] But the destruction in 1643 was altogether more calculated, public, and successful, conducted with the authority of the state. With parliamentary blessing, the beast was baited and humiliated, then violently destroyed, to the accompaniment of traditional expressions from the vocabulary of celebration. It went the same way as the books in flames, Prynne's picture frames, and the desecrated images of Charles I. Although the gloating iconoclasts would not admit it, their action had much in common with primitive notions of sympathetic magic and the assuaging or therapeutic effects of symbolic action.

VII

Episodes like these demonstrate how a culture performs itself, how meanings and values may be encapsulated in mimetic and metonymic acts. They indicate, in ways more familiar to anthropologists than historians, how metaphors and mini-dramas present and represent the messages of legitimacy and contest. Each incident originated in different circumstances, within particular contexts, but all raise questions about honor and mockery, symbol, substance, and the manipulations of power that go to the heart of the political culture of early modern England.

A more thorough inquiry might explore the gradient between unofficial and spontaneous action, of the sort that blinded the royal portrait, and official, sponsored iconoclasm of the sort directed against Prynne. It might further differentiate the nature of the target, the properties of the medium (such as fire), the interweaving of representation and action, and the peculiar religious and political stresses of the times. It is important to distinguish between the setting up of symbols and their pulling down, between the purposes of those who projected authority and the multiple responses of those who railed against it.

The events at Chester, Chichester, and Cheapside clearly have more in common than their beginning with the digraph *ch*. They came at moments of information overload, when participants in a deeply divided discourse embraced the rhetoric of knives or flames. It may not help to talk of homologies and similacres, floating signifiers and hegemonic referents, or polyvalent cross-referencing. But it might be worth asking if cultural theory can augment empirical history by illuminating the connection between the empty space in Cheapside, Edward's empty eyes, and Prynne's empty frames.

THOMAS R. HOLIEN

A Conversion and Its Consequences in the Life and Letters of Nicholas Sheterden

Near the beginning of a "talk" between the future Marian martyr John Bradford and Nicholas Harpsfield, the archdeacon of London, the following exchange is reported by John Foxe:

> *Harpsfield:*—"Well, then here is the matter; to know the way to . . . heaven."
> *Bradford:*—"We may not invent any manner of ways. There is but one way, and that is Jesus Christ, as he himself doth witness: 'I am the way.'"

With this exchange, their "talk" quickly and predictably turned from agreement to disagreement to judgment, with Harpsfield telling Bradford at one point that he was "far out of the way." Curiously, he never asked Bradford how he came to stray so far from "the true trail"; to put it another way, he never asked him about his conversion.[1] Like Harpsfield in this instance, historians of the early English Reformation have failed to investigate the phenomenon of conversion, at least in any sustained manner, a fact made all the more striking by the prominent role that conversion has played in the ongoing debate about the nature and pace of religious change during this period.[2] This lacuna in the historiography is perhaps most readily attributed to a deficiency of suitable evidence. And while it is certainly true that pre-Elizabethan conversion narratives are exceedingly few and far between, it is also true that those that do exist have not been subjected to close and comprehensive readings—Thomas Bilney's is a case in point.[3] Moreover, evidence for the incidence of conversion in the lives of many lesser known women and men has still not received the attention it deserves, despite the best efforts of John Fines.[4]

The bulk of this evidence comes from Foxe's *Acts and Monuments* and consists mainly of short biographies, examinations, letters, and prayers.[5] A careful reading of these documents with an eye for the study of conversion reveals their potential for opening significant new avenues of inquiry in this regard. To cite two examples: In the midst of the Fifth Examination of Elisabeth Young, a "forty and upwards" mother of three who had been charged with importing and distributing heretical and treasonous books,[6] the following exchange with the bishop of London's chancellor about the Real Presence and the interpretation of Scriptures is recorded by Foxe:

Elizabeth:—"Christ preached to the Capernaites, saying, 'Except ye eat the flesh of the Son of man and drink his blood, ye shall not have life in you': and the Capernaites murmured at it. And his disciples also murmured, saying among themselves, 'This is a hard saying, and who can abide it?' Christ understood their meaning, and said, 'Are you also offended? will ye also go away? What and if ye shall see the Son of man ascend up to heaven, from whence he came? will that offend you? It is the spirit that quickeneth, the flesh profiteth nothing.' I pray you sir what meaneth Christ by that?"

Chancellor:—"O, God forbid. Would ye have me to interpret the Scriptures? We must leave that for our old ancient fathers, which have studied Scriptures a long time, and have the Holy Ghost given unto them."

Elizabeth:—"Why sir, have you not the Holy Ghost given and revealed unto you?"

Chancellor:—"No, God forbid that I should believe so; but I hope, I hope. But ye say, ye are of the Spirit: will you say that ye have no profit in Christ's flesh?"

As this exchange and a number of others from Foxe suggest, conversion produced a difference in understanding about the Holy Spirit between converts from Catholicism and its defenders.[7] It also apparently produced a difference in the manner of speaking about God. In the following passage taken from a work written by a London rector named Thomas Mowntayne about his persecution during the reign of Mary I, Mowntayne recounted a conversation he had with Mary's lord chancellor, Bishop Stephen Gardiner.[8]

"My Lord (said I) I am no heretic, for that way that you count heresy, worship we the living God; and as our forefathers have done and believed, I mean Abraham, Isaac, and Jacob, with the rest of the holy prophets and apostles, even so do I believe to be saved, and by no other means." "God's passion! (said the bishop) did not I tell you, my Lord Deputy[9] how you should know an heretic? he is up with the 'living god,' as though there were a dead God. They have nothing in their mouths, these heretics, but 'the Lord lives, the living God rules, the Lord, the Lord' and nothing but the Lord."[10]

This is not, of course, the place to pursue the meaning of these differences—that would take several pages—but of their significance it can be said that at the very least they provide two new perspectives on why meaningful communication between both sides was all but impossible. The study of conversion during the early English Reformation, then, is not only feasible but long overdue. It must be quickly added, however, that any such study must of necessity be individualistic and impressionistic; it is not a phenomenon, as William James made clear long ago, that lends itself to generalization or precise analysis.[11] Even with these limitations, it is eminently worth doing if for no other reason than the most obvious one: the phenomenon of conversion played a part in this period.[12] A less obvious and more compelling reason is to be found in the flood of local studies that have appeared in the last 30 years, for in the same way that they have provided new and revealing perspectives on the character and course of the Reformation or Reformations, so, too, albeit on a drastically reduced scale, will the individual studies of those men and women for whom evidence of conversion has survived the centuries.[13] And it is with this purpose in mind, as well as the desire to acquaint a wider audience with an attractive if tragic figure from the sixteenth century, that I offer the following pages about Nicholas Sheterden.

At first glance, Sheterden does not appear to be a subject worthy of individual study: much of his life is lost to history, and his literary remains occupy less than a dozen fine print pages in Foxe.[14] It is known, among other things, that he was a convert to Freewill radicalism—that is, he rejected the doctrine of Predestination—and a casualty of the Marian reaction; he was burned with three others on July 12, 1555, at Canterbury.[15] The modest amount of attention that Sheterden has received from scholars has focused almost entirely on his status as a Freewiller, a subject about which there is some disagreement (i.e., did he convert from it?) and one that is carefully pursued in these pages. A few passing remarks have also been made about his performance under judicial fire during his heresy examinations. These proceedings, presented by Foxe as being recounted in Sheterden's own hand, are a fascinating mixture of doctrinal argument, legal wrangling, and personal reflection. They receive close readings here, as do two letters Sheterden wrote to his brother and mother before he died; a third to his mother, desperately seeking her conversion, is printed in full.

I

Both the facts of Nicholas Sheterden's birth and the forces that shaped his beliefs must be to some extent the subject of speculation. From three documents in Sheterden's literary remains, including two letters to his mother and a final prayer mentioning his children, it could be speculated that he died a relatively young man, perhaps in his late twenties to mid-thirties, an age range that would make him a child of the 1520's. Whether in this decade or an earlier one, Sheterden was almost certainly born in Pluckley, a textile town located southwest of Canterbury on the northern edge, or scarpland, of the Kentish Weald.[16] Pluckley was also the hometown of Henry Harte, the leader of mid-Tudor Freewill radicalism and quite possibly Sheterden's converter to the same.[17] Harte's first appearance in the pages of history was not as a Freewiller, however, but as a "favorer of the new doctrine." This was how the Canterbury Court of Quarter Sessions characterized Harte and five others in its indictment against them for "unlawful assemblies" in the spring of 1538, according to the Archbishop Cranmer, who wrote a letter on their behalf to Cromwell. Writing on April 29, Cranmer reported that the six men had been indicted "of none occasion or ground else but because they are accounted favorers of the new doctrine, as they [i.e., members of the court] call it." He then requested their release, characterizing them as favorers of God's word.[18] Henry Harte is not the only reform-minded person about whom something is known who may have influenced Sheterden's religious beliefs. William Lancaster, the parson of Pluckley from 1541 to 1554, was the subject of a deposition in 1543 for his disregard for Roman rituals and rites and, in one case at least, his disdain for an acquaintance who observed them. The record reads, "When [Lancaster was] told that Stephen Giles . . . blessed himself daily and nightly *In nomine Patris*, &c. and that he said a *Paternoster*, an *Ave* and a Creed in honor of God and Our Lady, &c., the parson [Lancaster] said that if he knew that Giles had used that form of prayer he would never accompany him or drink with him." As Andrew

Penny points out, the same exclusivist attitude was common among Kentish Freewillers during the reign of Edward VI, which is when writing about one of their number—Nicholas Sheterden—becomes a slightly less speculative enterprise.[19]

In late January 1551, the Privy Council ordered the arrest of Sheterden along with fourteen others from Kent and Essex in connection with a conventicle held during the previous month in the Essex town of Bocking. Their arrest was triggered in large measure by the testimony of their unwitting host, a weaver identified as "Upcharde," who told the Council that the men who met in his house on the day in question argued "about things of the scripture, especially whether it were necessary to stand or kneel, bareheaded, or covered at prayer." When Sheterden and eleven of his fellow conventiclers from both counties appeared before the Privy Council on February 3, they corroborated Upcharde's testimony, admitted to having absented themselves from communion for over two years, and revealed "divers other evil opinions worthy of great punishment." The record of the action taken by the Privy Council against Sheterden is unfortunately incomplete; he is listed as being imprisoned, but there is no information as to where or how long. Penny suggests that he may have been placed in custody in his native county where, he surmises, the investigation of the Bocking conventicle continued with the formal deposing of informants. The handful of depositions that survive not only document the previous existence of the Kentish conventicle—a deponent named William Greenlande "confess[ed] the congregation and [its] meeting at divers places"—but also demonstrate that while exclusivism and anti-intellectualism were certainly debating points for its members, opposition to strict Predestination was the centerpiece of debate and, of course, the reason for their identification as "Freewill-men" in Edward VI's and Mary I's reigns.[20] It was during the latter period that Nicholas Sheterden's name resurfaced, though this time not in Privy Council correspondence but in prison letters from John Bradford.

On August 16, 1553, not long after Edward VI's death and Mary's ascension to the English throne, Bradford, a popular Edwardian preacher, was arrested and placed in the Tower of London. He would remain there until March 24, 1554, when he was transferred to the King's Bench Prison in nearby Southwark, where he became one of the central figures in a famous dispute with the Freewill-men among his fellow prisoners as well as those who were incarcerated or in hiding elsewhere. Perhaps the most fascinating aspect of this dispute—and surely the most frustrating vis-à-vis Sheterden—is what Penny terms a "reclamation process" by which a handful of Freewill-men embraced predestination as an inherent part of Protestantism.[21] The frustration in relation to Sheterden arises from the fact that it cannot be definitively established if he was among them, which in turn has resulted in conflicting conclusions about his final faith. The only evidence that can be brought to bear on this question consists of his own writings, which will be considered last, and two prison letters from Bradford, who by all accounts was well suited to play the role of reconciler and reclaimer.

The first letter is addressed to Sheterden and to Robert Cole, a fellow conventicler from Kent and future convert to Protestant orthodoxy.[22] At the time the letter was written, most likely early in 1554, Cole and Sheterden were in the Freewill camp, although perhaps not firmly, as could be inferred from the lines following Bradford's opening in which he acknowledged their original letter as if it were one of personal inquiry rather than formal controversy. "Your letter though I have not read [it] myself . . . yet I have heard the sum of it, that it is of God's election; wherein I will briefly write to you my faith, and how I think it good and meet for a Christian man to wade in it." Bradford began with the basics, the Fall of "man" and his full redemption in Christ. He then turned to the terms of man's redemption—belief and faith in Christ—and after distinguishing between faith produced by miracles or induced by other means and "true faith, the justifying and regenerating faith," he declared, "I believe . . . that this faith and belief in Christ is the work and gift of God, that is, to those whom God the Father, before the beginning of the world, hath predestinate in Christ unto eternal life."[23] This declaration, of course, went to the very heart of the matter, and Bradford followed it by instructing Sheterden and Cole to search their own hearts for the presence of such faith. If they found it, he urged them to "praise the Lord." If not, he encouraged them to put off disputing about predestination ("too high a matter for you") "until," he wrote, "you have been better scholars in the school-house of repentance and justification which is the grammar-school wherein we must be conversant and learned, before we go to the university of God's holy predestination and providence."

Having set out a course of study that he believed would reveal to Sheterden and Cole the exclusive nature of God's role in salvation and—

he obviously hoped—produce in them evidence of their own, Bradford set about treating how "a Christian man" should "wade" in predestination. After reviewing his own approach to the doctrine and reiterating its main points, he rejected all challenges to the will of God that lie behind it, especially those mounted by reason. Reason, he wrote, "must needs be beaten down, to be more careful for God's glory than for man's salvation which dependeth only thereon, as all God's children full well see." These same children, Bradford averred, "know God to be a God which doeth on earth, not only mercy, but also judgement; which is justice . . . although our foolish reason cannot see it; and in this knowledge they glory and rejoice, though others, through vain curiosity, grudge and murmur thereagainst." Bradford's keen desire for Sheterden and Cole to know and see these same things, which is so evident in the preceding, is also present in the closing where he offered to write to them again.[24] What effect, if any, this letter had on either man is not known. Its value in Sheterden's case, however, is not limited to its message. Assuming the accuracy of the inference ventured above, and the potential of questioning as a prelude to religious conversion, this letter by its very existence is of considerable value in making the case for the reclamation of Nicholas Sheterden.

On February 16, 1555, exactly eighteen months after his initial arrest and roughly two weeks after his official condemnation, John Bradford wrote what turned out to be a rather premature farewell letter to some thirteen individuals—including Sheterden—and to "all other[s] that fear the Lord and love his truth abiding in Kent, Essex, Sussex, and thereabout."[25] The doctrinal persuasions of those named in Bradford's letter were first characterized by Miles Coverdale, who inscribed the letter: "To certain men, not rightly persuaded in the most true, comfortable, and necessary doctrine of God's holy election and predestination." The most recent scholarship is somewhat divided over the proper characterization of these men, with Penny arguing that Bradford was addressing himself to a doctrinally mixed audience (i.e., fellow "predestinators" and Freewill-men) and M. T. Pearse acknowledging this possibility but at the same time adjudging it "unlikely" owing to the contents of the letter.[26] Turning to the same, Bradford's salutation-cum-benediction reveals nothing about the composition of his audience, nor really does what comes next, his reason for writing: "to occasion you the more to weigh the things wherein some controversy hath been amongst us, especially the article and doctrine of predestination."

The passage that follows, however, could be interpreted as supporting the view that Bradford's audience was composed solely of Freewill-men. After recommending his tract, *Defence of Election*, and counseling reserve and restraint in controversy, Bradford wrote, "Do not suppose that any man by affirming predestination . . . [does so] either to seek carnality or to set forth matter of desperation."[27] He then sought to discredit this supposition by both explaining his own affirmation of the doctrine and by expounding at some length on what he apparently saw as the theological error responsible for it: the misapplication of the law and the Gospel vis-à-vis the old and new natures of the "man of God." He claimed that if they were applied properly (i.e., law to the old nature and Gospel to the new), "man shall be kept from carnality and from desperation also, and brought into diligence and godly peace of conscience."[28] He further claimed that if his counsel were followed, all disagreements and distrust "amongst" them would disappear, adding that he loved them in the Lord.

The remainder of the letter, which if anything strengthens the argument for a mixed audience, is by turns reflective and exhortative. He reminded his readers of what they shared with him—the same faith and fate—and why he was sharing his love with them, "that you might see my love, and thereby be occasioned to increase in love, and learn rather to bear than break." Continuing in this same vein, he commended unto his readers an unnamed though clearly much beloved "sister" whom he had recently converted to Predestination, imploring them to care for her and issuing the following caveat: "If you cannot think with her therein as she doth . . . molest her not, nor disquiet her, but let love abound, and therein contend who can go most before."[29] After making brief mention of another "good sister," Bradford filled his last lines with heartfelt words about avoiding the "Romish . . . religion," practicing the reformed one, and recalling the help and hope of those who did. Taking into careful consideration both the contents and context of this letter (i.e., Bradford's assumption that his execution was imminent), it seems reasonable to conclude that Bradford was writing both to his doctrinal opponents, whom he was trying to turn, and to his soul mates, for whom he sought to set an example. In regard to Nicholas Sheterden, such a conclusion removes this letter as an obstacle in making the case for his reclamation, leaving only two objections to it pending, the grounds for which are found in his writings.

II

Sheterden had been detained in Canterbury's Westgate Prison for some six months—beginning in the late summer of 1554—by the time Bradford finished the foregoing letter. While the circumstances of his apprehension are lost to history, the reasons for his imprisonment are to be found in the first of three examinations printed in the *Acts and Monuments*. Sheterden's examinations are of interest for a number of reasons, not the least of which being John Foxe's handling of them. Given the fact that Foxe suppressed evidence documenting the Trinitarian and christological radicalism of several victims of the Marian regime in Kent, it could be objected that he did the same thing in Sheterden's case, in effect posthumously converting him from Freewill radicalism to orthodox Protestantism. This objection cannot be completely discounted—proving a negative in this instance is impossible—although it can be persuasively countered. As Patrick Collinson concludes in his essay on the *Book of Martyrs*, "The pattern is now reasonably clear. Foxe was sometimes prepared to falsify his evidence to the extent of misrepresenting heretics . . . as orthodox and conformable if often confused and poorly-informed Christians of his own persuasion."[30] The fact of the matter is Sheterden does not fit the profile; he was anything but confused and poorly informed. Indeed, Collinson himself cites him as an example of Kent's "formally uneducated but often well-informed and highly opinionated" lay martyrs. Similar assessments of Sheterden or of his performance under questioning are to be found in all who have written about him. J. W. Martin calls him "articulate, well-read biblically, and spiritually sensitive." Andrew Penny claims he "handled himself with distinction in adversity," as does M. T. Pearse, who writes, "Sheterden gave a spirited and astute defense of his views to his persecutors."[31] None of these scholars, however, documents in any detail the basis for their assessments of him.

What then is it, precisely, that Sheterden said or did to lead historians to such conclusions? At least part of the answer emerges rather quickly in "The first Examination or Reasoning of Nicholas Sheterden with Master [Nicholas] Harpsfield, Archdeacon, and Master Collens the Commissary, for which they sent him to prison."[32] It began, like so many others in the pages of Foxe, back in the Upper Room with Christ's words, "This is my body." Harpsfield sought Sheterden's affirmation that these words "did change the substance, without any other interpretation or spiritual meaning of the words." Sheterden's response was nonsensical and deliberately so: "Then belike, when Christ said, This cup is my blood, the substance of the cup was changed into his blood without any other meaning, and so the cup was changed and not the wine." It led to an exchange about Christ's use of plain and figurative speech in referring to the bread and the cup (wine) and an exploration—initiated by Sheterden—of whether the priest's words or mind changed them into Christ's flesh and blood.[33] It also led, at least according to Foxe, to Harpsfield's exasperation and to Collens's declaration that, because Sheterden accepted bread as a "figure," his argument about the cup was against himself, in rebuttal to which Sheterden finally made his strategy plain: "My argument is not against me at all; for I do not speak it to prove that the cup is his blood, nor the figure of his blood, but to prove that the bare words being spoken of the priest, do not change the substance any more than they do change the cup into blood." This, of course, amounted to a denial of Transubstantiation, and it alone most likely landed Sheterden behind Westgate's walls.

The examination continued, however, with Collens's claim, based on John 3:13, that Christ's "manhood" was in heaven and on earth simultaneously.[34] Sheterden first reminded Collens that Christ was God and man, and when he persisted in focusing on the latter, warned him, "If ye will needs understand it to be spoken of Christ's manhood, then ye must fall into the error of the Anabaptists, which deny that Christ took flesh of the Virgin Mary; for if there be no body ascended up, but that which came down, where is then his incarnation? For then he brought his body down."

The examination concluded with an exchange about the anthropomorphic portrayal of God that reveals Sheterden's biblicism. At one point Collens asked Sheterden, "Why, doth not the Scripture say, that God is Spirit? and what hand can a spirit have?" He responded, "Truth is, God is a spirit, and therefore is worshipped in spirit and truth; and as he is a spirit, so hath he a spiritual power, so hath he a spiritual seat, a spiritual sword. . . . Because we know not what hand God hath, therefore, if we say he hath none, then it may as well be said, there is no Christ."[35] As this last line suggests, and as a letter to be considered later substantiates, Sheterden saw no value but instead real danger in debating such questions, questions which he believed were definitively answered in the Bible.

Sheterden's second examination—presented as being written in his own hand[36]—stands in stark contrast with his first one in the extent to which theological questioning is displaced by legal wrangling. Headed somewhat misleadingly by Sheterden "My first Answering, after their Law was established"—he did very little answering—it begins with his reason for recounting it: "Because I know ye will desire to hear from me some certainty of my state." Sheterden then moved directly to the proceedings: "I was called before the suffragan, and seven or eight of the chief priests, and examined of certain articles; and then I required to see their commission. They showed it to me and said, 'There it is, and the king and queen's letters also.'"[37] The passage that follows is of crucial importance, both for the information it contains and for the tone it sets. Sheterden wrote,

Then I desired to have [the commission] read: and so in reading I perceived, that on some notable suspicion he might examine upon two articles; whether Christ's real presence were in the sacrament; and whether the Church of England be Christ's catholic church. To that I answered, that I had been a prisoner three quarters of a year, and as I thought wrongfully: reason would, therefore, that I should answer to those things wherefore I was prisoner.[38]

Assuming that this examination took place within a month or so of Sheterden's condemnation (June 25, 1555), it can be established that he was placed in prison at some time in the late summer or early autumn of 1554. Sheterden raised the timing of his imprisonment after Bishop Thornden repeatedly refused to give him any reason for it: "For when I was cast into prison, there was no law but I might speak as I did: therefore, in that point, I could be no more suspected than you which preached the same yourself not long before." The law to which Sheterden refers reenacted three medieval statutes against heresy, thereby making possible the Marian persecution; it passed through Parliament in December 1554, well after Sheterden's imprisonment.[39]

Sheterden not only called attention to this illegality; he called into question the credibility of his examiner—and it would appear for good reason. Thornden, who had supported the religious reforms of Edward's reign, spearheaded their rapid reversion in Mary's in a volte-face that drew criticism even from a subordinate priest.[40] Sheterden alluded to Thornden's Protestant past twice more; challenging him, "Prove me suspect more than you yourself," and again when confronted with a letter he had written to his mother seeking her conversion, claiming, "In that I did but

my duty to certify her, I was not in prison for an evil. And that was before
the law also; and therefore no more suspicion was in me, than was in them
which taught the like."[41]

Legal arguments having failed them, one of Sheterden's examiners, a
master Mills, attempted another strategy, telling him, "If you were a
Christian man, you would not be ashamed of your faith being required."
This approach worked about as well as the first one did. Sheterden's reply
was at once unequivocal and tactical. "I am not ashamed, indeed, I thank
God, and if any man did come to me, either to teach or learn, I would declare it; but forasmuch as I perceive you to come neither to teach nor to
learn, I hold it best not to answer you." Sheterden put his perceptions
about his examiners' motives into words after they again equated his silence with shame. "Nay, . . . you shall well know I am not ashamed of my
faith: but because you do so greedily seek blood, I will answer only to that
you have against me." His defiance set off the following exchange:

> *Suffragan*:—"Nay, you shall answer to the articles, or else be condemned upon
> suspicion."
> *Sheterden*:—"I am content with that; yet all men shall know that as ye suspect
> and can prove no cause, so shall ye condemn me without a matter, and then shall
> know ye seek my blood, and not justice."
> *Suffragan*:—"No, we seek not thy blood, but thy conversion."[42]

These lines, for all intents and purposes, mark the end of this examination and for the most part encapsulate it. To the extent that there was a
winner, it had to be Sheterden. By virtue of his own wit or selective memory, he thwarted his examiners at every turn and in the process disclosed
virtually nothing about his faith. In the third examination—headed by
Foxe, "The Examination of Nicholas Sheterden before Stephen Gardiner,
Bishop of Winchester, then Lord Chancellor"—Sheterden is not only
forceful in demanding his rights but also forthcoming about his beliefs.[43]

The second week of June 1554 found Gardiner returning from a failed
embassy to the Continent. Even in his travels the aged prelate found no relief from the problem of religious dissent. At Calais he encountered "a haven of heretics," and in Canterbury he was told about Sheterden's recalci-
trance before the royal commissioners. Whether out of a sense of duty or as
Sheterden recorded him saying, "for the sake of charity," Gardiner delayed
his departure for London and called before him the thorn in Thornden's

side.[44] The proceedings began with both examiner and examinee describing the events in question. Gardiner stated, "I have sent for you, because I hear you are indicted of heresy; and, being called before the commissioners, ye will not answer nor submit yourself." Sheterden, of course, made up for the fact that Gardiner's description made no mention of his unlawful imprisonment; he also took issue with having been indicted, observing, "Neither did I know [of] any indictment against me. If there were any, it could not be just, for I was not abroad since the law [i.e., Heresy Law] was made." At first, Gardiner brushed aside the imprisonment issue ("Well, yet if such suspicion be of you . . ."), but after Sheterden raised it again, he held out the possibility of redress. "If thou wilt declare thyself to the church to be a Christian, thou shalt go, and then have a writ of wrong imprisonment." After declining the writ in favor of "right justice," Sheterden changed the whole direction of the examination by suggesting that prison would not change his conscience. He added, "Those things which I have learned were by God's Law openly taught and received by the authority of the realm." From the exchange that ensued—"And he said, it was never received that I might speak against the sacrament. I said, against some opinion of the sacrament it was openly taught"—it is clear that Sheterden was referring to his rejection of Transubstantiation and the Real Presence during Edward VI's reign. He explained why he rejected them in a self-revelatory passage that deserves quoting in full.

Their law did not only persuade me, but this most: when they preached unto us, they took pain to set out the word of God in our tongue, so that we might read and judge whether they say true or no; but now they take the light from us, and would have us believe it, because they say so; which is to me a great persuasion.

Here in the space of a single sentence—albeit a rather convoluted one—is a partial conversion narrative and a partisan commentary on the Marian regime.[45] At the center of both is the issue of doctrinal authority, and Gardiner was quick to question Sheterden's reliance on "a few" Edwardian preachers in the face of "the doctors and all the whole church." He asked him, "Now whom wouldest thou believe, either the few or the many?" Sheterden's answer—not unexpected, surely—reveals his thoroughgoing biblicism: "I do not believe for the few nor for the many, but only for that he [e.g., a preacher or a teacher] bringeth the word, and showeth it to me to be according to the process thereof."[46]

. After failing to entrap Sheterden with his own words ("Well, then if an Arian come to thee with Scripture, thou wilt believe him?"), or to entice him using "many words" about the Sacrament of the Altar ("But I let him alone, and said nothing"), Gardiner engaged him in a war of words about images. Sheterden began by pronouncing them outlawed in Scripture, and when challenged as to where, quoted a passage from Deuteronomy 4, which Gardiner mistook for an interpretation. Sheterden recounted what happened next:

Then was a Bible called for, and when it came, he bade me find it, and I should strait be confounded with mine own words; so that if there were any grace within me, I would trust mine own wit no more; and when I looked, it was Latin.

"Why," said Winchester [Gardiner] "can ye read no Latin?"

"No."

Then was the English Bible brought. He bade me find it; and so I read it aloud, and then he said; "Lo here thou mayest see; this is no more to forbid the image of God, than of any other beast, fowl or fish." I said it did plainly forbid to make any of these as an image of God, because no man might know what shape he was of. Therefore might no man say of any image, "There is an image of God."

What is especially noteworthy about this scene is not the spectacle of a layman with no formal education challenging a churchman with a formidable one, but its subtext: a layman who believed the Bible's true meaning was clear and made accessible through inspiration and study, challenging a churchman both far less sanguine about the text's clarity and fully committed to the church's historic role as its sole interpreter.

Shortly after this scene, Gardiner, who had written in 1546, "There was never [a] heretic, but boasted scripture," came to the conclusion that Sheterden was an unconvertible one ("At last he saw, he said, what I was") telling him that his charge of unlawful imprisonment would not protect him from prosecution for heresy.[47] He was right. Sheterden was condemned to die on July 25, 1555, by the bishop of Dover, Richard Thornden, because he would not answer all of the seven articles brought against him.[48] Both before and after this date, Sheterden wrote letters to family members and, like his examinations, these letters reveal his intellectual qualities and doctrinal commitments. These letters also reveal his personal religious faith and the persistent efforts he made to persuade his mother to make it her own.[49]

III

The first letter presented by Foxe, from Sheterden to his mother, is an amazing document, combining as it does anticlericalism, anti-intellectualism, dispassionate argument, and passionate exhortation. He began by wishing his mother "grace and godly wisdom, . . . [to] see and perceive the crafty bewitching of Satan our mortal enemy," reminding her, "he doth not openly show himself . . . but under color of devotion deceiveth them that keep not a diligent eye upon him." Showing his anticlerical colors for the first time, Sheterden charged, "For this is most true, that Satan . . . doth by his ministers make many believe, that those things which they compel us unto for their bellies sake, have many godly significations although they be most contrary to God's will . . . even as did the serpent in paradise to our first mother Eve." He then recounted the serpent's deception of Eve and followed it with a little dialogue of his own: "Even so our ministers now a-days, say, 'Hath God commanded ye shall not make any image or likeness of anything?' 'Yea, forsooth.' 'Tush,' say they, 'what harm can they do?' May we not remember God the better when we see his image or picture? for they are good books for laymen." Saying nothing about the didactic function of images, Sheterden dismissed them as moneymakers for the priesthood. He was not finished with them, however, and using Eden's other occupant, Sheterden sought to alert his mother to the dangers of images, specifically images of Christ. He wrote, "For Adam's eyes were so opened, that he lost both innocency and righteousness, and was become most miserable of all creatures: and even so we remember Christ so well by images, that we forget his commandments, and count his testament, confirmed in his blood, for stark madness or heresy." According to Sheterden, then, images of Christ were like the forbidden fruit: both brought sin and self-deception. In closing this part of the letter, he warned his mother that unless "we repent shortly" plagues would surely follow.[50]

What followed in the letter appears to have been an effort by Sheterden to answer any questions raised in his mother's mind about his competency to criticize the clergy and to condemn images. Prompted most likely by experience rather than expectation, Sheterden's effort took the form of a two-part attack, first upon the notion that only the learned were qualified to write about the doctrine and practice of the Church, and second upon the learning of the learned.[51] "But I know," Sheterden began, "the craftiness of them herein (I thank God) which will say, 'Where went he to school? Is he wiser than our great doctors that studied all their life?'" He did not answer either question, but rather addressed an issue raised by them: the long-standing expectation that the unlearned would never exercise independent judgment or challenge the judgment of the learned. Employing a pungent metaphor, Sheterden wrote, "And lo they say that it is good hay: although we smell it musty ourselves, yet must we believe it is sweet; and then pay them well for their so saying, and all is so safe." Moving from feed to bedding, Sheterden set up a learned straw man, challenging him, "What sir! be ye wiser than Christ, and God his Father, or the Holy Ghost? What, Sir! be ye wiser than the prophets and the holy apostles and all the holy martyrs? I pray you, sir, where had you your high learning?" These questions and those that followed them were, of course, a product of Sheterden's profound biblicism. He found the learning of the learned "strange" because he found so little of it in the Bible, venturing at one point, "I dare say, the greater half of their ceremonies were never commanded by Christ." And of course it was this perception which caused Sheterden to abandon the church and to work to convince his mother to do the same.[52]

In the remainder of this letter, he set about this task with a sense of urgency that is only surpassed by his last letter to her. He began this remarkable passage with an emotional plea: "Beloved Mother, as I have oftentimes said unto you, even so now I beseech you from my very heart-root in Christ, to consider your own soul's health is offered to you; do not cast it off: we have not long time here." He spent the rest of it answering a question that he himself posed: "Why should we condemn our fathers that lived thus?" This question, one undoubtedly that his mother had put to him, points to what must have been a powerful retardant to conversion during this period: the religious faith of forebearers. In his answer, Sheterden alternated between reassuring observations and what he obviously hoped would be stirring exhortations: "God forbid," he first observed, "that we should condemn any that did according to their knowledge, but let us take heed that they condemn not us." He then went on to claim that if their forebearers had "heard the word . . . and had been warned," they would have responded with greater gratitude than their own generations had shown. Again, trying to reassure his mother about the fate of their forebearers, Sheterden observed, "And surely look how many of them God

will accept and save . . . for our disobedience is more great than their ignorance." Following on with this last line, he claimed that God had shown
more mercy to them than he had to their forebearers. In the last lines of
this letter, amid talk of backsliding and backbiting friends, Sheterden gave
voice to his highest hope: "Would God we might be so knit in faith and
trust in God's word and promises here in this life, as we might together
enjoy the bliss and consolation of eternal life; which I desire and seek above
all worldly treasure."[53]

Worldly treasure occupied the opening lines of another remarkable letter that Sheterden wrote from Westgate Prison; addressed to his brother
Walter, it quickly moved from lucre to the subject of learning. The connection between them is to be found in an exposed bribery scheme that
Sheterden briefly outlined: "It is showed me, my brother, that ye willed me
by a letter made to a friend of yours to persuade with me, that I should be
ruled by mine uncle, which [*sic*] saith, he will bestow his goods very largely
upon me, if I should not stand too high in mine own conceit."[54] As the
next sentence suggests, he did not want to believe that his brother had such
little regard for the authenticity of his conversion. "But, my good brother I
trust ye do not judge so evil of me, that I should have a faith to sell for
money." Sheterden went on to make it clear to his brother that he valued
his faith above all else and would not allow anyone to interfere with his relationship with God. He was not finished defending himself, however, and
he immediately launched into a detailed defense of his learning—apparently not only his commitment but also his competency had been called
into question during the planning of the bribery scheme. He wrote, "For
though I be not learned (as the vain men of the world call learning), yet I
thank my Lord God, I have learned out of God's book." In these the first
few clauses of a long sentence, Sheterden established that there were two
kinds of learning and that his was based on the Bible. He went on to list for
his brother some of the things he had learned, including knowing "Christ
from his sacraments" and putting "a difference between the merits of
Christ's passion and his Supper." He pointedly concluded, "And not to
mix and mingle things all confusedly together, so that if one ask me a
question or a reason of my faith, I must say thus: 'I believe as holy church
believeth.'"

Having substantiated his own learning—and neatly turned the tables
on his brother in the process—Sheterden sought to undermine the learn-

ing of the learned. He introduced this effort by putting into words a thought that he suggested may have been on his brother's mind: "Why, they are learned; it were [a] marvel but that they know what is the truth, as well as others which never kept no such study." Responding, he wrote, "To that I answer, if they had studied God's word the author of truth, as they have done logic and Duns Scotus, with the legend of lies, they should have been as expert in the truth as they be now in bald reasons." Sheterden's words here are significant for a number of reasons, not the least of which being their status as the grounds for the final objection to his reclamation. The objection itself is easily explained. Sheterden remained a Freewiller because he continued to espouse an aspect of Freewill thought: anti-intellectualism. The fact that he did, however, does not preclude the possibility that he rejected the central tenet of Freewill radicalism, a belief in Freewill. Sheterden, then, was an orthodox Protestant with regard to Predestination, but one who had a deep distrust for formal learning.[55]

Sheterden closed this letter with a historical discussion of how those who ignored God's word were given over to error. Clearly with the leaders of the Marian church in mind, he wrote, "For it is evident enough to see how unlike their doings be to Christ's and his apostles: and that seen, either we must judge Christ's doings very slender, and theirs good, or else that indeed they be the very Antichrists which should come and turn all things out of frame." One wonders what Walter made of such talk . . .[56]

In the second of his three-volume history of the English Reformation, Philip Hughes observed the following about the Marian martyrs. "Oddities these men and women are, no doubt; unusual types, self opinionated, argumentative, dogmatic, intolerant; eccentric, it may be, and like all the autodidactic, so very, very sure of whatever they have themselves found out."[57] To be sure, Sheterden was all of these, but he was also reflective, intelligent, articulate, confident, and above all persistent, as the last letter from his hand attests. Written the day before he would die, it represents Sheterden's last effort to convince his mother to abandon the Roman Catholic Church. At once emotional and polemical, it captures the consequences of conversion for a son and his mother in Marian England.

O my good mother, whom I love with reverence in the Lord, and according to my duty, I desire your favourable blessing and forgiveness of all my misdeeds towards you. O my good mother, in few words, I wish you the same salvation, which I hope myself to feel, and partly taste of before this come [sic] to you to read; and in the resurrection, I verily believe to have it more perfectly in body and soul joined together for ever; and in that day God grant you to see my face with joy: but, dear mother, then beware of that great idolatry, and blasphemous mass. O let not that be your god, which mice and worms can devour. Behold I call heaven and earth to record, that it is no god, yea the fire that consumeth it, and the moistness that causeth it to mould; and I take Christ's Testament to witness, that it is none of his ordinances, but a mere invention of men, and a snare to catch innocents' blood; and now that God hath showed it unto you, be warned in time. O give over old customs, and become new in the truth. What state soever your fathers be in, leave that to God; and let us follow the counsel of his word. Dear mother, embrace it with hearty affection; read it with obedience; let it be your pastime: but yet cast off all carnal affections, and love of worldly things; so shall we meet in joy at the last day, or else I bid you farewell for evermore. O farewell my friends and lovers all: God grant me to see your faces in joy. Amen.—From Westgate, the 11th of July, 1555.

> Your child, written with his hand, and sealed with his blood,
> Nicholas Sheterden, being appointed to be slain.[58]

I V

The life and letters of Nicholas Sheterden have much to teach us— not only about the phenomenon of conversion during the early English Reformation but also about its further study. Many of the lessons are to be found in the letter above. The first and the most significant of these is that the study of conversion is not simply religious history; it is also social history. Through Sheterden's examinations and letters we meet his family— his mother and brother, among others—and we see the effect that his conversion had upon them, indeed, driving his brother to take part in a bribery scheme to secure Sheterden's abjuration. Other lessons are learned as well. In the first line of this letter, Sheterden claims that he is writing according to his "duty." Katherine Parr expresses similar sentiments at the beginning of her famous conversion narrative, *The Lamentation of a Sinner*.[59] What was this obligation they felt so deeply? Clearly, it was rooted in a number of things, not the least of which was the New Testament mandate to share one's faith—a rather novel idea in the sixteenth century and one that deserves further study.[60] (Implicit in this mandate was, of course, the ability to explain one's faith; it is a notion as shown above that Sheterden discusses at length and one that also merits attention.) Sheterden's warnings to his mother about the Mass bring to mind his words to his brother: "I have learned . . . to know Christ from his sacraments."[61] Clearly, Sheterden had a different conception of the person and work of Christ than his mother. What were the differences, and what difference did they make? These and other questions need to be pursued. Finally, after exhorting his mother to "give over old customs, and become new in the truth," Sheterden instructs her to forget about her fathers and to follow the "counsel of the Word." There are two important lessons here, beginning with the degree to which ancestors were a retardant to conversion, and here again, further study is warranted, especially within the context of traditional religious beliefs and practices. The second lesson is the degree to which individuals like Sheterden believed that the counsel of the Word was clear and could be apprehended by all readers and listeners. It is a conviction that cannot be explained apart from a definite view about the workings of the Holy Spirit, a topic, as noted at the outset, that still needs attention. It is hoped the preceding pages, and these few closing thoughts drawn from Sheterden's final words, will send the message that there is still much interesting and important work to be done on the phenomenon of conversion during the early English Reformation.

DAVID R. COMO

The Kingdom of Christ, the Kingdom of England, and the Kingdom of Traske

JOHN TRASKE AND THE PERSISTENCE OF RADICAL PURITANISM IN EARLY STUART ENGLAND

Modern historians have painted an ambiguous portrait of seventeenth-century English puritanism. On the one hand, thanks in large part to the efforts of Christopher Hill, everyone knows about the anarchic puritan scene of the English Civil Wars. Here is the colorful and sometimes spectacular puritanism of the Baptists, Levellers, Ranters, and Quakers, of the visionaries and radicals who turned the world upside down in the 1640's and 1650's.[1] This picture, however, represents only one side of the historiographical story. For some time now, scholars have been building an alternative vision of puritanism, particularly prewar puritanism, as a decidedly unradical phenomenon. Social historians, including Hill himself, have argued that throughout the early Stuart period, godly piety was favored by urban and rural elites, who saw it as an engine for discipline and social control in a time of increasing economic instability and dislocation. From a different perspective, but in a similar vein, political and religious historians have emphasized the extent to which godly personnel and values were successfully integrated into the political and ecclesiastical establishments. Thus, in his recent work, Patrick Collinson suggests that the Jacobean church came in many ways to be a puritan church, in which magistracy and ministry joined together in a war on sin.[2]

How then did the allegedly conservative puritanism of the early Stuart period transform itself into the exotic and revolutionary variants of the

Civil Wars? One of the few historians to tackle this problem is Christopher Hill, who recognized it as a serious contradiction in his own work. Hill hypothesized that there might have been a lineage of plebeian heresy and rebelliousness that began with pre-Reformation Lollardy, mutated into various forms of heterodox Protestantism—the Marian Freewillers, Familists, Grindletonians, and different flavors of separatist—only to emerge from beneath the blanket of mainstream puritanism during the Revolution.[3] While this thesis has remained largely untested, the publication of Christopher Marsh's pioneering study of the Elizabethan Family of Love has reopened the question. Marsh concluded that Familism betrayed few characteristics predicted by Hill; he found no ties to Lollardy, scant evidence of political or social radicalism, and precious little common ground between Familists and puritans.[4] The following paper continues the dialogue here set up between Hill and Marsh by examining the early career of a single individual, John Traske, and by using him as a window onto the problems of the origins of what has been called "radical puritanism."

On June 19, 1618, John Traske was sentenced by the court of Star Chamber to be whipped, pilloried, branded, mutilated, and jailed for life. Traske stood accused of conspiring to draw the king's subjects away from the established faith of the Church of England and of having written seditious letters to the king himself. More specifically, he had set himself up as the head of a sect of ultraprecise separatists who claimed that the Old Testament law, including the Saturday Sabbath and Mosaic dietary restrictions, remained in force for Christians. In late 1617, the authorities had caught up with the sect-master and his disciples, and six months later, Traske was tried, punished, and thrown into the Fleet.[5]

Rather than obligingly dying or disappearing, however, Traske recanted and returned to the ministry in 1620. He slid back into the London puritan community, only to emerge in the later 1620's as a pivotal figure in the city's antinomian underground.[6] Traske had thus gone from being a prophet of ultrastrict Jewish legalism to a role as an evangelical antinomian—that is, an adherent of the notion that true believers were free of the binding power of the moral law. Both at the time and in this century, this 180-degree shift has been seen as proof positive that he was an unstable drifter of no fixed intellectual abode. One of the goals of this chapter shall be to demonstrate that, although Traske's thought was more peculiar than anyone has supposed, it was neither unintelligible, hopelessly contradictory, nor empty. When we scrutinize his early activities and writings, not only can we make sense of this strange about-face, but we emerge with a portrait of an individual who had arrived at a series of positions that anticipated, sometimes uncannily, the most radical formulations of Civil War puritans. This, in turn, allows us to peer into the early Stuart godly community and to imagine how Collinson's "Religion of Protestants" might have become the altogether different religion of Clarkson, Walwyn, and Winstanley.

I

If we are to reconstruct Traske's theological peregrinations, we must step backwards and examine briefly the details of his life prior to his fateful appearance before the Star Chamber. Traske adopted the Saturday Sabbath in 1617, long after he had embarked on his career as a rogue minister and sect-master, and then only at the prompting of one Hamlet Jackson, a young associate who claimed to have received a fiery, spiritual vision concerning God's law. Jackson, a London tailor, had been well seasoned for this revelation. He was one of a band of loyal disciples who had come to regard John Traske as a prophet—a second Elijah, according to one account—and who had already followed Traske in resurrecting a number of Jewish ordinances, such as refraining from kindling fires and dressing meats on Sundays.[7] Yet even this progression into Judaic ritual represented only the culmination of a long process in which Traske and his followers had adopted increasingly unusual, even heterodox, opinions and practices that set them apart from mainstream puritans. Traske's now famous "Judaizing" phase was merely the latest and most ostentatious stop on a spiritual journey that had begun at least a decade earlier in his native county of Somerset.

We know almost nothing of the first 25 years of Traske's life. He was in all likelihood born in Somerset, c. 1584–85, possibly in the town of East Coker, to parents he would later describe as "godly." Having received what appears to have been a basic grammar school education, Traske became a schoolmaster in an unnamed gentleman's household in Somerset.[8] It may have been while serving in this capacity that he experienced the first of many encounters with the English courts, an incident that sets the tone for the rest of our discussion. In 1608, Traske was accused in Star Chamber of libeling Charles Best, a Somerset lawyer. Best claimed that a pair of "lewd" laborers had swindled him in a land deal. A series of legal wrangles and threats followed, during which time Traske, a companion of the two laborers, wrote and circulated a verse vilifying Best. The libel ridiculed the lawyer's ineffectual and hapless maneuvers, ending with a series of statements that reflect sentiments rarely articulated in early modern England: "alas poore foole it greives me now full sore. What? to be cosenned and a counsellor, low search bocrome bagge [a buckram bag was a generic description of a lawyer's tools, or in this case a lawyer's bag of tricks] is there noe knavery in store? well ever hereafter beware the clowted shoe by my consent, bycause thou hast plaid the foole, putt on longe coates and goe again to scoole." The word *clouted,* meaning patched, was again a generic description for the garb of the poor,[9] and there can be little question that (snide humor aside) Traske's warning—"ever hereafter beware the clowted shoe by my consent"—represents an unusually straightforward invocation of what can only be called class antagonism.[10] As we shall see, this strain of sympathy for the poor, and a parallel suspicion of wealth and power, would inform Traske's ministry in the years to come, giving shape to a strikingly egalitarian theological synthesis.

This synthesis would develop as Traske moved from his position as a schoolmaster, to a curacy within the church, to a role as a wandering, self-styled prophet. In 1611, two years after Best's suit, Traske would be ordained against the objections of the ecclesiastical examiner Samuel Ward, who suspected that Traske, a self-taught preacher who had never been to the university, was unfit for the ministry. Within two years, Traske had been suspended from his first Somerset curacy. He appears to have fled into the diocese of Exeter, where he assumed a role as household chaplain to John Drake of Axminster, Devonshire.[11] But by early 1614, he had left the Southwest, taking up the mantle of itinerant evangelist that he would wear for the rest of his career. That May, he appeared on the other side of England, where he was accused of unlicensed preaching in and around Ely.[12] This short stay in Ely will be discussed below, but for now it should simply be noted that Traske seems by this time to have abandoned the parochial structures of the Church of England in favor of peripatetic preaching. By November 1614, he had returned to Somerset, where he was charged with "running up and downe from parish to parish" as a "wandering minister."[13] He escaped, only to be arrested in Middlesex a year later, again for itinerant preaching.[14]

This rapid spiral into itinerancy and confrontation with the ecclesiastical authorities supports the claim, made by witnesses to the Traskite enthusiasm in 1617, that Traske had moved to a position of virtual separatism by the time he arrived in London.[15] His rejection of the authority of the church was accompanied by a parallel rejection of its doctrine. In early 1616, a preacher in Devonshire was forced to defend himself from the accusation that he shared "the erroneous fancyes" of Traske.[16] Fortunately, in 1615 and 1616, Traske managed to publish three tracts, which when carefully compared against the hostile claims of his critics, allow us to reconstruct these "erroneous fancyes." It should be pointed out, however, that the manner in which his ideas were presented was hardly straightforward. In order to get his works through censorship, Traske was forced to couch his arguments in terms that conformed to the conventions of mainstream Calvinist divinity. The peculiar aspects of Traske's message are therefore carefully submerged beneath a surface that was designed to avail itself of an orthodox reading, often emerging only as passing or opportune asides. Even more striking is the fact that Traske's two 1615 pamphlets were constructed as explicit attacks on various forms of *puritan* error, which undoubtedly lubricated the licensing process. The first treatise contained a passing refutation of anabaptism, as well as a critique of puritan pharisaism. The second is framed as an overarching attack on separatism and, more generally, on the godly obsession with the niceties of ecclesiastical government. Entitled *Christs Kingdom Discovered; or, That the true Church of God is in England, clearely made manifest against all Sectaries whatsoever* (1615), this short piece ostensibly followed a well-worn tactic used by nonseparating puritans to refute the claims of separatists, mimicking the classic godly argument that since the Church of England had nurtured within it true believers, it must necessarily be a true church of God.[17] Yet, as we shall see, Traske deployed this format not to defend the Church of England—which he had to all appearances abandoned by 1615—but to elaborate his own very unorthodox vision of Christ's Kingdom rightly construed. What follows, then, is an attempt to distill from his writings the distinctive or constitutive aspects of that Kingdom.

Our most extensive contemporary accounts of Traske's early ministry derive from a London puritan known only as "T.S.," a keen observer of the Traskite movement of 1617. T.S. claimed that prior to his adoption of Jewish ceremonies, Traske had hit upon an unusual soteriology, which differed from that of other divines and which he had used to distinguish himself from his fellow puritans. Having converted an obscure minister identified only as "Mr. Gr.," Traske had "marched like Jehu most furiously, making divisions in the church about London" with his innovative message. According to his novel soteriology, all people could be divided into one of three states: nature, repentance, and grace. In the first, unregenerate state of nature, humans were unaware of sin and utterly separated from God. To these, Traske preached repentance. In some ways, this resembled the standard puritan assumption that the ungodly needed first of all to hear the law preached in order to awaken in them a sense of sin and the attendant need for Christ. But Traske's notion of repentance went beyond a simple awareness of sin. Repentance was for him a state of intense sorrow and rigorous self-mortification, akin to what we might call a state of "penitence." Consequently, he enjoined initiates to crucify their flesh, apparently urging them to extremes of physical endurance, which included fasting, hard labor, the wearing of sackcloth, sexual abstinence, and possibly prolonged periods of sleep deprivation. It was, moreover, a period of waiting, in which the penitent sinner patiently mortified his or her flesh in expectation of the coming of faith.[18] This advent of faith brought the believer into the third estate, that of grace. Here, the rigors and miseries of the period of repentance were entirely wiped away, and the believer was "passed from death to life, they should have no more sorrow, all joy; sadness and sighing should be fled away."[19] This state of justifying faith brought with it complete assurance of one's election; on the account of T.S.—and here, his evidence is corroborated by two other independent sources—Traske also claimed that those so transformed could recognize one another's election infallibly and, perhaps most radically, that those in the state of grace no longer committed sin.[20]

It should be evident that if T.S.'s claims were accurate, Traske's message amounted to much more than a rigorous or exaggerated version of mainstream godly divinity. Several of the opinions described here—particularly the notion that the elect could infallibly recognize one another and that believers were free from sin—are among those identified by G. F. Nuttall as characteristic of the "spiritist" or "antinomian" modes of piety that emerged during the Civil Wars.[21] These are not the sorts of beliefs that we should expect to see from an ultralegalist who insisted that believers should perform every jot and tittle of the Mosaic Law. These are not the sorts of belief that one finds anywhere within mainstream puritanism at the time. Yet, indeed, when we examine Traske's early writings, T.S.'s account is not only verified but considerably amplified.

Traske's first pamphlet, entitled *A Pearl for a Prince*, represented a sort of charter for his ministry, a primer designed for "the little ones, for whose sake I penned it."[22] It was an introductory work, and as such it holds out tantalizing prizes rather than revealing the marrow of Traske's teaching. Nevertheless, its broad outlines confirm T.S.'s account. Thus, Traske explicitly claimed that repentance preceded, and ended with, faith. In a standard puritan maneuver, he urged his readers to examine themselves for the signs of a true faith:

The ground wher faith is sowen, is an humbled soule, a wounded spirit, or rent heart; to such God giveth the grace of Faith, as are so prepared for it. . . . Hast thou felt thy soule sick with sinne? Hast thou beene pressed downe with the burden thereof? Hath thine hart melted within thee, and thine eyes gusht cut with teares for thy sinnes?[23]

The miseries of repentance, however, were completely effaced by the joy that arrived with the coming of true faith:

Hereby thou maist trie thy selfe. Hast thou beene troubled, and terrified with the sight of thy sinnes? And art thou now at Peace? Hast thou mourned? And dost thou rejoyce? Hast thou hated God in his Word, in his Prophets, or poore children? And dost thou delight in his Law, receive his Prophets, because they are his Prophets; delight in the Saints, because they are children? . . . Hast thou feared death, and trembled at the time of dissolution? . . . And canst thou now wait with patience for the time of thy dissolution? Then maist thou take comfort to thy soule, that all the promises of God doe belong to thee, be thy nation, estate, sex or age, what it will.[24]

As this passage indicates, not only did Traske hold before his readers a rapturous vision of the effects of true faith,[25] but he did so in explicitly inclusive terms. The gospel was proclaimed to all without exception. There was nothing obviously unorthodox about this proposition, but Traske deduced from it a set of striking conclusions. He carefully used the notion of the universal promise to appeal to the most powerless members of early modern English society, the poor, women, children, and servants: "Here . . . by this, are discovered the darke courses of such as, dare impudently to affirme, that women have no soules: and that servants, are of no esteeme with God; or that children, shall bee damned."[26] While these claims were by no means novel in the context of early Stuart puritan divinity, there can be little question that in emphasizing the inclusiveness of the promise, Traske was extending an invitation to these most marginal of groups, a conclusion that is confirmed by his subsequent comments on magistracy. God's blindness to the particular state or status of individuals, and his willingness to confer salvation on them regardless of their condition, should be seen as a general pattern for human behavior: "The Magistrate may hence learne, to judge impartially, to execute judgement, without respect of persons, to deale uprightly, betweene the rich, and poore, the bond, and free. Hereby *hee shall draw neere to God* and be most like him: he is no respecter of persons, he not onely offereth, but bestoweth salvation upon all sorts indifferently."[27] Here, magistrates were warned not to allow their wealth or rank to pervert justice. This doctrine, he argued, "reproveth the practise of those Magistrates, that regard mens persons in judgement, favouring some for their riches, and oppressing others that are but of mean estate. Herein they differ from God, and do manifestly discover themselves not yet to be his."[28] These were strong words; from Calvin onward, reformed thought had been very much dominated by the notion that inequalities in wealth and power were not only to be tolerated but to be seen as an inherent aspect of the fabric of creation. While puritan ministers might employ similar rhetoric to upbraid usurers and grain-engrossers, or to remind magistrates of their duty to mete out justice fairly, they often counterbalanced such statements by emphasizing the fact that inequalities in wealth and power were ordained by God, citing the numerous scriptural passages enjoining obedience to superiors and portraying the Christian community as a body composed of diverse (unequal) parts. Traske's comments carried with them no such qualifications and hence tended to undermine, rather than support, the standard corporatist vision from which his rhetoric was drawn.

In a similar manner, but with even greater vehemence, he deployed the doctrine of the universal promise to attack what he perceived as hypocrisy and greed within the clerical establishment:

Such Ministers are reproved as flatter the rich, and fawne upon the mightie, but scorne the weake, and despise the poore. These swarme in all parts where the Gospell is preached: Not onely amongst those of Babels side, but also even here amongst us. Yea those that are so conversant about Touch not, Taste not, Handle not, these that would bee reformers of others, are herein most irreformed themselves. Oh, fearefull is the condition of such: surely the Lord never sent them; or if they say he did, they must prove it, by that they have such a commission, as Christ himselfe never had. He professeth himselfe to be sent to the poore.[29]

Traske had removed Christ's universal promise from a purely theological domain; he invoked it not only to challenge magistrates who exploited inequalities in wealth to their own advantage but also to attack the orthodox clergy. His vision of swarming, hypocritical ministers, bowing hungrily before authority, even as they lectured to the poor about the virtues of the moral law—a most curious claim, given Traske's reputation as an ultralegalistic Judaizer—represented a thinly veiled critique of the puritan ministry and (one suspects) a bald appeal to those who resented the domination of lay and clerical elites. Moreover, this critique suggested that the proper audience for the Gospel, indeed, the true heirs of the Gospel promise, were the poor, for whom Christ himself had exercised his ministry.

It was in Traske's second and third pamphlets, published anonymously and in rapid succession in 1615 and 1616, that his underlying message emerged most clearly.[30] As noted above, his second pamphlet, *Christs Kingdom Discovered*, was ostensibly directed against separatists. Traske thus set out to prove that the various scriptural passages referring to Christ's Kingdom, the Kingdom of Heaven, and the Kingdom of the Son of Man all referred to this life. This fact could be turned against those who claimed that the true church was not in England: "I heare one cry out for want of *Discipline*; others for *Order*; some for *Christs Officers*: one saith, *Here is Christ*; another, *there is Christ*."[31] Such puritanical preachers were false prophets and deceivers, unable to see that the true church was in England, because they themselves had no experience of Christ's Kingdom.

This was not, however, a straightforward anti-separatist tract. Religious writers often talked about the Kingdom of Christ as if it were immanent in the world, yet when they did so, they usually meant simply the church or its discipline. Traske had something very different in mind. Having adduced the immanence of the Kingdom to scold puritans and separatists, he shifted the terms of the argument to attack a second, entirely distinct opponent. The claim that the Kingdom was in this life was redeployed to refute not puritans, but those who claimed that the Kingdom of Heaven referred to the *afterlife*. Traske pointed out that the Scriptures explicitly used the present tense to describe the unshakable kingdom of Zion in Hebrews 12: "*We are come into it; not, we shall; but we are:* and, *we receiving a Kingdome:* not, *Seeing we* shall *receive a Kingdome;* but, *Seeing wee* doe *receive.* . . . What shall I say? Arguments of this sort are very many in holy Scriptures: yea, even those places which they most abuse to the contrary, do yeeld many plaine arguments to every impartiall Reader. . . . And let this be observed, that where the *holy Ghost* speaketh any where of the *life to come*, it is alwaies *in very short speeches*, or *briefe sentences*."[32] This, in fact, may be seen as the primary theme of the treatise. Traske argued, carefully but explicitly, that the Kingdom of Christ and the Kingdom of Heaven referred not only to this life but to this life *alone*.[33] The claim that the Kingdom of Heaven was a this-worldly estate, having nothing at all to do with the afterlife, is not one found frequently in the writings of pious puritans. In fact, it is so unusual and its implications are so peculiar and potentially radical that one wonders how it escaped the sleepy eye of the censor. For although Traske did not deny the afterlife, he most certainly sought to shift the emphasis away from it, and to transfer many of the privileges and transformations normally associated with heaven, to earth itself.

Predictably, then, Traske's vision of Christ's Kingdom bore no relation to any geographic or ecclesiastical entity. The Kingdom, he claimed, "is not *bounded* within any *Nation*, or *limitted* unto any *one People* or *Kingdom*. So that no man can say it is in this Company, and *no where else*, as divers false Prophets have assumed, and dared to maintaine."[34] Rather, it was a spiritual Kingdom, composed of all those who had passed from penitence to the joyful estate of faith, regardless of their nationality or ecclesiastical orientation. Those familiar with the terms used by seventeenth-century people to discuss the church will recognize that Traske was applying to the visible church terms normally used to describe the invisible church of true believers. Although this Kingdom was spiritual, it was immanent and plainly apparent to those who belonged as subjects. Only true believers, in short, could recognize the Kingdom and its subjects, and (just as T.S. had claimed) they did so infallibly and definitively. To use Traske's words: "The *onely way* to know that *Wee*, (that is, *the true Ministers of Christ*) are *in Christ*, is, by the *knowledge of your selves* to be *in Christ*: Giving us to understand thereby, that *none* can *truely know* a *Childe* of *God*, but he that is *in truth* the *Childe* of *God* himselfe."[35]

If believers could recognize each other, Traske reasoned, surely they could recognize the rules that inhered in the Kingdom. Once again, these rules had nothing to do with the institutions of church and state. In fact, Traske's kingdom was without governors of any sort; as he put it, "instead of *Officers*, thou shalt have *Peace*: yea, all the *Subjects* of this *Kingdome* are *Peace-makers*."[36] Traske thus rejected any notion of ecclesiastical oversight, whether presbyterian or episcopal. Outward means of church government were not necessary among the true Saints, who obeyed God's commandments willingly and without the coercion of ecclesiastical discipline.

This was Traske's rather utopian vision—a Kingdom without hierarchy, in which believers obeyed the dictates of God's law in purity, or near-purity, because the law was written in their hearts. But was Traske's vision of divine law the same as that peddled in puritan circles? Certainly, like most other godly ministers, he seems to have endorsed a strict legalism, in which the Scriptures were to be searched for eternal rules of conduct. As he argued from the Book of Malachai, "*Remember yee the Law of* Moses *my Servant.* . . . These are the *Lawes* of this Kingdom; to which whosoever shall adde, he is accursed of God. . . . And from which, whosoever shall take away, God shall take away his part out of the Book of Life."[37] This typically puritan attitude, when pressed to the perfectionist extremes suggested by Traske, helps to explain his ultimate passage into Mosaic ceremonialism. Nevertheless, there was one rule in his kingdom that sets him at odds with every other godly minister of his day: as he hinted at the end of his treatise on the Kingdom, the commandment to love one another entailed making goods common, either among true believers or more generally for distribution among the poor.[38] This strain of Christian communism, which has been overlooked by modern scholars, can be corroborated by holding various pieces of evidence side by side. The most vivid testimony comes from T.S., who recorded this passing comment on the Traskite enthusiasm: "Their silver and gold cast into the streets, as *bread upon the waters* given to the poor, (so did Master *Trask*). And some sold lands and goods, and distributed the price of them."[39] In 1619, the godly Somerset minister William Sclater had interpreted the same phenomenon in less flattering terms: "They must therefore that will be his disciples, take up this crosse; to keepe backe none of their temporalities from thier Paraclete; as hee said merrily, upon paine to forfeit their election." The results, Sclater mocked, were plain for the world to see: "What marvaile then if some besotted silly women, and servants, have purloyned from their husbands, and robbed from their masters, to maintayne this Saint-seeing-Saint-making-Saint."[40] To remove all doubt of the fact that (at least some) Traskites practiced a form of communism, we need only turn to the meditations of Returne Hebdon, one of Traske's disciples. While in prison following the routing of the Traskites, Hebdon wrote: "Therefore it is the judgement of the holy spirit, that whosoever is false in the common communion of goods, cannot hold the love in the holy communion of the body and blood of the Lord."[41]

Here, then, was a vision of the true church that is significant mainly in its departure from the orthodoxies of the time. But when Traske discussed the "Kingdom of heaven" and the "Kingdom of Christ," he did not refer solely to the order laid down by Christ for his church in this world. Rather, he veered back and forth between discussing it as an outward kingdom and as an inward kingdom, between a description of the ordinances of Christ and the subjective state of true believers. The tendency to discuss the Kingdom of Heaven as a subjective state of joy is most evident in his third pamphlet, aptly entitled *Heavens Joy, or Heaven Begun on Earth* (1616).[42] Once again, Traske denounced those who argued that the rapture of heaven was something to be enjoyed in the afterlife: "The Apostle plainly affirmeth, that such as have beleeved *do enter into Rest*, not *shall* hereafter, but *doe*."[43] This resting place was likened to a spiritual mountain: "so are the children of God at *quiet* when they sit down on the top of this *glorious mountain*, which with great difficultie they have climed."[44] As the subtitle of the pamphlet suggested, heaven was hardly a distant, other-worldly dimension. It was a concrete experience, to which believers had access while still on earth. At times, Traske seemed to hint that those who had been rewrought by grace were actually carried into heaven, where they experienced a privileged vision of God himself.[45] For the lucky recipients of grace, the "*Love* of Christ doth ravish the soule, and makes it to mount on high, yea, to be above in heavenly *Meditations*."[46] This rapturous "love of Christ" not only catapulted believers into a near-mystical state of bliss but, as we have seen, instilled in them a heartfelt and irresistible desire to obey God's law.

Yet this obedience was not one of bondage but of liberty. Indeed,

Traske's descriptions of obedience tended, as T.S. had charged, to veer off into antinomian excess. Thus, Traske claimed that "believers are no longer under a *Schoolemaster*, or a *Law* commaunding: but they having the Spirit of Christ, have libertie: yea, a glorious *Libertie*, which is not the least tast of *Heaven* upon *Earth*."[47] Here, using a conventional Pauline formula, Traske had carefully insinuated into his pamphlet the notion that believers were free from the commanding power of the moral law. Even though they obeyed the law out of the love of Christ, the faithful were nevertheless free from it as an external compulsory rule. Traske admitted that both experience and Scripture attested to the fact that believers suffered occasional lapses, but he argued that these peccadilloes were not sins: "Yet all this doth not prove that which some would urge out of these, and such like places, that they *commit sinne*, and this is most evident: for if they should *commit*, then were they still the *servants* of *sinne*, as it is written, *Whosoever committeth Sinne, is the servant of sin*."[48] On Traske's account, then, believers were free from the moral law and delivered into a state of sinlessness. As he put it, the Saints were "*holy Men and Women, pure, cleane, undefiled, and harmless*."[49] All of this was accomplished using ostensibly neutral Pauline phrases, glossed and arranged in a way that was thoroughly unacceptable from an orthodox perspective. Indeed, Traske used such tactics to argue that "the same minde is in [believers] which was also in Christ Jesus, *who being in the forme of God, thought it no robbery to be equall with God*."[50] Here, we see Traske at his most theologically radical, asserting the perfection of believers, indeed their identity with the person of Christ, even as they walked on earth. This tendency is likewise evident in the writings of Hebdon, who explicitly rejected the standard Protestant argument that perfection was something only attained in death, claiming "the new man must needs have a perfect birth, before it can be a new man, and so before the resurrection."[51] To put it bluntly, Traske and his followers enjoined perfect obedience to the Mosaic Law because they believed that by virtue of their peculiar unity with Jesus Christ they had attained something like a heavenly perfection in this life.

We have here arrived at a crucial point, both for understanding Traske's theological trajectory and more generally for understanding the nature of seventeenth-century English antinomianism. Traske argued that believers were free from the law and sin. But this sinlessness and freedom did not mean that the faithful could or would sin with impunity. Where unbeliev-

ers were guided by the external whip of the law, believers were guided by
the internal direction of the spirit, which led them inexorably to do God's
will. This notion—that believers had somehow internalized the law in a
way that made it superfluous as an outward rule—was perhaps the defining element of antinomianism both before and after the Civil War.[52] Freedom from the law meant obedience to the law, explaining how Traske's
early theology accommodated both explicitly antinomian and strenuously
legalistic elements. Hebdon attempted to articulate this paradox:

There is a Law of God holden in the worldly authorities, and the Law within in
the faithful in opposition: The worldly men make to themselves a light, and walk
in it, condemning the oppressed, as if they . . . did walke in darkenesse without
light. Thus carnall *Israel* in all things walke by sight in a visible worship of God,
persecuting and despising all that submit not to their glory: whereas the spirituall
Israel, though they seeme to this world, as living in darkness, and dishonour,
without the feare of men, and without the Law given by *Moses*, yet it is farre otherwise in spirit and truth, for God their God is a light unto them, they feare God
and obey him, and they are not without the Law of God, but the Law is within
them.[53]

Hebdon's quote, with its theological peculiarities and its denunciation
of the "worldly authorities," serves as an endpoint for our investigation of
Traske's message. Here was a mode of divinity that was as theologically
extravagant as it was socially radical. The so-called worldly authorities had
ample reason to be worried about Traske's Kingdom, for it left no space
for the doctrine and discipline of the national church, and its relationship
to secular authority was equivocal at best; of Christ's Kingdom, Traske had
written that "wheresoever it is, it hath the *preheminence*, or is *above* that
Kingdome or *Nation*."[54] There is good reason to believe, moreover, that
those in power recognized the communalistic, anti-elite tendencies of the
Traskite movement, contributing to the hasty and violent suppression of
the sect. Although Traske does not seem to have challenged the notion of
magistracy itself, his Kingdom had little room for those in positions of
wealth and power. Even as he argued that some of all degrees would enter
the Kingdom, he threatened that "the Scriptures doe make it plainely to
appeare, and plentifully doe confirme it, that fewest great and mighty ones,
yea, very fewe of them shall be saved."[55]

Had Traske and his disciples followed in the footsteps of Christopher

Marsh's Elizabethan Familists, practicing their faith quietly, and concealing clandestine books in sheds and chimneys, we might conclude that they represented little or no threat to the established order of church and state. But Traske, as we have seen, peddled his message with an almost megalomaniacal zeal. Not content to preach in pulpits, houses, and fields, nor to pitch handfuls of gold to the poor, he quickly decided to troll for the biggest fish of all, James I. In an apparent effort to convert the mightiest of the "great and mighty ones," Traske began in 1616 to send manuscripts and letters to the king, apparently offering among other things to heal the royal gout.[56] Needless to say, James was not amused, particularly since Traske took it upon himself to address the king using the familiar "Thee" and "Thou." A crucial document, recently discovered by Arnold Hunt of Cambridge, shows that Traske justified his familiar language by claiming "that the kinge would take no offence at it, because it was the manner of speeche, which was used to God himselfe."[57] Once again, we see Traske's deeply egalitarian vision of God, as well as his tendency to argue that God's stance toward people ought to be normative for human social relations in general.

James and his ministers recognized the threat inherent in Traske's hubristic rhetoric and posturing, and it was precisely this irreverence which led to his prosecution. When they decided, most emphatically, to punish him, they chose not the Court of High Commission, the venue reserved for the correction of doctrinal offenses, but the Court of Star Chamber, the venue for crimes against the state. And it was for crimes against the state that Traske ultimately suffered his gruesome punishment. The thinking (and the fear) behind this move was revealed by Lord Chancellor Bacon a week after the trial, when he warned the circuit judges to pay close attention to the proliferation of puritan sectarianism: "New opinions spread very dangerous, the late Traske a dangerous person. Prentices learn the Hebrew tongue."[58]

II

In the background, behind the terse utterances of Francis Bacon, we can hear the faint footfall of Traske's "clouted shoes." It should be evident at this stage that, by definition of the term, Traske's divinity must be described as radical—politically, socially, and theologically. I would now like to return to some of the larger questions I broached at the outset of the paper, to return to Christopher Hill and Christopher Marsh. First of all, how are we to characterize this radicalism? Where did it come from, and where did Traske stand in relation to mainstream Puritanism?

We have seen that Traske's so-called Judaizing represents merely the outward manifestation of a form of divinity that was peculiarly antilegal, if not antinomian. Let us consider for a moment the broad outlines of that divinity. First, as we have seen, Traske claimed that repentance was a state of self-mortification and humiliation that preceded, and ended with, the glorious onset of faith. Second, we have seen that Traske's desire to see his followers perfectly obey God's law flowed from his claim that true believers were, in some sense, perfect *in this life*. Indeed, they were free from sin and, sharing the mind of Christ, could infallibly recognize one another. Third, Traske showed a disdain for any notion of Christianity that tied true belief to a particular structure of church government, a particular mode of worship, or particular people. This attitude allowed him, somewhat disingenuously, to present himself as an opponent of puritan excess. Fourth, although he acknowledged the notion of an afterlife, Traske tended to argue that the Kingdom of Heaven (or Christ) was as much an internal, subjective state of rest, peace, and rapturous joy, experienced by believers while on earth, as a place of eternal future felicity; the thrust of much of his early writing was designed to show that little or nothing could be said about the afterlife, while very much could be said about heaven on earth. Fifth and finally, Traske enjoined his believers to give up their worldly possessions and to make their goods common, either to the poor or to other members of the Traskite community.

It should be pointed out that these arguments—repentance preceding faith, antinomianism, indifference to matters of ecclesiology, the tendency to allegorize heaven and hell as subjective states, and community of goods—are virtually identical to those habitually attributed to the Family of Love.[59] I would like to argue here that this was no coincidence, and to suggest, at least speculatively, that Traske's divinity emerged from exposure to Familism.

Let us return for a moment to one crucial biographical detail, alluded to above—Traske's curious appearance in the Isle of Ely in 1614. It has long been recognized that Ely had been a center of Familist activity in Elizabeth's reign, but only with the publication of Dr. Marsh's painstaking researches have these suspicions been confirmed and documented. Indeed, in 1609, Ely was the sight of what appear to have been the last two provincial presentments for Familism, when a pair of laymen were accused of possessing books by H.N., the messianic founder of the Family of Love.[60] Five years later, Traske, a young preacher whose activities had hitherto been confined solely to a fairly circumscribed area in the Southwest, suddenly appeared at the opposite end of the country, preaching without living or license, to conventicles in and around Ely. While none of those implicated in Traske's illicit meetings appear in Marsh's investigation of fenland Familism, there can be little question that these people personally knew members of the Family of Love. Indeed, two men who admitted to being present at one of Traske's clandestine "prayer meetings" would sit in 1616 on a four-person committee with one Luke Saunders, almost certainly a member of the Family. Another accused auditor of Traske, William Gunton of Sutton, was in all likelihood a relative of the Guntons of the Isle of Ely, who left behind an extensive trail of Familist connections throughout the region. A third man, John Thickpenny, also present at the aforementioned prayer meeting, bore the same unusual surname as the obscure Kentish cleric David Thickpenny, whose association with the Family had been exposed in the 1570's. Others who had gadded to hear Traske preach in Littleport hailed from the village of Downham, another site of Elizabethan Familist activity.[61] Although these connections are highly suggestive, it cannot be proved that any of these individuals were bona fide Familists. It is probably fair to assume, however, that they were operating in an environment where Familism was a live religious tradition, that they knew genuine members of the Family, and that they possessed more than a passing notion of what it meant to be a Familist, both ideologically and in practice. Traske's inexplicable presence amongst them may well provide a clue to the singularly strange style of divinity he would later promulgate both in print and in the pulpit. Either he was there because he was already keyed into an underground network of Familism, perhaps preaching his own messages to receptive ears, or he encountered Ely Familists in his travels, a confrontation that would shape his central teachings in the years to come.

This is not to argue that Traske was a member of the Family of Love, in anything like the sense outlined by Marsh. If we examine Traske's works, apart from the noticeable similarities outlined above, there are other areas where his teaching, indeed his entire style, seems to have run counter to the classic Familism of H.N. He appears to have rejected the Familist suggestion that the Resurrection was merely an allegory or metaphor for something that happened within the believer's heart, instead suggesting that the Resurrection of the Dead and Last Judgment were to be expected as all-too-real events in the future.[62] Similarly, although Traske occasionally lapsed into effusive descriptions of the ravishing power of the "love of Christ," there is very little hint of the bizarrely rhapsodic prose style of Hendrik Niclaes, with its continual, almost talismanic repetition of and resort to the image of Love.[63] More than anything else, we see in Traske a puritan militancy that is entirely alien both to H.N.'s writings and to the practices of his early followers in England. Traske's rigorous Sabbatarianism, the manifest biblical "primitivism" in evidence among his followers, and most of all his frankly volatile evangelical energy all bear the mark not of H.N.'s Familism but of the fervent, almost violent piety that subsisted at the edge of the puritan community, where presbyterianism shaded off into separatism.[64] For example, Traske's insistence that the perfection of believers implied perfect obedience to the Mosaic Law looks like a caricature or, at the very least, a distinctively godly misunderstanding of H.N.'s perfectionism. It is as if the antinomian and anthropotheic teachings of Familism had been glossed with the biblical literalism and moralism of extreme puritanism. I would submit that this is precisely what we are seeing in John Traske: Familist doctrine decoupled from H.N.'s writings and refracted through the prism of militant puritanism. The result was a deeply radical hybrid, a sort of evangelical Familism in which the most potentially destabilizing aspects of both traditions blended together to complement one another in a subversive heterodox stew.

From this perspective, we can easily see how Traske made the move from Judaizing to antinomianism. After his punishment in 1618, undoubtedly prodded along by the expectation of life imprisonment, he was forced to look long and hard at his opinions concerning the Mosaic Law. Not surprisingly, this reassessment led him to reject his strict legalism, a move that had the advantage of springing him from jail. Having repudiated his commitment to the Sabbath and the Law, what remained of his divinity was the antinomian core described above—his claim that believers were free from sin, his hints that they possessed the Mind of Christ, his exaltation of the transformative effects of free grace. And this, in fact, is what we find Traske teaching in the 1620's and 1630's, when he became a central figure in the spreading antinomian revolt against orthodox Puritanism. Having moved smoothly from heresy to heresy, he continued to itinerate, by all appearances retaining his commitment to preaching the Gospel to the "off-scouring of the world."[65]

We can now return to the question of the origins of radical puritanism, and to engage Christopher Hill's thesis concerning the survival of a heretical underground. Traske provides a case study in the assimilation of heretical ideas to mainstream Puritanism, an example of an individual who appears to have appropriated bits of Familist doctrine to create a syncretic mode of divinity that was uniquely his own. This allows us to qualify Hill's thesis. Rather than suggesting an unbroken genealogy of heresy, passing beneath the surface of English society as a hidden riptide, the genesis of puritan radicalism should probably be viewed as a development that took place within the godly community itself. In the example of Traske, we see a puritanism with permeable boundaries, a religious subculture in which various heretical or esoteric religious traditions were continually being absorbed into the seething world of religious enthusiasm and devotion that existed at the margins of the godly community. Here, particularly at the separatist fringe, foreign influences, such as Dutch Anabaptism and Familism, as well as homegrown theological innovations, were nurtured, debated, denounced, and integrated into normative puritan piety in order to produce new formulations. Puritanism should not be viewed as either radical or inherently conservative but as a heterogeneous community in which various styles of evangelism and piety competed for the affections of a Bible-addicted laity. In certain hands, and under certain political or social circumstances, the result could be virulently radical, as we have just seen. In John Traske's early ministry, more than two decades before the Long Parliament, we can detect almost every quality that would come to be associated with sectarian puritanism during the Civil Wars, from antinomianism and perfectionism, to the notion that the Kingdom of Heaven was somehow immanent in this world, to Saturday Sabbath observance, to communistic and egalitarian impulses. Indeed, his teaching is laced with "anti-formalism," or an opposition to all ecclesiastical or ceremonial forms of worship, recently proposed by J. C. Davis as a unifying characteristic of Civil War radicalism.[66] Traske was undoubtedly an extraordinary, indeed a unique, figure. But he was neither alone nor isolated. Throughout his career, which spanned 25 years and took him through at least seven counties, he consistently won friends and followers, ensuring his survival in a church that refused to give him a beneficed living. His uniqueness should not blind us to what he represented—the survival and transformation of a militant, and in some senses politically destabilizing, puritanism from its original Elizabethan context, to its explosive and revolutionary incarnation in the 1640's and 1650's. Both symbolically and in his person, he should be taken as a missing piece in the puzzle of English puritanism.

PART II

Diffusion and the Limits of Appropriation

J. SEARS MCGEE

The Mental World of Sir Richard Berkeley

During her progress in 1592, Elizabeth I and her court visited the home of a Gloucestershire gentleman named Sir Richard Berkeley. She had intended only to stay the night at his house in Rendcombe after being lavishly entertained at Cirencester, but "the extremitie of a great winde" forced a longer stay.[1] She had knighted Sir Richard at Bristol during an earlier progress in August 1574. It may not be altogether fanciful to suggest that the storm that forced the queen to extend her stay at Rendcombe had something to do with Berkeley's decision to dedicate a book he was writing to her. Or perhaps the queen's visit stimulated his decision to write the book in the first place. *A Discourse on the Felicitie of Man, or His Summum Bonum* first appeared in 1598, with a second edition in 1603 and a third in 1631. Furthermore, the book may have been part of his campaign for office in her government, even though, since he was two years older than the queen, he was no spring chicken.[2]

Berkeley's book is both odd and interesting. In the *Cambridge Bibliography of English Literature*, that bold attempt to place in appropriate categories every text that English literature contains, there is a category entitled "Jest Books, Comic Dialogues, Burlesques, Mock Prognostications and Drolleries." It contains such entries as a book entitled *Pasquil's Jests, mixed with Mother Bunches Merriments*, the first of whose several editions appeared in 1604. Nearby is Berkeley's *Summum Bonum*. The same book is listed, however, in another category, that of "Philosophical Writers."[3] Neither literary scholars nor historians of philosophy have, however, given Berkeley much attention. The few modern scholars who have mentioned him have not taken the trouble to find out anything about him that is not in his *Summum Bonum*—which is next to nothing.

This essay aims to answer three questions. Who was Sir Richard Berkeley? Was his book really so schizophrenic that it could be placed by the Cambridge literary scholars alongside both Mother Bunch's merriments and the writings of More, Bacon, and William Perkins? And what can we learn from it about its author's outlook on religious and political issues? This is, then, an attempt to describe a particular Elizabethan gentleman and his mental world.

First, a few words about Sir Richard Berkeley, a country gentleman who was a prominent figure in the politics and administration of his native county, Gloucestershire, from the 1560's. He served as sheriff in 1564 and on the diocesan commission for ecclesiastical causes in the 1570's.[4] In the decade preceding his death in 1604, he appears to have been aiming for preferment at Elizabeth's court. Elizabeth may have appointed him lieutenant of the Tower of London in 1595.[5] There are intriguing bits of evidence suggesting that he was under consideration for the vice presidency of the Council for Wales in February 1600, a council on which he is known to have served in 1591 and perhaps thereafter. According to a report to Sir Robert Sidney, Berkeley was hoping for the vice chamberlainship in September 1600.[6]

Berkeley's principal seat was not Rendcombe but Stoke Gifford, just north of Bristol, a manor that had been granted to Sir Maurice de Berkeley in the eleventh year of Edward III's reign. Sir Richard was probably born in 1531, and he survived his queen by only eleven months.[7] He was elected to serve as a knight of his shire to James's first Parliament, but died before the session convened. If he had not written his discourse on human happiness, we would have almost no way of knowing what sort of person Sir Richard was. He might have had a choleric temperament. An informant to Lord Burghley in 1574 described an incident in which Berkeley had a few years before "struck the High Sheriff before the Justice of Assize and travelled into Italy," presumably to evade punishment for his outburst.[8] By contrast, a description of his effigy in Bristol Cathedral says that his "expression shows refinement," although we have no way of knowing whether that was flattery by the artist or a genuine insight into Berkeley's character.[9] Berkeley's name appears in an undated letter to Burghley that included "a list of Gentlemen of good consideration in Gloucestershire." If this list is the product of one of those surveys of the country gentry that were compiled so that Burghley could identify reliable supporters of the government, especially in religion, then we have a further indication that Berkeley was considered a reliable conformist in religion.[10]

The preceding paragraphs contain the few scraps of evidence that can be gleaned about Sir Richard Berkeley's career and character, and the gleanings are obviously skimpy. They represent all we might know about him had he not written his discourse on human happiness, and we must now consider that intriguing mixture of jests and philosophy. As a philosopher, Berkeley was, as we shall see, no heavyweight, though the book itself is a hefty piece of work indeed—631 large quarto pages in the 1603 edition, a slightly expanded version of the first edition of 1598.

Even more impressive than its size is the range of erudition that the work displays. The book is a scissors-and-paste job on a grand scale, containing thousands of borrowings loosely organized into six "books." There is no evidence that Sir Richard studied at Oxford or Cambridge, but he certainly read Latin and Italian.[11] The sources that he mined most heavily are the Roman poets and historians, although he also dipped deeply into Greek writers (probably in the Latin translations that were in print in Tudor England). Virgil is quoted with great frequency; he was for Berkeley, as he was for so many others, simply "the Poet." Plutarch is his most important source for history, both natural and political, but Sallust, Suetonius, Livy, Pliny, and many others appear. Nor did he limit himself to Plutarch's famous *Lives*. He also loved to borrow from Plutarch's *Moralia* and from Cicero and Seneca.[12] Greek poets such as Homer, Hesiod, and Pindar also appear, although, predictably enough, Berkeley relied mainly on the Greeks for philosophy. Socrates, Plato, and Aristotle are the favorites, but many others also turn up: the seven sages of ancient Greece, Pythagoras, Diogenes, and so on. Berkeley also used numerous obscure classical writers: Claudius Aelianus, Aeschines, Anacharsis, Florus, Hierocles, Hipponax, Iamblichus, Valerius Maximus, Menedemus, and many more.

Perhaps 80 percent of Berkeley's quotations and stories come from pagan classical sources, but the remainder nevertheless are intriguing and must be mentioned. Besides the Bible, his main antique Christian sources were Jerome, Chrysostom, Basil, and especially Augustine. His interest in the other Fathers was slight. His only medieval sources were Bernard, Dante, and Chaucer, and he makes little use of them. His Renaissance writers include Petrarch, Guicciardini, Guevarra, Machiavelli, Erasmus, and More, and his Protestant divines, his own contemporaries, were Latimer, Calvin, Ursinus, Scaliger, and especially his fellow layman Philippe Du Plessis Mornay (1549–1623).[13]

On this mountain of reading, Berkeley erected a philosophical molehill. The book is an exercise in moral philosophy, and its argument is quite simple. According to Sir Richard, man's happiness consists not in bodily pleasures, wealth, honor and glory, or virtue but in salvation to eternal life in heaven. The "proof" of this argument is demonstrated by the piling up of examples, and he delighted in ribald, disgusting, or gory stories. Clearly, his method is based on the humanist dictum that history is philosophy teaching by example. He would have agreed with his contemporary William Blundeville, who wrote in 1574 that truth in political matters "is partly taught by the Philosophers in generall precepts and rules, but the Historiographers doe teach it much more playnlye by perticular examples and experiences."[14] Although Berkeley admired the Aristotelian ethic of moderation, his literary principle was that nothing succeeds like excess. Early in book one, for example, we read the story of the Roman emperor Heliogabalus, a "monster of nature . . . of whom grave authors write such matter as seemeth incredible, whereof a great part shall be passed over of me with silence, as not meet to be written." Nevertheless, four pages of detailed description of Heliogabalus's outrageous indulgence in food, wine, and sex follows before we learn that he was killed in his privy by members of his Praetorian guard and dragged through the streets before they threw his body in the Tiber.[15]

Berkeley had a particular fondness for stories in which a villain gets an ingenious comeuppance. He relates, for example, the story of one "Muleasses," king of Tunis, a man who was exiled from his own kingdom because of his addiction to whores. Upon his return, "that he might with more pleasure heare musicke, hee used to cover his eyes. But the judgement of God fell upon him." The kinsman who usurped his kingdom had Muleasses's eyes burned out with a hot iron so he could enjoy his music the better.[16] And then there was Justinian II, the Byzantine emperor who temporarily lost his throne to a usurper who cut off the emperor's nose. When Justinian regained power, each time he "had occasion to wipe his nose (if hee had one)," he had one of the conspirators executed.[17] Although some of the examples Berkeley offered were role models for Christian virtues, the vast majority are bad examples followed by spectacularly bad ends for the pathetic exemplars. We might think of Berkeley's technique as the obverse of medieval hagiography but with the same objective. He said as much in his preface to the reader:

It may bee profitable also to see the errours and passions of them discovored, by the disordered course of their life, and extraordinarie kind of death, [of those] that have set their felicitie in pleasures, riches, honor and glory, and such like worldly vanities, which to all, except they may be well used, are hinderance to felicitie, and have brought many to extreame miserie.[18]

The examples just quoted, which could be multiplied many times and with infinite variety, explain why Berkeley's discourse has been classified with jest-books as well as with philosophy. In the entire 631 pages, there is little that would pass muster with modern comedy writers. For misogynists and sadists, there are perhaps a few chuckles. Despite the great admiration all men held for Socrates, Berkeley tells us that Socrates's wife thought so little of him that after an argument she "poured a pisse-pot upon his head." Socrates quipped, "I thought after so great thunder we should have raine."[19] Then there was the man who, after hearing a preacher say that "whosoever wil be saved must beare his Crosse, ranne to his wife and layd her upon his shoulders." And there is his story of the emperor Severus Alexander's fiendishly clever punishment of an influence peddler. The man was trussed in the marketplace over a fire of green wood and wet straw. While he was slowly asphyxiated, the crier loudly proclaimed, "He that solde smoke, is stifled with smoke."[20]

Berkeley often described something as a "pretie taunt," a "pleasant story," or the remark of a "merry fellow." Instead of what we would consider a joke, however, what we read is a "gest" in the medieval sense of a striking or notable deed or incident. As Sir Keith Thomas reminded us in his Neale lecture, a characteristic of many such gests was that they were tales involving the activities of a trickster.[21]

One example, the examination of which gives us an entry into Berkeley's outlook upon political events in his own time, is his account of an incident that allegedly occurred in France in 1560. Berkeley relates how the pope wished to reward the cardinal of Lorraine, "a great maintainer of the Guisians faction" and a vigorous persecutor of the Protestants, for his services. He commissioned a painting of the Madonna by a great artist, personally consecrated the painting, and consigned its delivery to a mes-

senger. When the package arrived in France, the cardinal was so pleased
that he forebore opening it until he could assemble a party for the occasion. He invited the duke of Guise and many other worthies of the Catholic League for a splendid banquet and the unveiling of the papal gift.

When the longed-for moment arrived, however, the ingenious work of
the trickster—a Protestant, of course—manifested itself. To the horror
and confusion of the cardinal and his well-fed guests, the painting the pope
had sent had been stolen. The painting that was unveiled depicted the cardinal himself stark naked, with the queen mother, Catherine de Medici,
Mary Stuart, and the "old Dutches[s] of Guyse, naked also, hanging about
the Cardinalles necke, and their legges wrapped betweene his legges."[22]
Berkeley's source for this particular tall tale was probably *Le Reveille-matin
des François et de Leurs Voisins*, identified by Robert M. Kingdon as "the
most popular and widely circulated single piece of Protestant propaganda"
to come out of the St. Bartholomew's Day massacre.[23] There are others
Berkeley almost certainly drew from fifteenth-century Italian jest-books, a
staple of which was the lecherous clergyman (often a monk or a friar), se-
ducing the wives of laymen.[24]

The tale about the cardinal and the pope, however, also introduces an
important component of Sir Richard Berkeley's political and religious
outlook. There was a time when historians would have described Berkeley
as a Puritan, a man whose deep antipathy to Roman Catholics emanated
from his theology. To be sure, the *Discourse* abounds in corrosive criticism
of "quaffing," gluttonous, lecherous, blasphemous, and atheistic laymen
and churchmen, all familiar targets of Puritan preachers. Berkeley was not,
however, a Puritan even of the moderate variety that Patrick Collinson and
Peter Lake have identified in Elizabethan England. Dissatisfaction with
prayer book ceremonies and the amount and quality of preaching were essential characteristics of Puritans. Berkeley's snide references to "idolatry
and superstition" do not go beyond the usual Protestant rhetoric in such
matters, nor does he show much interest in the doctrines of predestination
and assurance that so fascinated Puritans. Nor was an Elizabethan Puritan
at all likely to write of late sixteenth-century England, as Berkeley did, that
"the sounde of Gods Word beateth continually against our eares. . . . In
every place is talke of divinitie, even among them that know not what belongeth to humanitie."[25] Puritans, by contrast, were utterly convinced that
too many dumb dogs who could not bark remained in pulpits all over the

land. Moreover, Berkeley's confidence that the days of papal dominion were over distinguishes him from Puritans who remained very fearful of the Counter Reformation. Berkeley seems not to have read Foxe's *Book of Martyrs*, and his occasional remarks about living in the "latter days" have a moralistic rather than a millenarian tone.[26] Also, it is significant that in his denunciations of the iniquity of papists (such as the assassins of Henry III and William of Orange), Berkeley's emphasis falls wholly on the political nature of their offense. Their religion is denounced more because it permits and encourages sedition and rebellion than because of its soteriological or ecclesiastical failings. In this matter, Berkeley sounds not like a Puritan but like Robert Burton, who in his *Anatomy of Melancholy* wrote of the "High Priest of Rome, the bull-bellowing Pope, which now rageth in the West, that three-headed Cerberus, . . . whose religion at this day is mere policy" and whose agents, the Jesuits, know how to employ "fasting and solitary meditation . . . to alter men's minds . . . to kill a King or the like."[27]

As we have seen, Berkeley was deeply interested in stories about the moral failings of Roman Catholic clergy. We read, for example, of a cardinal (or "rather carnall") of Este and his brother, who were in love with the same woman. When the cardinal learned that she favored his brother because of his beautiful eyes, he had his footman "plucke his brothers eyes out of his head." There was also a cardinal who loved to wash his hands in gold. Like many Protestant writers, he gleefully repeated the famous fable of Pope Joan, the English or German woman who dressed as a man and died after giving birth to a child after fooling all the cardinals for several years.[28]

In many of the most elaborate stories, however, popes especially are condemned for their political behavior. Berkeley depicted them as so desperate for power that they made Faustian deals with the devil and practiced necromancy to gain their ends. A lengthy section presented material from "their writers" (i.e., Catholic writers) purporting that a number of popes, including Benedict IX, Silvester II, Boniface VIII, and some eighteen others had used necromancy to gain the papal tiara for themselves. Boniface, for example, had spoken through a reed into Celestinus's bedchamber, saying that he must turn over the papacy to Boniface. Poor Celestinus, being a bit simple, thought he was hearing a voice from heaven and did what the voice bade him do. After Boniface's death, he was said to have

"crept in like a Foxe, governed like a Wolfe, and died like a dogge." When
Silvester II, who had connived with the devil to gain the tiara, died re-
penting and attempting to warn others against such temptations, he instructed that his body be placed in a cart drawn by unguided horses and
buried where they stopped. The horses stopped at the Church of the Lat-
eran, and thereafter his bones rattled and his tomb sweated shortly before a
pope was to die.[29]

At least as evil in Berkeley's mind as necromancy was the way that popes
and their minions had dealt with princes. "What is it but an excessive desire of glory," he asked, "that causeth them to make Emperours and Kings
kisse theyr foot, and hold theyr stirrop when they get up horse, and leade
him by the bridle?" Here follow stories about Celestinus, who placed the
crown on Henry VI's head with his foot, another pope who put a duke of
Venice and king of Crete and Cyprus under his table to join the dogs
chewing bones, the vicious Julius II who said that killing a Frenchman
would bring full and immediate absolution, and so on.[30] Almost level with
the papacy in Berkeley's disesteem were the regular clergy, especially the
Jesuits. After the assassination of the duke of Guise, "the Monkes and Fry-
ers, and the rest of that rabble of Cloister-men" were spoiling for revenge
against Henry III, but could find no one who "would consent to so vile an
act, to murder his Prince." Finally, a 22-year-old novice Dominican, a
"hare-braind fellow," was talked into attempting the deed. Even though
assured that he would be made a saint, he got cold feet and the Jesuits were
called in to reassure him. They did so, and the French king's murder followed in 1589. Although the news horrified the Catholics, Pope Sixtus V
nevertheless preached a sermon urging the young Dominican's canoniza-
tion.[31] Although Berkeley never mentioned the plots against Elizabeth's
life, none of his readers would have failed to think of them when reading
these sections of the book.

Another concern that pervaded Berkeley's political outlook was his belief that Englishmen had changed for the worse in his lifetime. In one of
the few places where, instead of quoting someone, he offers a personal observation, he says:

Fortie yeares and more I may with some judgement remember the worlde; in
which litle time I have found such a metamorphosis and alteration in mens minds
and manners, that if they should decline so fast from evill to worse after fortie

yeares more, it will bee a hard matter anie where to finde out a faithfull friende, or an honest man.[32]

An important symptom of the decline was the emergence of men (especially young men) who adorned, bejeweled, and perfumed themselves, practices which he thought had come into England recently as a result of the pernicious habit of imitating the styles and manners of foreigners, especially such wicked and corrupt foreigners as the sixteenth-century Italians and Spaniards. Machiavelli and Pope Alexander VI and his offspring frequently served to exemplify Berkeley's arguments in such matters. Here is a sample:

It may be wished men were not so much Italianated, whose habites many have gotten both of bodie and mind, and are become as artificiall apes, counterfeyting a formall kind of strangers civilitie: but that which some performe may rather bee called Divillitie. . . . The Italian hath an old proverbe: *Inglese Italianato, e diabolo incarnato*: An English man Italianated, is a Devill incarnated. Our Nation, although it hath received many great blessings from God, as no people in the world more, . . . yet . . . we imitate the Spaniards in their pride, the Italians in their dissembling and other vices, the Frenchmen in their rashnesse and inconstancie; the Flemings we beginne to follow in their quaffing and drunkennesse: and all these we counterfeit, or rather exceede in their vanitie of attires and gestures. Pride and excesse were two of the sinnes for which Sodom was punished. For many of our travellers bring us the worst of their manners, leaving the best behind: as the Spyder drawth poyson from the same flowre the bee sucketh hony.[33]

Just as the Italians had long since declined from the simplicity and virtue of the "old Romans," so Englishmen had declined from the virtue and simplicity of their ancestors. The elder Cato, for example, slept on goat skins and ate simply even though serving as the governor of Spain, whereas "the brave men and jolly fellowes of these dayes, that glister in golde and silver" take pride in "daintie and delicate meates, and spend whole dayes and nights in banquetting and quaffing. . . . [They] with their lascivious manners and effeminate attires, that passe their time in courting and carowsing."[34] Instead of pursuing learning, wisdom, and virtue, they pursued pleasure, profit, and power.

Predictably in light of his view of what had been happening to his fellow Englishmen for a generation, Berkeley saw a parallel corruption occurring in public life. In a passage added to the second edition in 1603, perhaps on the basis of his experience at court, he observes that "Machiavels rules are better followed in these dayes, then those of Plato, Aristotle, or Cicero." Indeed, he approvingly quoted the writer who said that Machiavelli's doctrines had become "the Courtiers *Alcoran*, seeing they have them in no lesse estimation, then the Turkes have the *Alcoran* and dreames of Mahumet."[35] Moreover, "kings in elder time" dressed like ordinary people and differed only in the quality of "their minde and inward furniture." One wonders what Elizabeth thought of this argument. Berkeley praised King Alfonso of Aragon, who rejected advice to dress grandly, saying that he preferred to outdo his subjects "in manners and authoritie, then in a Diademe and purple." He also praised Emperor Severus Alexander (225–35), son of the infamous Heliogabalus. Alexander refused to let his servants "weare any silke, cloth of gold or silver, and used often to say, that open excesse of apparell, and secret vice, were the destruction of Courtiers."[36] Berkeley also lamented the loss of the days when senates and councils always had "some excellent Philosopher" in residence, sometimes wise men "sent for out of farre Countries." Instead of them "and of learned Divines (who should supply theyr roomes among Christians) are brought in some excellent Machiavillians, as the meetest Counsellors for this corrupt time." Even princes themselves used to love learning and pursue it—but no more, except, of course, in the case of Elizabeth herself.[37]

Turning to the question of Berkeley's religious views, and having already concluded that he was no Puritan, the question of how to characterize his religious position remains. At the end of his book, aware that he had touched upon many theological matters, he inserted a caveat:

I tooke the matter in hand for my owne exercise and pastime, and have handled the same according to my talent. . . . And if I have written anie thing over much Philosophically, that dissenteth from the true professed religion (as in so spacious a field, and such insufficiencie of my selfe, I may easily wander out of the right path) I submit my selfe, and that I have written, (as becommeth a Christian) to the censure of the church of England, which I acknowledge and assure my selfe to be a member of the true Church of Christ.[38]

Berkeley's account of the creation of man and his fall and its consequences, which opens the book, is quite orthodox, emphasizing the impossibility of salvation by human efforts alone and thus the necessity of regeneration by means of God's grace. There are, however, places where Berkeley's soteriological language has a more "Arminian" ring to it. God "pro-poneth lawes to men with rewardes and punishments. He willeth him to embrace good and flee evill. To the doing whereof he denieth not his grace, without which we can doe nothing, nor refuseth our diligence and la-bour."[39]

Certainly an important part of Berkeley's religious thinking was his concern about the devil, about necromancy and about prophecies and prognostications. Although he never used the term *witchcraft* in his book, he returned time and again to its associates, necromancy and demonic pos-session. He was clearly fascinated by accounts, ancient and contemporary, of demonic possession, and he recounted them at great length: a Spanish nun at Cordoba in 1545, a Babylonian child born on March 7, 1532, a Frenchwoman in 1564, and so on.[40] The ancient oracle of Apollo also in-trigued Berkeley, as did all sorts of prophetic utterances. What Dame Frances Yates and others have taught us to regard as manifestations of the Hermetic tradition, he referred to as the "prohibited sciences." As in the case of some of the necromancers, Berkeley was ready to reserve judgment instead of rushing to condemnation. "This desire of vaine glory through singularitie of knowledge," he wrote, was not limited to the work of the devil in infidels but even in Christian prelates such as Albertus Magnus and Abbot Trithemius "to what perill of their soules I leave to the judge-ment of others." Only God himself knew "what their reward shall be at the day of judgement. . . . But to excell in these prohibited sciences, is not suf-ficient glory to these kind of men, except they also leave their knowledge in writing, to the prejudice of posterity."[41]

Berkeley lived in real fear of the machinations of the devil because the human appetite for happiness through the acquisition of pleasure, wealth, or power was as insatiable as it was misguided. As indicated earlier, his the-ology was fundamentally orthodox in Calvinist or even Thomistic terms. But there is an exception to this generalization. In his account of the Fall, Berkeley wrote that after Jesus Christ had restored humanity to God's fa-vor, the devil was very angry and began "to practise all manner of meanes to intrap him againe: and when he perceived that he could not deceive all, he handled the matter so, that the benefit of this promise might come to a very few, & that the greater part of the world should perish with him, by drawing them from the true knowledge and worshipping of God, to super-stition and Idolatrie."[42] The more orthodox way of putting it would be that Satan desires to seduce us from the truth but that he has no power over our wills. By saying that Satan "handled the matter so" that most would not enjoy the benefit of Christ's sacrifice, Berkeley gave Satan more power than the divines would have done.[43] Indeed, read literally, the statement that Satan brought down most men is a denial of the doctrine of double predestination.[44]

Was Berkeley aware of this problem when he wrote the disclaimer absolving himself from theological perfection and subjecting himself to the doctrine of the Church of England quoted earlier? Perhaps—but probably not. Let us remember that his education would have been largely complete before Henry VIII died. It seems likely that, despite the sincerity of his profession of Protestant belief, there remained a residual traditional element in his thinking that proved resistant, however unconsciously on his part, to the full implications of Protestant soteriology. He is best understood as an early example of a lay gentleman whose morality and soteriology is Protestant in its prejudices but also consistent with pre-Reformation attitudes and contemporary popular views that tended, as Peter Lake has argued, not toward Pelagianism but toward Manicheanism.[45] Broadly learned in the humanistic manner but still deeply impressed by the powers of Satan, Berkeley employed his learning to denounce what seemed to him a corruption of manners and morals that had taken hold during his long life. He dipped deeply into the medieval reservoir of anticlerical material, greatly swollen by Italian humanists, Erasmians, and Protestants. In a theological sense, however, his Protestantism was only skin deep.

That Berkeley was an anti-Catholic, an Elizabethan loyalist, and a "lukewarm" rather than a theologically informed and zealous Protestant becomes apparent when the nature of his providentialism is compared with that of zealous Calvinists. Berkeley certainly stated, as we have seen, that the retribution meted out to the men who lusted after pleasure or wealth or worldly glory of any kind came from God. The downfall of princes and great men as the wheel of fortune turned was, after all, a familiar topos for the Elizabethans, as was the belief that God's purposes were revealed in events. Medieval sermons and didactic histories such as the mid-sixteenth-century *Mirror for Magistrates* were filled with edifying examples of the kind that make up most of Berkeley's *Summum Bonum*.[46] Perhaps the two most widely read books in this genre in the seventeenth century were *The Theatre of Gods Judgments* (first edition, 1597, followed by three more) by Thomas Beard and *A Mirrour or Looking-Glasse, Both For Saints, and Sinners* (first edition, 1648, followed by four more) by Samuel Clarke. Clarke was a Puritan; Beard was not.[47] These works share Berkeley's anti-Catholicism and his providentialism, but they differ in important ways as well. Beard and Clarke delight no less than Berkeley in ferocious and ingenious punishments of the traditional deadly sins of lust, avarice, pride, and the like. But Beard organizes his book not around the traditional sins but around the Ten Commandments, while Clarke's gives considerable space to accounts of "joy in great afflictions" and examples of patience, meekness, compassion, charity, fortitude, and magnanimity. Clarke also recounts the stories of such heroes of the Protestant/Puritan movement as Lady Jane Gray, Anne Askew, the Marian martyrs, Gustavus Adolphus, and early seventeenth-century Puritans like Robert Bolton, John Dod, and William Gouge. Moreover Beard and Clarke draw heavily upon John Foxe's martyrology. Berkeley ignores Foxe. Beard and Clarke present multiple examples of judgments upon blasphemers, Sabbath-breakers, idolaters, apostates—sinners whose offense is against the Calvinist model of godliness. Berkeley shows no discomfiture about such iniquities and no interest in the models of Calvinist "godliness" that engaged the other two collectors of "wonders" and "providences."[48] Despite its continuities with the works of Beard and Clarke, Berkeley's *Summum Bonum* in important ways retains an older way of thinking, one that may even have outlasted the Puritans who crusaded against it.

Given the paucity of sources about Sir Richard Berkeley, it is difficult to come to a firm judgment about his purposes in writing his book and pursuing an office as exalted as that of the vice chamberlainship. Was his encyclopedic display of humanistic learning sincere in its denunciation of the manners and morals of his contemporaries, or was his jeremiad hypocritical—a device to gain royal favor and an office that he would exploit much as others did? Did he see himself as a man whose stoic, spartan values would enable him to lead a reform of the court and save his sovereign lady and his country from further decline? If he was not sincere at least in intention, then a book a third the size would have done as well. There is an almost manic energy about his omnivorous reading and hurried writing that works against the argument that he was a hypocritical flatterer grasping for a patron. He must have seemed a Polonius, or perhaps a Don Quixote, to the young peacocks swanning about the court.[49] If he had lived long enough to take his seat in James's first Parliament, he might have made speeches that would throw further light on this conclusion. As it is, we cannot be sure.

What we can do with Berkeley's unwieldy book is gain insight into the mind of a well-read country gentlemen at the end of the sixteenth century. One of his sources was the third-century Neoplatonist philosopher Iamblichus. The *Oxford Classical Dictionary* describes one of Iamblichus's books as "ill-written and philosophically worthless" but nevertheless "a curious guide to the superstitions of its age."[50] Applied to Berkeley, such a judgment is suggestive but far too dismissive. Berkeley was no eccentric recluse but an active and important county magnate and, briefly at least, a contender for high office in Elizabeth's court. After his death in 1604, his *Discourse* appeared seven times in the *Register* of the Stationers' Company. Thus printers were maintaining rights to it, although in fact no new edition appeared until 1631—when it did so under the aegis of that busy entrepreneur, playwright, and editor, Thomas Heywood. In his preface, Heywood wrote that "divers noble and well disposed Gentlemen" had asked him to publish it. This could mean that Berkeley's descendants paid Heywood to produce the third edition, as they might have done. His grandson, Richard Berkeley, was himself a politically active country gentleman of a scholarly and contemplative temperament, and his great-grandson, Sir Maurice Berkeley, sat for Gloucestershire in the Parliament of 1621 and married one of Sir Edward Coke's daughters. Nevertheless, a 631-page book would have been an expensive memorial. Furthermore, Heywood did, as he put it, add "such needefull ornaments . . . as best suit with the humour and fashion of the time."[51] He divided the book into chapters with headings that indicate the contents, and he translated some of the Latin poetry.

The evidence is not conclusive, but the continued entries in Stationers' *Registers* suggest that booksellers thought that Berkeley's *Summum Bonum* might sell. Even with a subvention from the Berkeleys, Heywood probably hoped to make an additional profit by reissuing it. Kevin Sharpe has shown that some of the attitudes Berkeley expressed were prominent in early Stuart court culture. For example, Ben Jonson excoriated vain courtiers in their "pould'ring, perfuming, and every day smelling of the taylor." Sir William Davenant's plays and masques contain lamentations about declining moral standards and increasing effeminacy and vanity, the latter due to "the influence of the French and of the court." In Thomas Carew's masque, *Coelum Britannicum,* performed on Shrove Tuesday in 1633, wealth and pleasure are among the worldly forces whose "claims are finally denied."[52] Simply by writing a tome such as the *Summum Bonum,* Berkeley departed from the model of the "typical" country gentleman. So did the Puritan preacher Ralph Josselin with his diary and the London artisan Nehemiah Wallington with his notebooks. Read with care, Berkeley can afford us insights into the thinking of other gentlemen, as have Josselin and Wallington for their callings and stations in early modern England. Berkeley's argument that "the luxuriousnesse used in feastes and garments, is a signe of a sicke Common wealth" and that spartan simplicity, stoic values, and love of religion, wisdom, and nation might restore it to health was widely held by gentlemen and noblemen in early Stuart England.[53]

"Prudentia ultra sexum"

LADY JANE BACON AND THE
MANAGEMENT OF HER FAMILIES

The later years of the Commonwealth were not the most propitious period for lavish tomb building. But there survives in Culford Church, Suffolk, a most unusual tomb, started in 1657 and probably completed in all its essentials before the Restoration [Fig. 1]. It memorializes a remarkable woman, Jane, Lady Bacon, daughter of Hercules Meautys and wife successively to Sir William Cornwallis and Sir Nathaniel Bacon, who died in 1659 at the age of 78, having contracted for the building of the monument two years earlier. By good fortune, the contract survives and reveals that Jane had a very clear view of her purposes. She agreed with Thomas Stanton of St. Andrew's, Holborn, that he would cut a tomb "all in whit and blacke marble, and touche fine polisht" and would follow the design "as it is nowe drawne and depicted in a paper drafte demonstrating the same, to which the sayd Dame Jane, for avoyding mistakes, hath sett hir hand." Although the "platt" does not remain with the contract and the tomb was not complete at Jane's death, there can be little doubt that it is her own choice of image that remains to us. Stanton's work usually followed a conservative format, and the seated funeral image is rare. Jane's inspiration may well have been drawn from the monument to Lord Chancellor Francis Bacon, erected at St. Alban's by Sir Thomas Meautys in 1640, the year that Meautys became Lady Jane's son-in-law.[1]

The tomb itself is so distinctive in character that it prompts even the most casual observer to ask why it was constructed in this form. As its centerpiece it has Lady Bacon, in flowing garments with a cowled headdress, holding on her lap a small child. To her left stand two boys and a girl, one behind the other, to her right two girls in the same arrangement. At her feet lies a full-size adult male, and beneath him the base of the tomb is carved with a lengthy inscription. Although the tomb is in its original position on the north wall of the chancel, the Victorians, in restoring the church, were not kind to it. They dismembered the monument to adjust its height to the altered floor levels, chipping the marble badly, and they replaced the wrong armorial cartouche when reconstructing it. Even then they had to allow it to rest at a lower level than the new chancel, protecting the inscription with an outer grill. It may be, however, that the restorers inadvertently helped to reemphasize the original structure of the tomb as conceived by Lady Bacon. Antiquarians, visiting Culford prior to its reedification, tended to invert the significance of the two adult figures, focusing initially on the male image: on the north wall, noted Blomefield in 1725, "is sculptured the figure of a man . . . lying on his right hand . . . behind a woman sitting, holding a girl in her lap." The man, Nicholas Bacon, Jane's younger son, obtruded before the floor level was sunk and was easily "read" as the center of the tomb group. Yet Nicholas died after his mother, and his addition to the monument must have been an afterthought, made possible by the generous marble slab at his mother's feet.[2]

Jane Bacon intended that her tomb *should* be a text to be read by observers, a text that moved beyond the usual expressions of familial piety and lineage identity or the articulation of pious platitudes about the spiritual and social worth of the interred. And since her life and attitudes are remarkably well recorded in a rich correspondence and dense supporting documentation,[3] it is possible to compare her self-fashioning in death with the construction of her social identity in a long and complex life. If we begin with the children who surround Lady Bacon on her tomb, some of these complexities immediately become apparent. Only one of the children, Jane Bacon, who had died in 1627, was a child of hers. Young Jane is accompanied on the right by Jane Meautys, the older child of Lady Bacon's daughter Anne, who had married a cousin, Sir Thomas Meautys, as her first husband. On the other side stand three great-grandchildren, the descendants of Lady Bacon's older son, Sir Frederick Cornwallis. And the delightful infant on her lap is the second child of Anne Meautys, but now

FIG. 1. Tomb of Lady Jane Bacon, Culford Church, Suffolk. Below: Detail of tomb. Photos by authors.

by her second husband, Sir Harbottle Grimston. We are therefore presented with the dead infants and young children (the oldest is ten) of three generations and of three families. They are differentiated and given individual personality and attributes by a skilled stonemason, presumably at the instance of Lady Bacon, who sits among them as the presiding matriarch. Some further reading of her purposes can be gained from the inscription on the base of the tomb: surely her own conception, although probably written by her son-in-law, Sir Harbottle Grimston. It begins, conventionally enough, with praise of an outstanding daughter, wife, mother, and woman, giving her lineage and descent. Then, having acknowledged her piety, charity, and prudence, it continues:

. . . qua temporibus difficillimis duas Familias antiquitate nobiles, quibus certissimo Divinae Providentiae nutu conjuncta fuerat, sola sustinuit, ab interitu vindicavit, et perpetuitatis spei Restituit, ingenti exemplo!

[. . . who, in the most difficult of times alone sustained two families of ancient lineage, to which she was joined by the will of Divine Providence; she saved them from destruction and restored them to enduring hope: a most marvelous example!]

Jane was the bond linking and sustaining the Cornwallises and Bacons, nurturing them and protecting them in times of trouble. The last, we may reasonably infer, was a reference to the crises of the Civil War, although we shall see that the families had repeated need of her skills before political disaster struck.

The children clustered around their progenitor should therefore be read in part as symbols of their particular families, all returning to the protection of she who had given them breath. But we can add something more specific to the choice of image when we discover that all the children had been born and had died at Culford, the estate that was part of the original property of the Bacons that Jane had inherited from her second husband. And, with the exception of her own daughter, all had died in the 1650's, after several decades of low infant mortality in both families. Thus Jane seems to have wished both to mourn the individual children, several of whom are commemorated with touching epitaphs on tomb slabs around the church, and to celebrate the integrity of the house that had endeavored to rear them. The solidity of her own image—an antique ma-

tron seated upon a classical chair, a figure that in other circumstances
might legitimately be taken for a nun—again suggests the desire to represent the abiding power of the mother who had sacrificed for the survival
of her lineage, but in sacrificing had become the rock on which the house
was founded.

The monumentality of Jane Bacon's ultimate self-imaging could scarcely be further removed from the other important visual icon that survives
her. Her second husband, Sir Nathaniel Bacon, was a celebrated gentleman artist whose sophisticated portraiture suggests a training in the Low
Countries. Only a few of his paintings survive, among them a small half
portrait of his wife, presumably painted in the early years of their marriage,
when she would have been in her thirties [Fig. 2]. It shows an elegant court
beauty, presented half face with more than a glancing reference to early
Italian Renaissance portraiture. The hair, pulled back into a fashionable
coif, has a distinctly copper tone, and the clothes reflect approved style for
the mid-Jacobean period. Only the imaginative choice of profile and the
sharply observed face, both presumably the stylistic determination of Sir
Nathaniel, differentiate this lady from a hundred more of her contemporaries.[4]

The dialectic between court elegance and sober matriarchy is not, of
course, unique to Lady Jane. Despite the uniform language of obedience
and submission assumed by the dominant, male discourse on female behavior, elite women in early seventeenth-century England frequently found
themselves negotiating between more complex roles. There was the tension between the dutiful dependence required of daughter and wife and
the probable obligation to assume significant authority as widow. To this
was added the newer dichotomy of court and country: women played
some significant part in the late Tudor and early Stuart court, and their
presentation also had to reflect this diversity. Some women showed themselves keenly aware of the nature of these contrasts. Lady Anne Clifford, in
the great portrait that she commissioned in the 1640's, articulated precisely this Janus-faced quality of youth and maturity, of courtly style and
sober widowhood, of dependence and authority. Mistress Jane Meautys,
who died as Lady Bacon, never attempted a synoptic representation at this
overt level of self-reflection. Yet, through a study of her life, we have an
unusual opportunity to trace the process of negotiation between the ideal

FIG. 2. Portrait of Lady Jane Bacon by her husband, Sir Nathaniel Bacon. Gorhambury House, Hertfordshire. Reproduced by permission of Lord Verulam.

and reality of gender roles. And we can pursue this theme temporally, as an intelligent and well-connected woman self-fashioned her career with increasing assertiveness.[5]

I

Mistress Meautys was born into East Anglian families with strong court connections and a reputation for Protestant godliness. Her father, Hercules, was the youngest son of Sir Peter Meautys, a gentleman of the Privy Chamber under Henry VIII, who was apparently closely connected with John Russell, first earl of Bedford. Her mother was born Philippa Cooke, granddaughter of the great Sir Anthony Cooke of Gidea Hall, Essex, one of the leading lay Protestants of his generation. Hercules died in

1588 when his children were still young, leaving behind a will of explicit godliness, a widow charged with rearing "my children and hers . . . as my only trust is in her," and an insecure estate, partly consisting of some loans to such unreliable debtors as his feckless brother-in-law, Anthony Cooke. The uncomfortable financial position of the Meautys family is suggested by the dispatch of the only son, Thomas, to learn a soldier's trade in Ireland at the age of fourteen. Thomas spent the rest of his life as a professional officer, always struggling for sufficient financial security to abandon his service in the armies of Europe. His younger sister, Frances, married early and only achieved late prominence in a series of seamy scandals as the mistress and, eventually, second wife of Robert Radcliffe, earl of Sussex. It was Jane, however, who embarked upon the most interesting initial career: at some time in the early years of James's reign, she became one of the women of the Bedchamber to Queen Anne. No detail of her rise from provincial obscurity to this desirable office survives, but her patron and later intimate friend was undoubtedly Lucy, countess of Bedford, wife of the third earl. It may be that the old affinity between Meautys and Russell provided the initial opening for a beautiful girl in the circles around the queen.[6] Early in 1609, Jane was the focus of court gossip, and a number of eligible young men, including the lord treasurer's gentleman-usher, "mad for . . . love" of her, were named as prospective suitors. Yet later that year she married not "young Garret" but Sir William Cornwallis, a widower more than 30 years her senior. Two years later, Sir William died, leaving Jane splendidly endowed.[7] This was the stuff of contemporary satire: the uxorious dotard who succumbed, physically and intellectually, to the charms of a young bride, and who was inveigled into financial arrangements for her benefit and to the detriment of his wider family responsibilities. There is much in Sir William's character that might support such a reading of his actions. He was viewed by his friends and acquaintances, not least by his own father, as complacent, "prodigal," and "too addicted" to the shallow pleasures of London. For most of his life he was a minor and inept player on the margins of the court and its intrigues. His well-placed connections were never, despite his reiterated and pathetic importunities—"so that I may be about her Majesty, I care not to be a groom of the scullery"—translated into patronage or preferment. He was a "loving, honest, kind," and utterly ineffectual man.[8]

Yet Sir William's lavish generosity to his young wife was not unmerited:

she provided him with a son. In 1593, his only surviving son by his first marriage had been killed in a riding accident, an accident for which Sir William partially blamed his brother, Charles. The latter, by virtue of the young man's death, became prospective heir male to the Cornwallis estates. Sir William's "malycyous thoughts" against his sibling were never substantiated, but they tell us much about the always-strained relationship between the brothers. Charles was the antithesis of William: an able man, but cold, suspicious, and tight-fisted, who eventually enjoyed the preferment—as James I's ambassador to Spain—that his brother sought in vain.[9] Upon the death of their father in 1604, the tension between the brothers burst forth. William moved to break the entail on the family estates that guaranteed Charles's inheritance, and the brothers sought to mobilize their court connections against each other. In 1608, upon his wife's long-anticipated death, Sir William immediately made plans to remarry.[10]

The marriage to Jane Meautys fulfilled his most extravagant hopes. Jane became pregnant in the summer of 1610, and in the following January the doting husband added another of the Cornwallis's East Anglian estates to her already substantial—particularly given the limited portion of £1,500 that she had brought to the marriage—jointure. In March 1611, she gave birth to a son, Frederick; a further assignment of lands from her husband, these at Wilton in Cleveland, followed on October 18: four days later he made a will that was also exceptionally favorable to Jane. By this date Sir William may have been sick, although his illness was not thought to be serious. However, on November 13, following treatment by the great court doctor Sir Theodore Mayerne—and, the cynical intimated, largely in consequence of it—he died very suddenly, "when neyther he nor any thought him so neere his ende."[11]

The death of Sir William left Jane rich. Her jointure was immediately worth £500 a year, and, since "by meanes of good friends" at court she acquired the wardship of her infant son, the control of the whole estate was hers. This, as a consequence of a remarkable clause in the settlement made by Sir William just prior to his death, she largely kept even after her son attained his majority. The Cornwallis legal advisers pointed out "howe small his sonnes living would be . . . when he should come of age" by virtue of his arrangements, but the old man was adamant. Yet there were heavy burdens, too. She was named executor, and Sir William's debts were considerable. She also felt the cold hostility of Sir William's family. She faced the resentment of Sir Charles, whose hopes of succeeding to Brome were shattered by Frederick's birth and who for more than a decade pursued a series of lawsuits and "fraudulent courses" designed to wrest control of the estate from his sister-in-law. Sir William's daughters by his first marriage, women much her senior who received nothing for themselves or their children in Sir William's will, although they had shared their mother's lands at her death, were also alienated from her. One, Lady Withypole, launched a bitter tirade against the settlement and against the entire patriarchal and primogenitural assumptions that underpinned it: "this hous, the thing so mutch respected, is it any thing but A desire to continew a mane's memory? hath not my father wrong then who hath bene led to breck the laws of god and nature, and to loose the particular memory of himself?" But one senses that the defense of the lineage, "that erthly imaginery eternyty" in Lady Withypole's bitter opinion, was not Sir William's sole priority. By his "child at second hand" he had finally outmaneuvered his clever, successful younger brother: it was one of his few achievements.[12]

What of Jane's views of the marriage? On Sir William's tomb, "the tribute of a loving wife to her very dear husband," the marriage was described as "optimo auspicio"—most successful. But, despite the request in Sir William's will that such a tomb be built, Jane postponed the matter until the year of her own death. This contrasts significantly with the expedition with which she memorialized her second husband, as does the "very remarkable" cool formality of Sir William's tomb with the lively and highly personalized monument to Sir Nathaniel Bacon.[13] Lady Jane's own tomb also suggests the difference in her perception of the two marriages. In her first, she was "given" in marriage with Sir William Cornwallis, in her second she was "joined" with Sir Nathaniel, and this seems more than the linguistic conventions applied to a single woman and a widow.

Chamberlain, reporting Sir William's death, tastelessly categorized Jane as a most tempting prospect, "a fresh widow . . . [with] the whole estate in her hands."[14] We do not know if she was besieged by the anticipated host of predatory wooers, but she certainly did not allow her opportunities to go to her head. She was keenly aware that attempts would be made to "entice my affections" by those whose primary motive was "my fortune." Her sense of her role as a young widow was appropriately decorous; "since Sir Willem Cornwaleys's death I neaver as yet had a thought of changing the course of life which I now lede," she wrote in 1613.[15] In that year she began to contemplate remarriage, but she did so with an independence, caution, and sense of responsibility that fully justified the exceptional trust that Sir William Cornwallis had reposed in her. The role she adopts in the negotiations with her suitor, Nathaniel Bacon, and his family was in many respects conventional; she expresses a demure diffidence at the prospect of remarriage and a pious resignation to God's will. But there is a hard edge to the discussion of financial arrangements. She knew the value of her estate. She dismissed the early offers made by Mr. Bacon and his friends, since her fortune deserved "farre greater offers," and even his assurance that "I should do with my own estate, beside my child's, what I would" did not at first suffice. She was determined that her future husband should bring an estate proportionable to hers into the marriage, and she was untroubled by an awareness that her demands might create tensions among the Bacon family, that Nathaniel's siblings might "envy" his enrichment.[16]

Her tough negotiating stance paid off. The Bacons, particularly Lady Anne, might recognize in abstract that "we must not laye out all our stocke upon one purchas, having so many others to provide for," but Nathaniel, the youngest of nine brothers, was a Joseph. His doting mother wrote of "the juill of our deer sonne" or, more tellingly, of "my deer Nath."[17] In the face of Lady Jane's demands, Nathaniel was promised the inheritance of the Bacon estates at Culford and Ingham, which finally came to him on his father's death in 1624; Lady Jane kept control of the Cornwallis inheritance.

Nathaniel's promise to Jane that she should manage her own property in marriage certainly vested: the later correspondence is full of references to Jane in London, handling her own affairs or pursuing their joint interests. She kept a close control on the daily business even of so remote a manor as Wilton in Cleveland, part of her augmented jointure from Sir William: there her steward on one occasion had to apologize for paying £10 for house repairs, apparently misled by Jane's general agreement when they had discussed the matter in London. In more traditional female style she maintained an equally tight rein upon the household: a superb household book, running from 1617 to 1629 covering Brome, Culford, and London, shows meticulous control exercised over routine expenditure. Nathaniel, though he assumed some share in business transactions, was often willing enough to remain in the country, nursing his rather delicate health, spending time with his parents at Redgrave or Culford, and painting. Jane, whose ill health equally seems to be an endless subject of discussion, nevertheless remained in London for long periods, especially when opposing Sir Charles Cornwallis's assaults upon her son's estate. No wonder that in 1624 her husband wrote to her in London, "I cannot but be fully perswaded of your moste great care & dilligence, whereby it [our business] hath attayned this present estate."[18]

It may be a mistake to identify Jane's growing assertiveness in the public defense of her property only with her marital experiences. To this specific context should probably be added her experience of the Jacobean court, particularly the formative friendship she established with Lucy, countess of Bedford. Lucy's lifestyle as confidante of Anne of Denmark, as patroness of writers, and as an independent woman whose complaisant husband preferred country pursuits and was usually willing to let his wife perform the courtly dance, cannot but have influenced the young Jane. It certainly taught her an interest not merely in the perpetual gossip of the Jacobean court but also in matters of state usually thought inappropriate for a woman. Lucy maintained a flow of letters to her friend, whose life was perforce passed largely in the country; she gossiped and talked of her own woes; she also commented on the Parliaments of 1621, 1624, and 1626 and on the political dispositions at the beginning of Charles I's reign. Her letters imply that she expected informed responses from her country friend, as did Jane's cousin Meautys when he later began to write of parliamentary politics and the Thirty Years' War. Jane's replies do not survive, but the tone of her correspondents clearly suggested that they valued her views. The country gentlewoman with these contacts had ample opportunity to reflect on the nature of power and to understand how to use connection to her advantage.[19]

Jane's activity as correspondent should probably be seen as a growing source of empowerment: an activity from which she derived mental stimulation and that affirmed her advancing control over her environment. The surviving letters to her were matched by her own flood of correspondence, very little of which now exists. All of this must have begun early in her career, before her first marriage: her brother referred in 1622 to "som 100 of yors [letters] that were rytten beinge a maide, a wyfe and a widdowe." Yet the construction of an archive that begins with her second marriage seems to mark some turning point in Jane's understanding of the importance of her literary efforts. We can be reasonably confident that it was her own choice to preserve these texts: when the Essex Record Office finally became the depository for the Cornwallis correspondence, some of the bundles were still bound and labeled in Jane's own hand. The sending and receiving of such material was, no doubt, a source of social pleasure: its preservation suggests in addition a perception of the importance of correspondence as an affirmation of her centrality in a nexus of family, kin, and like-minded friends.[20]

Finally Jane may have gained self-assurance at this stage of her career from the role she was able to play in the religious life of the locality. It is impossible to discover detail about her early religious training or attitudes, though all her family is likely to have been exposed to proper Protestant discipline. Her early adulthood, on the other hand, took her into a court environment in which Catholicism was becoming culturally legitimated, and her first marriage was into a family that had earlier been a powerful symbol of elite identity with the old faith. Only when she was freed as a widow and then as a second wife can we really begin to say anything about Jane's own faith. The key influence upon her was that of Elnathan Parr, rector of Palgrave from 1600 to his death in 1622, and as a godly Protestant a most unlikely choice of Sir Thomas Cornwallis as patron. Something of the strength of her attachment can be seen, even through the distortions of approved discourse, in the letter of consolation sent her by her household chaplain, William Greenhill, at Parr's death. "Your love," he writes, "was singular to this man, now god will, yea doth, make tryall of your love to him." Parr dedicated several of his published works to Lady Jane: the earliest, printed in 1614, speaks of her "sincere profession of the Gospell" and the "zeale in Religion" that has made her an example to many. Later Parr also included Sir Nathaniel in his praise, but he made it clear that it was Jane who "watered" his "studies with [her] countenance and beneficence." The affection was sustained even after his death: Jane made an allowance to Parr's much younger widow, which was still being paid in 1658, and one of the two clerical portraits that hung in her chamber was of Elnathan.[21]

Parr could judge of Jane's godliness at first hand and lead her along the proper paths of Calvinist orthodoxy. But her reputation was also known at a distance. When a remote kinsman, Sir Thomas Posthumous Hoby, intervened on her behalf in a tenurial dispute on her Yorkshire estate, he seized the opportunity to advocate that she install a preaching minister in the chapel on her lands because the people there labored in "palpable ignorance of the gospell of Christe." Bringing true Protestantism to Yorkshire was a ruling obsession with Sir Thomas, and he believed that he had an ally in Jane because she was educated in virtue and, significantly, because she had in her second marriage matched into "soe religious a family." The Cornwallises had allowed their Yorkshire tenants to go their own way, and the effective choice of minister had lain in the hands of the steward who, according to Hoby, was a listed recusant. Now the Bacon alliance could be invoked in the cause of the Gospel. The correspondence shows that Jane did intervene to dismiss the existing curate and order a collection amongst the tenants for the support of a new minister, but it may be that in the choice of the man the ingenious steward may have outwitted Hoby, for he rallied the tenantry to petition his mistress that they might choose "one that would be fit and willinge to teach their children" with no mention of the preaching of the Word.

Her role as godly patroness continued beyond her second husband's death. She badgered William Greenhill, who was tempted by the opportunity of a lectureship in London, to return to Suffolk, and in 1631 she presented him to the living of Oakley. In the city, Greenhill had developed close ties with the leaders of those who were opposing the increasingly dominant Arminians in the church. Lady Bacon associated herself more firmly with this group when, purely on the general report of his godliness, she appointed Jeremiah Burroughs, already in trouble for his vigorous preaching as lecturer at Bury St. Edmunds, to her living of Tivetshall. In 1637, both Greenhill and Burroughs were deprived by Bishop Wren for their refusal to accede to his demand for the performance of ritual innovations in their parishes, but not before Lady Jane had made every effort, through "great friends at Court," to protect her nominees.[22]

Yet it would be inappropriate to define Jane Bacon, in her second marriage, as driven exclusively by concerns for influence and control. The lady of Sir Nathaniel's portraits was also a lively and affectionate wife and mother, operating within the accepted parameters of her subordinate gender role. It would seem that her second marriage was a happy one. Bacon continued to write affectionate notes to his wife whenever they were parted by business, describing her as "sweet hart" and expressing appropriate wishes to return to her quickly. His letters are also full of warmth toward the children of the marriage, Anne, Nicholas, and Jane, seeking news of their well-being when he was in London or elsewhere, reporting their mi-

FIG. 3. Tomb of Sir Nicholas Bacon, Culford Church, Suffolk. Photo by authors.

nor doings when it was Jane who was absent. "Tell Nan," he writes in 1624, "I have bought her a fine new gowne, wherfore I shall expect great forwardnesse in her book at my retourne." Earlier in the same year when Jane was away, he reported on a domestic incident that suggests a daily closeness to his children: Nicholas, then six, "sends you word of a brood of young chickens, and of a disaster he escaped at my being with him; for he eate so much milk porrage at supper that he cryed out, (O Lord!) I think I have almost broake myne guutt; & I was fayne to walk him a turne or ii about the chamber to digest it." Moreover, he did not exclude his stepson, Frederick, from this intimacy: greetings and news regularly add his name to those of the younger ones.[23]

Jane's attitudes to her spouse are perhaps best detected in her approach to his art, which was clearly of critical importance to him. His letters often ask for the supply of materials when Jane was in London, and it was probably through her that he became an informal art consultant to the countess of Bedford. The latter was proud of her taste as a collector, and in

1618 she was pursuing Bacon to see if he could obtain any Holbeins from
his father, Sir Nicholas, who was rumored to be on his death-bed, or from
any other source. It seems to have been Jane's pride in her husband's skill,
as well as general affection for him, that moved her to commission the
memorial in Culford Church immediately after his death [Fig. 3]. A stylish
bust is surrounded by a carved border that incorporates a painter's tools:
the inscription lauds his artistic skill, and the conquest of Nature by his
brush. We have seen that she failed to be as demonstrative toward the
memory of her first husband. The lavish display of Nathaniel's pictures at
Culford is revealed in the inventory drawn up after her death, but it is also
noted in the poems of a suitor who came wooing her daughter in the
1630's. Philip Woodhouse reported that he saw:

> Some pieces were by forrayne Masters wrought,
> some by ye moderne pencills of our land
> Others from Italy were safely brought
> the best was drawne by his deer-loving hand
> who more than by Apelles arte had limn'd.

And finally the inventory of Culford, prepared over 30 years after Nathaniel's death, shows that Jane had carefully preserved his "shop" with his
painter's equipment intact, although there is no evidence that it was used
by any of his heirs.[24]

II

Nathaniel Bacon died in 1627, leaving a grieving widow in control
of the Culford estates as well as those of the Cornwallises. There is no suggestion in the surviving correspondence that Jane ever gave serious thought
to remarriage, although she was still a woman of some beauty if we are to
believe Philip Woodhouse. In his wooing poems to her daughter Anne, he
thought it wise to flatter the mother as well: she was

> . . . a stately Dame
> Who her meridian passed had of years,
> Yet she retayn'd a beautye might inflame
> the greenest object in her sight appears
> Beautye and vertue both did her adorne
> grave speeche and prudence gave her pleasing grace.

This heavy-handed compliment at least suggests that Jane had not permanently withdrawn into the role of the distressed widow. Instead, she presumably invoked those elements of self-construction that had served her well in the past to focus upon the duties of a head of house. She devoted her second and very lengthy widowhood to managing the family and property she had accumulated, while maintaining a measure of contact with the worlds of London and the court through visits and her lively correspondence with her cousin, Thomas Meautys. She had need of this form of relief, for her family were in the next three decades to provide challenges against which her earlier training was scarcely proof.[25]

It was the two boys, the heirs of Cornwallis and Bacon, who were to prove the greatest threat both to the fortunes of the families and to their mother's peace of mind. Some tension between the aspirations of a widow controlling her husband's estates and their future inheritor was always likely, but Jane was peculiarly unfortunate in the personalities and capacities of her sons. The early years were propitious enough in the case of Frederick Cornwallis. He was given early training in the Bacon household, where fragments from the letters suggest an adequate relationship with his stepfather. Mr. Greenhill trained him sufficiently in the classics for him to be sent to Cambridge in 1625. As befitted an heir whose parents identified with godly Protestantism, Fred was given into the hands of the great John Preston of Queens' College. Preston worked hard with his charge: he was reported by the faithful Greenhill to be calling Fred in three times a day to explain what he had studied. And his pupil seems to have liked Cambridge sufficiently to have stayed for three years. However, nothing in his subsequent career suggests that university had much intellectual or spiritual impact upon him. By the early part of 1628, Fred and his tutor were at odds: Greenhill reported that Fred had "given some distast to Dr. Preston through the height of his spirit." It was inevitable, he added, that Frederick should be deflected from study at times and "count it to much bondage to be held in a constant track of dutie." His old tutor was evidently fond of his charge and was the first of many apologists to his mother for the latter's fecklessness. From Cambridge, Frederick moved directly into service at court, and there the opportunities for rashness were immediately multiplied a thousandfold.[26]

It was a full decade after Frederick's arrival at Cambridge that his half-brother, Nicholas, though only seven years his junior, was dispatched to

St. Catherine's, another godly seminary under the headship of Richard Sibbes. Eighteen was an unusually late age for a fellow-commoner to start at university. A likely explanation is to be found in Nicholas's regular letters home to his mother, acknowledging payments of his allowance and giving brief news of his doings. The notes (they are scarcely more) are stilted and formal in language and are written in an immature hand. In one letter Nicholas expresses his affection and then adds: "I could as well expresse it in words as it is really in my heart: but your ladyship knoweth my dissability that way, and therefore I hope you will excuse all faults committed in the writing." Nicholas appears to be a slow learner, in marked contrast to his quick-witted siblings, and was presumably already a disappointment in a family in which both men and women prided themselves on their learning. His stay at Cambridge appears to have been shorter than that of his brother.[27]

The most onerous duty for the widow managing a wealthy heir was the arrangement of a suitable marriage. Here Jane's own experience was in principle beneficial. By the end of the 1620's, Frederick was reaching his majority, and his already expansive and expensive habits at court meant that he needed to make a sound financial as well as social alliance. Since much of Jane's own time was devoted to the younger children in the country, she employed go-betweens and advisers in London, for Fred was a prize to be offered in the national marriage market. Her principal agent was Dorothy Randolph, a cousin of the Meautys family and wife of an Exchequer official, who reported regularly on the availability of suitable matches. Dorothy was valuable as a commentator and postbox, but her standing was modest, and Jane also turned to gentlewomen of her own status, including that godly lady, Judith Barrington, for whom she had apparently performed similar services. Various candidates were trailed, without much sense of progress: "It is hard to meet with one whose person and portion is without exseption," Dorothy Randolph wrote with some exasperation in the winter of 1629–30. By then, Dorothy was keenly aware of the need for haste: meeting with Fred in December, she reported "a wandring humor in him . . . and a resolution this spring to go into France."

Frederick did something far worse than abscond for a Grand Tour: the next year he married without his mother's knowledge, and he married a woman who, though of impeccable social status, brought no dowry with her. Elizabeth Ashburnham, daughter of Sir John, was in Henrietta Maria's service and much favored by her royal mistress, who promised £3,000 from herself and the king in lieu of her own wealth. In personal terms it seems one of the few sensible acts Frederick ever undertook: Elizabeth emerges from her later correspondence with her mother-in-law as a woman of warmth and sound judgment, who endeavored to bring some stability into the life of her wayward husband. Financially it was, of course, disastrous: Frederick's expensive habits would have devoured even a mercantile fortune, and there was no hope that he could sustain himself on love and loyalty, especially as both he and his wife had to continue to live in the public eye of the court.[28] The marriage so explicitly contravened all Lady Bacon's prudential understanding of familial interest that it seems Frederick's relationship with his mother never fully recovered from the blow of his clandestine marriage, even though she gave unstinting support to his wife and children. She already mistrusted her son's sanguine temperament. A year before his marriage, William Greenhill had intervened with her when her son was in some trouble, advising careful handling of Frederick, who was convinced that his mother thought "there is no good to bee done with him but by harsh meanes and rugged usage, which he acknowledges worke outwardly uppon his nature." But this was no mere scrape or minor debt. It subverted familial authority as well as financial stability, and even with the direct intervention of the king and queen, pleading with a mother to forgive their respective servants, Jane was for a time unyielding. By the end of 1631, she was again sending her son money, and she had begun to receive his wife, while London letters from Dorothy Randolph continue to refer to his waywardness and his financial disputes with his mother. Only the arrival of children, born at Culford and reared there by Jane while their parents continued to serve at court, seems to have reconciled the family more fully.[29]

Frederick's court career continued to prove ruinously expensive, and he had received nothing in return save his dowerless wife, some minor grants, and lavish promises of future preferment. In consequence, by the mid-1630's he was deeply indebted to a number of importunate creditors, and Lady Jane was receiving a series of begging letters from her son—"I have bin faine to pay away all the litle monie that Mr. Morse [Lady Jane's steward] brought to stop some few people's mouths, & yet it will not half satisfie them; soe that I have not a shilling left . . . unless your Ladyship will be plesed to take mee into your consideration." Finally an expedient was found; the debts were paid off by a loan of £6,000 from his mother on the security of Brome, Oakley, and Thorpe Abbots, valued at £800 per annum. The arrangement was distasteful to Sir Frederick, who procrastinated and complained, but Lady Jane found an ally in an unlikely quarter: Frederick's wife, Elizabeth, had come to share her mother-in-law's low opinion of his fiscal competence. "My husband is very good," she began with touching loyalty. "But if he put his estat into a stranger's hand, I shall never looke to see any part of it again." She concluded, "The more tie you have upon him and his estate, the gladder I shall be, for I veryly believe it will be best for him." The arrangement did not terminate Fred's extravagance, and a series of additional loans were negotiated—*not* with his mother—in the late 1630's. On one occasion, Fred persuaded poor simple Nicholas to act as surety for him. But the 1636 arrangement did protect the Cornwallis lands in the Civil War period. The condition of the mortgage was that the lands would vest in Lady Bacon if, on six months' warning, Sir Frederick failed to repay the full sum plus interest. In 1650, when the Cornwallis estates were again targeted for sequestration, Lady Jane successfully claimed that the property was now hers. When she made her will in 1658, Lady Jane instructed her trustees to use the lands to supply Sir Frederick generously, but only on condition that he give security not to charge the estates with his debts; Brome and its ancillary lands were to be inherited by her grandson, Charles. Her belief in lineage was apparently reaffirmed by this reliable youth, reared under her own tutelage and inculcated with her values.[30]

Nicholas's situation, and that of the Culford estates, was more precarious. Lady Jane had a jointure interest worth about £300 a year at Culford, while Nicholas, upon achieving his majority, had succeeded to lands worth about £350 a year. He had borrowed some £2,800 on bonds in the 1630's and had acted as surety for money borrowed by Frederick. Lady Jane had paid off some of this in the late 1630's, gaining control of a portion of Nicholas's estate in the process and, as with Fred, protecting it from sequestration during the war. But the rake's progress continued. By 1645 Nicholas's debts totaled £6,600, what remained of his lands had been extended by his creditors, he had been outlawed, and he was imprisoned: those who had loaned him money were squabbling to ensure the priority of their claims on the estate. Ten years later, matters had been resolved. Lady Jane had recovered the Bacon lands, buying out Nicholas's creditors and what remained of his own interest in the property in a series of deals that, in the opinion of the parliamentary authorities, shaded the margins of legality.[31]

These later maneuvers were necessary partly because both Jane's sons had opted for the wrong side in the Civil War. Both joined the king at Oxford. Nicholas did little. He served as a captain of dragoons for a short period. He also somehow acquired a wife—a woman whose subsequent invisibility in the annals of the family suggests a wartime mésalliance. By the summer of 1645, Bacon had returned to London, where his efforts to compound for his delinquency and regain his sequestered estates were interrupted by his numerous creditors, who had him arrested and imprisoned at the end of 1645. Sir Frederick Cornwallis was far more actively engaged in the royalist cause. Elected as MP for Eye in 1640, he had voted against the attainder of Strafford and denounced Pym's alliance with "the enemy in our bosome," the Scots. He was expelled from the Commons in September 1642, accused of recruiting officers from the Continent for the king's forces. When he sought to compound for his estates in the summer of 1646, he emphasized that he had joined Charles in the north as his "sworn servant" and insisted that he had never borne arms; similarly he had gone to the west, where he was captured at the surrender of Exeter, merely as the servant of the prince of Wales. But his war was more eventful than this deliberately understated account might suggest. He had fought at Cropredy Bridge, gallantly rescuing Lord Wilmot; he had experienced personal tragedy with the death of his wife, who was buried at Oxford early in 1644. He had remarried in 1646, again without seeking parental consent— in this case, of the bride's family. Frederick remained suspect to the victorious parliamentarians; he refused to swear the Covenant; there were problems with his composition; he was imprisoned in 1655 in the round-up of royalists after Penruddock's futile rising. In 1656 he fled to the exiled court of Charles II, to return in 1660 to the rewards of loyalty, both office—treasurer of the household; privy counselor—and enhanced status— Baron Cornwallis of Eye. And he returned to a place in Cavalier legend. In 1688 he was embalmed in David Lloyd's hagiography of those "that suffered . . . for ALLEGIANCE to their SOVEREIGN"; he was fearless, debonair, frank; "a perfect . . . master of Courtly . . . raillery"; even "competently seen in modern languages." Pepys's more jaundiced view is not wholly incompatible with this encomium—"a bold prophane-talking man."[32]

By then his long-suffering mother was dead. In the 1650's she had offered a home to Nicholas and his regrettable wife at Culford; there, too,
Frederick's son, Charles, raised his young family under his grandmother's
eye and she mourned the deaths of two of his children. It was during the
Civil War and its aftermath that Lady Jane earned the inscription graven
on her monument: the savior of two families. Her general adherence to the
royalist cause is worth comment, given her vigorous Protestantism and her
country friendships with families like the Barringtons. We can only
speculate that she was in some measure led by the loyalty of her sons, with
their unswerving support of the king, although she had shown herself well
able to maintain a distance from their preoccupations. Perhaps her own
loyalties were rather formed by the memory of her old mistress, Anne of
Denmark, and by a sympathy for Elizabeth of Bohemia, kept alive by the
constant comments of her brother, who had served the Winter Queen. She
also seems to have wished to guard her own counsel; after 1641, the filing of
letters seems to have stopped as abruptly as it began, with only a little correspondence with her brother and sister-in-law dating from the early years
of the war. By the war's end she was probably too enmeshed in business to
concern herself with such matters. She kept the parliamentary demands on
her own property to a minimum. She relentlessly fought an assessment of
£2,000 from the committee of Haberdasher's Hall, taking every opportunity for procrastination and appeal until the authorities backed down and
apologetically reduced their levy.[33]

III

Two inadequate sons who were heirs to the two significant fortunes
she had nurtured must have been a bitter disappointment to Lady Jane.
But since resourcefulness had been inculcated into her by early experience,
she seems to have displayed considerable imagination in circumventing
these obstacles. In the Cornwallis family, it quickly became evident that
the next generation might be trained to displace the deficient Frederick. In
the Bacon lineage, this seemed much less likely. But there was an alternative in the female line, and one of the most intriguing aspects of Jane's view
of family was her willingness to turn to cognate descent when the agnatic
line failed. Her surviving daughter, Anne, began her career conventionally
enough. Little can be said of her early training: we have seen her in her fa-

ther's lifetime studying her "book," and it is probable that she shared the teaching given to her brothers by Greenhill and later by a Mr. Warwell. This would certainly have included instruction in the Protestant faith, and late in her life Anne impressed no less a judge than Gilbert Burnet, who spoke warmly of her "elevation and force" in discussing religion.[34]

Anne only appeared as a significant figure in the records when she approached marriageable age in the early 1630's. She had inherited much of her mother's beauty, if we may judge by the two late portraits of her at Gorhambury. She was also eligible: her father had left her some property in Timworth in her own right, and Jane was able to offer a significant portion. She was wooed passionately by at least one young gentleman, Philip Woodhouse, whose poems and letters to his love survive. Woodhouse met Anne, by his own description, while hunting "on Elden playnes" in 1632, and he was instantly enamored. He engineered an invitation to her mother's house, where Lady Bacon was "so noble and so debonayre" as to allow him an extended visit. He pursued Anne in ploddingly amorous verse after he had left the house:

> Goe blotted paper to the beauteous mayde
> Whom thy sad master would, but may not see
> Go therfore in his stead, be not affrayde,
> Thou hast no parent that inhibites thee.[35]

Philip was the heir to the Woodhouses of Kimberley, Norfolk, and as such someone who might have expected a hearing for his wooing. A letter written to Lady Bacon on February 11, 1633, suggests that he was indeed given some bare encouragement. Jane troubled herself to find out from her brother-in-law, Edmund Bacon, that an earlier possible alliance for Woodhouse had come to nothing. But his financial position was not good enough. In his second wooing poem he complained of "the All-mistris Gould" and lamented that another suitor, one of the Mildmay family, had the advantage of him. He attempted to respond by assuring Jane that he was seeking the financial advice of the "freinds of my affinitye" and by appointing proper go-betweens; all in vain. Did Anne even receive his wooing verse, bound up as it is among her mother's papers? The latter was certainly determined that her daughter should marry only where there was wealth at least commensurate with her own. The Mildmay match was also rejected. Anne was not married until after the end of the decade, and then she was allied rather surprisingly to her cousin, Sir Thomas Meautys, clerk of the Privy Council and close confidant of Lady Jane.[36]

Meautys was more than two decades older than Anne, whom he had known since her infancy. But the oddity of the match lies not so much in disparity of age as in Meautys's background. Sir Thomas owed his rise to the affection of Sir Francis Bacon, whose secretary he became in about 1616. He was one of the elegant young men with whom the lord chancellor delighted to surround himself, sycophants who, in Bacon's widow's tart phrase, by their "vicious courses did him great prejudice." But Thomas was distinguished from that throng by his willingness to act upon the fulsome expressions of devotion to his benefactor in the crisis of Bacon's fall in 1621. He became Bacon's "mainstay," working tirelessly to defend his master during Parliamentary inquiry, then to advance his schemes to recover court favor. Meautys was the preferred legatee of Bacon's will and assumed the executorship of the greatly encumbered estates. He erected the remarkable monument to Bacon in St. Alban's as an expression of his devotion and was buried at its foot. Meautys's courtly letters to Lady Jane suggest a mannered and whimsical personality, though his political observations are sharp and perceptive. Meautys was obviously fond of Anne from childhood, referring to her as his "pretious cosin Anne" and praising her beauty as a teenager in a series of elaborate conceits, but there is no hint in the letters that he courted her when there was serious competition for her hand in the mid-1630's. It would seem that Jane, having delayed in marrying her daughter, then chose a suitor for the personal security of a well-known familial relationship and for the possibility of advancing the Bacon interest, which would atrophy in the hands of young Nicholas. Meautys was a rich man by virtue of his posts in the royal administration, and through a series of tortuous and shady machinations he was steadily freeing his beloved master's Gorhambury estate of encumbrances to claim it as his own. And Gorhambury, the preferred home of Lord Keeper Sir Nicholas Bacon, could be seen as the foundation stone of the wealth and prestige of the Bacon family. Of Anne's view upon all of this we know nothing.[37]

The success of this alliance seems to have encouraged Jane Bacon to outface the difficulties of the Civil War years and do more than merely defend the existing financial interests of her families. In the 1640's, when Lady Jane and Sir Thomas Meautys and Anne were all living in Covent

Garden, Lady Jane assisted her old admirer in consolidating his claims on his patron's Gorhambury estate, lending him substantial sums on the security of the property. Sir Thomas died in 1648, leaving Anne with a life-interest in Gorhambury and their daughter, Jane, as his heir. When Anne married a widower, Harbottle Grimston, in 1651, Lady Jane Bacon was careful to guarantee the title of her daughter and grandchildren in the property, getting Grimston to buy out the interests of all others, creditors and distant relatives, who still had claims on the estate. But Gorhambury did not revert to the female Bacons. Anne's daughter by Meautys, "little Janey," who in one letter sent her love "to her dear Sir Harreby," died shortly after her mother's second marriage; her daughter by Grimston died in 1657: both, as we have seen, figure prominently on Lady Jane's tomb. By the time of Lady Jane's death, Anne was in her early forties and unlikely to bear more children. Gorhambury became the property of the heirs of Sir Harbottle by his first wife.[38]

The solidity of the fortune constructed by Lady Bacon in "the most difficult of time" must therefore be set in a matrix of biological failure and personal disappointment. Her obvious duty, as she moved from court to country, from marriages to widowhood, from the relative calm of the 1630's to the crises of the Civil War, was the defense of lineage, or in this case of three lineages, Cornwallis, Bacon, and her own Meautys kin. In the senior lineage there was no serious biological problem; although the beloved children of her grandson Charles were mourned, they were part of a large brood, the recitation of whose claims on the estates occupied many lines of her will. The failure here was that of the relationship between mother and son, which was so acute that Lady Jane clearly pinned all her hopes for the success of the Cornwallises on her eldest grandson, ultimately the main executor of her will and her residuary legatee. The crises for the Bacon dynasty were both personal and biological: Nicholas could neither produce an heir nor manage what he had already. He was allowed a life-interest in Culford, but all the deeds and even the stock of the estates were placed in the hands of Anne, and it is clear that she and Sir Harbottle had to hold Nicholas in a form of tutelage.[39]

Perhaps of most significance in understanding Lady Jane's attitudes is the evidence of her ability to transfer her dynastic hopes from the deficient Nicholas to the female line, afforced as it was by the Meautys connection. Young Jane Meautys was in her eyes an heir worthy of the struggle to purchase the Gorhambury property, and even her death does not seem to have diminished her grandmother's enthusiasm for her female lineage. And, even though her dynastic hopes were frustrated, there is some sense that her spirit did linger for a generation in the person of her daughter. Anne not only occupied the house of her distinguished cousin and inherited Culford after her brother's death. She also retained the best of her father's paintings, including the fine self-portrait that is a unique example of the self-representation of a seventeenth-century gentleman. In her later years she and her husband provided a home and support to Gilbert Burnet, and in his *History of My Own Times* he offers an encomium to his patroness. She was charitable to a fault, deeply concerned with relieving prisoners and educating the children of the poor. She was plain in her dress and modest in manner. When she spoke of religion, however, the vigor of her mother's personality was still present. Burnet also noted with disapproval that her religious views were imbued with "all the high notions for the church and the crown, in which she had been bred." This was surely a misreading of Anne's early religious education but a convincing summation of the character she had inherited from her mother.[40]

The pattern of Jane's life—court service, two husbands, difficult children, biological disaster, and Civil War crisis—could be replicated with variations in many other narratives of the landed elite in the seventeenth century. Was her response to these circumstances in any sense unique? Our analysis suggests that in most of the crises of her life she responded within the conventions of properly gendered behavior, managing her own affairs when there was approved opportunity to do so, protecting her family when widowed and in a logical position of authority. Her actions, insofar as they can be observed in her correspondence and family papers, are those of a woman who was able to achieve most of her goals by vigor of spirit, charm, and intelligent management. Yet in so doing she inverted many of the conventions of her culture: no virago she, but a woman to whom her distinguished sons-in-law deferred, a woman above all on whom many depended, both for breeding and for wealth. And her choice of self-imaging at the end reveals the extent to which she had internalized this sense of power and now sought to lend it permanent expression. Her tomb celebrates the nurturing strength of the matriarch, the integrity of the widow, and the strength of the lineage even in death.

ILANA KRAUSMAN BEN-AMOS

"Good Works" and Social Ties

HELPING THE MIGRANT POOR IN

EARLY MODERN ENGLAND

Historians have long recognized the role of the Reformation in the transformation of attitudes to poverty, vagrancy, and the relief of the poor. In its denial of the efficacy of works and its focus on justification by faith alone, Protestantism gave ideological force and articulation to a shift from private, religiously inspired relief to a more centralized, secular, and institutional system of provision for the poor. In their attitude to discipline and labor, Protestants also reinforced the assault on those deemed idle poor: vagrants, beggars, masterless youths who were to be given correction and punishment rather than relief. Protestants thus legitimized the punitive measures taken against the mobile poor in the decades following the Reformation. Harsh laws against vagrants, almsgiving, and the taking of inmates remained intact between 1600 and 1750.[1]

Perhaps the most striking aspect of this attempt by the Tudor and Stuart authorities to curb or control the mobility of the poor was its nearly universal failure. Despite the legislation and attempts at enforcement—and for all the condemnation of the migrant poor with which it was buttressed—mobility throughout the period remained ubiquitous.[2] As will be here shown, the mobility of the poor was sustained by an intricate network of ties that provided help on the road and upon arrival in new towns. It was based on ties of kin and neighborly relations, but also on looser and indirect contacts; occasionally it involved support to strangers and those deemed unworthy of relief. A contrast emerged between the Protestant assault on the vagrant poor and ordinary practices of help to those on the move, suggesting a divergence in attitude between those who preached and those who listened, and pointing in the direction of the failure of the Protestant understanding of poverty to take roots among the populace at large.

This chapter addresses this apparent divergence between the Protestant message and social practice and its implications for an understanding of the ways the Protestant message was received within the populace at large. As Paul Seaver recognized, there could be more than a single response to the standards of behavior set by the Protestants. Audiences could remain indifferent to the message preached, or live in perpetual anxiety over their failure to comply with the prescribed rules of conduct. Or they could respond more comfortably, since their social practices did not wholly diverge from what was preached.[3] There is yet another dimension to popular responses to what was delivered on the pulpit or in print. Since the meanings people may derive from what is conveyed to them depend on their social and mental habits, they may embrace the message but adapt it to their own needs. A reconciliation between theology and social practice is possible because those who listen derive different meanings from the ones intended by those who preach.[4] The difficulty in exploring this possibility is that only a tiny minority of early modern English women and men recorded their understanding of what was propagated and preached. For the vast majority of the population, we are left only with the record of the Protestant message itself, as it was pronounced from the pulpit or in print. An analysis of these pronouncements does not provide direct evidence of popular perceptions of the message, but it does allow us to assess the options made available to the audiences and how these could be adapted and used to fit a set of social practices and interactions.

The sections that follow take a closer look at the social ties that sustained the migrant poor and the Protestant pronouncements regarding vagrancy, charity, and the poor. Practices of support to the migrant, including occasionally those considered unworthy of relief, had force and vitality: they engaged the participants in a web of relations and obligations with which Protestantism could not easily compete. The tenacity of these ties in the two centuries following the Reformation suggests that ordinary people may have resisted or remained indifferent to the assault on the vagrant poor. But as the analysis of Protestant pronouncements on the poor indicates, ordinary people could embrace the message and still invest their actions with religious meanings, for the Protestant understanding of poverty and charity was itself amenable to differentiated interpretations.

I

In August 1624, David Jones was arrested for theft in Southampton. In his examination, the young man claimed that he had been an apprentice with a glover in Warminster for seven years, but after five years his master ran away from his creditors and Jones was forced to leave. He first moved to his mother's house in Warminster, where he remained the following winter. In early summer he decided to leave, despite his mother's objections. He traveled to Lovington in Somerset, where he stayed one night. The next day he walked seven miles to the small village of Calne, where he "lay one night in a barn." Next he turned to Somerton, where he also slept in a barn. And so he continued, "up and down the country," in places and villages "he knew not the names of." At one point he headed toward a fair near Winchester, where he stayed a few days, and where he also "lay upon a hill." Eventually he reached Southampton, where he was arrested for stealing clothes.[5]

For all the hardship and desperation that probably prompted him to steal, Jones was provided with some support in his wandering and what appears to have been a simple search for livelihood and work. It is likely that without the sense that survival would be had, Jones would not have left a mother who was reluctant to see him go and who may have given her tacit understanding that their house would remain a place to which he could return. Throughout the period servants moved frequently between annual terms of service that were also interspersed with moves into seasonal and daily labor. Moves into the parental home in the interim were routine.[6] Parents opened their doors to sons and daughters who fell on hard times: when they were unemployed or became sick, when their masters sent them away, when they themselves decided to leave. When the master of Thomas Burgess, a Bristol apprentice in the 1670's, complained at Quarter Sessions that the youth ran away three times, the first person the magistrates contacted was his mother, who was then living in the countryside.[7] Autobiographies and court records all point to the degree to which the parental home continued to provide a sort of safety net for children well after they left their homes or their service terms. Apprentices out of long-term services, married children who fell on hard times, daughters whose husbands went to sea, young preachers on the move—all returned to their parental homes for periods of weeks and months.[8] In the late eight-

eenth century, Joseph Mayett, an agricultural servant who moved among
no fewer than eleven masters in the course of his youth, returned home to
his parents at least three times when he was fired or sent away and was unable to find another master. One of his departures occurred during a particularly harsh winter, and like David Jones a century and a half earlier,
Mayett spent it in the house of his parents, poor laboring people in Buckinghamshire.[9]

Vagrants who were implicated in crime sometimes turned to parents for
help. Early eighteenth-century criminal biographies mention parental
homes as places to which youngsters returned time after time in their wandering and restless moves. Joseph Powis, who left for service in his mid-
teens, returned home for a year, then left and again was forced to come
back, to stay "but a short while."[10] Other accounts show parental homes
acting as a haven, where children implicated in crime—young and old—
returned and where they were given support, a place for hiding, information, and money to enable them to go on. "And being in some danger,
went to dwell with his father till his apprehensions should be over"—as it
was stated in one of these accounts.[11]

Beyond the parental home, vagrants and migrants on the road were
supported by more distant networks, all triggered by some form of personal contact. Lee Beier found 100 cases of people apprehended for vagrancy in late sixteenth-century Warwick who mentioned lodging in alehouses as well as with relatives, friends, gentlemen, and ordinary people.[12]
Witnesses in Southampton in the early seventeenth century also mentioned the help of kin who provided lodging and money during their travels in the countryside, before their arrival in the town.[13] Practices of hospitality among the gentry were documented by Felicity Heal, who showed
that large country houses continued to display public charity, in their gates
and barns, well into the eighteenth century and beyond.[14] Clergymen were
offering help, too. Henry Marshall, caught for theft in Southampton, testified about weeks of travel from London, in the course of which he met a
person who offered to travel with him, and then go to his kinsman, a clergy
in a neighboring village, where they could sleep and "it should cost [him]
nothing."[15] Scattered evidence shows clergymen keeping facilities for
sheltering vagrants in barns[16] and offering support to people on the road:
"I was relieved by the charities of the ministers from place to place," as one
deponent put it.[17] Friends and loose acquaintances provided help and re-

pose. "I continued shifting . . . for near a month; going to see first one acquaintance, and then another," as Joseph Powis recalled in 1732.[18] Community events allowed some rudimentary help to the passer-by: in the late sixteenth century, Puritan fasts offered lodging with the locals who allowed travelers to sleep in their barns.[19] Harvest and sheep shearing, revels, Christmas and other holidays, churching, funerals—all allowed the outsider temporary access to private and communal displays of largesse.[20]

Some of these customs and festivities, such as funeral doles and ales, dwindled in the course of the seventeenth century, but many others remained intact. Wakes, for example, lost their religious character and became rare in the south, but they retained their character in the summoning of friends, relatives, and guests well into the nineteenth century; funerals retained their generous entertainment long after 1700.[21] A widespread network of local fairs offered some avenues for eking out a living for a few days.[22] Fairs were mentioned in the testimony of David Jones in Southampton in the early seventeenth century, and a century later fairs were still mentioned in criminal biographies as places where the vagrant could find food, some services, and odd work in return for lodging.[23]

Private houses could sometimes offer temporary shelter to strangers, as evidence tracked by Lee Beier on poor widows and artisans taking in vagrants shows. Sometimes this was done in return for some services, such as odd jobs around the house, as is evident in a case in late sixteenth-century Southampton.[24] Shelter was also offered in barns. The evidence for the practice is sparse, but what there is suggests that attitudes toward the outsider poor had a dual face. On the one hand there was fear, suspicion, and exclusion; on the other, hospitality and support. Migrants who infiltrated barns without the permission of the owners risked punishment and expulsion by householders, neighbors, and local officials who pursued legal action against them. But there is also evidence of householders who provided open hospitality in their barns, at times to as many as twenty and more people, and for the space of weeks and months.[25] A lenient attitude appears prevalent. In his wandering in the countryside in the early eighteenth century, Joseph Powis remembered losing his way in a large Common and finding shelter in an "old cow-house," where the farmer found him in the morning asleep. Having listened to his tales, the farmer became friendly and then "put me in my road."[26] Other accounts of criminals in the early eighteenth century show them being offered sleeping accommodation in a "little tenement belonging to an inn," in haylofts, servants' lodgings, and "outhouses."[27] Commons are mentioned, too: in one account the prisoner arrived at a house "on a Common" where he saw a woman and a boy. He asked her for some beer and told her about his previous arrest and his escape, whereupon "she readily gave him some and ask'd him to eat some victuals."[28] This type of casual help to the stranger on the road continued. In the mid-nineteenth century, barns were still offered to huge numbers of people on the road. The census of 1851 included a separate category for "vagrants and others in barns." Among them were females and males, some children of extremely tender years, and many in their teens; they counted some 20,000, or 13 percent of all those under the category of "no special occupation."[29]

I I

Towns in the course of the period became more distinctive in their landscape, rhythm, and size, while networks of support for the new arrival in them differed to some extent from those in the countryside. Alehouses were more prominent, and their numbers rose substantially in the sixteenth century. These establishments, consisting often of no more than a room or cellar run by a poor laborer, an artisan, or a widow, were located in the poorest neighborhoods and catered to the needs of growing numbers of poor arriving in a town. Unlike barns and private houses, alehouses offered lodgings in return for payment—a market exchange. But some forms of informal support in them was extended: information, contacts regarding masters and employers, lodging in return for services and jobs.[30] Some court testimonies in early seventeenth-century Southampton show entrants to alehouses sleeping on benches, presumably without paying for it.[31]

Of prime importance were other types of networks: those of kin as well as a host of other relations, sometimes loose and indirect, all based on some form of personal contact. Over a third of female migrants in late sixteenth-century London had kin living in the town, and the importance of kin for new arrivals in towns is evident in scattered cases in urban courts throughout the seventeenth century.[32] Kin were also involved in arranging apprenticeships, and not only among the well-to-do. In their autobiographies, Edward Barlow and Richard Norwood, who both became apprentices, wrote about the extensive help that was offered to them by their kin when they first arrived in London: Barlow lived with his uncle and aunt for almost a year, until he settled as an apprentice at sea.[33]

Life stories of criminals at Newgate in the early eighteenth century still referred to help provided by kin upon their arrival in the capital: "an uncle of his, after long solicitations got him to come up to town," in the case of John Cartwright; "she came to an aunt, much against her father's will," in the case of Jane Holmes.[34] Witnesses' accounts at the Old Bailey show town dwellers helping their kindred in other ways, especially with money, thus guaranteeing some sort of security upon their arrival in town. In one case, a landlady testified that she gave her lodger credit "till her uncle came." In another, the witness claimed to have been invited by a friend to go to his aunt, "of whom he expected to have had some money."[35] In still another case, the witness told the court that when her husband went to meet his brother who had just arrived from Northamptonshire, she was afraid he was going to give him money.[36] Kin continued to provide some form of support and security in the form of temporary lodging, shelter, and contacts with prospective employers well after migrants came and settled in towns, as a study of domestic service in late eighteenth-century London indicates.[37]

Beyond kin, migrants used a host of contacts, at times close and well known, at other times loose and indirect. Thomas Hardy arrived in London in the early eighteenth century with an introduction from his previous master in the countryside, "to Mr Kerr . . . with whom he lodged the first night, and with whom he maintained afterwards the most friendly intercourse."[38] In other cases, word of mouth sufficed. A witness in Southampton described how he received food and clothes when he arrived in the town from people to whom he delivered the recommendations of his neighbors back home.[39] Fellow natives who moved to towns and sometimes clustered in specific neighborhoods offered help. In many towns, scores of youngsters were arriving year after year from the smaller towns and villages that surrounded them; formal associations based on the migrants' county of origin developed as a consequence.[40] By the end of the seventeenth century, London's newspapers were advertising dozens of "county feasts" that were designed, among other things, to help fellow natives just arriving in the town.[41] Help was extended by natives informally. An account at Newgate in early eighteenth-century London showed a newcomer who went directly to the street "where he met with some of his countrymen."[42]

Looser networks were also at work. London's population between 1550 and 1650 nearly quadrupled, and by 1800 it had doubled to an estimated 960,000. Although long-range migration contracted in the century following the Restoration, seasonal migration continued to supply London with poor migrants who filled its expanding suburban periphery.[43] As can be gleaned from eyewitness accounts at the Old Bailey in the early eighteenth century, a web of relations were formed on the road or in the first encounters at town. No previous long-term contacts were involved; much was triggered by conditions of travel on the road, by personal spontaneous contacts and alliances, by crammed living spaces in the town. People became acquainted on roads, carts, and ships on their way to the capital.[44] They formed liaisons upon arrival in the town[45] and grouped together to hire lodging in houses and rooms, often sharing rooms as well as beds, as several accounts indicate.[46] Some testimonies show migrants inviting their fellow new arrivals to "lye in" their rooms, cabins, beds, stables, and cellars. "I had no beds, but I believe they might lye in the stable" was how it was described in one account.[47] The cost of lodging houses, on a nightly or weekly basis, was cheap.[48] At times, lodging and victuals were offered in return for "odd charrs, running errands, watering horses"—as it was claimed in one case.[49] Shoes, food, and a warm fire on cold days were offered, too. "The prisoner came into the house and desired me to let him warm himself by the fire, for he said he had been with a cart to Edmunton, and was very cold. He begg'd an old pair of shoes."[50] As some of these accounts suggest, almsgiving was by no means extinct in the early eighteenth-century metropolis.[51]

Neighborhoods became extremely vital in creating an environment where migrants could thrive. Courtroom witnesses in the early eighteenth century made constant references to hospitality they provided each other,[52] as well as to neighbors' acquaintances who had just arrived from the countryside. They show neighbors sharing meals, tools, and any other "necessaries," as one deponent described it, as well as animals for travel and expensive clothes.[53] Frequent references were made to assistance provided at work and during illness, following accidents and assaults, at home, in the street, and in the alehouse.[54] Witnesses provided valuable information to one another about work and employment, places for lodging, employers and their character.[55] They introduced newcomers and supplied information, temporary lodging, and help to their neighbors' acquaintances coming from afar. "They were recommended to me by Mr Baily, my next door neighbour" was a typical remark.[56] Norms of giving temporary shelter to new arrivals are evident in these accounts, too. One witness described sitting "at the Parlour window" when a neighbor approached and asked her to let a young woman who had just arrived from the countryside lodge with her "for two or three nights." Having at first refused, she soon yielded, for her neighbor "would take no denial."[57]

This interchange between the neighbors underlines some of the features common to many of the interactions described above. The neighbor's initial reluctance to provide lodging to a person she had never met points to the limits and boundaries of informal networks of support: the greater the social distance, the fewer the obligations to provide help. But her eventual consent also points to the dynamics and force of social ties. Her neighbor appears to have evoked a sense of mutual obligations: between neighbors one was not supposed to deny requests for favors. Most types of interactions between migrants and those who helped them could be described in similar terms: personal exchanges that entailed some expectation of benefits and returns, material or otherwise. The returns could be immediate or at a future point, and they could be reciprocated by the migrants themselves, by those they knew, or even by the community at large. In a society in which many people moved frequently, support and hospitality to those on the move entailed long-term (albeit uncertain) benefits in the form of help to oneself or one's offspring and kin. For all the uncertainties, such benefits gave social ties intensity and force. Even relatively weak ties, such as those with strangers, could become indispensable and binding.[58]

III

Within this immensely varied set of social contexts and interactions, the Protestant message, with its views on poverty and charity, was pronounced. Protestant understanding of poverty and charity drew on a distinction between two categories of poor: those who deserved the support of the community and those who did not. The first category included those considered unable to work—children, the old, and the infirm; the second category included those judged able-bodied but unwilling to work.

The migrant poor, especially those wandering from parish to parish for longer periods of time, tended to fall within the latter category. This distinction between two types of poor was not novel: it formed the basis of late medieval thinking on poverty and vagrancy, and it was articulated by early sixteenth-century Christian Humanists who stressed the value of prudence and discrimination in the relief of the poor. Henceforth those categories were embedded within official responses to the poor in a series of laws that culminated in the Elizabethan poor laws of 1598 and 1601. The legislation laid the foundation for a comprehensive system of relief based on the imposition of compulsory rates, but at the same time it stipulated severe penalties on those considered unworthy poor. Begging was restricted, and vagrants were to be prosecuted and put into houses of correction.[59]

Protestants gave these notions of discriminate giving greater poignancy and legitimation by providing a conceptual frame within which to understand and justify the denial of support to the undeserving poor. Since for Protestants poverty was no longer sanctified, the poor themselves were held responsible for their plight, especially those deemed "idle." Wickedness and sin were conceived as the roots of poverty, and begging became an offense against the law of God. Because of their indulgence in sin, it was claimed, the idle poor excluded themselves from the right to charity, and the church had no duty to help them. A host of sins were associated with vagrancy: idleness, fornication, drunkenness, robbery. Indiscriminate giving was condemned as oblivious to the ill effects that it had on the poor, encouraging them in their idle and loose ways.[60] Puritans were particularly prone to single out the sins of the poor, especially those of the young: unruly, rude, easily drawn to stealing, and shying away from diligent and honest labor, youth were the archetype of the shiftless, unworthy poor. Puritans also placed greater stress on the needs of their own local poor, on the community of believers, and the imperative to care for the "household of faith" or the "fellowship of the saints." According to Sears McGee, Puritans were also more inclined to emphasize first table duties, such as avoiding idolatry and the profanation of the Sabbath, than second table duties, such as charity.[61]

The Reformation thus sanctioned the shift away from private, personal giving toward institutional relief that allowed the proper control of the recipient in her needs. It gave respectability to refusal of casual alms at the door, and it evoked a sharper sense of the boundaries of local communities by instigating the fears and suspicions of outsiders. Denunciations of the idle poor could reach a "collective paranoia," as Felicity Heal referred to it, and the campaign against vagrants was particularly fierce when Puritan magistrates were involved.[62] The shift away from private to more institutional relief was also reflected in private charities that aimed primarily at the establishment of hospitals, almshouses, and schools.[63] Among the populace at large, the assault on the sturdy beggar also bore some fruit: scattered evidence shows that people could deny food on the premise that their obligations to the parish were fulfilled or that the poor person was an undeserving beggar who needed to be dealt with by the official representatives of the state. Fears of the undesired stranger could be instigated by preachers who mobilized ratepayers against unwelcome newcomers.[64]

Yet the trend toward discrimination and institutional relief remained incomplete. Concerned as they were with the classification, control, and suppression of the poor, Protestants were also absorbed with questions relating to the nature and justification of charity itself. The gains of giving engaged their hearts and minds no less than the effects of receiving charity. Here the reformers faced a problem: since good works and acts of charity no longer constituted reciprocal relations with the Almighty and had no effect on salvation, charity and compassion to fellow Christians had to be invested with novel meanings and rewards. The question was not only who should benefit from charity but why perform good works at all. Preachers and theologians appear to have acknowledged the exacting demand involved in the forsaking of the traditional rewards for charity, and they emerged with an arsenal of arguments to uphold and reinvigorate the value of good works. Countless preachers exhorted their congregations to give to the poor, and argued forcefully that generosity to the poor was evidence of election, of Christian sharing, care, and protection of fellow brethren. Charity was elevated as a duty to God, a mark of humility that procured to the poor what was their natural right.[65] Some Puritans were less forthright in the denunciations of indiscriminate giving and tended to emphasize charity to all.[66] Many urged discipline, piety, and self-examination, but also a spirit of sacrifice for the sake of the community over and above selfish needs and interests.[67]

The result was that passionate pleas for charity focused on benevolence and compassion, and notions of generosity and sacrifice as a Christian duty could then take priority over issues of discretion and prudence in the distribution of relief. The basic imperative of charity could be reiterated over and above the methods and means of implementing it. This was particularly evident in catechisms in which the fundamental teaching of the Church, rather than elaborate theological issues, were inculcated to generations of Protestants. Thomas Cranmer's Catechismus (1548) provided the model: "We ought to love and dreade oure lorde God above all thinges, so that for His sake we hurt not our neighbour . . . but that we aide, comforte and succour hym in all hys necessities and afflictions."[68] Catechisms written from the late sixteenth century onwards all made the distinction between the first and second table commandments: the first four related to "godliness towards God," and the remaining six to "charitie toward our neighbour." Second table commandments taught the believer, according to Alexander Nowell, the "duties of mutual charitie or love among men," which were embedded in the Holy Scripture as "the principal partes of Religion."[69] Along with thrift, diligence, and husbandry, catechisms urged their readers to "help the poor in miserie."[70] In their exposition of the Commandments, catechists broadened the range of obligations entailed in each, and they increasingly came to emphasize not only the sinfulness of breaking the Law but the duty enjoining it.[71] The eighth commandment— do not steal—included not only the prohibition on all "deceitful" dealing but also the positive injunction to "labour that every man have his owne" and to "relieve the poor, to succour widows and fatherless."[72] Nor were "neighbours" interpreted narrowly or classified as those belonging to the fellowship of believers and those who did not, or even put into categories of deserving and undeserving poor. In a section devoted to the meanings of "love thy neighbour," Nowell glorified "brotherly love among Christians," the bond "wherewith God hath coupled together all mankynde." To the question "How far extendeth the name of neighbour?" he replied, "The name of neighbour conteyneth, not onely those that be of our kinne and alliance, or friendes, or such as be knitt to us in any civile bond of love, but also those whom we know not, yea and our enemies."[73]

Much space was devoted to the value of good works. Catechists articulated and amplified the benefits that charity had for the donor rather than its effects on the recipient. They addressed the believer who was perplexed by the idea that good works had no impact on salvation: Why perform good works that had no effect on the afterlife? Answers were not in short supply. Many catechisms stressed the value of good works as a testimony to the thankfulness, faith, and love of God, to His blessing in man and glory upon earth. Others pointed to the value of works as acts prompting remembrance of human sin and helplessness. Still others talked about good works as training: in faith and humility, in humbleness before God, in diligence, and the "forsaking fleshly and evil affections."[74] Good works were a "schoolmaster to Christ."[75] Sometimes charity was described as bringing the believer closer to God, providing some assurance in the goodwill of the Lord, hence, though not affecting salvation, making it "certain to ourselves," and at the same time helping "to winne our brethren to Christ," as it was phrased by Edward Dering.[76] Occasionally the afterlife could be evoked more explicitly. "The lawe teacheth us our dutie towardes God and our neighbour, promising everlasting life to suche as do fulfill thee lawe, and threatnyng eternall damnation to such as doe break the same."[77] There were variations between writers, with the predestinarians tending to emphasize good works as proof of election.[78] But all catechists shared and conveyed the conviction that, although good works had no role in salvation, they were the inevitable product of a saving faith. As a recent study of catechistic literature in the two centuries following the Reformation shows, this conviction pervades catechistic literature throughout the period.[79]

Puritans themselves sometimes interpreted the injunctions regarding charity and good works in terms of private giving and alms at the door, of giving to individual poor rather than to institutions controlled by the representatives of the state. If the overseers failed in their responsibility to relieve the poor, it was their personal obligation to help them.[80] There were Puritans whose self-examination and account of daily deeds and sins were constructed in terms of private acts of charity and personal interactions rather than of donations to institutions or the parish system of relief. Samuel Ward reproached himself for failing to remember the poor—"never remembering our poor brethren," or "not taking order to give to poor women"—as he noted in his diary.[81] Acts of giving to the vagrant poor at the door were a moral resource on which some Puritans drew when they constructed their past experiences, providing a model of training for themselves and their children: "I remember [being] sent to the door with victuals to a poor body," as Edward Terrill recorded in the late seventeenth century.[82] Quakers drew on their acts of charity toward the beggar as signs of their distinctiveness among their neighbors, and memories of denial of food for themselves or their children were incorporated within their descriptions of their suffering in their path to salvation.[83] In the early eighteenth century, Elizabeth Ashbridge remembered how in her childhood she was overwhelmed with compassion and love for the poor—who were "blessed of the Lord," as she referred to them. She described how she used to go and visit the poor, give them money and other necessities, "remembering that those that give to such went to the Lord."[84]

Reputation for charity was also couched in terms of the benefits of giving rather than caution and prudence in the distribution of support. Writers of autobiographies enhanced the character of a dead parent as generous, charitable, merciful. They emphasized the capacity to give without thought of consequences and returns, rather than prudence and calculation. In his eulogy for his mother, James Fretwell remembered how she reacted to ungrateful responses for her charity: "I don't do this out of respect to them [i.e., the poor], but because it is my duty." He also made explicit reference to the fact that she provided services and support to neighbors as well as to strangers.[85] Funeral sermons in the seventeenth century also magnified the qualities of compassion and generosity. Since charity was a testimony to the glory of God, it had to be proclaimed and made known by the "praising or dispraising of persons," as one preacher explained it.[86] Much of this praising was couched in terms of the capacity for largesse, generosity that extended to individuals no less than to institutions, to strangers and not only to kin or friends. "He was that hand that handed out relief to orphans, widows, strangers in their grief," as it was said in one sermon. Other similar pronouncements in funeral sermons abound.[87]

In the two centuries following the Reformation, the transition to institutional relief and to an emphasis on the public control of the poor remained incomplete. The early eighteenth century witnessed a transformation in philanthropic donations from posthumous bequests to lifetime contributions, which gave donors greater control of the recipients in their needs. Preachers continued to denounce the sturdy beggar, and the language of discrimination regained a central role: "If [the poor] would not work, neither should they eat." But throughout the late seventeenth century and early eighteenth, the gains and benefits of the charitable act were argued with vigor in a surge of sermons and publications. All stressed the value of benevolence and the gratification that came from charity to the poor. The religious value of almsgiving was advocated, and the social and practical gains of the charitable act increasingly came to be stressed. Many preachers continued to espouse sacrificial giving and open generosity "even to those who may be wicked or to those from whom we can expect no advantage."[88]

I V

For all the official emphasis on discrimination, classification, and control of the poor, practices of private support to the migrant poor among the populace persisted. Generations of preachers conveyed to every parish the shame and stigma of poverty, legitimizing the occasional denial of support to the poor, and instigating suspicions of the outsider and strange poor. But among the populace, the provision of help to migrants, with no apparent consideration of their worthiness, did not wither. Based on a multiplicity of interactions and reciprocal obligations, networks of support continued to be sustained in the countryside and in towns, where loose ties provided help, and crowds of beggars continued to obtain some form of casual help at the door and in the street well into the eighteenth century and beyond.[89]

The Protestant assault on the vagrant poor does not appear to have taken deep root in the populace at large. In a society in which most people were at some point in their life migrants for shorter and longer duration, the message had its obvious limitations. Many among the poor must have derived their notions of help to one another from the bonds of mutual obligations that their social ties entailed, and they remained indifferent to the Protestant assault on the idle poor. There was also the problem of applying notions of discrimination to concrete circumstances, of the accidental confusion of the "honest" migrant with the "sturdy" beggar. The distinctions could become even more blurred, since the period witnessed the gradual recognition of a third category of poor: able-bodied but still deserving support.[90] Most vagrants had occupations, and many had social ties in some of the communities they entered. If it was difficult to deny help to someone whose whereabouts and background were unclear, it was even harder when the person had an identifiable vocation, or if she was kin, neighbor, or a distant relation of closer circles of friends.

But the Reformation did not simply widen a gap between theology and social practice. The Protestant message regarding the poor was double-edged: it sanctioned the classification of the poor and withdrawal of support from those considered sinful, but at the same time it elevated a spirit of charity and compassion to the poor. Charity was the normative base, and discrimination was a more elaborate qualification of it. The two injunctions were not incompatible, but there was always some tension between them: between the catechist urging his flock to give to the poor, including strangers, and the preacher's insistence on the priority of the local poor or the "household of faith"; between the evocation of the brotherly bond of all mankind, including those who wronged us, and the insistence on the shame of vagrancy and the sin of begging. There was a strain between a more open understanding of Christian charity and appeals to generosity, and more exclusive tendencies and appeals to prudence, caution, and calculation in the distribution of charity. In the course of the period, the tendency for exclusion became increasingly more prominent, but it never wholly acquired a single authoritative voice.

Under such circumstances, there was scope for divergent interpretations and emphases. Among the devout, some people continued to take pride and derive a deep sense of gratification from face-to-face giving to kin and neighbors as well as to strangers. There is no reason to suspect that similar reactions and emotions could be evoked among the poor. People could embrace a more exclusive view but also a more open understanding of charity and good works. These could be adapted to a variety of interactions with the migrant poor in the street, the barn, or the house. Those who occasionally denied help to beggars, strangers, or even neighbors and kin found solace and exculpation of guilt in the preachers' denunciation of the sturdy beggar. For many others, the words written and preached could be appropriated and adapted to fit practices of help to migrants, be they strangers or not. Protestantism provided a language with which to communicate the benefits of giving, and this could endow an intricate system of informal support among the poor with meanings and a sense of moral worth that did not always conform with the meanings and intentions of the preachers.

Godliness, Commemoration, and Community

THE MANAGEMENT OF PROVINCIAL SCHOOLS BY LONDON TRADE GUILDS

Late medieval Christians energetically maintained spiritual links with the dead. Chantries were perhaps the most elaborate and structured method by which the living could remember the dead—and seek to relieve their souls in Purgatory—but numerous other means were available in parish churches, including the annual requiem for benefactors of parish charities, the weekly prayer for those whose names were listed on the parish bede-role, and the use of commemorative items during worship. Eamon Duffy suggests that the meticulous care with which parishes handled such memorials "really did ensure a sort of immortality" not simply because it was owed to the donors but also because preserving the names of the dead "was integral to the parish's sense of identity, both in conserving a sense of shared past and in fostering a continuing commitment to the religious ideals and the social and religious structures embodied in the parish church."[1] Before the Reformation, London trade guilds (or "livery companies") took similar steps to commemorate deceased members. These included the participation of freemen in their brethren's funerals, the administration of members' chantries and obits, and the management of charitable institutions created by company benefactors. The Reformation's attack on such traditional expressions of the affinity between the living and the dead threatened to sever the links between company members and their collective history.[2]

Companies faced that challenge with considerable creativity. They developed innovative ways to commemorate deceased members including constructing tables of company benefactors in their halls that were reminiscent of parish bede-rolls. They also commissioned paintings and statues of famous company members and sometimes displayed their coats of arms in stained glass in their halls.[3] Such post-Reformation commemorative practices could reach into the distant past. In 1566, the Mercers' Company memorialized famous members such as Mayor Richard Whittington (d. 1422) and Dean Collett, who entrusted St. Paul's School to the company's care in 1510. In 1613 it built a monument to Alderman William Dauntsey (d. 1550).[4] There was considerable interest in this sort of commemorative activity in the late sixteenth and early seventeenth centuries, and the rebuilding of company halls after the Great Fire of 1666 provided opportunities for companies to reaffirm their commitment. The Clothworkers' officers arranged for the replacement of their commemorative table, stained glass, and "effigies" in 1669, and the Brewers' governors ordered the coats of arms of the twelve leading contributors to their rebuilding efforts carved on their restored hall's walls in 1673; the Drapers' officers were unable to finish replacing destroyed memorials of company benefactors before 1700.[5]

Individuals participated in this process by viewing their companies as a reliable means for perpetuating their own memories. A common practice involved giving their company a commemorative gold or silver plate on which they might inscribe their arms or bits of verse. Some even specified how the plate should be displayed, such as when Sir Thomas Leigh presented a covered cup to the Mercers' Company in 1571 with the requirement that it be used at the annual election of its master. In case anyone forgot Leigh's instructions, he inscribed the cup "To elect the Master of the Mercerie, hither I am sent, and by Sir Thomas Leigh for the same entent."[6] In times of financial distress, a company's officers could liquidate its treasures, but on such occasions they would acknowledge their responsibility to maintain the donors' memories. When the Haberdashers' officers sold several commemorative pieces in 1621, they ordered that a detailed description of such items be kept so they could be replaced with identical pieces in the future, thereby continuing to commemorate the donors.[7] Facing a financial crisis in 1627, the Skinners' officers decided to mortgage some of the company's plate, but they encouraged company members to claim any pieces donated by their ancestors or friends, presumably hoping to dampen criticism that they were forgetting their responsibility to preserve the donors' memories.[8] When the Goldsmiths' governors sold several commemorative plates in 1637, they kept a detailed log of the liquidated pieces that filled four full pages in their court book and included illustrations as well as inscriptions, such as "George Smithe's gone, this gift remains behind; no brother to his company more kind," and "Keep me clean and bruise me not for I am Richard Croshawe's pot." The company began replacing these pieces after the Restoration, but was forced to sell them—and record their details—in the aftermath of the Great Fire.[9] The Drapers' officers melted down several pieces of plate to raise funds for a loan to the Crown in 1696. Over the next four years they took steps to replace all the items donated by company benefactors, although they substituted pieces they thought "more useful" to the company but "of equal value to that melted down and the benefactor's name engraven thereon as if it had been the piece . . . first made."[10] Clearly they considered it no breach of trust to alter the physical form of a commemorative gift so long as its value—and spirit—remained the same.

The companies' interest in commemoration may have prompted members to entrust them with larger charitable benefactions. Before the Reformation these often included chantries and obits, but from Queen Elizabeth's reign onward they generally involved the almshouses, lectureships, and schools in London and the provinces that typified the well-known quest for godly reform.[11] To encourage that effort, the Goldsmiths' officers decided in 1618 to display the arms of benefactors of company charities in their hall not only to honor their memories but also to "stir up others hereafter to the like works of charity and piety." The Haberdashers' governors acted on a similar impulse in 1652 when they agreed to display a table of benefactors in their hall as a commemoration of them and as an example to those "whose hearts God shall stir up and incline to works of this nature."[12] All concerned appreciated that while the maintenance of charitable benefactions could enhance the reputation of a company, the neglect of such a trust would have the opposite effect. The Grocers' Company faced this problem directly in 1680 when, as a result of its poor financial health, several of its benefactions had fallen into arrears. The company officers therefore urged their members to support the "piety and charity" of "their ancestors" by contributing to the resuscitation of the company's "holly and pious" charities.[13] Such charitable endowments therefore had three objectives that echoed the goals of pre-Reformation commemorative donations: to increase godliness generally, to preserve the memories of the benefactors, and to bolster the reputation and communal solidarity of the companies that would manage them.

Livery companies may have taken great care to maintain charitable institutions and to commemorate their benefactors, but it remains to be seen how successfully the charities achieved their ends. In order to assess the commitment of livery companies to the pursuit of their benefactors' intentions, this chapter will analyze their management of provincial grammar schools, one important subset of their charitable endowments. During the sixteenth and seventeenth centuries, ten livery companies were involved in governing 25 grammar schools in provincial England and Wales.[14] As we have seen, companies often had difficulty maintaining the commemorative objects in their direct possession, but that was a relatively easy task compared with the administration of complex institutions scattered across England and Wales. In addition to the financial pressures mentioned earlier, when managing provincial schools company officers faced the challenge of communicating and, more important, cooperating with people they often had not met in places where they seldom had ventured. Such circumstances often tested their resolve to preserve the memories—by enacting the wishes—of company benefactors.

I

The principal authority that school benefactors could give company officers was the power to appoint schoolmasters and their assistants, who were known as "ushers." In theory, all schoolteachers were appointed by bishops, but in practice there seemed to be little interference with company discretion in this area. Upon learning of a staff vacancy at a school for which they were the patrons, guildsmen could solicit nominations from a variety of sources. They sometimes considered references from Crown officials, but more commonly they relied on recommendations from Oxford and Cambridge colleges.[15] This emphasis on university-educated schoolmasters was obvious when the Goldsmiths' officers rejected an applicant for a post at their school at Stockport, Cheshire, in 1645 because he did not hold a degree from either university and so would not, in their opinion, be able to prepare students for university life. Similarly, in 1604 the Fishmongers' officers preferred a candidate for the mastership of their school at Holt, Norfolk, who had letters of recommendation from several Cambridge fellows over another who was "only reported to be an honest discreet sufficient man" by several unnamed people attending their meeting. Sir Andrew Judd, who founded the Skinners' school at Tonbridge, Kent, even specified that the company should hire only schoolmasters who held the MA from All Souls, Oxford.[16]

University degrees and strong references were not always sufficient qualifications for school posts. Companies sometimes also required candidates to be examined by a panel of experts. During the early seventeenth century, the Haberdashers' officers routinely appointed a committee of London preachers and schoolmasters to examine candidates for posts at their schools. The examinations addressed an applicant's ability to teach as well as his intellectual capacity, and not every candidate passed the test. The records of such examinations tend to be cursory, although they suggest a fair degree of rigor, such as the decision of the panel appointed by the Skinners' officers to test candidates for the Tonbridge schoolmaster's post in Latin and Greek as well as on "many deep questions."[17]

Since a schoolmaster's success depended largely on his maintaining the support of his school's local community, guildsmen also considered the views of villagers, townspeople, and provincial gentlemen with local ties when filling staff vacancies. In 1593, the Drapers' officers asked a candidate for the post of schoolmaster at Barton in Staffordshire to certify that he had local support. During the early seventeenth century, the Clothworkers' governors asserted their authority in appointing the schoolmaster of their school at Sutton Valence in Kent, although they allowed the local people to send a nominee to stand in election in London. At the same time, the guildsmen were in the habit of making the appointment of the school's usher contingent on the approval of the "townsmen" and those of "the country."[18] The Grocers' officers relied on Sir Walter Mildmay—a Privy Councilor and founder of Emanuel College, Cambridge, who sat in the Commons for Northamptonshire from 1557 until his death in 1589—for advice concerning their school at Oundle in Northamptonshire, while the Fishmongers' governors turned to Sir Christopher Heydon—an astrologist, former MP for Norfolk, and a member of an important family in that county—when appointing the master of Holt School. In 1639, the Haberdashers' governors hired an usher for their school at Bunbury in Cheshire who had been nominated by several leading parishioners there, and in 1664, they appointed William Morris to be master of Monmouth School because he had letters of support from several townspeople as well as some gentlemen who lived in the area. Nonetheless, such local support did not guarantee lasting success. Seven years after hiring Morris, the haberdashers considered several complaints against him from the mayor and other people of Monmouth, and took the occasion to remind the townsmen that the company had appointed Morris principally because he had been their nominee. The Londoners then suggested that in the future the town should avoid involvement in the appointment of masters because the company was "likely to provide better for them than they can for themselves."[19]

No matter what course they chose, companies were always careful to maintain—and to display—their control over the appointment process. The Goldsmiths' officers took particular care in this area, insisting throughout the early seventeenth century that applicants for positions in the schools they managed appear in person at one of their court meetings. This proved a hardship for nominees from both Deane in Cumberland and Stockport, who often complained about the expense and duration of their journeys to London, which could take at least seven to ten days each way, depending on the season. In reply, the guildsmen typically reminded applicants that the right to appoint staff members rested with the company alone, and they suggested that they would reimburse the expenses of those who traveled to London and, upon examination, were appointed to school posts. In addition to making applicants appear at court, the goldsmiths insisted on placing other candidates in election against those nominated by the people of Deane and Stockport. Such elections may have been largely ceremonial; for example, the goldsmiths put William Donkan forward in three elections between 1648 and 1652, and he lost each time. For the schoolmasters who made the long journey to London, the ritual was doubtless another indication that, despite their provincial support, their employers were in London.[20]

A dispute between the Drapers' officers and the people of Kirkham in Lancashire displayed the potential inflexibility of guildsmen when appointing provincial staff members. In 1684, the Londoners considered a letter from the minister and 30 other residents of Kirkham on behalf of James Woods, a candidate to be the school usher there. Along the side of the letter was an endorsement from the schoolmaster, but according to the company's record of the incident, the manner in which the schoolmaster recommended Woods suggested that he believed the local people had the right to choose the usher. As a result, the guildsmen refused to consider the nomination of Woods and ordered their clerk instead to inform the people of Kirkham of their mistake and require them to submit another letter acknowledging the company's sole right to make such appointments. When the corrected letter arrived a month later, the drapers appointed Woods without further comment.[21] Such incidents reminded all parties that London guildsmen could be rather authoritarian in the management of provincial schools entrusted to their care. It made no matter that, in nearly all of the cases discussed thus far, the guildsmen ultimately hired the provincial nominees, for the affirmation of the appointment process itself seemed as important to the Londoners as its outcome.

I I

Upon hiring schoolmasters or ushers, guild officers had to establish means for monitoring their performance. Companies sometimes dispatched inspection parties to visit their schools, instructing them to examine the efforts of the staff members and to make any necessary reforms. These company-sponsored junkets could be the occasion for guildsmen to enjoy the pleasures of the countryside with their wives and friends or to partake in "very worshipful and good entertainment with good store of venison" at their colleagues' country homes, but they usually dealt with serious matters as well. Such visits enabled Londoners to remind schoolmasters and students alike of their responsibility to maintain their benefactor's memory, an act sometimes buttressed with an order to hang his portrait in the schoolhouse or to display his coat of arms on its gate.[22] Inspectors also evaluated the performance of a school's staff and students. If company officers did not feel competent to do so on their own, they would appoint experts to accompany them on their inspections. In 1589, the Clothworkers' governors instructed their inspectors to bring "some learned man" with them when visiting Sutton Valence in Kent, and the Skinners' officers usually appointed a London clergyman to accompany them on their visits to Tonbridge.[23]

Such visits would not always produce an accurate assessment of the state of school affairs. In October 1617, the Haberdashers' governors received a favorable report from an inspection party that had recently returned from Monmouth, but a month later they heard allegations that the negligence of that town's schoolmaster, John Owen, had led to a decline in the school's enrollment. The guildsmen therefore wrote to the town's mayor and common council, asking them to submit their own evaluation of Owen's performance, and they summoned the schoolmaster to appear at their court. Owen traveled to London in January and, upon hearing the townspeople's allegations, admitted he had neglected his duties at the school and promised to vacate his post by Lady Day. After the Londoners appointed Henry Crewes to be the new schoolmaster in early March, they learned that Owen had revoked his resignation, and so they dispatched their clerk to Wales to investigate the matter further. The controversy dragged on until November, when the company negotiated a settlement by which Owen would receive £20 annually for three years out of Crewes's salary as well as a loan of £50 from the company to help him to secure a position elsewhere.[24]

Infrequent inspection trips could not adequately provide company officers with a sure sense of a school's condition, and this encouraged them to develop close ties to local people. When cultivating reliable provincial contacts, guildsmen often turned to clergymen. Clerics played an active role in school governance across the country. From the perspective of Londoners, clergymen would seem especially qualified to supervise school activities due to their standing in their local communities and because during the early modern period provincial clerics were increasingly likely to be university graduates who could be expected to have some expertise in educational matters.[25]

The governments of provincial schools managed by London guilds, whether designed by the founders or by subsequent guild officers, sometimes assigned local clergymen a formal role as overseers. When London mercer Richard Collyer called for the establishment of a school at Horsham, Sussex, in his will of 1532, he intended it to be jointly administered by the Mercers' Company and Horsham's vicar, churchwardens, and parishioners. Draper Thomas Russell, who founded the school at Barton in 1593, appointed the local parson to join with three gentlemen from the area to visit the school annually and report their findings to London. After the Drapers' officers became governors of schools at Kirkham and Goosnargh in Lancashire in 1673, they empowered the local inhabitants to appoint six persons to join with their vicar and neighboring ministers in inspecting the schools annually.[26]

Even when clergymen did not have formal positions in school management, company officers often turned to them for advice. When the Clothworkers' governors needed information about the school they governed at Sutton Valence, they usually addressed their correspondence to "the vicar and townsmen" or "the minister, churchwardens, and parishioners" there. Furthermore, guildsmen often turned to provincial clergymen for evaluations of applicants for teaching posts. In 1660, when the schoolmaster of Holt wanted to hire an usher, the Fishmongers' officers ordered him to obtain certificates of the applicant's good character from several local ministers. Throughout the seventeenth century, the Haberdashers' governors accepted the recommendations of their preachers at Bunbury when hiring new masters for their school there.[27] Guildsmen also asked local clergymen to assess the performance of established teachers. During their visits to Tonbridge, the Skinners' officers often employed the local pastor to examine students, and occasionally they invited other local clerics as well. When a committee of Fishmongers' governors visited their school at Holt in 1657, they noticed that the enrollment was smaller than expected and—out of concern that the schoolmaster's performance was to blame for the school's decline—they asked the minister of Holt to examine the students and the books they used. In 1658, the Haberdashers' officers received word that the schoolmaster at Monmouth had accepted an ecclesiastical living in Herefordshire that would prevent him from continuing in his post. Before proceeding to the election of a new schoolmaster, the Londoners first wrote to their lecturer at nearby Newland and asked him to inquire into the teacher's activities.[28]

Perhaps no one was more aware of the authority that guildsmen gave ministers over teachers than William Hickes, schoolmaster at Oundle. When a committee of Grocers' officers inspected the school in July 1650, they found that Hickes was held in high esteem by local people. After dining with him, the local minister, and "other friends," the guildsmen returned to London seemingly content with the state of affairs at Oundle. Their mood changed rapidly two weeks later after they summoned Hickes to London to explain certain theological differences that he had with the minister. The company's records offer no details about the nature of the dispute or how the minister communicated his concerns to the company after apparently making a favorable report to the Londoners during their recent visit. In any case, Hickes was unable to rebuff the minister's allegations, and so the guildsmen summarily told him to find himself another post.[29]

The reliance of company officers on provincial clergymen for information relating to their schools was undermined by the need of many teachers to seek clerical employment in order to augment their meager salaries. The ability of a schoolmaster to combine educational and clerical duties was accepted by the founders of some of the earliest provincial schools entrusted to London companies. When goldsmith Edmund Shaa planned the disposition of his estate in 1488, he called for his livery company to establish a grammar school in Stockport, his birthplace, and specified that the schoolmaster was to be a priest who would say mass twice a week at the parish church to benefit the souls of Shaa, Shaa's parents, and all Christians. Fellow goldsmith Bartholomew Reade followed Shaa's example when establishing the guidelines for his school at Cromer, Norfolk, seventeen years later. As the sixteenth century progressed, the chantrylike qualities of schools fell away, and school statutes increasingly emphasized that schoolmasters were to be university educated and skilled at instructing boys in grammar, rather than insisting that they be ministers.[30]

However, because by the late sixteenth and early seventeenth centuries the proportion of clerics who were university graduates was growing more rapidly than that of schoolmasters, well-qualified applicants for school posts often would have been in holy orders, and their economic needs would have encouraged them to pursue clerical employment.[31] In 1614, the master of Tonbridge School complained that his enrollment had fallen because of sickness in the area and the use of private tutors by gentlemen. As a result, he was forced to preach in order to augment his income, a development that the Skinners' officers seemed to take in stride. Of course, problems would arise if local people felt their schoolmaster was diverting too much time and energy away from his teaching duties. When inspecting the school they governed at Colwall, Herefordshire, in 1663, the Grocers' officers learned that schoolmaster Henry Walwin often preached at a nearby church in order to supplement his teaching salary. Although some of the local people whom the Londoners interviewed thought highly of Walwin, others testified that he neglected his teaching in order to concentrate on his position as a preacher, which was the more lucrative of his occupations. The guildsmen ultimately admonished Walwin to take more care with his teaching, but they did not prohibit him from preaching.[32]

While company officers could tolerate occasional preaching by schoolmasters, they often discouraged them from taking on more burdensome clerical work. The Mercers' officers were informed by the local patron of their school at West Lavington, Wiltshire, that the schoolmaster's annual salary of £10 was so small that he had to combine the post with the vicarage in order to attract able candidates. The Londoners therefore agreed to pay future schoolmasters a yearly gratuity of £5 to avoid such pluralism. The Haberdashers' officers consistently warned their schoolmasters not to accept ecclesiastical livings and, tellingly, when both the schoolmaster and usher of Monmouth School applied for the vacant position of town lecturer, the guildsmen did not schedule interviews for them.[33]

Other companies adopted a more flexible attitude toward schoolmasters who also held clerical positions. In the late 1630's, a parson of a parish near Holt reported to the Fishmongers' officers that their schoolmaster there was "old and weak" while his usher was "very old and unfit both in body and learning." He therefore offered himself as a replacement for the usher, claiming that he would allow the schoolmaster to stay on and that he had the support of some local gentlemen for such a move. The guildsmen rejected the plan because, in their view, the duties of a parson and those of a schoolmaster each required "a man's whole time and diligence conscionably to discharge," and so they resolved not to give the schoolmaster's post to "any man that had cure of souls." However, 50 years later economic realities led another generation of fishmongers to adopt a different policy. In March 1686, they learned that the Holt schoolmaster held two clerical posts in other places, which had led to the school's decline. In response, the schoolmaster claimed that he was forced to seek other employment because the local inhabitants were generally poor and because curates in the country near Holt had taken students to bolster their incomes. A local gentleman then told the guildsmen that the advowson of a living near Holt was for sale for around £80 and that, if it were added to the schoolmaster's post, it would ensure that they could attract an able teacher for their school. The company officers agreed to the plan and told him to proceed with the purchase.[34] Similarly, in 1559 the Goldsmiths' officers hired the vicar of Cromer to be their schoolmaster there after they had received evidence of local support for his appointment. However, the liability of having one person hold both posts became clear to the guildsmen in 1643, when they learned that the man who was serving as Cromer's vicar and schoolmaster had accepted yet another post several miles away and had hired someone else to teach at the school. Apparently the situation had existed for several years before some local people brought it to the guildsmen's attention, at which point they promptly hired a new schoolmaster. By 1670, the company's officers again consented to the combination of the two posts because the local people reported that their schoolmaster was "usually the minister of that town."[35]

The combination of the posts of schoolmaster and minister placed London-based school governors in an awkward position. While they may have been pleased that their school was thereby better able to attract a qualified master, it increased their reliance on one man for information. Ideally, a community's schoolmaster and its pastor would work together in propagating godliness; they would also keep a keen eye on one another, thereby increasing the likelihood that the school's governors would learn about a decline in their school's fortunes before matters deteriorated too greatly. However, the presence of both a schoolmaster and a minister in a town or village was no guarantee of a school's success. Indeed, as we shall see, rivalries between two such local authority figures could make the school governors' task all the more challenging.

III

Their reliance on provincial clergymen could place London-based school governors in the middle of parochial disputes. As mentioned earlier, the government of the school at Horsham called for the local vicar, churchwardens, and parishioners to work collectively with the Mercers' officers in governing their school. This system seemed to work well initially, but in August 1629 a letter from the vicar and churchwardens to the guildsmen nominating one Edmund Pierson for the vacant schoolmaster's post was followed immediately by another from the vicar alerting the mercers that this appointment was likely to prove controversial because several parishioners supported another candidate. This warning proved well founded. Two weeks later, a large number of parishioners appeared at Mercers' Hall, some of whom supported Pierson while others claimed the vicar had nominated him without their consent and instead recommended Thomas Robinson. By December, the guildsmen formally installed Pierson, but less than a year later the Londoners received another communication from the parishioners asserting that Pierson's selection had been fraudulent and threatening to sue the company officers if they refused to overturn their earlier action. Finally, in November 1631, Pierson resigned his place and the mercers hired Robinson with the consent of the vicar and churchwardens, though there is no indication of how enthusiastically the vicar participated in this decision.[36]

The possibility of coming out on the wrong end of a local dispute could well encourage a clergyman to approach school controversies cautiously. In April 1661, the haberdashers heard a complaint from some inhabitants of Bunbury against their schoolmaster. When the guildsmen asked their lecturer there for his opinion on the matter, he informed the Londoners that it had sparked "great division" among local people. He therefore requested that instead of relying on him for information, they might appoint a committee of parishioners to investigate the schoolmaster. In the end, he may not have been able to avoid involvement in the conflict. In February, some of the schoolmaster's supporters accused the lecturer of neglecting his duties, and such ongoing local tensions may have encouraged him to resign his post two years later, which was three years before the company finally dismissed the schoolmaster.[37] The company's lecturers at Monmouth and Newland learned a similar lesson twenty years later. Relations between the haberdashers and the Monmouth magistrates had been strained throughout the Restoration period, with frequent clashes over issues such as the appointment of almspeople to places in the company's disposal. Against this backdrop, in July 1678 the guildsmen asked their two local preachers to investigate a complaint from the usher of Monmouth School against his master. Two months later, the lecturers exonerated the schoolmaster, and so the company's officers dismissed the usher rather than risk further tensions between the two teachers. Such efforts proved futile. The following April the haberdashers learned that Monmouth's magistrates had intervened with the bishop of Hereford on behalf of the dismissed usher, and they therefore dispatched their lecturers to try to dissuade the bishop from becoming involved in the matter. The lecturers' efforts may well have contributed to the erosion of their local positions, for the Newland lecturer resigned reluctantly in November 1681, and by September 1682 the haberdashers were trying to persuade the Monmouth magistrates to stop impeding their lecturer from preaching. The usher finally resigned in December 1682, but the Monmouth lecturer followed his example two years later.[38]

The battle lines were more clearly drawn in a dispute between vicar Richard Clegg and schoolmaster Richard Taylor of Kirkham at the turn of the eighteenth century. Taylor's tenure began poorly. Clegg and the parishioners had supported another candidate for the post, but the drapers rejected him in favor of Taylor. Within four months of the schoolmaster's appointment, the guildsmen received a complaint that he had admitted girls to the school, to which they responded by ordering Taylor to dismiss the girls, but only after allowing them to remain a while longer. Shortly thereafter, the drapers rejected Clegg's suggestion that they reduce the schoolmaster's salary. There then ensued a flurry of petitions and counterpetitions that shed some light on the nature of the dispute. It appears that the vicar enjoyed support among the churchwardens and a considerable portion of his parishioners, and one petition from his allies accused Taylor of threatening that "he will have the vicar's gown off his back or his own." Subsequently, however, some of those whose names appeared on this petition claimed that they had supported it before they understood its full contents. Furthermore, the school's usher testified at great length that his master had never sought a feud with Clegg. Instead, he reported that well before Taylor arrived in Kirkham, Clegg had established a reputation for being quarrelsome and that, perhaps unwittingly, Taylor soon sided with the vicar's enemies in the neighborhood. In the end, the guildsmen determined that all of the charges the vicar brought against the schoolmaster were groundless. While the drapers had the power to keep Taylor in place, they could do nothing about Clegg, and so the two continued to live and work together rather unhappily ever after.[39]

The dispute between the schoolmaster and the vicar of Kirkham may have been a particularly passionate one, but it indicates how easily a school could become a flash point for tensions in a community. Together with the other controversies discussed here, it highlights the risks involved when a schoolmaster or a clergyman appeared to lend his authority to one side of a factional dispute involving a school. At the same time, it displays the limited extent to which a livery company's officers could trust a clergyman to assess a schoolmaster's performance objectively.

Even if guildsmen could find reliable local contacts, the success of their provincial schools still required the support of local people who decided whether or not to enroll their children as students. As discussed earlier, the officers of London companies used their authority over school staff appointments to maintain the classical curriculum that school founders sought to encourage. However, no matter how well trained a schoolmaster might have been, his ability to implement a classical curriculum was limited by the willingness and ability of provincial people to have their children educated in this manner. The resolution of disputes between guildsmen and provincial people over the nature of their schools offers perhaps the clearest indication of the willingness of London guildsmen to invest themselves in the success of charities in their care.

The Clothworkers' officers worked with the residents of Sutton Valence throughout the seventeenth century to make their school better suited to local needs. In 1620, the guildsmen ordered schoolmaster Job Davenport to reform his ways in response to complaints from local people that he had only five students because he used "overmuch severity" in his teaching. Twenty years later, schoolmaster Thomas Philpot asked the clothworkers if he could teach English as well as Latin in the school. After they checked their records, the company officers concluded that the school's founder had expressed no intention regarding the teaching of English, and so they left the matter to the schoolmaster's discretion. Nevertheless, they warned him that his decision should advance the reputation of the school and please the local inhabitants "for whose benefit" the school was intended. However, Philpot's successor, Thomas Carter, resigned after little more than a year on the job because the unwillingness of local parents to have their children learn Latin discouraged him from teaching there. The issue came to a head in 1684, when a group of local people traveled to London to complain that schoolmaster Richard Forster had refused to admit any students who did not intend to study Latin. The company officers resolved the controversy in 1685 by concluding that since the local residents were "for the most part mean people and not able to breed their children to be scholars," the school usher should teach children to read and write English to prepare them for employment in trade.[40]

The Goldsmiths' Company supported comparable reforms at Cromer. At the request of a local gentleman in 1652, the company's officers investigated whether the school was being run in accordance with the wishes of its

founder, Bartholomew Reade, who died in 1505. The results of their in-
quiry indicated that although the schoolmaster was prepared to teach
Greek and Latin, for several years he had no students in those subjects.
However, since "almost all of the inhabitants" were content to have their
children attend the school to learn arithmetic and how to read and write
English—subjects "more consistent with people of their condition" than
Latin grammar—the Londoners endorsed the change in the school's character carried out by the local people. The only obstacle appeared to be the
will of the founder, which had allocated a £10 annual salary for a "grammar
school master," but the goldsmiths concluded that Reade had intended his
estate to support the children of Cromer in their "several callings" and that
the "revolution of time" had reduced the local inhabitants to a condition
in which they would not benefit from the study of classical grammar. They
therefore ordered the schoolmaster to continue teaching English and math
so that the local youth would be instructed "according to their parents' desires" and their own capacities until "it please God that some may be capable of learning grammar."[41] Similarly, when the skinners learned that no
students had left Tonbridge School for the universities in 1688, they in-
quired into the effectiveness of schoolmaster Thomas Roots. Three years
later, they determined that the school was "of little advantage" to Tonbridge because only three or four students there were interested in Latin.
The guildsmen therefore recommended that the school's usher begin
teaching English and math to local children so the school would be "more
useful and beneficial to the town."[42]

No matter how much legal authority London guild officers may have
had, their power to direct provincial school affairs was quite limited. They
relied heavily on accurate reports from local informants, without which
they had virtually no idea what was taking place in the provinces. While
they may have hoped that schoolmasters and clergymen would cooperate
with them—and with one another—in striving to bring godly reform to
the provinces, guild officers learned at their cost that rivalries and controversies in local communities would greatly limit their ability to govern
their schools effectively. Even more important, no matter how strongly
Londoners may have supported a schoolmaster, if he did not meet the
needs of his local community, he was doomed to failure.

IV

It is clear that all of the schools discussed here had a considerable influence on their local communities, but it is very difficult to measure whether they contributed greatly to the Puritan effort to spread godliness throughout the provinces, an effort with which historians have often associated them. Obviously schools like the ones just described were unable to provide steady streams of classically trained young men to the universities to become preachers. Furthermore, school staff members and local clergymen could quarrel over the direction of school affairs, thereby making the schools sources of controversy and contention rather than of godliness. At the same time, however, they all doubtless contributed to increasing lay literacy, which would have enabled some to read the Bible and godly tracts and thus broaden the boundaries of their spiritual lives. As the schools shifted their emphasis away from the classics and toward the imparting of basic skills, they also prepared provincial young people for participation in the world of commerce, which was of course the world of London guilds. Either way, the management of schools by London livery companies enhanced the already considerable influence of the metropolis on the rest of the nation, but the cooperation between Londoners and provincial people supports recent studies suggesting that such influence was filtered through the screen of localism.[43]

Whatever their provincial impact might have been, the maintenance of such charities contributed to the spiritual lives of the livery companies themselves. Whether or not their efforts to pursue the school benefactors' objectives and to maintain their memories bore the desired fruit, the considerable time, energy, and money a company's officers expended on their charities displayed their commitment to maintaining the ties to the company's past. Even if the officers pushed the limits of their mandate in transforming a school's curriculum—just as they did when exchanging a commemorative plate for a more useful one—they strove to remain true to the donor's memory and therefore true to their company's traditions. The Reformation may have overturned chantries and obits, but the commemoration of godly benefactors remained an essential part of efforts by company officers to offer their members a sense of community that would confer upon them "a sort of immortality."

Remembering the Puritan Past

JOHN WALKER AND ANGLICAN
MEMORIES OF THE ENGLISH CIVIL WAR

> The memory of the just *is* blessed: but the name of the
> wicked shall rot.
> —Proverbs 10:7

> Much memory, or memory of many things, is called
> *Experience.*
> —Hobbes, *Leviathan*

"Whatever you do, don't mention the war." Sadly these words can still guide Americans through their British holidays. Americans believe in progress, and while they admire Britain, it saddens them, for the specter of decline haunts it, and when they look west for escape as Americans are wont to do, they see Northern Ireland. The land of hope and glory seems buried in the painfully recent, still-remembered past. When the pilots of the Royal Air Force flew up to fight the Luftwaffe in 1940, Winston Churchill promised that if they won, they would achieve Britain's finest hour. His line quickly came to describe the collective memory of World War II in Britain, and ever since then Britons have struggled against the nostalgia of that optimistic and imperial promise. In the wake of both victory and the Empire's end, Churchill's Whiggish and rhetorical praise became a cynical elegy, a curse that implied inevitable declension and pessimism. If Britain cannot forget the war, can it amount to much again?

Historians are not sometimes too removed from such a momentous question. They ease nostalgia when they put forth a less glorious and climactic past. As if after a suitable mourning period for Churchill, many historians in Britain began to taint such notions as finest hours and revolutionary changes, perhaps to make their present more palatable. In the realm of Stuart England, the most revisionist of these historians stripped the Revolution from the English Civil War and left it with few great lasting effects. In their accounts, the Revolution sunders the seventeenth century no longer. It no more separates the early modern period from the modern than it distinguishes the age of divine-right monarchy from parliamentary government. It neither beckons modern toleration nor parts the age of Scripture from that of reason and science. In their vision, the seventeenth century has become a seamless series of civil wars, rebellions, and sectarian insurrections.[1] Because the Civil War did not extinguish the religious conflicts that caused it, religion remained at the center of the later Stuart period, complicating things all over again.[2] Where historians once saw one Restoration, in 1660, and one crisis, the Exclusion Crisis of 1678–81, their successors now see several restorations, 1660–65, 1681–85, and 1688–94, or several crises, 1660–64, 1667–73, 1678–83, 1685, 1687–89, and 1712–15.[3] Or both: a Restoration Crisis.[4] This revision of the Restoration has overlapped that of the last Stuart years, which likewise forsook older accounts of an ideologically defused political stability, and stressed instead the denominational dynamics within a confessional state.[5]

As long as they remembered it, the English Civil War remained the standard by which English men and women judged religious strife, and so it haunted British politics.[6] Many historians of the late Stuart period now preach the need to remember the war, and while Jonathan Scott has preached the loudest, he has not preached alone. Mark Goldie has characterized the crises of 1667–68, 1672, 1679–80, and 1687–88 as reversions to the 1640's, and Tim Harris has shown how the war's memory drove Whig and Tory propaganda during the Exclusion Crisis.[7] J. G. A. Pocock and the late J. P. Kenyon have written about how memories of the war determined the political consciousness of the governing classes in 1688–89 and the subsequent two decades, when any political dispute could likely "swoop back without notice to the 1640's and 1650's, where the contestants had to fight the Civil Wars all over again."[8] The war's religious conflicts have crept ever closer to the Enlightenment, snatching even the American Revolution from its grasp.[9] Seventy years after Sir Keith Feiling, historians have gone "right back past the sterner upland fields where Strafford labored," to the conflicts within English Protestantism that began with the Reformation.[10] Historians have diag-

nosed the amnesia of Whiggish historiography that forgot about Protestantism when it hated liberty of conscience. They have then prescribed a threatening cure: the chronic recurrence of early modern religious conflict and a
revisionism dependent upon it.[11]

Consequently, the religious conflicts of the Restoration no longer por-
tend toleration. The Restoration church was not a Whiggish way station
on the road from Puritanism to the Age of Reason. Instead, it was a
Laudian, vindictive, and coherently premodern church granting no latitude to schism.[12] Until the Glorious Revolution, it sanctioned coercion as
Augustine did, against Nonconformists' Lockean protests that they could
not help what they believed.[13] After 1689, toleration did not erase the fact
of their schism, and Anglicans did not act as pluralists who saw the future,
"acknowledged the fact, and changed the political theories they held."[14]
Toleration helped Freethinkers and some Dissenters to discover popish
priestcraft within Anglican sacerdotal authority; they then deployed anti-
Catholicism against it. Where the Restoration once did away with serious
religious conflict within English Protestantism, it now appears to have
only refined it instead.[15]

Martyrologies, the proof-tokens of the wars of religion, flourished.
Quakers began to compile their Book of Sufferings.[16] Presbyterians and
Congregationalists compiled lists of ministers who had suffered ejection
and abuse after the Restoration rendered them Nonconformist. Their stories of suffering fortified the communal courage of religious minorities by
proving that their travails wrote but the latest chapter in the persecution of
the true church, which stretched from the early Christians through the
Reformation and the Restoration. The stories hearkened back to John
Foxe, the greatest of all English martyrologists, whose *Acts and Monuments*
inspired Dissenters to search for the hidden meanings of their own sufferings, in order to find typological equivalents proving them to be members
of the chosen people of God. The church responded decisively. Against
Dissent, learned Anglicans across the ecclesiological spectrum wrote various histories of the church, and unprecedented historical scholarship was
achieved.[17] Parish ministers preached upon the past in anniversary sermons, and themes of martyrdom, repentance, and deliverance were annually repeated.[18] The London press sent forth newspapers devoted entirely
to popery and the Civil War, as weekly heaps of history were proffered to

the public.[19] Few people in late Stuart England, it seems, were eager to amount to much.

Even after 1700, English men and women still remembered in detail the sufferings it inflicted. These memories munitioned one of the principal conflicts between Anglicanism and Dissent in the first decade of the eighteenth century: that between Edmund Calamy and John Walker. Calamy, a Presbyterian with impeccable Puritan bloodlines, published an abridgment of Richard Baxter's *Reliquiae Baxterianae* in 1702. Within this abridgment he added a chapter consisting of brief biographies of the clergymen ejected by the Act of Uniformity in 1662. These accounts drove the book's success. Continued demand led to a second and greatly expanded edition in 1713, in which the ejected ministers received their own second volume.

Far too many Anglicans remembered the war differently to allow Calamy's accounts to stand unchallenged. Calamy provoked Walker, an Exeter clergyman, to plan his own account celebrating ministers who had been sequestered during the Civil War and Interregnum. Walker distributed queries for his project through the church and received nearly 1,000 letters in response. The children of "loyal Church of England men" wrote about their families' sufferings; clergymen and parishioners sent scathing reports of abuse that lumped Presbyterians, Independents, and more radical sects together. They remembered the violence of the war above everything else. Parliamentary soldiers and Puritan ministers had destroyed churches, murdered their episcopal enemies, and assaulted their families. Anglicans collapsed any distinctions among military, religious, and domestic violence, attributing all three to the nature of Dissent. They remembered the intruding ministers for their inferiority, their heresies, and their moral repugnance. They found Dissent's errors to be inherent and not localized to the abuses of wartime. In an age known for its internecine disputes at Convocation, Anglicans of widely divergent ecclesiological beliefs united around Walker's project, affirming both its necessity and its methods.

Walker's methods mark a telling change in the intellectual history of denominational conflict. For while he wanted his audience to remember the Anglican ministers of the war, he worked diligently to ensure that they would not be remembered after the martyrological fashion of Foxe and his

Nonconformist imitators. Walker and his Anglican cohort hated Calamy's martyrological bent. From the letters he received, Walker digested their discrete memories into an attack upon Dissent that mixed his own Anglican loyalty with empirical confidence. If Walker could prove Calamy wrong in his numbers and characterization of the ejected Nonconformists, he believed he could demonstrate the fundamental dangers that Dissent still posed. Walker and Calamy both sought to prove that their respective denominations had suffered more than the other. Each thought himself the better accountant of suffering and the more dutiful to truth. Both men were correct in their own way because their truths were different: they depended upon different views of how the past informed their present. Walker's high-church loyalties mingled freely with his empirical claims to veracity; this combination competed ultimately against Calamy's martyrology for the sanction conferred by the memorial authority of the Civil War. Against the Foxean pasts of Calamy's men, Walker provided the memorial and empirical case for religious intolerance. By memorializing the Civil War in such a fashion, Walker played a curious part in the movement of British thought away from theology and toward an empiricist style of moral philosophy.

I

Calamy commemorated "men of eminent piety, great ministerial abilitys, excellent in their tempers, successful in their labours, & particularly in their sufferings." He wanted posterity to honor them, to "know what manner of men they were."[20] He chose Baxter's life as the vessel through which he would pour out his defense of Nonconformity, abridging the autobiography to this end.[21] In the ninth chapter of his abridgment, Calamy alleged that 2,000 ministers had been ejected by the Act of Uniformity, and then he listed as many of these as he could. Such a large number, Calamy protested, testified to the injustice of the act. Anglicans concerned about occasional conformity had charged Dissenters with inflating the number of the ejected ministers, and Calamy thought that this charge "had a tendency to blacken their memory, if they were not clear'd by a just representation." While his purpose was straightforwardly partisan, Calamy appealed to numerical evidence in order to prove how narrowly the Restoration church had defined itself against Presbyterian efforts for comprehension within it.[22] He lumped the unofficial ejections that occurred at the Restoration with the formal ones of two years later. His biographies, culled from printed lives, funeral sermons, memoirs, and his own memory, all portrayed the ejected ministers as eminently tolerable within the church. His memorial to Civil War Puritanism idealized his own Nonconformity. It was Presbyterian, loyal to a more comprehensive church and to monarchy and opposed to the excesses of the Laudian church in its prewar and Restoration iterations.

At every turn, Calamy celebrated the moderation, learning, and prestige of his men, whom Anglicans tended to remember as unlettered extremists scorned by the upper classes. His Nonconformists saved Colchester from the Ranters and rescued Marple from the Quakers. They opposed the military rule of the Protectorate by guarding their pulpits against officers who claimed the authority to preach. Such men refused the Engagement as steadfastly as they later refused the Act of Uniformity.[23] John Owen and John Ray received encomia that emphasized their scholarly writings, and Calamy praised other men for their traditional academic qualifications. Thomas Gilbert "had all the school-men at his fingers-ends," and Calamy's own father, himself an ejected minister, commanded all of Aquinas.[24] Calamy repeatedly connected their learning to their irenic hopes, mentioning every Nonconformist he could who had participated in the Westminster Assembly or the Savoy Conference. His biography of the schoolmaster Joseph Halsey boasted of how he had "his house thronged with gentlemen's sons of the best rank; who tho' averse to Nonconformity, thought themselves happy in having their children under his roof." He described Francis Holdcraft as the son of a London knight, the beneficiary of the earl of Anglesey, and the friend of Archbishop Tillotson. These prestigious ties stood high above Holdcraft's own achievements, which Calamy did not bother to mention, presumably because such gentle associations lent more credibility to Calamy's case than anything Holdcraft might have accomplished on his own.[25]

In Calamy's memorial vision, the ejected Nonconformists had suffered under the Laudian church before the war and endured similar travails afterward during the Restoration. Thomas Ford had preached against the "Laudensian faction" at Oxford and Cambridge and had escaped Laud by serving in Germany as chaplain to George Fleetwood's regiment under Gustavus Adolphus. He returned to England to serve in the Westminster

Assembly, and when war came, he reformed Exeter against "those mad errors" of enthusiasm. He refused the Engagement and was ejected from Exeter cathedral, but Calamy noted boldly that Ford "enjoyed for about thirteen years great quiet and comfort" in his ministry until his ejection in 1662. Ever the moderate during the Restoration, he distrusted those who obtained licenses to preach under the Declaration of Indulgence in 1672. Calamy's depiction of Ford typified his memorial method: praising a Presbyterian who endured Laudian and Cromwellian hostility with the same steadfast moderation, only to suffer finally at the hands of a neo-Laudian church where "church musick" was always "justling out the constant preaching of the word."[26] Calamy's Nonconformists exuded theological moderation, irenic hope, erudition, and social respectability; narrow neo-Laudians had spurned these qualities by ejecting them.

Finally and most flamboyantly, Calamy invited his readers to think of his men in martyrological and providential ways. He seized upon any connection between Nonconformists and the Marian martyrs. Consequently, John Flavel prevented a shipwreck off Portland through the power of his prayer.[27] Providence indulged other Dissenters with more peculiar favors. Thomas Rowe escaped arrest in 1665 for preaching to conventicles; after ridiculing Rowe's preaching on mortification at the Dorset quarter sessions, a J.P. got his comeuppance when he died with his "members perfectly mortified." Later, when the Declaration of Indulgence was suspended, an order was sent to disturb Rowe's service, and the wife of the officer appointed to execute it fetched her husband from church immediately. Calamy reveled in the result: the woman was seized "by the distemper that goes by the name of appetitus caninus, or Dogg Appetite, insomuch that she ravenously devour'd whatever came near her that was eatable," forcing her husband on to poor relief. For Calamy this evidence confirmed "God's making good his word to his people . . . and is known by his judgments that he executes, in remarkably cutting off such as molest and trouble them."[28] The symbolism of Rowe's revenge mattered more to Calamy than the accuracy of its circumstantial details.

Calamy produced a Foxean martyrology. His portrayal of Nonconformists and their sufferings served ultimately to support their membership within the tradition of English martyrs to the true church. The brute facts of persecution interested him less than what those facts could symbolize. By implication, his prosopography characterized the Nonconformists as the new ancient Christians and their Anglican persecutors as the new Romans. Calamy would show that Presbyterians and other Nonconformists had acted "in the main upon the same principles with those who have been most eminent for serious religion ever since the Reformation," or more succinctly, since Foxe.[29] By placing its sufferings within a historical narrative that reached back beyond the Civil War to the Reformation, he sought to remove the memorial burden of blame for the war under which Dissent still labored in the early eighteenth century. Calamy's accounts, their typological descriptions of suffering, and their claims to divine favor were as repetitious and formulaic as his historical perspective was savvy. It allowed him to assert that rather than causing the Civil War, the Puritans had endured the excesses that had caused it, and suffered from these same excesses during the Restoration. Calamy commemorated the ejected Nonconformists with a Foxean belief in what their ejection meant. Persecution was the particular lot of the godly, and their suffering authenticated them as such. To strengthen the faith, Calamy supplied the proper historical perspective.[30]

II

Calamy's account appeared in 1702, the same year which saw the first volume of Clarendon's *History of the Rebellion* emerge from Christ Church and which heard Tory sloganeers proclaim, "No moderation!" during elections. Calamy infuriated Walker and his Anglican friends. One thought that Calamy's "head seems very thick & capable of no other impression than that of a sizeable oaken stick."[31] For most Anglicans, the suffering that the Nonconformists had endured did not validate their claim to persecution; that claim was reserved for the orthodox. Anglicans had sought to recapture providence from what they believed were Puritan abuses of it throughout the Restoration, and Calamy's account provoked them anew.[32]

Thomas Long, prebendary of Exeter cathedral, a formerly sequestered minister and champion of Anglican intolerance, struck first.[33] Long had criticized Baxter's autobiography when it was first published in 1697. Seven years later, he published *A Rebuke to Mr. Edmund Calamy*, attacking as nonsensical any comparison between the ejected Nonconformists and the suffering churchmen of the Civil War and Interregnum.[34] Long knew

Walker, the rector at St. Mary More in Exeter, and suggested to him the idea of an Anglican memorial project to counter Calamy. By March 1703, Walker had begun soliciting materials to that end.[35]

Meanwhile, a fellow minister, Dr. Charles Goodall, had begun searching out information on sequestered Anglicans through the press, and for two years Walker and Goodall pursued their projects as rivals, competing for the attention of John Hudson, the Bodleian librarian.[36] By September 1704, Goodall's health was failing, and he sent Walker his collection, which consisted mostly of pamphlets concerning the sequestrations.[37] For all his own industry, Goodall's contribution shrank to very little before the prospect of Walker's intent: to list all of the ecclesiastical livings that had been sequestered throughout England, Scotland, Ireland, and Wales.

Yet Walker did not seek to better Calamy at his own game. If previous Anglicans had tried to recapture providence from Dissent, Walker planned to dispense with providence altogether. He never intended his account to substantiate Anglican typological claims to divine favor. While Walker would memorialize the sufferings of the Anglican faithful during the Civil War, he sought with equal fervor to abandon the Foxean glosses of such persecution. To this end Walker composed a list of queries and asked the archdeacons to distribute copies of it to each minister in his diocese at the next visitation. These queries asked the name of the predecessor, his parish, and its value; whether he was formally turned out of his benefice, harassed out of it, or forced to compound for it; a brief summary of his character, "either for morals or learning"; and his university degree. This information would allow Walker to count the minister as formally sequestered. Walker next asked how the minister was sequestered (whether for refusing the Covenant, by the Triers and Ejectors, or by "any other more arbitrary and violent way"); how he suffered afterwards, whether by the commissioners, by the "succeeding irregular minister," or by "the soldiers, or the Mob"; and whether he had recovered his benefice at the Restoration. Walker solicited anything in print that could help him compose a biography of the man, such as funeral sermons, biographies, or the minister's own writings. Because most of these sequestered ministers had died by the time Walker began working, he asked for references to any surviving friends or relatives who could confirm the present minister's own reply.[38] In these queries Walker was trying to draw upon evidence that existed beyond the realm of theological dispute. He was seeking facts of Anglican sufferings that revealed the human virtues of the sufferers.

These facts would also display the moral failings of the Puritans who had persecuted their Anglican victims. Walker focused the second half of his queries on the "irregular and illegal minister": his name, how he gained the benefice, and whether he had been turned out by the Act of Uniformity. If he had conformed to the Act, or if it had not specifically ejected him, then Walker could strike him from Calamy's list. Walker asked whether the interim minister had been episcopally ordained or if at all, and if "they had ever been to any University, or were tradesmen." Against the Presbyterians, Independents, Anabaptists, Brownists, and Fifth-Monarchists, he asked for accounts of "their ridiculous praying and preaching; their canting, formal, or immoral practices; what factious or furious, and virulent things, they either did or said against monarchy, episcopacy, the Church, the King, the Bishops, the Clergy, the liturgy, the Lord's-Prayer, the Ceremonies, and the Royalists." Walker also sought similar information regarding the commissioners who had ejected the episcopal predecessor. Through his queries Walker planned to gain as detailed an account of each parish as he thought possible. Their bent against the "irregular and illegal" ministers is clear, as it was intended: Walker's questions sought answers of a sort most damaging to Dissent. He nonetheless demanded a standard of veracity from their respondents. Walker asked them to name their sources and describe "whatever else the relator's condition may be that renders his testimony credible," desiring "nothing but what you have good grounds to believe is true." In closing, Walker noted the approval of the bishop and archdeacon of each diocese and their request for each minister's assistance.[39]

Where Calamy aspired to Foxe, Walker aspired to Sir Francis Bacon. His queries strived to determine the authenticity of the sufferings of Anglicans by following Baconian rules for determining the reliability of observations, rules which others were to embrace in evaluating stories of marvels, monsters, and miracles.[40] Because they were verifiable, Walker thought the facts of Anglican sufferings to be more important than whatever putative providential meaning men such as Calamy might dream up for them. Walker scorned the martyrological character of Calamy's account as strenuously as he sought to discredit the Dissent it supported.

For all his empirical ambitions, the idea of returning to the Civil War did not charm all of Walker's correspondents. John Prince, an antiquarian of Devon, thought it might "stir an hornet's nest about the ears," and others suspected that many clergymen would not cooperate.[41] Some tried sabotage: one "very forward busy person, & employed . . . by the superior governors of the Church to disgrace the service of the choir and make it seem ridiculous," had burned Walker's queries "to prevent as far as in him lyes, your good and laudable design."[42] Reticent clergymen provided terse accounts or bare lists and closed their letters by asking for anonymity.[43] Some denounced the project as divisive and vindictive, evincing a low-church sensitivity. Humphrey Prideaux, dean of Norwich, thought it resembled "the Devil's office," and Robert Berkley wrote that he would rather serve as "an instrument in the closing up than fomenting our unhappie divisions," citing Stillingfleet as an exemplar who sought the same.[44]

Generally, Anglicans who disliked Walker's project blamed Laudian excess for the war. James Owen blamed the churchmen for their "honor and interest," which, by tying them to the king and his court, obliged them "to vindicate those extravagances, whereof they were the principal causes & instruments, as having abetted and consecrated the violation of the laws and libertyes of England." When war broke out, men became "flushed with blood and victory" and unrestrained as "the complexion of the war was at length greatly changed and it was pursued far beyond the first design." Yet subsequent excess did not absolve the guilt that Laudians still bore for causing the war and making it necessary "by force to withstand the torment of arbitrariness, that bore down all powers before it." Owen doubted that all episcopal clergy had been silenced or sequestered: "many of them connived at and preached all along those times," and many were debauched and ignorant. He scoffed at the idea that their sequestration "was any great curse to the nation," and refused to parallel their past misfortunes with those of the Nonconformists, whose Restoration sufferings seemed more authentic and justified. "The violence of Bishop Laud and other bishops of that time was so great" that many ministers were forced into exile, prosecuted, suspended, and ruined.[45] Owen's potted history neatly describes a low-church view of the war shared by churchmen such as Gilbert Burnet, who disapproved of Walker's project.[46]

Still, such replies were few. Far more letters trumpeted Walker's project as necessary and long overdue. During a decade known for division be-

tween high-church country clergy and low-church bishops, the memory of
the war's suffering churchmen provided a cause around which the church
could gather and bemoan its descent from national to established. Walker's high-church sympathies were clear, as were those of his bishops, Sir
Jonathan Trelawny and Offspring Blackall. Churchmen of similar beliefs
most frequently wrote to Walker. John Newte gave portraits of Laud and
Charles I to his alma mater, Balliol College, and raised money to build in
Tiverton the first organ in the west country since the Civil War. Newte's
love for the beauty of holiness made him a devoted correspondent. He sent
numerous accounts to Walker and reported to him from Convocation.[47]

Yet most of Walker's correspondents did not associate Walker's project
with high-church nostalgia. Whiggish bishops remained bishops: men
such as White Kennett, the bishop of Peterborough and himself a historian, sent many lengthy reports. Rank-and-file Anglican ministers responded assiduously to Walker's queries, apparently unconcerned that
some of his questions were "designed for peculiar purposes."[48] They
sought out parishioners who could remember the war, and recorded their
reminiscences about the sufferings of Anglican ministers and the exploits
of their persecutors. Some ministers scrawled their answers on the back of
the queries themselves, obeying Walker's admonition to keep them at
hand when questioning parishioners.[49] Their letters intertwined praise for
the Anglican cause with condemnation for its enemies past and present,
the Puritans of the Civil War and their dissenting descendants. In most of
the letters, there is a greater concern with the "usurping minister"; because
many churchmen fled their parishes after losing them, they figured less in
the memories of parishioners than their successors did. Most who wrote to
Walker thus concerned themselves more with memorializing the errors of
the interim ministers than with extolling the virtues of Church of England
men. Their missives, while vindictive, did not all fly from high-church
fury.

In the wake of the Revolution settlement, Anglicans felt they needed a
new weapon against Dissent. The Toleration Act rendered irrelevant the
political, ecclesiological, and theological theories for religious intolerance
that had composed the political theology of Restoration Anglicanism.
Against both Latitudinarian and neo-Laudian opposition, Dissenters
gained political rights and legal sanction for their worship beyond indulgence; the magistrate could no longer help the Anglican minister by co-

ercing the wayward into the church.[50] Walker thought he could remedy this situation. Anglicans would respond to his queries with facts about sufferings. From these symptomatic facts of Dissent Walker would deduce its pathology, by an ethical calculus that took Dissenters' manifest violations of the law, of the social order, of gender relations, and of religious decorum into account. He would demonstrate the etiology and symptoms of perverted religious zeal like an epidemiologist. He would not advance a rival assertion of supernatural, providential sanction for the Anglican Church against its sectarian rivals. Against Calamy and his Foxean plea, Walker supplied facts to provide a memorial and empirical case for religious intolerance.

I I I

Walker sought to demonstrate the superiority of Anglican suffering, and his correspondents praised the empirical dimension to his work. One such champion asserted that "induction, among all logicians, is lookt on as a very sound sort of argumentation; and few, or none, will be able to confute you, when your work is founded, upon true historicall relation, and pure matter of fact."[51] The most pressing matters of fact concerned violence. Anglicans did not discern theological violence from military violence; they commingled Puritanism with the military force that imposed it and characterized Dissent through violence itself. The violence done to Anglican ministers, their churches, and their families was the most convincing demonstration of Dissent's many dangers, and memories of this violence provided the evidence. Walker's correspondents remembered the wars with bigotry. Yet assisted by his Baconian queries, they remembered it with bigotry empirically defended.

Walker's intentions were clear, but that clarity disturbs, for how authentic were the stories that Walker's correspondents recounted? The murder of Walter Raleigh, dean of Wells, rector of Chedzoy, and chaplain to Charles I, provides a case in point. Raleigh was murdered by his jailer in October 1646, and his status as an Anglican martyr was guaranteed in 1679 when Simon Patrick published his works.[52] By 1704, Patrick was bishop of Ely, and he wrote Goodall to complain that he had not received any information about Raleigh for Goodall's work.[53] Nonetheless, Goodall and Walker received letters from other sources that provided separate accounts of Raleigh's death. A Mr. Westry summarized Raleigh's sequestration from the Wells Deanery, his imprisonment there, and the County Committee's refusal to allow him to see his family. When his jailer demanded to see a letter Raleigh was writing to his wife, Raleigh refused, and after a brief skirmish, "the Gaoler drew [a sword] & ran him thro' the belly, of which he died." The Committee, "to consummate their barbarity, turned his wife and children out of doors."[54] Mr. Corry, the minister at Chudleigh, provided a more detailed account of the murder. According to Corry, parliamentary soldiers had plundered Raleigh's parsonage at Chedzoy, seized his cattle and horse, and turned out his family. After General Goring was defeated in the west, they jailed Raleigh as his family fled to Bridgewater. Corry named "one Barret, a shoe-maker of that town," as the jailer who refused Raleigh's request to see his family, but nonetheless brought him before the County Committee to plead his case in vain. The next morning Raleigh, "having some urgent business with his wife," began writing the letter; Barrett entered his room "with his sword drawn, before the letter was finished, demanded a sight of it, but the Doctor holding it fast in his hand, Barrett run him through the belly to the back-bone, of which he tumbled out of his chair dead." Corry then related how Raleigh's son George secured Barrett's arrest, but the Committee released him, restored him as J.P., and arrested George, who later escaped. After Raleigh's burial, the County Committee arrested Mr. Standish, a vicar, "till the hour of his death" for burying Raleigh according to the Book of Common Prayer.[55]

Had Westry and Corry poached their stories from Patrick's brief life of Raleigh, or had they followed Walker's instructions to seek out what Raleigh's contemporaries themselves remembered? Walker cited Patrick's work in his published account, and Patrick in turn cited *Mercurius Rusticus*.[56] Yet neither work revealed that Barrett was a shoemaker or that Standish nearly died for reading from the prayer book: these details came from the letters alone. And where Patrick asserted that Raleigh died several weeks after Barrett's attack, the letters claim with more drama that Barrett killed him on the spot.[57] Corry's account described Raleigh's murder with details that precisely condemned Raleigh's persecutors: the County Committee had raised and restored Barrett, a mere shoemaker, to the office of a J.P.; they had arrested Raleigh's son and released Barrett; and they had almost killed Standish for performing Anglican burial rites. The devil was in the details. If they assisted him and stood independent of typological interpretation, Walker included them in his account.[58] If they did not on either count, he elided them. When soldiers set upon John Edsaw, the minister of Chaley in Sussex, he cut them apart with a hedging bill before succumbing to arrest. Walker noted Edsaw's imprisonment at Ely-house, but he did not mention his active resistance.[59]

The language of many letters resonated with the intolerance of Restoration Anglicanism. During the 1670's, Long and other churchmen had written works comparing the Dissenters to the Donatists, the fourth-century schismatics denounced by Augustine; 30 years later, even in the wake of Toleration, that comparison remained on the tip of high-church tongues. William Prior wrote to Walker with an account of how "the Circumcellian round-head souldiers" had crippled his father, the rector of Evetham in Hampshire. The Circumcellians were a militant terrorist faction of Donatists, and they came easily to other high-church minds as antecedents to the parliamentary soldiers.[60] Such violence justified the Restoration's expulsion of schismatic Presbyterians. "Let them our Dissenting brethren," wrote Prior, "determine whether (2 Kings 12.13 captrs) the conspirators who slew King Joash, or King Amaziah, who slew those conspirators, were the blood guilty." Prior thought Charles II as righteous as Amaziah for ejecting "those first invading preachers, as on our bolder regicides," by turning the same wheel of retributive justice upon them.[61] Anglicans such as Prior combined biblical history and early church history with that of the war, divining the same faction in each. Yet Prior's storming vehemence may have clouded his memory; although he swore he knew this story from "my father's widow, his manservant, and other evidences," he mistook his father's parish for Collingburne in Wiltshire.[62]

Anglicans implicated the judges of the Civil War in its violence as well. J. Whitefoot sent Walker an account of the trial of Thomas Cooper for conspiring to deliver Norwich to the royalists in 1650. After executing the plot's ringleaders on December 23, 1650, the judges, led by Philip Jermin, justice of the Upper Bench, pursued the case further. Lacking evidence, they offered pardons to prisoners who would testify against their fellows. The judges used William Hobart, a gentleman, to testify against Cooper on Christmas Day, "to add to his affliction." They found him guilty and condemned him to die. The next day, the judges used a third prisoner, Armstrong, to testify against Hobart, whom they also convicted. Their convictions were "said by some of the judges to be for convenience to have one black coat, and one red coat, meaning one Gentleman, and one minister to suffer among the rest." Cooper was executed in front of Holt School, where he had been an usher since 1643. Hobart enjoyed hope of a reprieve, because his friend Matthew Lindsey was mayor and one of the judges. He had mistakenly cast the deciding vote for Hobart's execution, but Jermin refused to recall it. This injustice "struck Mr. Lindsey into so sad an apprehension of his mistake, as that about a fortnight after he fell sick and died."[63] Walker's printed *Attempt* neatly elided the providential conclusions that Whitefoot had stressed.

Walker's treatment of Whitefoot's account reveals the epistemological divide that separated Walker from many of his earnest correspondents. Whitefoot sent Walker a true account of Puritan persecution according to his instructions. Better still for Whitefoot, it revealed with stark typology the war's conflict. In it, Puritan judges abused reverent men and eschewed holy days; divine justice struck when the guilty consciences of mistaken accusers such as Lindsey led to their own deaths. Whitefoot took these typological conclusions for granted, and assumed Walker sought such conclusions as much as he did the facts supporting them. Yet where Whitefoot thought in typological terms, Walker conscientiously did not. He felt that such providential and typological details sounded too much like Calamy's to be included in his own account.[64] The distance between Foxean readings of persecution and Walker's Baconian calculations was too wide to span, for it was the same distance that separated Calamy from Walker.

The typological habit was hard to break. People condemned entire communities for abetting the sufferings of sequestered ministers. Richard Towgood recalled how the "cursed first born bats of hell" in Bristol, who feigned "pure sanctity and true holiness," had chained his father and other prisoners together "like so many dogs" in one room where they were "forced to discharge the necessityes of nature."[65] Against a hostile community, congregations could come to the rescue. Sarah Rudkin remembered how soldiers had dragged her father, Christopher Barron, from his church in Dickleborough to Norwich Castle, but his "flock followed him and rescued him and hid him a long time after." When the earl of Manchester offered to restore Barron to his benefice if he would take the Covenant, he declined, preferring "to suffer affliction with the righteous [than] enjoy the pleasure of sin for a season." Manchester's soldiers rifled through Barron's house and took away his corn and plate; when they returned to carry away the rest, they found that Barron's neighbors had spirited it away to preserve it for him.[66] In Staffordshire, a soldier named Bullock shot Mr. Bourne, the minister of Canock, while he was preaching upon 2 Timothy.[67] Some women aided him while others in the congregation hauled Bullock to the stocks, where he furiously promised that he "would kill Bourne, for he had a Devil, for nothing but the Devil could tell him of those sins Bullock had been guilty of, which Mr. Bourne had reprooved hereupon." Bullock was cashiered and sent to Stafford jail, where he lived out the rest of his days. Bourne visited him in prison, prayed for him, and tried to induce him to repent, but Bullock obstinately continued to want to kill him.[68] Bourne's story presented another stark and typological account of the moral superiority of Anglicanism, but Walker did not include Bourne in his printed *Attempt* because he could not confirm the story. Walker typically exercised such restraint, trying to remain truthful and often at his own expense.

Walker's correspondents would not distinguish religious from military violence, and Anglicans remembered them as one. During the war, soldiers on both sides occasionally preached; even Calamy euphemized the war as "those times of confusion, when soldiers were preachers."[69] The parliamentary soldier-preacher Mr. Tucker "preached up sedition, and rebellion . . . and was ready to join with the Devil to execute it too." Lacking "the sword of the spirit, he preached with a long keen-sword lied by his side; and was ready to draw it even in the church for the promotion of the good old cause," and once he beat an elderly cavalier who took issue with his "mad idle doctrine, and dangerous principles."[70] The inversion could work both ways when preachers fought as soldiers: Joshua Reynolds alleged that Baxter himself had shot a royalist officer during the war.[71]

When correspondents recalled the physical abuse of an Anglican minister, they reflexively stressed the symbolic importance of such violence. A servant of Lewis Alcock remembered how a soldier came to Alcock's house near Southampton and rifled through his belongings. Alcock remained unmoved until the soldier found his surplice, put it on "before his face . . . girt his sword upon it, and so rode off in triumph through the parish." This caused Alcock to weep uncontrollably, and shortly thereafter he may have lost his mind. He refused to leave the parsonage house and slept in the parlor with his guns loaded, "and declared himself not to deliver up the possession of his house to the usurper but with his life." Several gentlemen of the parish pitied Alcock and persuaded the new minister to allow him to stay in the parsonage house until he died in 1647.[72] Robert Warren, the rector of Melford in Suffolk, suffered a similar humiliation. His neighbor, a former J.P., remembered how some Presbyterians had forced him out of his pulpit during his service and marched him home while beating "a frying pan before him in derision, saying this is your saints bell."[73] John Ferebee's tormentors seized his prayerbook and surplice while he was baptizing a child. "Tearing the one and wearing the other," they stripped him naked and marched him into a makeshift jail in Gloucester.[74] Some described the abuse of Anglican ministers as if they were Laudian statuary. After soldiers "pulled and halled" Thomas Howell, the bishop of Bristol, out of his palace, they pulled down its lead roof, even though they knew his wife was there in childbed. After exposing Howell's wife to the skies, "in the cathedral they robb'd the sepulchres of the dead and barbarously diggd up many dead bodyes for the sake of the lead," besides the usual obliteration of the communion table, rail, and the prayer book.[75] Although lead was valuable both in peacetime and war, its heightened wartime value did not rationalize its theft; on the contrary, it convinced Walker's correspondents that violent zeal rather than need for ammunition had provided the motivation.

Iconoclasm justified retaliation in kind: if soldiers were to strip churches, churchmen could resist as soldiers. Thomas Mason served as a captain in the royalist army in 1643, before becoming the rector of Ashwell in Rutland the next year. In September 1644, a parliamentary cornet named Sewel took the surplice and common prayer book out of Mason's church, tied them to the tail of his horse, and dragged them through the town. Mason killed him in July 1645, and his son made no apologies in his relation. Sewel had blasphemed before the Directory replaced the Book of Common Prayer in January 1645, thus allowing the younger Mason to assert that Sewel lacked even "the pretence of one of their illegal ordinances for what he did." In defiance of any law, wrote Mason, Sewel claimed only "the right of furious zealots."[76] When Walker's correspondents remembered the plundering of churches and parsonage houses for lead, or that of ministers' estates for plate and corn, they assumed these crimes had come from the anti-Arminian violence of their most extreme perpetrators. Memories of religious war wedded military and theological violence.

And the violence of Dissent was not confined to men alone: the remembrances sent to Walker conspicuously emphasize violence done to women. While he subordinated accounts of families' sufferings to that of the ministers themselves, many of his correspondents reversed this priority.[77] When sequestered ministers landed in jail or fled their parishes, their families often stayed behind. Their responses to Walker often recounted the travails of their mothers more extensively and pathetically than those of their fathers. Beyond this pragmatic reason there was another dimension to this focus on women. Domestic violence struck many of Walker's correspondents as the most damning aspect of Puritan ascendancy, and they pathologized it to show what they believed were the inherent dangers of Dissent.

Puritan ministers beat their own wives: if the English family were a little commonwealth, the domestic violence recounted by Anglicans demonstrated beyond doubt the political danger of Dissent. Andrew Williams, a servant of Mr. Moyne of Ashford, related how his violence to the king was reflected in the violence toward his wife. When Moyne heard news of the regicide, he joyously told his wife about it, but she fell weeping at the news, whereupon Moyne flung a stool at her, pursued her around the house, and broke down three locked doors to get at her before she could be rescued by neighbors. Moyne believed that Williams would have killed his wife, had not her neighbors come to her aid. Christopher Lee, who replaced the incumbent minister at Bovey-Tracey in Devon, tried several times to kill his servant, who had often prevented Lee from killing his own wife as well.[78] Even Presbyterians who opposed the mad errors of enthusiasm were dangerous, as opposition to extremism did not void the fact of their schism. A Mr. Tuchin falsely accused a gentleman of being an anti-Trinitarian and refused to baptize his child, traumatizing its mother so badly that she died in childbed soon afterward.[79] Violence accompanied heterodoxy, which in turn caused more violence.

Anglican wives fared far worse. Thomas Smith, the rector of Richards Castle in Hereford, was turned out of his living in 1647, and he retreated from the parish, but his wife remained in the parsonage house. When his replacement, William Woodward, came to take possession, Mrs. Smith clenched her arms around a bedpost. Woodward ordered soldiers to remove her, but they refused; he, "more merciless than they, went to her, and to compel her to loose her hold, he (having a new pair of shoes on) kicked her upon the belly, with that violence, that it gave her a rupture, whereof she never recovered, but died within little more than a year." The author of this account noted that as late as 1690 Woodward was still "clamouring against our Church as a persecuting church" in his conventicle.[80] As with heterodoxy, violence intertwined with hypocrisy.

Often, the victims of such violence were pregnant. The trauma of sequestration frequently caused women to miscarry and even die. Soldiers turned John Heslehead out at gunpoint from Warkworth Church in Northumberland; they marched to his vicarage house and then expelled his family. His daughter died in childbirth soon after, "occasioned as 'twas thought, by the hurry and fright of her sudden removal."[81] During a bonfire at Uxborough celebrating a parliamentary victory, a tailor called one of Emanuel Sharpe's sons "a priest's bastard"; hearing of the insult, his mother "showed so much resentment of the matter that it was the cause of an abortion." This only provoked those of "the adverse Godly party," who shouted that "the calf was dead, and if the cow had died also they would have made a bonfire that should have reached to heaven."[82] When a soldier ordered the wife of Thomas Barker out of the parsonage house in Baxterly, Warwickshire, she asked him for his commission; he referred her to his pistol and "turned her out of doors, and set a cradle with a young child in it upon the dunghill."[83] Shortly after miscarrying, Susan Temple was cast out of her husband's parsonage house at Bourton on the Water in Gloucestershire. Soldiers carried her out into the churchyard; when she asked for mercy, "the soldiers told her she must go agrazeing."[84] Many of these letters nearly excluded the sequestered minister. Richard Cox provided a terse biography of his episcopal predecessor, Thomas Rawson, before lamenting at length the death of his wife, a woman of quality who had endured repeated abuse and had died shortly after giving birth to her fourteenth child. Walker received scores of such letters.[85] Puritan ministers killed pregnant women, parliamentary soldiers tried to rape the daughters of Anglican ministers, and old women suffered in jails infested with disease.[86] Prototypical stories of suffering and martyrdom do not appear to have informed Walker's correspondents, who could have lifted them from Foxe or from atrocity pamphlets describing the Irish Rebellion and the war in England.[87] Evidently they obeyed Walker, for the numerous stories of suffering and pregnant women do not repeat each other beyond the blunt facts of death or miscarriage.

Yet as with other acts of violence, the sufferings of Anglican women not only condemned the sins of their persecutors but allowed those relating them to elevate such women into models of Christian mercy and forgiveness. Griffith Vaughan's grandson remembered that on the day they came to sequester his paternal grandfather's estate in Pitsford, his mother fell into labor. The women assisting her begged the soldiers for mercy: while they allowed her some rest, "before my mother had lay'n in her month," they came again, gutted the house and took her wearing linen, and threatened to make her "proud heart come down." Vaughan's grandson remembered how often his mother had remarked that "she had a secret joy within her at that time, and all the time they were abusing her in this manner." Her own father had also suffered as a sequestered minister; after the war, Mrs. Vaughan took pity upon one of his worst persecutors and "was one of his best friends, and constantly for some years gave him weekly relief."[88] As Anglican ministers forgave their tormentors, Anglican wives provided them with sustenance.

The trauma of childbirth allowed other clear moral contrasts between Anglicans and their enemies. Dr. Turner was sequestered from Felsham in Surrey and replaced by Mr. Fisher; when Fisher came to take the parsonage house, Turner's pregnant wife begged him to allow her to stay, until she had given birth and recovered; but "like a true member of that faction," Fisher forced her away. When Turner reclaimed Felsham after the Restoration, Fisher's wife was pregnant, and Fisher "had the face to request that for her, which he had denied before to Mrs. Turner." Turner replied, "'Though you showed little of Christianity, you shall see that I am (I thank God) a Christian,' and let her in God's name stay for long in the house and well come."[89] Grace abounded amid such traumas.

When Anglicans remembered the violence wrought by Puritan ministers and parliamentary soldiers, their desecration of churches, and their abuse of ministers and their wives, the distinctions among the actors faded before the light of their actions. They did not distinguish nontheological violence from theological violence in their memories. They commemorated the victims of true persecution, true because they had suffered for their orthodoxy. They would expose Calamy's men as "the men who make themselves saints by calling themselves so," whose claims to persecution were as poorly grounded as their theological tenets.[90] To the people who wrote to Walker, toleration, whether as a principle or as an expedient against popery, was possible only as a product of forgetfulness.

IV

Against Calamy's idealized portrayal of the ejected Nonconformists, Walker received enthusiastic responses detailing the manifold errors wrought upon congregations by interim ministers. These replies stressed the intellectual superiority of Anglican ministers against their replacements. They recounted stories of Puritan preaching that struck them as ridiculous and even dangerous; these often ribald accounts assisted Walker in his efforts to condemn the late Stuart heirs of Civil War Puritanism upon evidence outside the realm of theological dispute. The behavior of Puritan ministers certified their moral inadequacy and their hostility to the church. Taken together, these memories created an Anglican pathology of error for Dissent founded upon the truth of the things remembered, in their particular details.[91]

Walker's correspondents relayed smugly how their episcopal predecessors had bested their unread enemies. Answering charges of insufficiency before the Gloucestershire sequestrators during the war, Mr. Hurst defended his reputation as a scholar at New College, Oxford, and as rector at Hawling. He asked them to judge the fitness of his accusers, whom he suspected were illiterate. The sequestrators granted Hurst's wish and requested "his neighbors (shepherds and plowmen) to come near him." Hurst had purchased a hornbook that morning, which he described as a new English book "which cost him but a penny," and offered to accept the testimony of any of them who could read it. But when he held the book out to them, his accusers fled "like dogs with their tails between their legs," and without further disturbance, "home vamped Mr. Hurst to Hawling again."[92] Francis Fern sent Walker a transcript of one of Cromwell's letters, announcing proudly that he had duplicated exactly its errors in spelling and grammar.[93] Walker's correspondents related such evidence of ignorance with exactitude.

Shepherds and plowmen were easy targets, and their examples meshed well with the stupid ministers who served them.[94] If sequestered ministers were learned and pious, their replacements personified ignorance and impiety. John Lawrence recounted how all four men who succeeded his predecessor at Yelverstoft were "mean illiterate men" except the last, who mustered enough literacy to flatter Cromwell in print.[95] One Mr. Chapman wrote Walker about the travails of Thomas Gibson, who so nettled the Puritans that they charged that "he preach'd Ormanism," but the "Fools meant Arminianism."[96] Walker and his correspondents often referred to Calamy's men by their unscholarly trades, complaining of how "good schollars and able good men [had been] turned out to make room for Taylors & others."[97] The message of Puritan ignorance did not need to be stated explicitly.

Calamy's enemies lambasted him for claiming that the Nonconformists excelled in scholarship. Humfrey Smith wrote Walker to discredit the reputation of the Independent John Flavel, whom Calamy had celebrated in his account.[98] Having perused Flavel's works, Smith showed how Flavel had falsified quotations from various commentaries upon the Pentateuch and was "a wretched astronomer" to boot, although he "would have his readers think him deeply skilled in that science." He was guilty of "preaching up Calvinisticall tenets without either a sufficient knowledge of them, or of the art with which the patrons of them are wont to manage them." Nonetheless, Flavel was "a great master of Cant . . . he had a peculiar faculty of delivering his sermons to the satisfaction of his auditors, having a clear voice, much action, and sighs and tears at his command."[99] Others followed Smith's tactic of showing the connection between bad scholarship and worse theology. Mr. Bury believed that Easter was misplaced on the calendar, for according to his exegesis, it was too cold at that time of year for the Easter biblical stories to be credible. His opponent did not refute him "from the Jewish keeping of Passover, but from the difference in climates" between Shropshire and Jerusalem, and asked Bury if he knew the latter's latitude. This put an end to the argument.[100] Another letter asserted that Bury was merely a tailor. Although Calamy had asserted that Bury had attended Oxford, Walker replied that if he had, it was only as "one of the garrison."[101]

Anglicans' memories of blasphemy and excessive zeal provided evidence of the theological errors of Dissent and pointed to the danger these errors posed. One of the most notoriously remembered preachers was Christopher Jellinger, a German émigré in Devon whose unusual parochial style combined nightwalking with extemporaneous prayer. Jellinger's lawyer wrote Walker to describe how Jellinger broke into the bedroom of a newlywed couple on their wedding night, came to their bedside, "prayed . . . and kept close to the work of the night: where praying for the good success of the opus tenebrarum, he sayd 'Give them Lord thousands, & tens of thousands; millions, Lord and tens of millions.'" At this point the husband screamed at Jellinger, "Old Doctor, you overstock my barton!" An old servant of the same couple witnessed Jellinger preaching in their house and complained of how its "noyse being terrible in a calm night and I understanding never a word, did sweat with fear." Jellinger's caterwauling sermon so affrighted the wife that she miscarried and almost died. Because her husband was a "red-hott presbyterian," and she "a fire-hott papist, and not apt to be easily terrified," the lawyer mistrusted the elderly servant's information. He confirmed it separately upon the credit of some Anglican gentry before concluding this episode had occurred.[102] Dissenters were not reliable witnesses. One Mr. Wilcox came to Walker's house and told him that Jellinger used to pray for his horse; presumably, Wilcox was Anglican.[103]

Peasants and servants were incredible witnesses, and when "tailors and others" took the pulpit, their preaching lacked trustworthiness. Such assumptions themselves testified to how credibility often depended upon one's social station.[104] Walker's correspondents knew of Calamy's frequent protestations supporting the gentility of Nonconformists such as Francis Holdcraft. Anglicans distrusted Nonconformist scholarship for reasons that were similar to their diagnosis of Puritan zeal. Overconfidence in their intellectual abilities led Puritans to scholarly error, as their unread and egotistical sense of their own religious callings to ministry led them to extemporaneous prayer. Catholics might have dissembled for their own protection, but at least they were canny in their deceit. Nonconformists were simply liars.[105]

Devon abounded with characters such as Jellinger.[106] The always dependable John Newte sent Walker an account of his father's replacement as rector of Tiverton, Theophilus Polwhele. Polwhele enjoyed the Angel Inn in Tiverton perhaps too much. When a couple came to the inn to ask him to marry them, Polwhele, dressed "in antick garb like a mountebank," kept ceremony to a minimum not out of Puritan severity but for alcoholic reasons. Asking only if they would take each other for man and wife, he pronounced them so, and "turned away and went in again to his company" for another round.[107] Newte's father had been sequestered for malignancy upon the evidence of one of Polwhel's friends, Lewis Stuckley, another "infamous independent preacher." To discredit Stuckley's evidence, Newte pointed out Stuckley's ridiculous command, to "never reckon you pray, read or meditate aright till you clap about the neck of Jesus Christ; till he kiss you all the kisses of the lipp."[108] John Tindall relayed the rude expressions of Walter Shute of Cornwood, who preached in February 1649 that "Now I plainly see that Hell is pav'd with the skulls of Kings and Princes," and modified the Lord's Prayer to read, "You may go to hell with our father which art in Heaven.'" Shute pulled down the loft at Cornwood, broke its painted windows, and ruined the vicarage house and glebe lands.[109]

Anglicans thought the rantings of Presbyterians, Independents, Anabaptists, and others revealed not only flawed theology but mental illness as well. Restoration anti-Nonconformists as diverse as Hobbes, Sprat, Tillotson, and Stillingfleet had diagnosed the insanity of Puritanism; Walker's correspondents offered similar if less erudite analyses.[110] John Chamberlin thought the preaching of the Independent ministers disturbed "the hearer's brains and makes them cockoheaded and run from one religion to another and never understand the true worship of God."[111] One attacked the "reverence some deluded people have for the memory" of Calamy's ministers, and clergymen who made such references to delusion meant them seriously.[112] They took extemporaneous prayer in particular as a sure symptom of mental illness. When J. Potter questioned his uncle about the war, the old man was "so strangely sunk in his intellectuals, that his relation was all over incoherence and confusion, much like the language of extempore prayer."[113] William Wake, the future archbishop, remembered Nicholas Gibbon as an addict recovering from extemporary prayer. Gibbon was rector of Sevenoaks in Kent, but during the war he quit the church, set up a separate congregation, "and greatly showed his gifts of praying by the spirit." One of his former parishioners hired a secretary to transcribe Gibbon's prayers. After one service, the parishioner, Mr. Culliford, presented the transcript to Gibbon and asked his opinion of it. Gibbon replied as a schizophrenic might: he declared the transcript blasphemous, asserting that "no person of any Christian principles could justify it but must be ashamed of it and beg God's and the people's pardon." Culliford then told Gibbon that the prayer was his own: shocked by this epiphany of the "strange strain he was fallen into," he forever after stuck to a formulary prayer.[114]

The ignorance and error of interim ministers often led them down the path to moral depravity, and the communities that endured them long remembered their infamies. Mr. Tray of Horsely refused to preach on

Christmas, thinking the day idolatrous. To show his ire at the town's festivities, he "caused a turd to be put into paste, & sent it to the common bakehouse upon that day, which spoil'd a whole oven full of Christmas pys." A ditty arose in Horsely from Tray's offense: "Parson Tray, on Christmas Day/To help on reformation/Instead of the word did bake a turd/and poyson'd his congregation." The man who relayed this story to Walker allowed that "a rogue wench" who lived with Tray might have ruined the pies instead. Either way, Tray was guilty.[115] Thomas Edwards of Badby in Northamptonshire described its interim minister as a "terrible drinker" who kept a pitcher of ale near his pulpit, and "constantly went out to make water when the psalm was a singing."[116] In Oxfordshire, it was commonly reported that Captain Butler, an army chaplain who took over the rectory of Heyford, "destroyed his wife (who was a comely person) by giving her the French disease," which eventually killed them both.[117] Such turpitude could send parishioners beyond their limits. Newte sent Walker what he remembered of Theophilus Hart. Besides preaching while seated and having his gardener read from the prayerbook for him during services, Hart maintained a reputation as an adulterer. Newte recalled staying at Hart's house while Hart committed adultery with a servant; he had several bastards by this woman, and all the neighborhood knew "that when his wench got too big with child he would take her to London to give birth." Hart's daughters lamented that he rarely missed going to London on such trips for fifteen or sixteen years. He paid for his immoralities in 1686, when he was found in bed with the wife of a butcher. The butcher demanded an answer for the affront, but upon receiving none, he took the broadax he happened to be carrying and cleft Hart's head wide open. Newte regretted only that the butcher was hanged for the murder.[118]

Hart held Wappenham for 40 years; his predecessor had fled to Ireland and stayed there at the Restoration, and Hart bribed the bishop's secretary into passing his examination for orders and institution afterwards. His tenure continually reminded all the parish of the clerical abuses of the Civil War. Walker's correspondents took care not to distinguish the Puritans of the war and Interregnum from their Restoration brethren and the Dissenters of their own time. Fifteen years after the Glorious Revolution, many of Walker's correspondents sincerely feared that Dissent might foment another civil war. One asked Walker,

Is it come to '40 again? Are the saints to reign in this century? Why was such a fa-
natick suffered to put out such a list? Why does not the London clergy arraign
such a varlet, if not for the list, yet for laying so many and grievous imputations
upon the Act of Uniformity. . . . I wonder what the young Saint [Calamy] means,
at this distance of time, to show such spite and malice not only against the Church
of England, to which he is a sworn enemy, but also against the present government, for at this distance of time, the memories of those great men which that
wicked crew turned out, is almost forgot and also the intruders too.[119]

James Dixon provided a eulogy of his father, who had been sequestered
for refusing the Covenant. But in the same breath he lamented "the Revolution and Revolt of 88," when his brother "ran with the multitude, and
saved his bacon (the more shame for him) instead of suffering as our father
had done." Dixon boasted that he had not "bowed to the Baal of those
times," and kept the "principles, not of my father only, but of all our fathers—and to this moment pay double taxes—yet am no papist, I assure
you."[120] One nonjuror sent in an account of himself. Such mistakes, however amusing in hindsight, came not only from nonjurors whose loyalties
stemmed from "a superstition as stupid and degrading as the Egyptian
worship of cats and onions."[121] Rather, their mistakes revealed the sensi-
bilities that had caused them. Across the ecclesiological spectrum, Anglicans remembered the Civil Wars not only as an unprecedented catastrophe
but as one whose upheavals had allowed the timeless errors inherent in
Dissent to erupt. In the first decade of the eighteenth century, many Anglicans still feared another eruption.

Yet Walker's methods of Anglican remembrance were utterly inappropriate to demonstrate the existence of such a pathology of Puritan error.
The replies to his queries repeatedly exceeded what Walker had requested.
While most respondents dutifully followed the letter of Walker's instructions, most violated their spirit: consistently they responded to his queries
in providential and typological terms. Walker's correspondents obeyed his
instructions, but they drew their own conclusions. Fired up against Dissent, they understandably misunderstood the character of Walker's memorial mission.

v

Walker took the accounts he received and combined them with his own empirical ambitions to create his book. Devoted to memorializing Anglican sufferings, it did not take on Calamy's account directly. Walker had planned such an attack, which he titled *Adversaria Calamistica,* and referred to it in his notes as "the second part of my book," but this part was never printed.[122] Walker's notes for this second related project describe a memorial that was the reverse of the *Attempt,* a threefold attack upon Calamy's account. Walker first defended the Act of Uniformity against Calamy's charge that it was unduly harsh. Next, he compiled a list of the Nonconformists whom he disqualified from Calamy's alleged total of 2,000. Walker's near obsession with reducing Calamy's number shows how seriously he took the quantitative dimension of his work. The Act of Uniformity, which reestablished the Church of England, still loomed large in the memories of many Anglicans. If Walker could prove that the Act had ejected far fewer ministers than Calamy asserted, Calamy lost his quantitative attack. And third, when Walker could not disqualify a minister, he provided evidence sufficiently discrediting his character to justify the ejection. Beneath a letter describing the exploits of a Presbyterian, Walker wrote, "Note this story as a proof of the factiousness of lecturers."[123] Walker believed he could demonstrate the dangers of Dissent empirically. He also believed he could prove that Calamy had lied.

Walker thought Calamy's portrayal of the Act of Uniformity was deceptive, that it was only intended to scandalize the church. That scandal in turn was a dodge: by reducing the differences between the church and Nonconformists to those of clerical conformity, Calamy had skirted the more damning fact of their schism. No matter how Calamy criticized the act, all Nonconformists remained schismatics.[124] Walker did not distinguish the Nonconformists of the 1690's and 1700's from their Puritan predecessors. He lamented that Calamy's work was published "in the selfe same age with Harrington's Oceana, Ludlow's Memoirs, Milton's Works and Life, Oate's Picture of King James . . . Christianity not Mysterious . . . the world never saw more blasphemous books."[125] For the 1690's had seen the "Principles of 1641 (and even those of 1648 [1649]) . . . plainly and openly revived . . . afresh recommended, or now first handed to the world."[126] Nor did Walker distinguish the republican principles of Puritans such as Ludlow from those of "deistical republicans" such as Toland, much less from the alibis of Titus Oates. If republicanism occurred in all of them, Calamy's protestations of the Nonconformists' loyalty to the government lost their trustworthiness.

This suspicion determined Walker's defense of the Act of Uniformity. He would stress its necessity in light of the violence done to the church during the war. He would prove that Calamy's men were the ones truly guilty of the retribution they "with unparalleled impudence charge on us."[127] Walker resolved to find sources that could obtain this end: the journals of the Rump Parliament and committees for the sequestration of ministers, accounts of the Triers and Ejectors, and those of Cromwell's commissioners at Oxford. He would search the Bodleian, the private libraries at Oxford and Cambridge, and the lists of wards and sequestrations. He usually followed these resolutions through, obtaining records such as John Nalson's transcripts of the Committee for Plundered Ministers.[128] Against Calamy, he would consider the acts, ordinances, proceedings, covenants, and engagements of the Interregnum to show how they were more cruel than the Act of Uniformity. In short, he would turn all of Calamy's own arguments against him.[129] Walker was convinced of his own objectivity in this regard. His standards of truth, combined with his Anglican piety, would conquer Calamy's martyrological ambitions. As a litany he circled the following command in his notebook:

To be sincere in the search for truth. Not to stifle and suppress the truth. Not to varnish over and aggravate what is truth beyond its due degree. To use no arguments which if turned I should not receive. TO use none which may be resented. TO say nothing only for the sake of wit. TO have constant regard to charity. Not to contemn and despise the adversary. To have a steady eye to God's word and continually beg his help, &c.[130]

Against Dissent and Calamy's frequent violations of "epistemological decorum," Walker would maintain a standard of truth appropriate to the gentle station of Anglicanism.[131]

If Walker did not always succeed in restraining his hatred, he at least recognized the need to do so for the sake of impartiality. The crimes against the church during the war, presented impartially, would justify the Act of Uniformity where drier debates over its interpretation had not.

Low-church writers such as John Ollyffe and Benjamin Hoadly had taken the latter route in their responses to Calamy. Ollyffe had sought to distance himself from both sides, against those who supported the "rigorous impositions complained of by the nonconformists" and against Calamy's overly literal interpretation of the Act's terms.[132] Walker defended the very vindictiveness of which Ollyffe complained by resorting instead to the recent and remembered past.

For his second attack upon Calamy, Walker went about reducing the number of ministers that Calamy alleged had suffered ejection under the terms of the Act of Uniformity. The denominationally motivated historical debates of his time required Walker to pay obeisance to truth and impartiality.[133] Yet his concern with an empirically quantifiable argument that was rooted in evidence from the war distinguished him from more talented Anglican contemporaries such as Burnet and Stillingfleet, who pursued more distant topics. Walker filled a notebook with the names of Nonconformists whom he thought he could disqualify from Calamy's list, based upon what he had received in response to the queries.[134] If a Nonconformist had been ejected but later conformed, Walker struck him from Calamy's list. He did the same if a Nonconformist had left his place at the Restoration in 1660: where Calamy had not, Walker made a firm technical distinction between the de facto ejections of the Restoration and those explicitly demanded by the Act of Uniformity. If a Nonconformist gave up his position voluntarily, Walker refused to admit him as ejected. If he were an Anabaptist or an Independent and consequently lacked episcopal ordination, Walker disqualified him, on the grounds that he held it illegally to begin with, thus invalidating Calamy's claim to ejection. Such ministers could not have held places according to the Elizabethan Act of Uniformity, Walker pointed out.[135] Finally, Walker examined the precise definition of the benefice held: if a Nonconformist held "only a curate," Walker disqualified him.[136] Walker suspected that more Nonconformists had lost their benefices as a result of politically exclusive legislation such as the Corporation Act than by the Act of Uniformity. He reduced Calamy's numbers to "500 at the most," which by his own calculations was one-sixteenth the number of Anglicans turned out during the war.[137]

If Walker could prove that the Act of Uniformity had ejected only one quarter the number of ministers that Calamy asserted, then it became more difficult for Calamy to describe it as vindictive and immoderate. And thus

Walker thought he would deprive Calamy of his quantitative attack upon the Act of Uniformity. The methods that Walker employed to reduce the number of Calamy's ejectees allowed him to typify them as extremists beyond hope of comprehension. Calamy had included scores of ejected ministers theologically beyond the Presbyterian pale, in order to achieve his number of 2,000; Walker turned this tactic against Calamy by showing how it contradicted his rendition of Nonconformity as moderate. These methods allowed Walker to discredit Calamy as a historian, by showing how his inflated numbers and his characterization of Nonconformity offended the truth. Inflation and partiality condemned historian and subject alike: for just as Walker's correspondents distrusted evidence supplied by old Puritans and their servants, Walker became convinced that Calamy could not tell the truth.

For his third rebuttal of Calamy's account, Walker planned a qualitative comparison of the Nonconformists and the episcopal clergy. His notes reveal a man viscerally inflamed by Nonconformist nostalgia, yet also calmly resolute in his empirical efforts against it.

Not soe many such prophane and sacrilegious intruders into the ministry, such factious, rebellious, virulent, heterodox, ignorant, hypocritical, fellonious & thievish, canting rogues in any 2000 ministers in the world as those 2000, which from the bottom of my heart I do believe to be a truth. So many were unordained. So many had eate the bread of starving familys so many had forwarded murder rebellion &c. compute each kind.[138]

Walker suspected that Calamy had falsified the number of Nonconformists, distorted their factiousness into irenicism, truncated their extremity into moderation, and transformed their ignorance into erudition.[139] Joshua Reynolds, Newte, Richard Davies, and White Kennett all criticized the character of Calamy's men and disqualified their legal right to their benefices.[140] More moderate churchmen shared Walker's contemptuous tone in assassinating Calamy's characters. Walker noted interim ministers for their humble trades, their lack of learning, or their scandalous lives. Yet he admitted to himself that "where a story seems improbable or is not certaine . . . there say I have been told, [or] I have heard it is reported." He refrained from putting questionable stories forward as true.[141] The descriptions Walker appended to the entries in his list of Calamy's Nonconformists ranged from simple disqualification to ranting, excursive, polemical biography. Moses Hodges received a line attesting only that he had conformed, whereas Walker spent eight pages attacking the infamous Cornelius Burges of Wells. He annotated both with references to letters and books that had mentioned them, especially Anthony á Wood's *Athenae Oxonienses.*[142]

In the *Adversaria Calamistica,* Walker digested the discrete memories of his correspondents into an encyclopedic refutation of Calamy's case for moderate and respectable Nonconformity. His biases were clear, but so was his industry: he was painstaking in his cross-referencing, annotation, and solicitation of letters, books, journals, and other sources. Walker believed he could demonstrate the menace of Dissent with certainty, as forcefully as he believed in the imperative need for such a demonstration. The *Adversaria* also suggests that Walker realized the shortcomings of his earlier attempt to better Calamy. The account of Anglican suffering that he intended to produce with his queries and the *Attempt* perhaps seemed too much like a martyrology to serve as a convincing refutation of Calamy's work and his methods. Such a realization may have led to his plan for the *Adversaria,* for though it was never published, the latter work provided a less ambiguous and more appropriate vehicle for his ambitions to impartiality and his empirical methods. This sort of critical history was rapidly becoming a favored genre for associating establishment propaganda with empiricism, science, reason, and gentility.[143] In the *Adversaria Calamistica,* Walker found a way to reject explicitly the old, providentialist paradigm which was itself too symptomatic of the Puritanism that had monopolized it in the public imagination. But he began working in the older, martyrological framework, at least formally, and never fulfilled the empirical plan of the *Adversaria.*

After twelve years of work and a decade of others goading him to finish, Walker finally published his *Attempt* in 1714. The first part provided a virulent high-church history of the Civil War, culled from Clarendon and royalist polemics published during the war and Interregnum. The second part presented the fruits of Walker's queries, an impressively extensive compendium of the sequestrations and ejections of Anglicans from their positions in the cathedrals, the universities, London, and the parochial parishes. Bishop Blackall of Exeter awarded Walker a D.D. for his efforts, but Walker's timing was wretched.[144] The death of Queen Anne in the same year brought an end to the dominance of the Tories in the government and their high-flying allies in the church. Nonetheless, Walker kept on working, receiving and collating letters as late as 1721, which suggests that he intended to publish a second edition. The Tory press hailed him as a successor to Foxe and recommended that his book be chained up in all churches.[145]

The compliment probably annoyed Walker. He attacked the Nonconformists as incessant memorialists in the first part of his *Attempt*. Yet something more than denominational bigotry motivated Walker's attack. In his opinion, the Nonconformists were not only idolaters of their own sufferings but empirically irresponsible idolaters as well. Their techniques of martyrology resembled "the undertaker's equipage, which serves indifferently for all funerals." Calamy offended the worst because he had been the most ambitious: his account had furnished Dissent with a calendar "beyond that of the Roman Church, with more than five times as many saints as there are days in the year."[146] Unwittingly Walker had miscalculated as well. In spite of his Baconian intentions, he compiled an Anglican memorial that even his fellow Anglicans and Tories perceived as an old-fashioned martyrology. Although he intended to memorialize Anglican sufferings from the war, he worked with equal earnestness to erase their Foxean glosses.

Walker's project and the letters he received testify to how vigorous the memory of the English Civil War remained 60 years later. Anglicans united around their own memories and those of their parishioners to ascertain the danger of Dissent. For Anglicans, this was a truth beyond the war's boundary. In pursuing this truth they created a pathology of error that ascribed intellectual, theological, and moral inferiority to Dissent as its inherent characteristics. Walker combined his fellow Anglicans' discrete and zealous memories with his own empirical ambitions. In trying to make this combination work, he took on a problem he could not solve; his anti-martyrology failed to dissociate the war from English habits of martyrological remembrance. His methods and failure illuminate the changing attitude of the Anglican establishment toward the meanings of sufferings and ultimately of historical facts themselves. Walker memorialized the war in a new way that rejected martyrology, in order to revere the war's memory in what he thought to be a superior fashion. Despite the assistance of the church and his many correspondents, his efforts ultimately failed, as his work faded almost immediately into obsolescence and obscurity. Yet his efforts against Calamy remain a salutary reminder to historians who study the effects of the Civil War. Walker's visceral loyalty to the church and his empirical faith in its superiority reinforced each other. That combination is not merely some relic from some "long twilight of sophistry" somehow separating the Age of Scripture from the Age of Reason.[147] Lest we forget, that is how many Anglicans first met the Enlightenment.

PART III

Religion and Locality

MURIEL C. MCCLENDON

Reconsidering the Marian Persecution

THE URBAN CONTEXT

The Reformation has long had a reputation as an era of intolerance and conflict. G. R. Elton characterized it as a period that "sharpened all conflicts and augmented persecution."[1] As western European Christianity began to fragment in the sixteenth century, early expressions of support for some type of religious tolerance from humanists gave way to religious bigotry and warfare. German peasants interpreted Luther's message to support their aims at social reform. This led to the bloody Peasants' War of 1524–25, in which thousands died. In England, Henry VIII executed Carthusian monks who refused to swear fealty to the Church of England of which he had declared himself Supreme Head in 1534. In France, the 1572 massacre of Protestants in Paris on St. Bartholomew's day spread throughout the country, taking thousands of lives. Religious tolerance, according to traditional interpretations, unfolded only gradually from the end of the sixteenth century, emerging out of a variety of factors such as skepticism and widespread exhaustion from confessional combat.

As real and dramatic as religious bigotry was, some scholars have recently challenged the conventional view that such prejudice and intolerance were hallmarks of the Reformation era.[2] Rather than concentrating on theorized expressions of the complete religious freedom that tolerance has come to represent in modern western societies, these scholars have sought to redefine and understand religious tolerance as a practice and to place it in its local, political, and social contexts.

Bob Scribner has found that in sixteenth-century Germany, incidents of what we now understand of tolerance arose out of a number of practical and contingent considerations, including concern for the maintenance of political and social stability, the inability to enforce religious uniformity and the toleration of religious minorities whose services proved economically beneficial. Scribner has also identified the existence of a practical toleration among ordinary people, "a good-natured acceptance that common folk could hardly be expected to agree on matters of belief since theologians could not reach any form of agreement."[3]

In sixteenth-century Strasbourg, the focus of Lorna Jane Abray's research, although city magistrates feared that religious diversity imperiled the stability of the city, they often tolerated confessional diversity to avert some larger disaster, which rendered such toleration unstable and erratic.[4] I have argued elsewhere that in England, the magistrates of Norwich also tolerated spiritual diversity as part of a pragmatic strategy to keep religious conflict from exploding into public controversies that would draw the English government and church authorities into the city's affairs and undermine civic autonomy and independence. This tolerance was never expressly articulated or codified in law and was also unstable and could not always be maintained.[5]

Such findings about the possibilities for different measures of religious tolerance and coexistence in the sixteenth century point to the need to reevaluate received notions about the Reformation era simply as "the age of a 'persecuting society.'" Just as tolerance depended upon varied and contingent circumstances, so too did persecution. Scribner has argued that persecution was often a matter of short-term conjunctures or expedience, rather than a permanent feature of European social, political, and religious life. Sixteenth-century Europe was subject, then, only to moments of persecutorial activity.[6]

This chapter will explore and highlight the contingent nature of religious persecution in the sixteenth century by focusing on events in England, particularly in the city of Norwich, during the campaign against Protestant heretics conducted between 1555 and 1558 by the government of Queen Mary Tudor. By the time of Mary's accession in 1553, Norwich was one locale where Protestantism had already put down strong roots.[7] It was also the seat of the diocese where more than 40 people were executed as heretics under Mary. Only in the diocese of London were more people put to death. Despite the strength of Protestantism in Norwich and its location in a diocese where heresy was hotly pursued and punished, the city largely escaped the full force of the Marian persecution. Only two residents of Norwich died as Protestant heretics and the records indicate that only one other was examined for unorthodox opinions. While Mary's government launched the most intense religious persecution that England had ever seen—nearly 300 people were put to death as heretics and thousands more were arrested and examined—the evidence from Norwich demonstrates that religious persecution was nevertheless piecemeal and limited. The legislative directive to arrest, examine and execute Protestant heretics did not result in a "sustained national campaign, masterminded from the centre," as Christopher Haigh has noted.[8] The Marian persecution of Protestants was conducted chiefly at the local level, and the process was shaped by a variety of local, political, and social factors. Consequently, persecution cannot be understood as the simple logical extension of religious antagonism rooted in doctrinal conflict. It was a phenomenon that must be placed in its local political and social context.

I

Mary Tudor ascended the throne of England in July 1553 determined to restore Roman Catholicism as the established religion and thus reverse the Protestant religious policies of her late half-brother, Edward VI. The religious innovations of Edward's six-year reign are well known. His government overturned the conservative religious legislation passed during the last years of Henry VIII's reign, including the Six Articles, the act restricting access to the Bible and heresy statutes. It also prohibited several customary ceremonies, such as the use of holy water and ashes, and dismantled all intercessory institutions, such as confraternities and chantries, at whose foundation lay the traditional Catholic doctrine of purgatory. The Edwardian regime replaced traditional religious practices with Protestant forms of worship. Parliament permitted the marriage of priests and passed two Acts of Uniformity in 1549 and 1552, which authorized and imposed the First and Second Books of Common Prayer, respectively. The 1549 Book introduced an English Mass service for the first time. In 1552, the Second Edwardian Prayer Book abolished the Mass and replaced it with a Holy Communion service. The Communion service lost the sacrificial character of the Mass; from 1552 it was deemed a memorial of Christ's original sacrifice. The doctrine of transubstantiation was thus rejected and the priest no longer performed the miracle that had been at the heart of the Mass.

Mary Tudor had remained a committed Catholic during her half-brother's reign, openly refusing to use the two Protestant Prayer Books imposed by his government. It was thus widely anticipated that she would seek England's official return to the Catholic religion when she became queen. Shortly after her accession, Mary showed the direction in which her government would move when she issued a proclamation on August 18, 1553, that expressed her desire that her subjects should follow her in the practice of the religion that "she has ever professed from her infancy hitherto." If the return of Catholicism was now certain, the persecution for which Mary's reign is often remembered was not, for she also promised not to compel her subjects about religion.[9]

Mary's first Parliament made her intentions in the realm of religion considerably clearer when it met in October 1553. It passed the First Act of Repeal, which rescinded Edwardian religious legislation, including the statute sanctioning clerical marriage, and reinstated Henrician religious worship. The following year, the queen's government took other major steps to complete the reversal of the Reformation. Mary issued royal injunctions to the bishops in March that covered a number of issues, from the suppression of "evil books" to the restoration of traditional clerical discipline to the reestablishment "all manner of processions of the Church" and the "laudable and honest ceremonies."[10]

In November 1554 the queen's third Parliament met. While earlier legislation had rescinded Henrician and Edwardian religious mandates, it did not nullify the break with Rome, which the queen so ardently desired. The process of reuniting England with the Roman Catholic Church picked up speed when England received Reginald Pole as a Cardinal and a papal legate. Pole came ready to lift the papal sentence of excommunication imposed on England when Henry VIII broke with the Church. To help smooth the way for Parliamentary repeal of all remaining antipapal legislation, Pole brought with him a papal dispensation allowing the current owners of former monastic lands to keep their new properties. With that assurance in hand, Parliament passed the Second Act of Repeal in November 1554, which formally restored papal supremacy in England.[11]

The third Parliament also passed a law against heresy, which dictated death for those who refused to submit to the Roman communion, a customary penalty for religious deviance across Europe.[12] That legislation not only encouraged the self-imposed exile of nearly 800 English Protestants that was already under way, but also set the stage for the trial and execution of Protestants that began in January 1555 and only ceased with Mary's death in 1558, and for which the queen's reign is often chiefly remembered.

As Christopher Haigh and Susan Brigden have pointed out, the nearly 300 executions carried out under that legislation went far beyond the queen's original expectations.[13] During the last official flurry of activity against heretics in England before the Reformation, bishops found that public abjuration and penance, combined with the execution of a handful of Lollards, served to suppress those heretical communities for years.[14] In 1554, the queen, her advisers, and churchmen undoubtedly believed that the course of persecution would be much the same.[15] A few extremists would be put to death, some more would publicly recant and these demonstrations would serve as a suitable warning of the dangers of religious schism, driving the remaining heretics back to the true faith or, at least, public conformity.

The queen and her churchmen hoped for reconciliation much more than they desired execution and martyrdom. Imprisoned Protestants were exhorted numerous times by their examiners to abandon their heresy. Sometimes they were visited in jail by a host of theologians, bishops, friends, and family, who tried to induce them to accept Catholicism as the one true religion or simply beg them to recant to save their own lives.[16] Some Protestants were initially released from episcopal custody with hopes for future conformity. Obstinate heretics had to be put to death and more than a few loyal Catholics were willing to participate by accusing and testifying against Protestants, sometimes even when they were neighbors, friends, or family members.

Unlike the Lollards in the earlier sixteenth century who had more readily retracted their opinions and disappeared from public life, the Protestants persecuted by Mary did not. They were too widespread and their church had just recently been England's official religion. The executed became martyrs, known for often being cheerfully willing to die for their beliefs. Their surviving coreligionists were, in fact, driven to worship in secret cells and conventicles. Rather than breaking them, the persecution only strengthened their commitment. In addition, the burnings often inspired sympathy for the victims and a reaction against the queen, thus encouraging still more criticism and defiance of her rule. Mary's examiners quickly learned that Protestant disobedience had become more resolute and organized as a subversive underground, and this only magnified the imperative to burn willing and unrepentant heretics. From there the cycle accelerated, turning initially hesitant examiners into eager participants in the persecutorial process, which only created more martyrs for the Protestant cause. And so the burnings stretched from February 1555 until just before the queen's death in November 1558.

II

As the burnings of heretics began in early 1555, the city of Norwich was surprisingly quiet. Since the reign of Henry VIII there had been interest in religious reform and Protestantism among the city's residents, some of it fairly vocal. The controversial Thomas Bilney had occasionally preached in the city from the late 1520's. He was later executed there as an obstinate heretic in 1531, although most scholars now agree that Bilney's views were not, strictly speaking, unorthodox.[17] The cleric John Barret, an early convert to Protestantism, settled in Norwich in the mid-1530's as a member of the cathedral staff. The sermons he delivered soon after his arrival aroused considerable controversy.[18]

Local records also indicate that the city was the site, from the mid-1530's, of various conflicts and disputes over religious matters among local residents. During Henry VIII's reign, they questioned the nature of the priesthood, criticized official changes to religion enjoined by the King's government and violated traditional religious observances.[19] Under Edward, many local Protestants had been vocal in their support for the changes in religious doctrine and practice sanctioned by the King's government. Some even expressed their belief that religious reform had not gone far enough. Norwich mayor's court records contain several accounts of local iconoclasm, neglect of traditional religious observances, and conflicts over changing religious doctrines and practices among local residents.[20] The overwhelming majority of these controversies over religion in Norwich were handled by city magistrates, who actively contained them before they escalated out of control and attracted the attention of outside authorities, such as the local ecclesiastical hierarchy and the Crown.

Religious conflicts continued during the first year of Mary's reign, although they were muted. Fewer disputes came to the attention of city magistrates than during King Edward's lifetime. The magistrates handled most of these cases as they had in the past, working to check religious controversy, although there were a few notable exceptions.[21] However, when the heresy law passed in Parliament in January 1555, religious conflict virtually vanished from the pages of the mayor's court books. If religious nonconformists among city residents eluded punishment in the mayor's court after 1555, they also largely evaded prosecution by the central government and ecclesiastical authorities charged with eradicating Protestantism.

I I I

On July 13, 1557, Elizabeth Cooper was burned as a Protestant heretic at the Lollard's pit outside Norwich's Bishop's-gate. Cooper's execution followed scores of others around England since the implementation of the heresy statute in 1555, but hers, remarkably, was the first of a Norwich resident. Elizabeth Cooper was a pewterer's wife who had earlier forsworn her Protestant beliefs and then become "greatly troubled inwardly" by her actions. One day she interrupted a service at Saint Andrew's parish, the scene of her recantation, and publicly revoked it. She told the assembled worshipers that "she was heartily sorry that she ever did it [i.e., recanted], willing the people not to be deceived, neither to take her doings before for an example." An irate member of the Catholic congregation, "one Bacon," whose identity cannot be definitely established, insisted that city sheriff Thomas Sotherton, who was present at the service, place Cooper under arrest. He exclaimed, "Master sheriff! will you suffer this?" Sotherton placed Cooper under arrest and she was later condemned to death. She went to the stake along with one Simon Miller of King's Lynn, on July 13, 1557. Miller had been turned over to diocesan authorities by an unnamed "evil disposed papist" in Norwich, according to the martyrologist John Foxe, after he had arrived in the city and asked a group of people leaving a church "where he might go to have the communion."[22]

In the crowd that attended Miller and Cooper's execution was a young woman who exclaimed that "she would pledge them of the same cup that they drank on." That woman was Cicely Ormes, the wife of a worsted weaver from Saint Lawrence's parish in Norwich. Also in the crowd was "Master Corbet of Sprowston by Norwich," the former city recorder. Upon hearing Ormes's remark, Corbet turned her over to the chancellor of Norwich diocese, Michael Dunning.[23] Dunning examined her, inquiring into her views on transubstantiation. In response to the question "What is that that the priest holdeth over his head?" Ormes retorted, "It is bread: and if you make it any better, it is worse." Dunning sent her to the bishop's prison, where she was subjected to further examinations. He offered Ormes her freedom "if she would go to the church and keep her tongue," but she refused, "for God would surely plague her." Although he was reluctant to condemn "an ignorant, unlearned, and foolish woman," Dunning sentenced Cicely Ormes to death. He committed her to the custody of sheriffs Thomas Sotherton and Leonard Sotherton, who placed her in the Guildhall prison, where she lingered for over a year. Ormes recanted her beliefs at one point, but recommitted herself to Protestantism. She died bravely, according to Foxe, on September 23, 1558, before a crowd of 200 spectators.[24]

Cooper and Ormes were the only two Norwich inhabitants put to death in the Marian persecution. A third person was examined for heresy by ecclesiastical authorities in 1558 and then abjured the "errors, heresies and damnable opinions" of which he stood accused. In a signed retraction, the grocer Thomas Wolman, of Saint Andrew's parish, repudiated his belief that the Protestant martyr Thomas Carman, who was executed in Norwich along with two others in May 1558, had "died well for that he did affirm and say that he did believe that Christ was not present in the Sacrament of the altar." Carman, a plowright from nearby Heigham, was sentenced to death for pledging support for Richard Crashfield, a Protestant from Wymondham, Norfolk, who was burnt at Norwich in August 1557. Wolman was released after abjuring his opinions and came to no further harm, dying in the early days of Elizabeth's reign.[25]

These three incidents involving Cooper, Ormes, and Wolman occupy little space in John Foxe's *Acts and Monuments*, commonly called the *Book of Martyrs*. Despite East Anglia's reputation for Protestant fervor, none of the three Norwich victims of persecution became well known. Nevertheless, Foxe's narratives of their tribulations, based on correspondence and interviews conducted in the early days of Elizabeth's reign, provide important evidence for understanding the exceptional nature of persecution in Norwich.

A close examination of how Cooper and Ormes were discovered, accused and then responded to examination (there is no information concerning the apprehension of Thomas Wolman) reveals the very tenuous structure of the persecutorial apparatus in Norwich. The stories we have from Foxe of their arrest and execution are highly unusual. In contrast to many other communities where the persecution was more systematic and aggressive, the two executions in Norwich only occurred because of several peculiar contingencies. Indeed, the two victims' public self-incrimination was instrumental in this respect, making it seem that with a little bit more discretion there would have been no executions of Norwich residents.

Elizabeth Cooper and Cicely Ormes were arrested only because they stood up, Cooper in church and Ormes at Cooper's execution, and publicly announced their adherence to Protestantism. No one had betrayed them or reported their heresy to the authorities, nor had the civil or ecclesiastical powers discovered them through an investigation. Cooper was not being examined when she renounced her recantation; she walked into a "popish service," as Foxe called it, and incriminated herself before the entire congregation of her own free will. This was only barely enough to bring her down in Norwich. When the irate Bacon complained and forced sheriff Sotherton to arrest Cooper, Foxe tells us the Protestant sheriff "was very loath to do it," for he and Cooper "had been servants together before in one house, and for the friendship he bare unto her, and the more for the gospel's sake."[26]

Ormes's apprehension was much like Cooper's. She acted in a similar manner, voluntarily announcing her support of Cooper, the outsider Simon Miller, and their beliefs in full view of the townspeople, including civil and ecclesiastical officials, assembled for Cooper's and Miller's execution. This public statement must have been heard by several people who would have wanted to see her punished. However, it is worth noting that, as Foxe tells the story, John Corbet, a former city Steward and Recorder, was the one who immediately detained Ormes and turned her over to Chancellor Dunning. One wonders if Ormes would have met the same fate had Corbet not been present. As it happened, Ormes was executed for her indiscreet public remarks about Cooper's execution, which occurred only because Cooper incriminated herself in open church.

The chain of serious persecution under the heresy statute in Norwich depended on the weak links of self-incrimination, bad timing, and Ormes's reaction to Cooper's execution. The third victim of persecution at this time, Thomas Wolman, was also detained for his reaction in support of a burned heretic who was an outsider. In much of England, this kind of chain reaction against executions set in motion more investigations, examinations, and executions. This did not happen in Norwich, where no heresy hunt followed Cooper's and Ormes's executions. Their executions serve to underscore the rarity of such persecution in Norwich. The special contingencies on which their executions depended highlight the problem of understanding how and why Norwich, a well-known home of many Protestants, escaped large-scale persecution.

I V

Unlike Elizabeth Cooper and Cicely Ormes, most of the Marian martyrs were taken into custody through the efforts of lay authorities. Philip Hughes's analysis of the circumstances surrounding the capture of martyrs listed in Foxe's *Acts and Monuments* reveals that secular officials were responsible for close to 60 percent of those arrests. When secular magistrates were not involved, the next most common way in which Protestant suspects were apprehended was betrayal by a family member, friend, or neighbor. Hughes found that such betrayals accounted for almost 13 percent of the executions.[27]

If the burnings ultimately had the effect of turning many English people against Mary's religious policies as many historians have claimed, it was nevertheless the case that magistrates and lay people played a critical role in making the Marian persecution possible. As David Loades has commented, "the persecution involved a massive administrative and judicial effort by both the ecclesiastical and secular authorities in East Anglia and the Home Counties, with thousands of detections, investigations, and interrogations behind the hundreds of trials."[28] The system of lay courts, church courts, and royal commissions could be set in motion by just a single accusation against a suspected Protestant.

The diocese of Norwich was active in hunting down and trying heretics throughout Norfolk and Suffolk, but not in Norwich. Ralph Houlbrooke has described the nature of the persecution in Norwich diocese as "spasmodic" and "geographically limited." Official persecution was intermittent, with four major eruptions of activity: the spring and summer of 1555, the spring of 1556, the winter of 1556–57, and the spring of 1558. Houlbrooke relates the first two waves to diocesan and metropolitical visitations, but suggests that the last two were motivated by local concerns. The majority of the diocese's victims were from rural areas. Consequently, Houlbrooke writes, "the major towns of the diocese, with the exception of Ipswich, were hardly affected." Ipswich, he notes, was home to a large number of Protestants, but this leaves us to wonder why other towns with many Protestants did not see nearly as many investigations and executions. Houlbrooke adds that Bishop Hopton, the chief proponent of the diocesan persecution in 1556, even departed from Ipswich before completing his investigations, "much preferring to deal with heretics from rural mid-Suffolk."[29]

Although Houlbrooke's study of church courts does not include detailed histories of the diocese's many villages and towns, he suggests that the persecution's irregular geographical pattern was rooted in local historical circumstances, even during the first two waves of examination sponsored by the bishop's and archbishop's offices. He observes that "it is significant that according to Foxe's account there were a large number of persecuting justices of the peace in Suffolk," where the suppression of Protestantism was fast and furious. This again highlights the important role of civil authorities and local sociopolitical conditions in the campaign against heresy. Although Norwich was the diocesan seat and known to harbor many Protestants, all of the evidence indicates that the civic authorities who resided in the shadow of the bishop's palace abstained from participation in the Marian persecution of Protestant heretics.[30]

It is tempting to speculate that the reason that Norwich's civic authorities did not participate in the Marian persecution is because they formed a solidly Protestant body that sought to protect the strongly Protestant local population. However, that was simply not the case. The civic leadership in Norwich had been religiously divided since the 1530's, and the available evidence indicates that such divisions continued into the Marian era as well. The only evidence concerning magisterial religious allegiances in Norwich comes from wills, and thirteen survive that were composed in the Marian period.[31] These documents are subject to a number of interpretative problems. On the one hand, Protestant testators who opposed the prevailing religious settlement could have been hesitant to declare their religious sentiments openly. They might have been even more reluctant to do so once the burnings began. Neutral will preambles (i.e., ones that committed a soul to God alone or to God and Christ with no mention of the saints or the Virgin) would not have aroused suspicion and potentially exposed family members to persecution. On the other hand, even committed Catholic testators might have been averse to making provisions for traditional services or to leaving money for traditional church ornaments in their wills, fearing a future reversal of Mary's religious policies. Despite these inherent difficulties, the wills written during Mary's reign nevertheless indicate that there was not complete agreement among Norwich's magistrates on religious matters.

Eight of the thirteen aldermanic wills offer evidence of Catholic allegiance. Their testators invoked the saints and/or left money for masses to be said for their souls. The religious sentiments of the remaining five testators are more difficult to evaluate, as they neither called upon the saints nor bequeathed money for anniversary masses. While there are some small clues about these writers' sentiments—alderman Thomas Gray left a small legacy to the clergyman John Barret, who reembraced Catholicism under Mary—it is clear from the surviving wills that there were Catholic aldermen in Norwich who could have participated in the Marian efforts to eradicate Catholicism if they had so desired.[32]

While Norwich was the home to a substantial Protestant community, Catholic residents also could have taken part in the suppression of Protestantism if they had chosen to take the initiative. In addition, the examples of Elizabeth Cooper and Cicely Ormes make clear that, in each case, one person secured the arrest that ultimately resulted in their executions after they incriminated themselves. John Corbet alone took Ormes to the diocesan chancellor for examination after her outburst at Cooper's burning. When the Saint Andrew's parishioner Bacon insisted that the reluctant sheriff arrest Elizabeth Cooper, Sotherton had to comply or risk serious danger to himself. Thus, not only did the magistrates fail to root out Protestants, but their willingness to accept religious heterogeneity appears to have had some support from the populace.

Thus, the Marian persecution simply did not get off the ground in Norwich. Despite the presence of ample Protestants and Catholics, only two Protestants were executed, few were even examined, and only one is known for certain to have gone into exile.[33] What factors, then, contributed to the unusual course of persecution in Marian Norwich?

There are few, if any, extended analyses of urban politics and religion during the Marian persecution, and so it is difficult to compare Norwich with many other towns on this point. Indeed, it might be that the Marian persecution was lighter in towns than in the countryside, despite the usual association of Protestantism with urban areas. Ralph Houlbrooke's study suggests that most towns in Norfolk and Suffolk escaped the brunt of the persecution because of reluctant local authorities. In Bristol, Martha Skeeters has found some evidence that the "mayor and aldermen had attempted to dissociate themselves from the burnings" of the four to eight residents put to death there. As evidence she points to the magistrates' refusal to worship at the cathedral whose chancellor directed Bristol's heresy trials and the consequent reproach that the magistrates received from the Privy Council on the eve of the last execution in the city.[34]

The city for which there is the most research on religion and politics during this period is London. According to Susan Brigden, London experienced more burnings than any other place in England, and more local residents were executed than any other locale. The difference between Norwich, where there was so little persecution, and London probably cannot be explained by the depth or intensity of religious belief, either for Catholics or Protestants. There was no shortage of unhappy Protestants in Norwich during Mary's reign, just as there was no shortage of unhappy Catholics during Edward's. Instead, it is necessary to identify the conjunctural factors of politics, society, and belief that made persecution possible in a given time and place. Thinking about persecution as a practice, differences in such local factors as familiarity, trust, civic solidarity, the presence of central government and the political traditions of urban ruling groups helps to explain why London and Norwich followed such different courses during the Marian persecution.

In her study of religious conflict in the capital, Brigden estimates that 32 Londoners died in the fires. Hundreds more were investigated and examined for heresy.[35] London's population was probably eight to nine times greater than Norwich's in the mid-Tudor period, but sixteen times the number of Norwich victims were executed in the persecutions, and the proportion arrested for religious reasons was many times greater.[36] In addition, approximately 40 more men and women from other parts of England were also put to death in the capital. Still more were sent there for examination. This illustrates London's central role in the persecution. The heresy statute originated there, more victims came from London than any other town, and the number of outsiders who met their deaths in the capital exceeded the number of native martyrs. Some of these outsiders had moved to London or were passing through, but others were transported to the capital for their interrogation and trial. London attracted many immigrants from around the country because it was England's biggest and most cosmopolitan city and its economic and political center. Because it was the seat of central authority, London also pulled the unwilling into its administrative hands. In both ways, London differed consequentially from Norwich.

Norwich remained a provincial city in which the distinction between city residents and migrants from the countryside appeared sharply maintained in the differential treatment given outsiders, as the case of Simon Miller suggests. London, on the other hand, could not so readily uphold a similar sense of corporate unity and civic identity. Its population was much more mobile and expanding than Norwich's and, as the seat of the kingdom, London had to play host to visitors from around the country and from the Continent. Brigden's study of London during the Reformation tells us much about conflict and the breakdown of community caused by confessional division. Yet, as this study of Norwich and several others of Continental towns show, the fact of confessional division alone cannot fully explain urban disturbance. A more focused study of urban society and its institutions in London shows that the challenges to community were not just religious and that, in some important ways, communal solidarity survived.[37] This could help to explain Brigden's seemingly contradictory conclusions about the pervasiveness of religious conflict during the Reformation and some Londoners' reluctance to accuse one another during the Marian persecution.

As the country's administrative center, with heretics from around the provinces being brought there for examination, the anti-heresy campaign could not possibly have bypassed London as it did Norwich. Edmund Bonner himself was painfully aware of the expectations placed on him during the persecutions, for as bishop of London he had to examine many suspects, many of whom were sent to him directly by the Privy Council. In the early days of the burnings, he was hesitant about his responsibilities in the persecutorial effort. The bishop lamented to the future martyr John Philpot that the vigilance of the Court limited his ability to avoid the unpleasant task of pursuing and punishing heretics. Bonner was right, for he was later officially scolded for allowing too many heretics to slip from his grasp undisciplined.[38]

Bishop Bonner's personal history also illustrates the dynamic cultural process of persecution. From his initial reluctance to burn Protestants, Bonner became a most eager proponent of the practice. First he had been forced to start because of his position in London, then he became the target of Protestant criticism. As Brigden observes, "the wilfulness and obduracy and teasing of the godly goaded him."[39] This same process of constructing a culture of persecution affected many others from the queen down to some local magistrates and residents. Practicing such a draconian policy inherently tended to raise the stakes of the game for all involved. Once Protestantism was defined as heresy and Protestants were identified and executed, their threat to Church and state only increased. In addition, once the process of apprehending heretics had begun, the failure to follow through would potentially endanger one's own safety. For this reason, the process of hunting heretics was very difficult to stop once it gained momentum. Even the reluctant Sheriff Sotherton in Norwich felt compelled to arrest and preside over the July 1557 execution of the unfortunate Elizabeth Cooper, more than two years since the first burning in London and after 28 Londoners had already been consumed by the flames. Perhaps if the Marian burnings had continued, instead of slowing to a halt just before the queen's death, the pressures to persecute would have become overwhelming in Norwich. As it happened, civil and ecclesiastical officials found the pressure to persecute irresistible in London from an early date, while those in Norwich did not.

London officials and residents may have been more responsive to the Marian call for persecution partly because they had engaged in comparable acts in the past, though with less serious consequences in the cost of human life. London's magistrates had long been involved in efforts to impose religious uniformity. During Henry VIII's reign, they presided over the arrests and imprisonment of hundreds of Londoners under the terms of the Six Articles. Under Mary, hundreds of Protestant suspects were routinely arrested by aldermen's deputies and sergeants.[40]

Brigden's interpretation of the Marian burnings is subtle and often difficult to track, especially on the subject of how heretics were betrayed and how cross-devotional solidarity emerged in the face of the persecution despite her emphasis on the Reformation's destruction of community. While Brigden notes that Marian persecutors such as Bonner typically took action "upon information given to them rather than searching out and arresting suspects themselves," she reports that the identities of the informants are still mostly unknown. She reports that certain "Judas-like promoters" of Catholicism were identified as betrayers by chroniclers such as Foxe, but she adds that "of Londoners delating their fellow citizens there is almost no evidence." When Protestants were reported, as during the 1554 visitation, it was often the troublemakers, disliked for other reasons than their religion alone, who were named.[41] She appears to be distinguishing between common Londoners and the most devoted advocates of Catholicism, between Protestants persecuted only for heresy and those who troubled Catholics in additional ways, as well as between persecution in general and the rash of burnings under Mary. As Brigden explains, "Citizens might draw back from accusing their neighbors of heresy" when the punishment was death, "but the old suspicions and grievances harboured against confessional enemies did not go away."[42] Cross-devotional solidarity in London only went so far, as it nevertheless led the country in burnings.

If Catholic Londoners were sometimes reluctant to send their neighbors to the stake, Brigden recounts how they "found other ways of persecuting the gospellers," forcing them, for example, to finance the reequipment of parish churches for Catholic worship or harassing them with other charges.[43] In the end, Brigden reports that "the Marian persecution, and its aftermath, left much bitterness and much guilt."[44] Persecution once started, institutionalized, and sustained in London would not subside so easily. But in Norwich, where there was so little persecution during Mary's reign or before, there were only slight grounds for lingering resentments.

RICHARD L. GREAVES

The "Great Persecution" Reconsidered

THE IRISH QUAKERS AND THE
ETHIC OF SUFFERING

The concept of the "period of the great persecution," to use Gerald Cragg's phrase, has shaped much of the thinking about the era from 1660 to 1689.[1] The persecution was real enough, but how extensive and intense was it? This chapter will examine the evidence with respect to the Friends in Ireland, most of whom were of English descent, and their ethic of suffering. Other Nonconformists experienced varying degrees of persecution in this period, but none of them maintained systematic records, making it impossible to compare their degrees of suffering with those of the Friends. In general, however, such evidence as we do have suggests that all Protestant Dissenters had the benefit of de facto toleration throughout most of the period under review, although the Scottish Presbyterians less so because the government perceived them to be a threat to security.

Recent historiography about persecution in early modern Europe has demonstrated that toleration did not develop progressively,[2] and late seventeenth-century Ireland was no exception. As in the sixteenth-century European context, toleration in practice was pragmatic, "a working compromise that could be altered if and when circumstances allowed."[3] Toleration in late Stuart Ireland was broken by intermittent waves of persecution that typically were responses to political threats. The Irish situation, I shall argue, was no less marked by generally divergent attitudes toward Quakers and other Nonconformists on the part of civil authorities, who were normally tolerant, and Church of Ireland clerics, most of whose leaders maintained a drumbeat of protest against toleration.

I

From the beginning, the Quakers defined themselves in oppositional terms, as proponents of the inner light against the forces of darkness,
of spiritual worship against human inventions, of the true church against
the congregations of Satan, of spiritual baptism against baptism by water,
of holy living against reputed holy days, of plain speaking against oaths
and artifices. As participants in the Lamb's War, they looked on the world
in militant terms—an arena in which they engaged for the truth against the
legions of darkness.[4] "My Bretheren," John Perrot exhorted the Friends in
Ireland, "yee have a Battayle to fight." William Penn employed similar imagery to urge Quakers to remain steadfast: "As an Army with Banners his
Glorious power may make you, Against whome none of the many Weapons formed against you may prosper." And from James Nayler, this advice:
"Fight against whatever would draw you from ['the Way . . . into the Kingdom of Heaven'], and with violence break through it, and take the Kingdom."[5] Similar rhetoric peppers Quaker writings.

The corollary to this confrontational stance was an expectation of—and
a need for—suffering. Indeed, like other Nonconformists the Friends developed an ethic of suffering.[6] To undergo persecution was a necessary,
even a somewhat welcome element of their being. The more a believer is
persecuted, averred Isaac Penington, the greater the spiritual blessing.
"The World's Dislike, Enmity and Persecution is an evidence of God's
choice, and of a Removal from it towards God." The only true disciples,
Penn insisted, were those who bore the cross daily, following Christ
through afflictions, trials, and temptations. "No cross, no crown," he entitled one of his books.[7] "Better to suffer outwardly in prisons, and holes,"
reflected John Audland, "& have the love and presence of the Lord with us,
then to disobey the Lord, and walk contrary to his gift, and so suffer inward anguish and sorrow of heart, and something separate us from the love
of God." As prisoners in Dublin awaiting banishment in 1656, Francis
Howgill and Edward Burrough exhorted Friends in Ireland to "fly not the
Judgement: but dwell in it."[8] The early Quakers used their sufferings in a
theological *apologia* to justify divine retribution on both rulers and ruled in
repressive states. "In our sufferings," Burrough explained in May 1660,
"must be filled up the measure of the iniquities, both of Rulers and People

in this Nation, that the Lord may over-turn them with his hand, when their measure of oppression is finished, and the burden of its guilt falls upon them."[9] Suffering was providential. The Quakers also needed some persecution as confirmation of their status as children of the light, as proof that their campaign in the Lamb's War was not moribund and as the context in which they could freely fulfill their duty to testify against oppression. Suffering was a public act, a necessary, visible manifestation of their inner commitment to God. "Dissent was a drama," as Sharon Achinstein aptly reflects, "in which preserving the inner realm of conscience alone was not enough to define human freedom; actions in public mattered."[10] To testify was, in part, to suffer.

Notwithstanding the importance of the ethic of suffering and the Quakers' fundamental opposition to everything that was not in harmony with the Spirit, their ability to develop a rational organizational structure and to expand in Ireland owed much to the government's willingness to grant them de facto toleration during most of the late seventeenth century. Indeed, some persecution occurred, but it was sporadic and largely local. As early as late 1656, government officials began to discount the Friends as a serious threat. Barry Reay's contention that fear of the Quakers was a powerful factor in bringing about the Restoration[11] does not apply to Ireland, where references to the Friends in this context were inconsequential.

I I

Virtually from their arrival in Ireland in 1654 in search of converts, the Friends challenged the Cromwellian authorities to heed their prophetic call to repentance. The first historian of those events, the Quaker Thomas Wight, remarked only that Miles Bateman, Miles Halhead, and James Lancaster "had some service with the chief rulers and officers of the army," but judging from the brevity of their stay, their reception must have been chilly.[12] In the meantime, the ex-soldier William Edmundson, who had emigrated to Ireland at his brother's suggestion to become a trader, quietly began to gather believers into the country's first Quaker meeting. When John Tiffin visited the island later in 1654, he and Edmundson traveled about in search of converts, and "the priests and people began to be alarmed and in a rage." Other Friends followed, including Elizabeth Fletcher and Elizabeth Smith, who persuaded Captain James Sicklemore and Lieutenant Robert Sandham to embrace Quaker tenets. Additional officers, including Captains Edward Cook, Thomas Holme, William Morris, and Robert Wilkinson, made similar commitments.[13]

The initial reaction among the authorities was mixed. At Dublin the lord mayor imprisoned Smith and Fletcher, and at Lurgan the governor had Edmundson beaten. In Derry, however, the governor attended two meetings convened by Edmundson and Richard Clayton, acknowledged the truth of their message, and treated them kindly. Similarly, the governor of Cork, Colonel Robert Phaire, dealt amicably with the Friends and permitted them to proselytize among his troops.[14] Deeming the Friends the spiritual descendants of the Puritans and proponents of an ongoing spiritual reformation, Major Richard Hodden, governor of Kinsale, urged Henry Cromwell, commander of the Irish army, to reward virtue by looking with sympathy on the Quakers. They should be encouraged to settle in Ireland, a "wast Land" that Hodden envisioned as a place of "Comfortable habitations for Religious English men."[15]

Some two months after Hodden wrote this letter, Howgill and Burrough arrived in August, and almost immediately Howgill sent an epistle to the magistrates and people of Dublin, warning them to heed the word of God. In an undated epistle "to all the dominion of Ireland," probably composed shortly thereafter, Howgill likened the governors, magistrates, officers, and soldiers to an ax that God used to cut down his enemies:

He cut them off, to plant you in, he threw them downe, to raise you up, as he hath done the most of you, from a low Estate, to a high, and hath given you power. Now you are abusing of it, to the Exalting of yourselves, & your wills. . . . Are not you in the Same Nature, they were?

Howgill lashed out at their defense of professional clergy—hirelings whom they supported, he averred, because their gospel allowed authorities to persecute Dissenters. The powerful were not to attempt to suppress the Quakers, "for doe what you can, they will grow upon you, as Israel of old."[16] Writing to essentially the same audience in October 1655, Burrough was no less uncompromising in his jeremiad, admonishing rulers, magistrates, and judges that if they did not heed his call to repent, their blood would be on their own hands and their posterity forever.[17]

By mid-December, ten months after his father had issued a proclamation in England directed against Quakers who disturbed the services of other Christians, Henry Cromwell had heard enough. At that point he was still seeking to reconcile moderates and radicals, especially Baptists, whose principal strength was in the army. Cracking down on the Quakers, whose efforts to win adherents from the gathered churches had sparked animosity, was politically popular. On December 17, Cromwell ordered the arrest of Friends, and in the ensuing wave of persecution the government cashiered Quaker officers and soldiers, imprisoned Friends, and banished some of them. Explaining his actions in February 1656, Cromwell contended that Quaker principles were inconsistent with military discipline and to some extent even with civil government. Moreover, the Friends' "counterfeited simplicitie" made him suspect that they were plotting against the state. Limerick's governor, Colonel Henry Ingoldsby, was of the same mind, deeming Quakers a "wild yett subtill & designeinge generation off people."[18]

Howgill and Burrough were among those sent to prison and ultimately banished, but they remained obdurate. While incarcerated, they penned a defiant epistle to the military officers and "all the honest hearted" in Dublin and elsewhere, insisting they had been falsely convicted and demanding to be tried by the law of equity and righteousness. In a separate epistle to Cromwell, the Council, and their "Teachers," Burrough castigated them as perverters of God's law: "The hand of the Lord god in Vengeance is against you, and will upon you be accomplished."[19] Not surprisingly, therefore, the Friends saw the Cromwellian administration in Ireland in a harsh light, as an enemy of God and an impediment to the proclamation of truth. Nevertheless, as persecution declined after 1656, the Friends concentrated their attacks on fellow sectaries and the populace in general, not the magistracy and the military. The recorded number of imprisoned Quakers dropped sharply, from 77 in 1655 to 15 in 1656, 5 in 1657, 3 in 1658, and 1 in 1659.[20] Once the Friends had been removed from the ranks of the military, the government no longer considered them a security threat.

Unlike their counterparts in England, Friends in Ireland left little record of their expectations and reactions at the Restoration, perhaps because of the rapidity with which it occurred.[21] A military cabal seized Dublin Castle in December 1659, ending half a year of radical rule. On February 15, 1660, Sir Charles Coote and 54 officers issued a declaration that included a condemnation of Quakers and Baptists. Two months later, the Friends were expelled from Galway, and throughout the island Quakers were imprisoned—at least 124 in this year of restoration.[22] The suddenness with which the events and the accompanying crackdown on the Friends occurred is reflected in Edmundson's terse comment: "Now was King Charles coming in, and these Nations were in Heaps of Confusion, and ran upon us, as if they would have destroyed us at once, or swallowed us up."[23]

In a letter to George Fox dated August 17, 1660, Thomas Loe provided an overview of the persecution, including its uneven impact. By the time Loe wrote, some Friends in Dublin had been in prison nearly three months, and coreligionists were also jailed at Cork, Limerick, Bandon, and Waterford. Yet he knew of none who had been confined for anything except refusal to pay tithes, and meetings in central and northern Ireland were actually increasing in size.[24]

The beleaguered Quaker community in southern and western Ireland received support from several leading Friends. Burrough returned in June 1660, a month after composing a powerful work entitled *A Visitation and Presentation of Love unto the King, and Those Call'd Royallists.* In it he castigated the Interregnum rulers as hypocrites who had failed to liberate the people from their yokes of bondage. At the outset of the Civil War, the parliamentarian cause had not been unjust, he insisted, for the king had been responsible for "a great measure of Iniquity and Oppression." Yet Charles's opponents "went beyond (in Violence and Cruelty upon you) what the Lord called them unto." Victorious, they became oppressors, casting down and exalting whomever they wished, "rowling up and down in Confusion" while the nation groaned under a vexatious burden. Burrough shed no tears at the fall of the Interregnum government.[25]

For Burrough, Charles's restoration was not only reasonable and equitable but also divinely ordained. "It is Equal as in the Lord, that he should be restored who hath been removed & cast out by such as have pretended to Govern & Rule better than he, but have ruled in Oppression & Injustice, & not answered the cause wherefore he was cast out; & that he should come in to be a Scourge upon these, this is just." While acknowledging Charles's headship over the nation in civil matters, Burrough put the new regime on notice that if the king ruled tyrannically or unrighteously, the Friends would speak out against him but not seek his overthrow by physical force. Like all Quakers, Burrough refused to recognize royal supremacy in the church or accept the government's power to enact laws concerning faith and worship. Rather than obey unjust commands, the Friends would suffer.[26] The ethic of suffering was thus conjoined with the recently formulated peace principle to provide the foundation for Quaker behavior in the civil state. This is the message Burrough took with him when he returned to Ireland in June 1660. He reiterated it in a classic jeremiad to the people of Ireland entitled *The Everlasting Gospel of Repentance and Remission of Sins.*

John Perrot, who had been in Ireland in 1655–56 and subsequently remained in contact with Irish Friends, was unable to return in 1660 because he was a prisoner in Rome. Nevertheless, from his cell he sent an epistle on July 3 exhorting them to "keep your meetings & let the zeale burne in the house of god, . . . & minds will be melted, & the drose Cast back, & god increased in the furnace" of persecution. He would return to Ireland for several months in early 1662.[27]

I I I

The fate of Quakers—and Protestant Nonconformists in general—rested largely in the hands of the Convention and then of the successive lords lieutenant: the duke of Ormond (1662–69), John Baron Robartes (1669–70), John Lord Berkeley of Stratton (1670–72), the earl of Essex (1672–77), Ormond again (1677–85), the earl of Clarendon (1685–87, following the brief administration of Archbishop Michael Boyle of Dublin and the earl of Granard), and the earl of Tyrconnell (1687–89, technically as lord deputy). Generally, the lords lieutenant pursued a policy of de facto toleration, especially toward the smaller dissenting groups, namely, the English Presbyterians, the Congregationalists, the Baptists, and the Quakers. This was not a policy rooted in a theory of toleration but the outgrowth of pragmatic considerations, tempered only when Nonconformists were viewed as a security threat.[28] Because of the Scottish Presbyterians' numbers (approximately 22,000 in some 88 congregations), their concentration in northern Ireland across the narrow channel from Scotland, and their links with dissidents in that country, they provoked the greatest concern in government circles, whereas the smaller bodies were worrisome only when conspiracy threatened. Particularly in the Dublin area, the Quakers earned a solid reputation as businessmen and artisans, especially as the guilds were gradually opened to them in the 1670's and 1680's. The de facto toleration of Quakers and their economic success were inextricably related, as each had the practical effect of encouraging the other. For the most part, Church of Ireland clerics argued against toleration for Dissenters. Their hostility stemmed partly from religious principles, particularly their commitment to the ideal of a united Protestant church, but they were motivated as well by anger over their treatment in the 1650's and, especially in the north, concern about the destabilizing effect of the Scottish Presbyterians. Jeremy Taylor, bishop of Down and Connor, mocked what the king himself had referred to as liberty for tender consciences, likening it to a disease that

must be cured by anodynes and soft usages, unless they prove ineffective, and that the Lanncet [then] be necessary. But there are amongst us such tender stomacks, that cannot endure Milk, but can very well digest Iron; Consciences so tender, that a Ceremony is greatly offensive, but Rebellion is not; a Surplice drives them away as a bird affrighted with a man of clouts, but their Consciences can suffer them to despise Government, and speak evil of Dignities, and curse all that are not of their Opinion, and disturb the peace of Kingdomes, and commit Sacrilege, and account Schisme the character of Saints.[29]

Directing his anti-toleration arguments primarily against the Presbyterians, John Bramhall, archbishop of Armagh, warned that Presbyterian polity would lead to the oppression of common people by high commissions in every parish and to the imposition of tyrannical authority on everyone, including the monarch. Nonconformists in general, he charged, failed to distinguish between "essences and abuses" in churches and thus plunged kingdoms into bloodshed because of disagreement over innocent, legally established rites.[30] From conventicles, a manifestation of schism in the church, came sedition in the state, admonished George Wild, bishop of Derry. Such examples could be multiplied many times over. Yet the wall of opposition against toleration among Anglican clerics had a few cracks, as reflected in the grudging willingness of Robert Price, bishop of Ferns and Leighlin, for the state to grant a degree of liberty to all Protestant Dissenters except Presbyterians as long as they were peaceful and disturbed neither church nor state. The same could not be granted to the Presbyterians because they were "a restlesse generation" that could only be "managed" by legal coercion.[31]

In contrast to this nearly monolithic hostility to toleration for Nonconformists, lay leaders tended to repress dissent only when the regime's stability was shaky, as at the Restoration, or threatened, as by the 1663 Dublin conspiracy, the Galloway and Bothwell Bridge rebellions in Scotland, the Rye House plotting, and the Argyll and Monmouth insurrections. In 1660 and 1661, there was a flurry of concern about those Ormond referred to as "Phanatiqe & disaffected persons."[32] Indeed, even the Presbyterian minister Samuel Cox warned about "giddy phanatick spirits," but in January 1661 the lords justices and Council lumped Presbyterians with Quakers, Baptists, Independents, and Catholics in a ban on illegal assemblies.[33] Because the Quakers proved to be no threat, by December 1661 Ormond was focusing his concern on Catholics and "Anabaptists."[34] The discovery of the Dublin plot sparked a widespread crackdown on Dissenters, particularly the Presbyterians, but even in these circumstances Ormond and the Privy Council differentiated between seditious conspirators and quiescent Nonconformists. The Friends came under closer scrutiny, perhaps in part because the principal conspirator, Thomas Blood, allegedly escaped disguised as a Quaker.[35] More so than at any other time during this period, one catches glimpses of frustration among some in the political nation. John Thompson, one of Ormond's correspondents, referred to the Quakers' "stifneckednesse and untoward ways," while another writer complained to the bishop of Kildare that Ormond's recent proclamation against conventicles "doth so litle ingage them to Conformity, that it hardens them, & hightens them in their sin."[36] As the security precautions eased in 1664, Thompson grumbled that the Quakers believed persecution had passed, "from which suposition they take so much Confidence that ther is no liveing by them in quietnesse."[37]

This pattern continued in the ensuing years. The Galloway rebellion in the autumn of 1663 prompted serious security concerns in Irish government circles, but again this was directed toward the Presbyterians, especially in the north. In Munster the earl of Orrery, keeping a wary eye on both English dissidents and Gaelic Irish, prepared to use a militia of 2,000 horse and 3,000 foot to keep order, whereas Viscount Conway urged the implementation of liberty of conscience, which he believed would be conducive to the growth of trade and manufacturing—an early example in the Irish context of a theoretical argument for toleration. Baron Robartes's lord lieutenancy, in fact, led to an increase in tolerance, even for Presbyterians, finally prompting Charles himself to order Robartes to be more discreet in distinguishing moderates from dissidents.[38] Although Robartes's leniency to Nonconformists sparked criticism, Charles replaced him in 1670 as part of his move toward closer relations with France, not because of a change in religious policy. Robartes's successor, Lord Berkeley of Stratton, a Catholic sympathizer, had instructions to moderate the zeal of those who disquieted church and state, but his tenure, while involving more tolerance for Catholics, marked no significant change toward Protestant Nonconformists. As lord lieutenant, Essex too dealt moderately with Dissenters, opting not to take strong action even against the Covenanters. Although he banned conventicles in garrisons for security reasons, he licensed Nonconformists who agreed to worship in specified places.[39] The aim was indisputably to maintain peace, not to enforce ecclesiastical uniformity. Although clerical hardliners were outspoken in condemning such leniency, Essex fell in 1677 as a consequence of the maneuverings of his political enemies, especially the earls of Ranelagh and Danby, not his religious policy.

When Ormond resumed the lord lieutenancy, he opposed the establishment of new Nonconformist congregations and meetinghouses, but he permitted existing groups to worship. The Bothwell Bridge uprising necessitated heightened security, but Ormond, with Charles's approval, repressed only the Covenanters. Moderate indulgence remained the policy, the upheavals in Scotland notwithstanding. Dissenters who lived peacefully could "Exercise their calling without disturbance," opined Ormond, whereas factious Dissenters would have to be "remove[d] from burdening & misleading the people."[40] The duke was in England when the Rye House plotting was disclosed, but his son, the earl of Arran, reacted by prohibiting all conventicles. When the Quakers refused to obey, Arran rightly adjudged them no threat, although a number of them, including William Edmundson and Anthony Sharp, were briefly imprisoned. News of the plotting persuaded Ormond to endorse a firmer policy against nonconformity, but even in the aftermath of the Argyll and Monmouth rebellions, Clarendon left quiescent Dissenters alone.[41] Although Tyrconnell did not trust the Nonconformists, he dutifully implemented James's indulgence policy, enabling Friends to take their places in municipal government.

Thus in the three decades under review, the Quakers, as irenic Nonconformists, enjoyed a substantial degree of toleration, although it was uneven and offered no protection for their refusal to pay tithes and church rates. They benefited from the fact that both lay and clerical leaders concentrated on the Scottish Presbyterians, whom they deemed, in varying degrees, a security threat. The policy toward Nonconformists in Ireland altered primarily with reference to the activities of militant Protestants in the three kingdoms, but the preoccupation of Dublin Castle with the potential for Gaelic Irish unrest clearly provided the context for the concentration on security.[42]

I V

Thus the crackdown on Irish Friends at the Restoration did not become the norm for ensuing decades. As in England, persecution was sporadic, both chronologically and geographically. From Cork, Burrough observed in late August 1660 that despite "the rage of men, . . . the little flock" of Quakers had been preserved and was even growing "in victory and dominion."[43] Again, as in England the full scale of persecution is probably beyond recovery because the records are incomplete. Whereas Joseph Besse reported only 61 Quaker recusancy convictions in Norfolk for the period 1664–85, John Miller found evidence of 776 in the same period.[44] As I have demonstrated elsewhere, the Irish material poses similar problems. Of the 32 prosecutions for conventicling reported in the minutes of the Moate men's meeting for the period 1660–63, none are noted in the Great Book of Sufferings. Moreover, only 13 of 25 cases pertaining to tithes and church rates at Moate in the same period are recorded in the Great Book.[45] We need an exhaustive cross-check of the Great Book; Abraham Fuller and Thomas Holme's *A Brief Relation of Some Part of the Sufferings of the True Christians, the People of God (in Scorn Called Quakers) in Ireland* (1672); William Stockdale's *The Great Cry of Oppression* (1683), which supplements Fuller and Holme; Holme and Samuel Fuller's *A Compendious View of Some Extraordinary Sufferings of the People Call'd Quakers, Both in Person and Substance, in the Kingdom of Ireland* (1731), which builds on the earlier publications; Besse's *A Collection of the Sufferings of the People Called Quakers* (1753), which also uses some of the preceding material; the records of Quaker meetings; and civil records and other relevant documents.

Until an exhaustive compilation has been undertaken, we can use the data of the Fullers, Holme, and Stockdale to formulate preliminary conclusions about the nature and extent of Quaker suffering in Ireland. In England (including Monmouthshire), there were an estimated 39,510 Friends around 1715, or approximately 0.73 percent of the population. They were organized into 672 meetings. About the same time, the Quaker population in Ireland, where the number of meetings had grown from 30 in 1660 to 53 in 1701, was approximately 3,000, or 0.11 percent of the population.[46] The ratio of non-Quakers to Friends, in other words, was 138 to 1 in England and 933 to 1 in Ireland around 1700. The Congregationalist minister Thomas Jenner of Carlow had exaggerated when he complained in 1670 that the number of Quakers had "in a short space increased to be many thousands."[47]

Although the meeting for sufferings was not founded until 1676, Friends had been recording their tribulations since 1653. In 1670, an anonymous Quaker author claimed that more than 8,000 Friends had been incarcerated since the return of Charles II. Of these, 173 had perished in captivity, 138 had been banished, and more than 600 were in prison at the time he wrote. These figures probably exclude Ireland, for the systematic submission of information on Quaker suffering there did not commence until the meeting for sufferings was established.[48] John Whiting subsequently claimed that 9,437 Friends had been jailed in England and Wales between 1660 and 1680 for attending conventicles or refusing to take oaths. Another 624 had been confined for recusancy, and 198 had been banished. By 1680, moreover, 243 Friends had expired in prison. Neither author provided lists of names, but it is probable that apart from the numbers who died, these figures refer to the number of arrests, not the number of individual Quakers, some of whom would have gone to prison several times.[49] (A total of 369 Friends accounted for the 776 recusancy convictions noted by John Miller.)[50] Unfortunately, no such general estimate was made for Quaker suffering in Ireland.

Persecution occurred in waves in both England and Ireland, but judging from the preliminary figures, the pattern was not identical. In Ireland, repression was coterminous with the Restoration, whereas in England it commenced in the widespread suppression of sectaries following Thomas Venner's abortive rebellion in January 1661.[51] Further repression in England occurred following passage of the Quaker Act in 1662, but in Ireland the number of arrests began to decline, remaining low through 1668. In the meantime, fresh waves of persecution struck English Friends in the aftermath of the Northern Rebellion (autumn 1663) and the resulting Conventicle Act (May 1664), and again following the Second Conventicle Act (May 1670). Irish magistrates were responsible for a substantial increase in Quaker persecution in 1669, but unlike their counterparts in England, the Irish Friends experienced relatively modest persecution in the turbulent years that culminated in the Tory Reaction.[52]

In the aftermath of Venner's insurrection, the scale of repression was greater in England than in Ireland. In March 1661, Howgill, who was collecting records of sufferings, told a Durham Friend that he knew of nearly 4,000 Quakers, 500 of them in London, who were in prison in England.[53] The same year, *A Brief Relation of Some of the Cruel and Inhumane Usage*, which Howgill may have written, counted 4,257 victims. For Irish Friends, whose numbers were a thirteenth of their English counterparts, to have suffered on a comparable scale, some 325 of them would have had to be confined in 1661. Edmundson reported to Margaret Fell in April of the same year that many had been jailed at Cork, Limerick, Maryborough, and Waterford, but again the north seems to have escaped the tribulation.[54] Holme, Abraham Fuller, and Besse record 118 imprisonments in Ireland in 1661, but they also refer to unnamed others in five of the fourteen cases. (Sixty-eight names appear in these records, seven of them twice.)[55] When Holme and Samuel Fuller tabulated figures in the early eighteenth century, they concluded that 135 Friends had been imprisoned in 1661.[56] The actual number was probably higher, although it is impossible to know by how much. It is inconceivable, however, that it could have been anything like 325, and the proportional scale of suffering in England must have been two or three times that in Ireland in 1661.

The degree of persecution in the two countries seems to have shifted several times in the ensuing years. When a group of Friends in English prisons petitioned for release in 1663, a companion document, possibly prepared in January of that year, noted that 463 Quakers were incarcerated in 32 towns and counties.[57] Holme and Samuel Fuller show 47 Friends in Irish prisons in 1662; hence by the end of that year the proportion of jailed Quakers was higher in Ireland than in England.[58] But the average for the period 1662–70 was 35 per annum in Ireland and approximately 445 in England, or proportionately the same in the two countries. With the impact of the Declaration of Indulgence in England (1672), the relative degree of persecution in that country decreased in the decade 1671–80. The average number of jailed Quakers in England was 140 per annum compared with 17.5 in Ireland, even including the anomalous year of 1680, when 276 Friends were behind bars in England according to Whiting, but only 1 in Ireland according to Holme and Samuel Fuller.[59] Following the disclosure of the Rye House plotting, which only tangentially involved Ireland, the pattern shifted substantially. In London and Middlesex alone, 841 Friends were arrested in 1683–84 for attending conventicles, but in all of Ireland Holme and Fuller record only eighteen prisoners in 1683 and eight in 1684.[60] Clearly, the degree of persecution was dramatically altered by factors extraneous to the Friends.

To gauge Quaker suffering more accurately, we need to know something about the duration of the confinements and the value of distrained goods. For Ireland, the data on length of imprisonments is too vague and incomplete to use quantitatively. Most confinements ranged from a few days to six months, although some stretched beyond a year or more. Richard Poole died in the Wexford jail after spending two years there for refusing to pay tithes, and Francis Randall was in the same lockup more than two years for recusancy and refusal to pay to have his children christened. For declining to pay tithes, John Bennet spent more than four years in the jail at Naas, county Kildare, and Thomas Chanders was in the Carlow prison for nearly as long.[61]

According to the figures of Holme and Samuel Fuller, the value of distrained goods rose steadily from the 1650's to the early eighteenth century: £17 6s. 8d. per annum in the Protectorate; £109 5s. 2d. during Charles II's reign; £395 18s. 7d. in James II's reign; £1,055 14s. 7d. while William and Mary ruled; £1,349 19s. 7d. under Anne; and £1,731 16s. 6d. in George I's reign.[62] When adjusted for inflation, the real value of confiscated possessions rose by a third under James II and doubled by the mid-1720's. We can obtain a better sense of the impact of distraint by looking at average amounts for the period 1660–70 using the figures of Holme and Abraham Fuller. As I have shown elsewhere, in 66 tithing cases Friends in Ulster sustained the heaviest losses (£135 16s. 6d.), followed by their coreligionists in Leinster (£41 9s. 4d.) and Munster (£13 1s.). Throughout the country, the average loss was £2 19s. 8d., but the burden was heavier in Ulster (£4 4s. 11d.) and lighter in Leinster (£1 3s. 9d.). In the ensuing four years, 1671–74, the value of distrained goods increased sharply, from £190 6s. 10d. in the period 1660–70, to £410 2s. 3d., but the average distraint dropped by more than half, to £1 6s. 6½d. The number of cases in these four years rose dramatically, from an average of six per annum in 1660–70, to an average of 77.25 per annum between 1671 and 1674.[63] The scale of the increase was probably the result at least in part of better recordkeeping by Friends.

Records of sufferings kept by the Dublin monthly meeting indicate that distraints for tithes and church rates were selectively imposed. The determining factors in most cases seem to have been the relative zeal of parish ministers and churchwardens on the one hand and the relative wealth of individual Quakers on the other. The wealthiest Dublin Friend was almost certainly the clothier Anthony Sharp, who emigrated to Ireland in 1669 and by the time of his death in 1707 had amassed a fortune that enabled him to bequeath estates worth at least £10,000 to his eldest son as well as substantial holdings in England, New Jersey, and Queen's County (Laois), and 29 houses in Dublin to his other children. Among the other opulent Quakers were the merchant Samuel Clarridge, the linen-draper Robert Turner, who emigrated to Philadelphia with seventeen servants, and the linen-draper James Fade, whose finances collapsed by 1701, leaving him £1,652 in debt.[64] According to the Dublin records, the somewhat zealous ministers and churchwardens of St. Catherine's parish distrained Sharp's goods fifteen times between February 1671 and June 1687, but not at all in eight of those years. Altogether, he lost possessions valued at £13 17s. 6d., mostly pewter and cloth, for refusing to pay tithes and church rates of £12 3s. 8d. Clarridge suffered almost identical distraints—£13 5s. 8d.—though over a slightly longer period (1670–88, but with no confiscations in the period 1673–78). Turner's deprivations are harder to assess because on three occasions he did not cite the value of the distrained goods, although he lost at least 24s. between 1673 and 1682 (with no distraints in three of those years). Finally, the Dublin records indicate that the authorities seized Fade's goods only once during Sharp's years in Dublin, namely, in 1683, when he lost 17s. worth of items for refusing tithes of 15s.[65]

The usefulness of these statistics depends, of course, on whether or not they are complete. Perhaps the best indication that the figures are tolerably accurate is the fact that Quakers who had their possessions seized had no motive *not* to disclose this to their meetings. Failure to report would only have fueled suspicion that they had tendered tithes and church rates or that they had relied on companions and family members to remit them on their behalf, both of which practices the Quaker leaders denounced. Moreover, like many others, Sharp, Clarridge, and Turner insisted they had not paid tithes. Turner and his wife, Martha, for instance, wrote in 1680: "We doe hereby testify and declare thatt we never paid tithes or paid preists wages directly or indirectly, itt being Contrary to the Gospell day and Manyfestation of god in our Consciences." Sharp's statement was similar, as was that of Clarridge, who qualified his attestation only by confessing that he had paid a professional priest when he married for the second time.[66] It is, then, probable that the Dublin account of distraints is reasonably complete. Several observations are therefore in order. First, even with these high-profile Quakers, who were obvious targets of parsons and churchwardens, distraints were irregularly collected. Second, contrary to the impression conveyed by Besse's examples, the value of the items confiscated was normally not substantially higher than the tithes and church rates that were owed. (At least one exception occurred in the period 1681–84, when Sharp reckoned that Friends in the diocese of Ferns and Leighlin suffered distraints of £173 15s. for refusing to remit tithes of £34 12s. 5d.)[67] Finally, considering the wealth of these men, the average annual distraints were very modest: 16s. 4d. for Sharp (1681–87) and 14s. for Clarridge (1670–88).

Although the average distraint was probably bearable for most Friends, some experienced heavy losses. Francis Robson of county Armagh lost five cows and a bull worth £9 in 1665. For refusing to pay church rates of 10 s., Edward Kemp of Limerick was excommunicated and lost his house, which was worth £20. In 1666 an entire flock of 62 sheep as well as cattle valued at £18 were confiscated from John Marsh of county Armagh.[68] These are, of course, extreme cases, but Friends who lived through this period would have experienced the *Angst* that such penalties might be visited on them.

Quakers could also be punished for a variety of other offenses, including recusancy, refusal to take an oath, disdain for hat honor, declining to toast the king's health, and failure to observe holy days. In Dublin, Quaker shops were regularly stoned during the Christmas season.[69] Some Friends were fined because they refused to pay the customary fees for baptism, funerals, and the churching of women following childbirth, notwithstanding the fact that Quakers did not observe such rites.[70] In addition to fines, distraint, and incarceration, Friends might be subjected to physical abuse from magistrates or their agents. In 1660, two troopers in county Cavan dragged Thomas Lunn between their horses for two miles and then beat him, and a decade later Quakers were kicked and pummeled at Athy, county Kildare.[71] When Christopher Hillary of Shankill, county Armagh, refused to bear arms in the militia in 1670, he was forced to sit on a wooden horse with three muskets at each leg while four inches of match were burned; after this scare, he went to prison. For proclaiming the Friends' message in the cathedral at Cork the same year, Solomon Eccles was whipped from one end of the city to the other, sustaining at least 87 lashes.[72] For a similar act in the parish church at Ballinakill, Queen's County (Laois) in 1669, John Edwards was beaten with a staff until it broke, struck on the head with one of the pieces, and placed in the stocks for two hours on a cold winter day. Miles Gray was thrashed at Carrickfergus and Downpatrick in 1663.[73] Numerous other cases appear in the records. Victims of physical punishment had typically engaged in some form of public behavior that antagonized or offended non-Quakers.

v

Without denying the reality of persecution in Ireland, its scale must be placed in perspective. As refuges opened up in New Jersey and Pennsylvania, Friends from Ireland did not flock there in appreciable numbers, nor did the government attempt to prevent them from doing so. Although Audrey Lockhart has claimed that the exodus of Quakers from Ireland was notable, Richard Vann's examination of family lists found no substantial migration in the seventeenth century.[74] Of 615 first purchasers and reputed first purchasers of land in Pennsylvania, only 35 (5.7 percent) were from Ireland, and several of these, including Sir Henry Ingoldsby and Sir William Petty, were not Friends.[75] In the decade 1681–90, the Philadelphia meeting received 75 certificates from Friends in England, 6 from Wales, and only 5 from Ireland. (Provided by the monthly meetings, the certificates indicated their approval for the Quakers to relocate and, as appropriate, their freedom to marry.) In the following decade, the numbers were 66, 5, and 1, respectively.[76] In the period 1682–87, 31 (12.2 percent) of the 254 indentured servants who went to Pennsylvania were from Ireland, though not all of these would have been Quakers.[77] This figure is enlightening given Lockhart's belief that indentured servants may have constituted a majority of the emigrants from Ireland to Pennsylvania and New Jersey.[78] Kerby Miller may be correct in claiming that approximately 3,000 Irish Friends emigrated to America between 1682 and 1776,[79] but few left before the 1690's, and most who did were probably more interested in economic advancement than in escaping persecution. Quakers, of course, were not supposed to flee from persecution but to confront it.

From the late 1650's to the outbreak of war in 1689, the scale of persecution was substantially tempered by a surprising amount of de facto toleration. Perhaps nothing could have reminded non-Quakers of the Friends' presence and activities more than the meetinghouses they constructed and sometimes expanded to accommodate growth. They built one in Cork in 1678, and by 1700 it was commodious enough for 200 worshipers. Friends at Castledermot in county Kildare constructed a meetinghouse in 1675, and their colleagues in Waterford did so in 1694. Quakers at Lurgan enlarged their meetinghouse in 1691–92.[80] By 1701, 27 of Ireland's meetings had their own houses of worship, while the remaining 26 meetings still gathered in private homes.[81] The most interesting example occurred in Dublin, in full view of the country's principal governors. Dublin Friends used houses at Bride's Alley from 1657 to 1687 and at nearby Bride Street from 1657 to 1692. Commencing in 1677 they also leased a house in New Row from a Dublin alderman; city authorities obviously knew what Quakers were doing. In 1683 William Brabazon, earl of Meath, leased them property in Meath Street, where they erected a two-story meetinghouse that was completed in 1687.[82] All of these properties were within a fifteen-minute walk of Dublin Castle, St. Patrick's Cathedral, and Christ Church. In addition, the Friends had their own burial ground near fashionable St. Stephen's Green, and when this was full they acquired space near Dolphin's Barn, southwest of the city center.[83] They made no attempt to conceal their burials, for they marched, several abreast and in silence, through the streets when it was time to inter a deceased member.[84]

The Friends also had sufficient freedom to operate their own schools. The first appears to have been the one founded at Moate, county Westmeath, by Lawrence Routh in 1677; after a month he relocated to Trade's Hill, King's County (Offaly).[85] Shortly thereafter, Quakers in Cork founded a school, as did those in Dublin in 1680. Five schoolmasters attended the six-months meeting in 1681.[86] At least in part because Quaker teachers refused to use many of the Latin classics owing to objectionable content, they attracted few non-Quaker students.[87] Nevertheless, some attended, hence the work of the schools had to have been known outside Quaker circles. Moreover, some Friends apprenticed their children to non-Quakers, and some Quaker masters accepted apprentices who were not Friends. The extent of this interfaith cooperation between masters and apprentices was enough to spark the half-yearly meeting's concern.[88]

Throughout the period, Friends were able to crisscross the island seeking converts, buttressing the faithful, sharing news, and helping to organize meetings. Over the space of a year in 1682–83, Benjamin Bangs traveled 1,746 miles by his own reckoning, holding 180 meetings ranging from Antrim to Cork; although other Nonconformists met scarcely or not at all in this period, he suffered no persecution.[89] Six times John Banks trekked across Ireland between 1670 and 1682. John Tiffin came to Ireland nine times; Benjamin Brown, three; Roger Longworth, five; Robert Lodge, four. Burnyeat made numerous trips around the island. An anonymous (and incomplete) eighteenth-century Quaker document lists the names of 78 people (plus two anonymous women) who traveled through Ireland as public Friends (essentially ministers) between 1669 and 1688; 20 of these people made two or more journeys. During these two decades, the average number of public Friends on the move each year was at least five and probably double that number.[90]

Generally these public Friends seem not to have been hindered by magistrates. In June 1660, however, Burnyeat, who had been jailed at Armagh, reported that "it is very hard to Travel in this Nation for us," and in the early 1670's John Stubbs was confined by the mayor of Cork and threatened with whipping.[91] Yet after journeying some 2,000 miles through Ireland in 1660–61, Burrough reflected that he had enjoyed "very free passage in the principal cities and towns."[92] When George Fox visited Ireland in 1669, he traversed the island for three months, claiming he often had to do so in secrecy to avoid magistrates determined to arrest him. Yet he converted the mayor's wife at Bandon; brazenly rode past the door of Christopher Rye, Cork's hard-line mayor; attended the six-months meeting in Dublin, which was anything but secret; and was finally escorted by nearly 100 Quakers to the ship that would take him back to England.[93] At no point in this period did the state government attempt to stop the movements of public Friends; the only efforts were made at the local level, and these were very sporadic and ineffective.

Unlike some of the other Nonconformists, the Friends made virtually no attempt to act surreptitiously. The principal exception was the periodic effort on Fox's tour to keep his movements secret. Otherwise Fox himself

exhorted Friends "to bee as Huldah the prophetesse who instructed both
the King and his princes & priests in the Law of God in the Old Covenant,
soe they should bee much more diligent to search & instruct in the new
Covenant."[94] Early in 1674, Fox sent Friends in Ireland and elsewhere
copies of a book—probably *The Case of the People Called Quakers Relating
to Oaths or Swearing* (1673)—which he instructed them to give to members
of Parliament, the nation's governors, justices of the peace, mayors, judges,
and bailiffs.[95] The prominent Dublin Friend Anthony Sharp did not hesitate to challenge Alderman Enoch Reader in 1680 when Reader criticized
the Quakers for refusing to conform and take oaths.[96] Sharp even wrote to
Charles II, insisting that Friends were an innocent and industrious people,
and contending that the king should preserve the righteous, for it was because of them that God spared the nation.[97] This was nothing less than a
firm lecture to the sovereign.

Like their coreligionists in England, Irish Quakers did not hesitate to
seek redress for their grievances. There was no suffering in silence. In May
1687, for instance, the six-months meeting instructed Edmundson, Sharp,
and six others to petition the lord deputy for relief from the quartering of
soldiers in their homes, the sentences of episcopal courts against those who
refused to pay tithes, and the losses sustained because Quakers could not
take oaths when wills were proved.[98] The Friends regularly attended assizes
and quarter sessions "to doe servis for truth."[99] Over the years Sharp made
numerous efforts to assist imprisoned Quakers, appealing directly to a
wide variety of magistrates and ecclesiastics, including the governor of
Wicklow, whom he advised to "wash [his] hands From persecuteing the
true English protestants." In the reign of Charles II alone, Sharp also intervened with the Privy Council, the duke of Ormond, the bishop and consistory court of Meath, the Hanaper of Chancery, the archbishop of Armagh, the bishops of Ferns and Raphoe, and a host of lesser magistrates.[100]
Other Friends were involved in similar endeavors. Such activities would
have been a constant reminder to the authorities—if they needed one—of
the Quakers' opposition to the established church, tithes, church rates,
oaths, and the rites of baptism and burial. Notwithstanding such opposition, they enjoyed remarkable access to many in positions of power.

The Friends in Ireland earned a substantial degree of de facto toleration
by their behavior, industry, and economic success. Viscount Conway,

whose wife was a Quaker, welcomed them as tenants: "They have gott a generall reputation through the Kingdome of paying their Rents well when all others have failed."[101] In discounting Friends as a threat in 1683, Longford noted that most of those in Cork were among the city's greatest traders as well as peaceful people.[102] Although Sharp was one of the most prominent wool merchants in Ireland and a highly visible man in Dublin, he was incarcerated only once, for approximately 48 hours.[103] Despite being subjected to the distraint of his goods, as we have seen, he was left free to practice his religion in part because he was a good citizen and one of the city's major employers (with a workforce of some 500), and in part because he eschewed provocative forms of testimony, such as witnessing in the Church of Ireland or "going naked for a sign."[104] Apart from the early 1660's and the crackdown in 1669, other prominent merchant-Quakers in Dublin, such as Turner and Clarridge, fared similarly,[105] as did the Dublin Quaker community as a whole. In 1687, Sharp and Clarridge were named aldermen in Dublin, and other Friends served as aldermen in Cork, Cashel, and Limerick and in some corporations as burgesses. Moreover, the weavers' guild elected Sharp as its master in 1687, a year after he became a member of its governing council.[106]

V I

It would be erroneous to deny or minimize Quaker suffering from the late 1650's to the outbreak of war in 1689, or to slight the psychological stress caused by living in the shadow of persecution. But to refer to this era as "the period of the great persecution" implies an intensity and breadth of repression that did not exist for Irish Quakers. Relatively few Friends suffered extensively, and none were executed or confined for truly long periods, as were William Dewsbury, John Bunyan, and Francis Bampfield in England. The time of heavy suffering was still on the horizon, in the horrors to which the Friends were subjected during the war between James II and William III. Quaker losses in that conflict may have been as great as £100,000, a staggering sum for a small religious community—an average of perhaps £40 per member. Some of the misery stemmed from religious enmity, but most of it was caused by the depredations of war. Notwithstanding their small numbers, the Friends survived this cataclysm because of the organizational structure they developed in the 1670's and 1680's,[107] and that development might not have been possible without the substantial de facto toleration they enjoyed in the decades before the war.

However experienced, suffering was fundamentally a communal act. As Michael Walzer has rightly noted, suffering is a shared experience in which the victims "come to know one another in a special way."[108] Compulsion thus has the effect of fortifying a sense of community among those who are its targets. This was certainly the case with the Quakers, whose sense of being a suffering community transcended state boundaries and helped to sustain their identity as a transnational society with members in America, throughout the "British" Isles, and on the Continent. Their first major history, written by the Dutchman Willem Sewel, reflected the movement's international flavor and entailed the collaboration of Friends beyond the Netherlands. The sense of transnational community was reflected in other ways, as in the financial assistance provided to English Quakers by their associates in Ireland in the early 1680's and in the reciprocal aid extended to Friends in Ireland by their colleagues in England during the time of troubles.[109]

Yet the persecution in Ireland was never so severe that it prevented the Quakers from experiencing and contributing to what Jim Smyth has called "the formation of an 'Anglo-Irish' identity."[110] Notwithstanding their suffering at the hands of a Protestant government, prodded especially by prominent clerics in the Church of Ireland, the Friends maintained a sense of identity with other Protestants vis-à-vis the Catholic majority. When the former Quaker Joshua Bows accused Sharp of complicity with Catholics for his service as a Dublin alderman during James's reign, Sharp angrily retorted that he had possessed no greater religious or civil freedom at this time than any other Protestant, that he was as much a heretic in Catholic eyes as other Protestants, and that he was a Protestant landowner whose possessions in England included dissolved abbey lands. Moreover, during the time of troubles, as Sharp pointed out, the Friends "hazarded themselves to Save and help the protestants besides charitable collection for poor prisoners and dressing Sick and wounded."[111] From a different perspective, the Quaker leaders never succeeded in persuading all members of their movement to eschew marriages with other Protestants; in fact, Clarridge himself twice wed non-Quaker women. The Friends were thus members of two communities—the transnational Quaker movement, to which they accorded their higher loyalty and for which they suffered, and the Protestant community in Ireland, whose identity was essentially framed in opposition to the Catholic majority (for political and economic no less than religious reasons) and to whose ultimate triumph in the early 1690's they contributed through their economic success and civic participation. Their membership in the latter community moderated the extent to which they suffered in the former, and the leavening agent most responsible for this was probably the increasingly important involvement of the Friends in the world of commerce where profit was more significant than religious differences.

Local Politics in Restoration England

RELIGION, CULTURE, AND POLITICS

IN OLIVER HEYWOOD'S HALIFAX

In the recent historiography on Restoration England, apparently contradictory conclusions have been reached about the nature of divisions within Restoration communities. On one hand, scholars studying dissent in its many guises are keen to stress that all but the most radical Nonconformists lived alongside their Anglican neighbors in relative harmony for most of this period. Persecution, while real enough in some places and at some times, was not characteristic of most communities, and when it did take place it was often either a response to external pressures or the work of a narrow group within the community.[1] On the other hand, scholars exploring the emergence of party strife in England during this period have argued that the political and religious tensions and the periodic crises they engendered were not simply affairs of high politics played out at Westminster. Ordinary residents of communities as diverse as London and Yarmouth thought of themselves as Whig or Tory and acted accordingly.[2] Since one of the important themes of this work is to remind us of the religious component of what have often been treated as purely constitutional questions, we are left with the contradiction. If Dissenters lived happily alongside their neighbors, there can hardly have been highly polarized party identities based on religion emerging in the same communities at the same time.

This contradiction suggests that there is a degree of complexity to local political and cultural identities in the Restoration community that has not been sufficiently appreciated. The purpose of this essay is to explore this complexity through the diaries of Oliver Heywood, a Presbyterian minister in the parish of Halifax, Yorkshire, between 1654 and 1702.[3] Heywood's corpus is particularly well suited to this purpose. He was a prominent figure in northern nonconformity, related by ties of kinship and affinity to most of the leading Presbyterians in Lancashire and Yorkshire and respected by Nonconformists throughout England.[4] Moreover, Heywood's public role meant that—as a good providential Calvinist—his duty to record and interpret God's plan extended to the broader canvas of community and nation as well as the more traditional Puritan diarists' focus on the individual and family.[5] Thus Heywood's writings contain a particularly wide-ranging and scrupulously honest account of the fortunes of a Nonconformist divine, his congregation, his community, and his nation in the turbulent decades following the Restoration of Charles II in 1660.

An analysis of this material will show that we cannot think of Restoration England as a divided society in any kind of simplistic sense. Undeniably, there was fierce opposition in Halifax between Dissenters and Anglicans, between supporters of discipline and supporters of conviviality, and eventually between Whigs and Tories. Undeniably, these religious, social, and political ideas overlapped in the minds of individuals in ways which created relatively coherent cultural "packages." Yet the clarity of this opposition was muddied by a large and complex middle ground composed of individuals who did not take on board the complete "package" offered by either side. Even a model of local politics that envisions two poles separated by a neutral middle is not sufficient, for in Halifax, those in the middle held quite definite, if not necessarily orthodox, political opinions. Moreover, we also have to incorporate evidence which suggests that these opposing cultures were themselves undercut by competing polarities.

By way of a conclusion, I will argue that one methodological tool which can help us understand the complexity of political and cultural identity in Restoration communities is local history. On one level, the point is obvious. The evidence examined below suggests that cultural conflict in Halifax in the Restoration era was shaped by the particular history of the community and more generally by the economic and social structures of the parish. However, we can and must go further, for in a very real sense, the political and cultural identities of the Restoration community were created by the interactions of "local" and "national" in the experiences of individuals and groups in a particular place. The contradiction between accommodation and opposition was thus real enough, but it is only a contradiction if we assume that individuals and groups in a community were the passive recipients of the archetypes of high politics, putting them in a position, as it were, to get it "wrong." We can indeed find evidence that people acted like Whigs or Tories, yet we must recognize that the "Whig" or "Tory" identities people adopted had local as well as national roots and that those local roots might well lead them to act in apparently contradictory ways at other times.

I

Although the source used here quite naturally highlights religion, there can be little doubt that cultural identities in Halifax were rooted in religious beliefs and spread, like so many ripples, out to politics and society. The point is clearest with respect to Dissenters, a group whose culture was centered around their profound disagreement with the theology, practices, and personnel of the Church of England.[6] In seeking examples of the fundamental corruption in the Anglican Church, Oliver Heywood and other Nonconformists in Halifax had to look no further than their own vicar, Dr. Hooke, an active crusader against Nonconformity and one of Heywood's chief persecutors. Hooke's personal failings included greed, duplicity, and vindictiveness, faults compounded by his pastoral, doctrinal, and political errors.[7] Several entries note Hooke's failure to provide adequate preaching at the parish church. Such inaction encouraged his parishioners to spend their Sundays "clubbing" for ale instead of listening to a dull reading from the Book of Common Prayer.[8] Equally problematic were the doctrinal implications of the fulsome funeral sermons he was in the habit of preaching for drunkards, fornicators, liars, and profligates.[9] Worse still, Hooke was insufficiently concerned with the threat that popery posed to the Protestant religion. A curate of his went unchastised for saying he "would rather die in the Pope's bosom than in the Presbyterian faith," and when news of the Popish Plot broke in Halifax in November 1678, Hooke did nothing more than preach a rather generic sermon (one he had used the week before!).[10] Multiplied throughout the church— Heywood relates stories of papist priests holding livings, stories of pluralists, stories of bad doctrine preached to the people, stories of the lack of preaching—these failings made the church's active persecution of Nonconformists all the more unbearable and unjust.[11]

The Dissenters' critique of the Church of England and its clergy was closely linked to their understanding of the political landscape of Restoration England. Hooke's failure to react properly to the news of the Popish Plot in 1678 was but one of a number of national political events recorded in Heywood's diary.[12] Many entries suggest the extent to which religion and politics were joined in his mind. A volume Hooke published in 1684 entitled *The Royal Guard* horrified Heywood not only because the vicar argued that Dissenters were "greater enemies to the king and Christ than papists," but also because he advocated the creation of a standing army to be used against schismatics and supported by fines collected from them.[13] Heywood's fear of Charles's absolutist tendencies is also evident in a comment recorded in 1664 that equated the newly imposed hearth tax with the principles of arbitrary government—principles which Heywood knew all too well were to be expected from those influenced by popery.[14] Indeed, though grateful for the toleration that was extended in 1672 and again in 1687, Heywood was none too easy about the circumstances in which it came. Not only did Charles's and James's declarations encourage papists, but being done against the will of Parliament, they raised constitutional questions that made Heywood and his circle quite uncomfortable.[15] Significantly, all of these examples reveal the extent to which Heywood's reading of contemporary political issues was rooted in the history of the Civil War and Interregnum. Indeed, Heywood was busy creating a historical reading of his own times by marking the anniversaries of particular events in ways that put Dissent into a good light.[16]

Finally, there was a close connection in Heywood's political consciousness between government and society. Included in a list of twenty reasons why he thought that a "land-destroying judgment" was imminent was the following comment:

the national sins openly acted by governors: disowning the cause of God, casting off Christ's interest and government, building again what was destroyed: covenant breaking, making snares for tender consciences: want of execution of justice punishing sins, . . . for Menasseh's sins was Judah ruined.[17]

Such sins were identical to those which had so exercised Puritans earlier in the century.[18] Drunkenness deserves note as perhaps the most commonly mentioned sin. (Here, too, religion and politics were not far away, for Heywood considered brandy to be a popish innovation that was "too hot for English bodies.")[19] Fornication, adultery, and bastardy—"light skirts" was the phrase Heywood used on one occasion—were other sins given some prominence in his jottings.[20] While it is hardly surprising to find a Presbyterian minister moaning about the sinfulness of the world, the fact that he so explicitly criticized the local magistracy for failing to correct such behavior is of more interest.[21] Indeed, not only were the gentry lax in controlling these assaults upon good order, but they were often the worst offenders. Sir John Kaye, a West Riding justice, was known to have had a servant in his household give birth to an illegitimate child.[22]

As the preceding discussion has hinted, the worldview of Heywood's opponents was no less coherent and systematized. Indeed, the vehemence of the belief on one side that persecuting bishops, lax justices, and immorality were the agents of the devil was matched in intensity by the belief on the other side that Presbyterian factiousness was an affront to God and king and the first step down the road to civil war and anarchy. Part of the motivation of those hostile to Dissent was their perception that Nonconformity was a threat to the nation because it was a threat to the church. Given its pulling power in contemporary polemics, popery was used as part of this argument. One of Hooke's sermons compared the Nonconformists to papists, and the vicar of the nearby parish of Burton, incensed that many of his parishioners had participated in a prayer meeting to cure a melancholy woman, contrasted the church of God with the chapel of the devil where popish miracles took place. (His suggestion for a cure was to put the young woman in with "merry company.")[23]

There was also a more overt political strand to these beliefs, for the Dissenters' refusal to obey the law made their continued existence a political danger of the greatest import.[24] A sermon Heywood published in 1672 was carefully studied by his enemies because it criticized the Act of Uniformity. Since criticizing the law was tantamount to criticizing the king, the sermon might have been grounds for a charge of sedition, and in any case it provided further evidence that Nonconformists had designs upon the monarchy.[25] Indeed, such was the connection between Presbyterianism and sedition that during a particularly severe bout of persecution in 1683, Heywood could not stay at home for fear of being arrested nor could he go abroad for fear of confirming rumors that he was involved in a plot.[26]

As was true in Heywood's case, his opponents based their critique of Dissent upon a particular reading of the nation's history. On at least two

occasions that Heywood records, the vicar explicitly blamed the Nonconformists for the murder of Charles I, and anniversaries were celebrated and
even created with an eye to their political message.[27] The local schoolmaster, for example, set his pupils to writing essays about how the Presbyterians killed Charles, and told them that the Popish Plot was merely a Nonconformist forgery.[28]

The association made between Nonconformity and the excesses of parliamentarian rule serves as a reminder that it was the *combination* of religious and political dissent which made Nonconformists dangerous. Heywood paints a fascinating picture of a theological debate between Dr.
Hooke and several other curates and Mr. Samuel Maude of Sowerby. Although serious, this discussion was taken by everyone except Heywood as a
form of entertainment: Hooke and his curates may have accused Maude of
being a heretic for denying the doctrine of original sin, but they also drank
toasts to him. For our purposes, the crux of the story came when Hooke
quipped that Maude would make a good Presbyterian preacher because of
his zeal. Maude countered, "Some Presbyterian preachers are honest men."
Whereupon Hooke's curate retorted, "How can they be honest men that
obey not the king's laws?"—a comment which perfectly illustrates the distinction incipient Tories drew between mere heresy and sedition.[29]

Rounding out this comprehensive critique of the dangers inherent in
Dissent was the threat they posed to good order in the society. In Don-
caster, the justice giving the charge at the sessions held in 1684 "expressed
himself with great fury against Dissenters . . . saying if those Dissenters
were but once rid out of the way we should all be quiet."[30] What he meant
by "quiet" probably has to do with the Nonconformists' penchant for
minding other people's business with their constant harping on what others saw as harmless recreations such as maypoles, rushbearings, horse races,
cockfights, even stoolball.[31]

Yet for all that these two coherent cultural packages stood in clear opposition to one another, we have to recognize that they were undercut in numerous ways. Not least is the fact that both of these cultures appealed to
almost precisely the same goals—the preservation of the Protestant religion, the extirpation of popery, the maintenance of good order in the society, and the success of the monarchy—as justification for their vehement
stance. The result was an inevitable confusion about who stood for what,
which opened up these apparently coherent ideological systems to the in-

fluences of other kinds of polarities. It is this complexity and ambiguity which I shall examine next, looking at the incomplete and often contradictory ways in which the two oppositional cultures described above were taken up within the community.

Of course, it must be said from the start that there are many examples in the diaries which show the opposition between conformist and Dissenter being played out by the residents of Halifax's many townships. When elected as churchwarden for the township of Hipperholme in 1664, Stephen Ellis "belched out grievous threatenings, how he would punish the fanatics in the place . . . [and] work a greater reformation than ever Heywood could do"—a pointed reference to Heywood's attempt to establish Presbyterian church discipline during the Interregnum.[32] The opinions of this well-to-do yeoman were clearly shared by a broader, more diverse social group, for Heywood and other Dissenters were often intimidated and threatened.[33] Dissenters were no less willing to express their views. One marvelous entry tells of a letter delivered to Jeremy Brooksbank, a man hired to serve as church warden in Shelf in 1678, who had threatened to prosecute all those attending Heywood's sermons. The letter warned him that he was attacking "Bethel," not "Babel," reminded him of the Scots' release from the "burden" of a "service-book," accused him (or the Anglican curate) of drunkenness, and threatened him with divine judgment if he did not stop troubling "such as would live peaceably." In the brouhaha that followed, the blame was pinned on Samuel Midgley, a man, Heywood explained, "odd and conceited in some notions, yet a professor, and sometimes comes to hear me."[34]

Yet even in this story there are hints that these two oppositional cultures unraveled in the real world of the community. Samuel Midgley was only an occasional visitor to Heywood's congregation, and Jeremy Brooksbank had not always been hostile to Dissent: "Thou hast been a friend to some in the day of their calamity to keep them from the heat of the flames." Moreover, the two were already embroiled in a dispute about a trespass (quite independently of their religious differences) which was eventually resolved through the mediation of two individuals, one who was a member of Heywood's congregation, the other who was not.[35]

Further evidence of the complicated nature of Restoration politics in Halifax is that elements of the Dissenters' critique of the Church of England were shared by many who were not convinced Nonconformists.

Heywood makes several remarks that suggest the people's preference for preaching over more formulaic or ritualistic religious services, and he was apparently not alone in feeling that Hooke's response to the Popish Plot was insufficiently vehement.[36] Elsewhere we sense that parishioners were quite prepared to make the comparison between Heywood's devoted service to the Lord and the assiduous way in which conformist clergymen pursued the fiscal rewards of their offices.[37] The conclusions they drew, however, were not always to Heywood's liking. A woman in Kirkburton, disgusted by her vicar's insistence on collecting his fee for baptizing a newborn too sickly to make the journey to the parish church, considered joining the Quakers.[38]

These examples prompt two observations. First, ordinary folk were quite capable of making their own judgments about matters relating to religion, a point wonderfully illustrated by David Harley's work on the differences between Anglican, Nonconformist, and popular understandings of the causes and theology of melancholy and possession.[39] Second, popular criticism, though it had doctrinal and ecclesiological implications, was primarily directed at the behaviors and attitudes of particular clergymen. One senses that the residents of Halifax were careful judges of the practical qualities of the clergy, and one must assume that Heywood's popularity outside the ranks of committed Nonconformists was because of his mastery of "practical divinity"—a term encompassing everything from the quality and relevance of the minister's preaching to his willingness to visit the sick or pray for women in childbirth.[40] However, while their exclusion from the church may have made practical divinity something of a necessity for nonconforming clergymen, they did not have a monopoly on such dedication. A vicar from Lincolnshire, in Halifax on account of his health (unlikely as that may sound), was very popular among the parishioners, perhaps because he was a competent and conscientious preacher. Hooke, however, discharged him after six months, an action which "astonished" the chief inhabitants of the town when they learned about it.[41] Indeed, the fact that Heywood related the story in this way shows that despite his utter disdain for the hierarchy and policies of the national church, his commitment to practical divinity might lead him to overlook the conformity of men whose hearts were in the right place. The curate of the township of Sowerby received warm praise on two occasions for resisting his parishioners' demands to hold a rushbearing festival, and one of the many curates who came through Coley after Heywood's ejection was identified as a man who was sound on the essential doctrine of salvation and a good and conscientious preacher.[42]

In the same way that Heywood's approval of some conformist clergy suggests that the Dissenting culture was not perfectly coherent even at its core, the respect which he was shown by individuals we might otherwise expect to be his enemies reveals similar ambiguities at the heart of the conformist culture. On his death bed, Samuel Mitchell, a member of a prominent family from the township of Northowram whose members get frequent mention in the diaries for their dissolute behavior, put the word out that he would like a visit from Heywood to seek assurances about the fate of his soul.[43] Heywood visited an Anglican curate in similar circumstances, and the fact that the call came in the immediate aftermath of the Exclusion Crisis makes it all the more significant.[44]

Turning from religion to politics, more evidence suggesting the complexity of local politics is found in the many stories that record the tacit or even active support that Heywood and other Dissenters received from the churchwardens and constables charged with their persecution. The officers who sent warnings of impending raids or simply refused to act were by no means all active Nonconformists.[45] Indeed, once Dr. Hooke tried to force all the churchwardens in the parish to give him the names of those who did not receive the sacrament at church, but they refused en masse. Although their subsequent prosecution for perjury only resulted in a fine of five shillings each, this collective action by a disparate group of men is surely significant, for it suggests that ordinary householders were quite willing to make an independent judgment about the political threat that Dissent posed to the parish and the nation.[46]

There are also hints of a more proactive political stance on the part of the people. When Heywood's goods were distrained in 1670, no one would buy them.[47] Since the story cannot be explained by sympathy for Heywood's religious beliefs—there were not *that* many Dissenters in Halifax—we must consider the possibility that this boycott was an indication of widespread popular support for Heywood's populist politics. Here it is worth bearing in mind that many of those attending Heywood's sermons were not committed Dissenters, and what they heard on those occasions often had an explicit political message.[48]

Two other incidents reveal a similar degree of independence in the political judgments of Halifax's residents, an independence which allowed them to bridge the gap between Dissenter and conformist with surprising ease and which often had them explicitly or implicitly criticizing the state or its policies. In 1675, Heywood recorded the proposal floated by "the heads of the chapelry of Coley . . . to give me a call to preach in public, say[ing] things will not be right till I be brought to it again."[49] It was an utterly preposterous notion. In addition to the vicar's implacable opposition, the fact of Heywood's nonconformity could not simply be overlooked. The proposal is all the more significant because it was made by the leading individuals in the community, not a narrow faction. The idea was raised again in 1682 and debated by the vicar and four residents of the chapelry. Of the four, one was a longtime member of Heywood's congregation, two others were not members but had links to his circle, and the fourth was related by marriage to two of Heywood's most active opponents within the chapelry.[50]

The second example reveals the same kind of support within a different segment of the community. The passage of the Test Act in 1673 meant that the governors of the Halifax grammar school, a group which included representatives of all the important families in the parish, had to get a certificate attesting to their acceptance of the Anglican communion service. The evening before the appointed Sunday, they met as a body and resolved to attend the service and receive the sacrament but not in their capacity as governors—a neat dodge which let them comply with the act without endorsing its intent. The vicar, however, laid a trap. In the middle of the service, he announced that all those who wanted a certificate would have to come and kneel at the high altar, something which many refused to do. The crucial feature of this story is that the governors were a religiously mixed bunch. One, Mr. Horton of Sowerby, was a great friend to Dissenters, but others, including Mr. Samuel Lister and Mr. Ramsden, were not particularly associated with one side or another, and some, including Mr. Daniel Greenwood and Mr. Jonathan Hall, were even associated with the antagonists to Dissent, the latter being described as a recent "convert to the prelatical way."[51]

This same political independence is found in the ranks of Heywood's persecutors, and it led them to take actions which reveal a degree of ambiguity among those most identified with the conformist cause. Sir John Kaye, half in jest, asked the man at whose house the prayer meeting for the melancholy woman had been held if he was keeping a conventicle; when the man explained what had happened, Kaye approved, adding that a good prayer (not the vicar's suggestion of "merry company") was exactly what he would have tried.[52] On another occasion, Kaye went out of his way to ensure that a summons Heywood had received for holding a conventicle came to naught at the Quarter Sessions.[53] Yet this was the same man who at other times had lashed out at Nonconformists in his capacity as a JP and whom Heywood chastised (in the privacy of his diary) for keeping open house during the Christmas season and for allowing fornication by his servants.[54] Another instance concerns Sir John Armitage, Kaye's colleague on the West Riding bench, and Stephen Ellis, the wealthy yeoman from Heywood's chapelry. Although they were closely allied in their persecution of Nonconformists, Armitage went to court in 1669 to prosecute Ellis for slander. He was high sheriff of Yorkshire in that year, and Ellis had supposedly told Armitage's son, "I am as good a man as thy father, but that thy father has some more means. And that which he has he got by his poor tenants by racking them. I got not mine by cozening and cheating."[55] Thus precisely the kind of factious disrespect for authority that was held against Dissenters is found here in the heart of the opposing camp.

I I

As I suggested above, one way to approach the complex and often ambiguous divisions we find in Halifax's political culture during the Restoration era is to pay attention to features that suggest the presence of alternative polarities around which individuals and groups might construct their political identities. One obvious factor was the parish's economy. Halifax was part of the West Riding woolen district, and many households in the parish made a living—for some a relatively comfortable living—producing cloth within the domestic unit as a supplement to a small (usually pastoral) agricultural holding. The availability of this income coupled with the abundance of freehold and secure copyhold tenures helps explain the economic underpinnings of the evident political independence of many residents of the parish.[56] It also suggests that attitudes toward wealth—how it was obtained, how it was used—might well affect emerging political identities. Consider, for example, the close similarity in the sentiments behind Stephen Ellis's accusation that Sir John Armitage had

made his money by "cozening and cheating" his tenants and the many stories Heywood told of the providential judgments that afflicted those who
were covetous. These antagonists thus seem to share—along with many
others in the community—a sense that wealth must be acquired and used
legitimately.[57]

Another factor we must consider is the way in which the political
structures in the parish created a context that conditioned the ways in
which the issues and positions of high politics were received and interpreted. A classic upland parish of the type described by Thirsk, Everitt,
and Underdown, Halifax lacked a strong or unified resident gentry.[58] The
influence of what few gentlemen there were was circumscribed to at most
one or two townships, leaving local government largely in the hands of a
host of middling and wealthy yeomen of whom Stephen Ellis is a typical, if
well-to-do, example.[59] Given these facts, it is not surprising to find him
lashing out verbally at the son of Sir John Armitage. To a man such as Ellis,
Armitage might be perceived as an unwelcome outsider throwing his
weight around in matters that did not concern him. The same kind of sentiment is revealed in a brawl at a cockfight in Halifax occasioned by a gentleman's disparaging comments about the quality of his opponents'
cocks.[60]

The vicar's position in the parish's political structure was equally tenuous. Inevitably an outsider and often appointed for political considerations
(Halifax was a relatively wealthy living in the gift of the king), it is hardly
surprising to find that he was not necessarily seen as a natural leader in the
community. Thus the many examples of popular sentiment against
Hooke, particularly as expressed by the "chief inhabitants" of the parish,
may have been instances in which the parish's natural leaders took advantage of particular strands of the Dissenting critique of the Anglican
Church to put Hooke in his place. The refusal of the grammar school governors to take communion while groveling on their knees before Hooke at
the high altar can be read in the same way, but that story can also take a
slightly different spin. It may have been that the governors were expressing
their resistance to the centralizing tendencies of the late Stuart monarchy—not because they were incipient Whigs but out of an interest in
maintaining local autonomy.

The same sort of tension between local and national is also evident one
rung up the political ladder in the highly idiosyncratic way in which Dis-

sent was prosecuted in Heywood's Yorkshire. Although the English legal system in the late seventeenth century was hardly a model of bureaucratic regularity, it is nonetheless striking that Heywood, who was almost constantly in flagrant violation of various statutes of the Clarendon Code, escaped prosecution and imprisonment for so long. Obviously the warnings of neighbors and officers helped, but more intriguing is the evidence that the upper echelons of the county's legal system—men as a rule hostile to Dissent—were quite willing to bend the rules in his favor. Kaye and Armitage did this on occasion, and another instance was Heywood's release from prison late in 1685 apparently on little more than the whim of the high sheriff. Such men might well react to national affairs in ways which expressed their sense that "their" county was "their" property, and there are even indications of an inverse correlation between the peaks and troughs of persecution in Yorkshire and the royal policy toward Dissent during those periods.[61]

All of these examples, while alerting us to the overlapping fissures that divided the community in an uneven and often incomplete way, also suggest ways in which lived experience and national political rhetoric were combined as individuals actively constructed their political identities. As a final example illustrating this point, consider Heywood's account of his first exposure to the terms *Tory* and *Whig*. A few months after the last Exclusion Parliament, he was visiting a Mrs. H. in Chesterfield and was told

about a new name lately come into fashion for Ranters, calling themselves by the name of Tories. . . . I hear further . . . that this is the distinction they make instead of Cavalier and Roundhead, now they are called Tories and Whigs, the former wearing a red ribbon, the other a violet—thus men begin to commence war, . . . and the Tories will hector down and abuse those they have named Whigs.[62]

The connection Heywood made between a group he already knew as "ranters" and this new name of "Tory" is significant for two reasons. First, it illustrates that contemporaries perceived a direct line of descent linking Cavalier with Tory and Roundhead with Whig. Second, and perhaps more important, it suggests that these oppositional political categories (originating elsewhere) were taken up by (or applied to) groups defined by other criteria. Specifically, the term *ranter* was one Heywood used to describe people, usually gentlemen, who engaged in excessive drinking, carousing, gambling, dancing, and brawling, and it is often associated with his criticism of the gentry's failure to take seriously their responsibilities as magistrates and leading citizens to provide discipline in the community.[63]

Given that it is impossible to read the account without imagining gentlemen "trying on" these new identities (and ribbons) to see if they liked the fit, the story provides a wonderfully concrete example of why political identities in the Restoration era were often so unstable. On one hand, it allows for the possibility that some embraced the connection between experience and rhetoric offered by this new "fashion." Gentlemen who "ranted" in the period leading up to 1681 (or for that matter commoners who played stoolball on Easter) may well have *intended* to offend a strict moralist like Heywood, and after the Exclusion Crisis they may well have seized the opportunity to give that social commentary a more explicit political point.[64] At the same time, the story leaves open the possibility that others might have rejected this new "fashion." Heywood, though hostile to both ranters and Tories, was clearly not about to think of himself as a Whig, for he was equally troubled by their role in these confrontations.[65]

Although possible, then, the connection between political rhetoric and lived experience was not necessary, and in some instances it may have been quite ambiguous. Was the curate of Sowerby who had been reviled by his parishioners (they broke down the chapel doors and called him a "cobbler") for not allowing a rushbearing going to side with the Whigs against "ranting" or with conformists against Dissent? Did his parishioners— obviously in the "ranting" camp—really mean to attack the established church and thus ally themselves with Dissenters?[66] The questions are rhetorical, but they indicate the potential for shifting and unstable political identities in Restoration communities that become visible if we take local history seriously as a mode of analysis.

Obviously, doing local history cannot mean taking the particular features of the political culture of Restoration Halifax as a model to apply to other communities. However, to avoid, at the other extreme, a descent into isolating antiquarianism, I would suggest that taking local history seriously means undertaking an analysis which seeks to identify the factors that were interacting in particular communities during the Restoration, for here we may find patterns that are not evident if we examine the particular outcomes of those interactions.[67] Among the factors suggested above as being important in Halifax are several that emerge in other studies of Restoration communities. For example, in Jonathan Barry's work on

Bristol, it is apparent that individuals otherwise sympathetic to the Crown bridled at the domineering tactics of an outsider, the marquess of Worcester, invoking the urban version of the upland autonomy evident in Halifax.[68] In Mark Goldie and John Spurr's study of the parish of St. Giles Cripplegate in London, the vicar—a low-church, Presbyterian sympathizer—was attacked by a group of high-church parishioners. This was an inverted version of situation in Halifax but one that clearly reveals the importance of examining the vicar's relationship with his congregation.[69] Finally, in P. J. Norrey's study of the West Country, we see economic issues merging with political ones in local resistance to the hearth tax and its collection.[70]

By identifying such factors in their local context, we can begin to appreciate the way that individuals and groups holding definite and often fervent opinions on a range of subjects—from rushbearing and preaching to sedition, covetousness, and local autonomy—sought to express those ideas in the terms of the (changing) political rhetoric that was available to them. That political rhetoric came packaged from Whitehall and Westminster in neatly oppositional categories, but those categories could be filled with any number of different meanings in different local contexts.[71] The end result of this approach will be a more complex picture of the Restoration period and its politics, for this approach recognizes the active political identities of a wide range of English men and women as well as the potential fluidity of those beliefs, and by so doing, it allows us to better appreciate the nature and causation of the cultural and political changes of this era.

KATHARINE W. SWETT

"Born on My Land"

IDENTITY, COMMUNITY, AND FAITH AMONG

THE WELSH IN EARLY MODERN LONDON

When in 1605 Sir Thomas Mostyn, a north Welsh gentleman, joked to his in-laws that their young grandson was "of the humor that other servingmen be and giveth me warning every day that he will go to London to seek service," Mostyn was referring to a common phenomenon.[1] London's rapid growth in the sixteenth and seventeenth centuries was almost entirely fueled by migrants from Britain's provinces, including distant regions such as Wales and England's north and west. In huge numbers the capital attracted men and women, both "betterment" and "subsistence" migrants; that is, those who aspired to strike it rich as well as those trying to survive another winter. But how exactly most individuals arranged their long-distance moves to London, and how upon arrival they adjusted to the metropolis and constructed new lives for themselves there, are intriguing questions to which we have few answers. Yet answers are important, because so many early modern Londoners had been themselves formed in the very different social settings of villages and small towns: each act of migration began a reciprocal process that changed not only the individual migrant but also, incrementally, the capital itself. How the Welsh, for example, found aid, community, and success in London can further our understanding of London's dual role as both a multicultural metropolis of migrants and a city with its own powerful civic culture. While scholars such as Paul Seaver have begun exploring the influence of social rank on this role, early modern ethnicity remains largely a mystery.[2] This article uses city and provincial evidence to survey the significance of Welshness in Welsh migrants' adaptation to London life.

In *London and the Country Carbonadoed*, Donald Lupton's entertaining 1632 survey of the city and its people, he remarked admiringly and with considerable truth of the capital's diversity, "She's certainly a great world, there are so many little worlds in her."[3] Londoners new and established might form ties with one another based on neighborhood, parish, guild, occupation, or religion. Indeed, scholars have noted the influence of religion as a vital, if imperfect, cohesive force for a number of immigrant groups in the capital such as the French, Dutch, and Irish. From the mid-sixteenth century, Huguenot and Calvinist Dutch refugees fled the continent to escape religious persecution and were permitted by the English government to establish communities with their own Presbyterian churches. Welsh migrants, however, had no institutional focus in one of London's "stranger" churches, and their motives for migrating were primarily economic.

Yet categories of immigrants ought not to be presumed rigid, for economic factors were important even in "religious" migration. Trade conditions on the continent affected French and Dutch migration levels, and their value as skilled artisans increased the English government's willingness to accept Protestant groups from abroad. Outbreaks of xenophobia by the London population were linked to the state of the English economy rather than to actual numbers of immigrants. Thus perceptions of immigrants by the host community did not always reflect reality but could significantly shape migrants' experiences: foreignness was for these Protestants more a potential source of problems than religion. Once in London, French and Dutch immigrants had a practical incentive to stay church members, as their consistories generally had good relations with the city authorities and frequently intervened with them on their members' behalf. Nevertheless, their church ministers struggled against the gradual attrition of their congregations.[4]

For the Welsh we have no such ready measure of assimilation. Nor had they an obvious source of community in a particular guild, occupation, or neighborhood in the city.[5] Most city sources, such as parish records, lists of guild members or aldermen, and apprentice and freemen registers, show Welsh dispersed across the spectrum of occupations and social ranks from cooks and carpenters to prominent merchants.[6] The Welsh were also very well represented at all levels of the royal court and the Inns of Court. The funeral lists for Queen Elizabeth and for King James I are particularly striking in this regard.[7] This very wide distribution points decidedly toward their successful adaptation to metropolitan life. But on what terms?

The Welsh did share with one another both a distinctive ethnicity and its popular caricature. Although a recognizable speech pattern and a background of rural poverty also describe other long-distance migrants, the Welsh were set apart from the English by their unique history, culture, and language. Yet in England they suffered no legal and tax disadvantages, no periodic outbreaks of xenophobia as did aliens. Since the Acts of Union which brought Wales fully into the English polity between 1536 and 1543, the Welsh were simultaneously, in one writer's memorable phrase, "the nearest of foreigners and the most distant of provincials," with some characteristics of both groups.[8] Moreover, a robust satirical stereotype that touched on their social, economic, cultural, and linguistic differences with the English also signaled Welsh distinctiveness.

Popular representations of the Welsh would suggest that in them the English saw some things to marvel at, some to mock, little to fear, and nothing to envy. For example, issues of social rank and status were integral to English images of the Welsh. While purportedly Welsh tendencies toward superstition, greed, theft, naive rusticity, casual sexuality, and strong kin attachments all may be traced back to associations between Welshness and intense rural poverty, what seems to have been regarded as particularly Welsh was the juxtaposition of poverty with an utter lack of social humility, with assertions even to gentle status. This intersection of poverty with gentility contributed a great deal of comic mileage to English playwrights and pamphleteers, who at least in print claimed to have difficulty distinguishing a Welsh gentleman from a Welsh beggar.[9]

Scholars have argued that popular characterizations of the Welsh show that they were a familiar presence, a known ethnic group, in London. Several note the relative mildness of their literary caricature, considering it a rather straightforward description of the real Welsh or calling it "tolerant" or "affectionate."[10] This assessment is disputable, but it is true that sly, pedantic, foolish, or immoral Welsh characters in plays such as *The Merry Wives of Windsor* and Middleton's *A Chaste Maid in Cheapside* or in Sir Thomas Overbury's sketch of a "Braggadocio Welshman" mostly lack the overt hostility evident in attitudes toward the Scots or the Irish.[11] Several stereotypically Welsh traits were not incongruous in the capital. We might surmise that the combination of poverty, grand aspirations, and sturdy self-regard was ideal for producing new Londoners determined to succeed, while Welsh respect for rank and descent was reassuringly conservative.[12]

But even light mockery may demean status, and certainly being Welsh in London was different from being Welsh in Wales.[13] Shortly after lawyer James Price quarreled with his manservant in the capital in 1620, the latter disappeared with his master's horse and 40 pounds in gold and silver. Price went looking for him, without success, and vented his frustration in front of Londoners who knew a Welshman when they saw one:

He came to inquire where his man bought fine clothes and there he railed upon the man and woman and called them "whores." All the women in the street hard by Holborn Conduit did beat him very sore and abuse him vilely: they called him the "foolish Welsh justice."[14]

Outside London's theaters, in the street, vestry, and guildhall, how might stereotype or prejudice have colored the lived experience of Welsh ethnicity?

I

The adjustments and choices faced by Welsh migrants offer some gauge to how our subjects perceived both London's social climate and their own best interests. Did they find a basis for community in their foreignness, retaining ties with one another and with Wales as they adapted to metropolitan life? In *Micro-cosmographie* John Earle was dismissive of such connections:

The poorest tie of acquaintance is that of place and country. . . . These are only then gladdest of other, when they meet in some foreign region, where the encompassing of strangers unites them closer, till at last they get new, and throw off one another.[15]

If Earle was right, prejudice might further compress this process for the Welsh. If acceptance seemed to call for anglicization and assimilation, we might expect migrants to scatter and avoid one another in the metropolis.

The strategy of gradually melting into the larger population was feasible, for Wales's population was tiny and could not generate huge numbers of migrants. Vivien Brodsky Elliott calculates the Welsh composed only

3.4 percent of apprentice enrollments in the reigns of Elizabeth and James I, and 5.3 percent of Inns of Court members.[16] Their small total numbers would certainly have ensured many daily points of contact with non-Welsh Londoners. For example, the institution of apprenticeship was the main way in which the middling and upper ranks of migrants were integrated into London society. For Welsh boys it served also as an instrument of anglicization, because most of them had English masters. The enrollment of freemen from the Haberdashers' Company between 1547 and 1613 shows a minority of new journeymen of Welsh origins entered by patrimony or by Welsh masters. But the vast majority, 58 out of 75, had spent their seven years in an English household and were sponsored by Englishmen; obviously these men had achieved an adequate working relationship.[17] Some such bonds were stronger still. When Humfrey Lloyd, a London apprentice, came home to Shropshire to die in 1611, he left his master, Martin Smythe, a bequest of a clock. Householder and mercer Gilbert Lloyd asked his old master, John Prowde, to oversee his will, and Robert Geoffreys, a highly successful haberdasher and merchant adventurer originally from Caernarfonshire, left legacies in his will to his master's children, although his apprenticeship had ended 35 years earlier. Sir Richard Clough changed his will at the eleventh hour to leave most of his estate to his former master's disposition, including the support of Clough's wife and children.[18] We know next to nothing about the language preparation of nonelite Welsh migrants, but households mixing Welsh and English turn up readily in London records, and they would surely have improved the spoken English of apprentices and of domestic servants of both sexes. Joanna Davis from Oswestry and Elizabeth Evans from Flintshire were both servants to Evan ap Howell, clothworker of St. James Garlickhithe, in 1582. Dudley North is known to have employed a poor Welsh lad whom Richard Grassby describes as "kept to very hard labor and a thin belly."[19]

Parish records can also be used to demonstrate the integration of Welsh natives into London neighborhood life, which was particularly important because many Londoners may have had very limited familiarity with most of their large city.[20] In them Welsh appear across the parish social spectrum. While years of membership on the vestry are unsurprising in the cases of prosperous businessmen such as John Williams the goldsmith, who lived in St. Peter's Westcheap and did work for the court, or Robert

Geoffreys, who became an alderman while remaining active on the vestry in St. Michael Bassishaw, humbler householders of Welsh origins such as William Bowen and Gilbert Lloyd also worked their way up to positions of respect in their communities. A ratepayers' assessment list for repair of the church in St. Dunstan in the West in 1613, for example, includes Morris Powell, Evan Lloyd, William Griffith, and Robert Lloyd. Welsh names also crop up on parish poor relief lists. Lewis Powell, a recipient of aid in St. Peter's Westcheap for several years, obviously had an established, if unenviable, place in parish life.[21] Their litigation records, though evidence of conflict, indicate many Welsh Londoners' successful functioning in a mostly English environment, having forged and being called upon to defend extensive ties with neighbors and business partners. Lawsuits in which Welsh were allied with English associates against one another also demonstrate their activity in the larger society.[22] Sir Thomas Myddelton, the only native Welsh lord mayor in the Tudor-Stuart period, was too extremely successful to be considered typical, but he grew rich on ventures with English and Welsh partners and by lending money to both Welsh and English.[23]

Not only English masters and neighbors but also English in-laws were not unusual. Marriages between Welsh and English in London appear to have been quite common, and they indisputably ensured important points of contact. What Jean Howard terms the "inevitable cultural miscegenation of metropolitan life" was probably accomplished most efficiently within the family, where the face of Wales became a familiar and even a loved one.[24] In the absence of a recorded marriage license, intermarriage is easier to trace for the mothers, sisters, and daughters of male migrants than for the Welshmen themselves. For instance, we might guess from her use of his patronymic that Edward ap John and his wife, Anne ap John, Londoners who died in the 1650's, were both Welsh. Yet Anne may have been English, French, Dutch, or even Irish. Their daughter almost certainly married an Englishman in Giles Reason, and in another generation her family's Welsh descent would be hard to detect.[25] However, female connections should not be overlooked. Humphrey Toy, the apparently English printer of the Welsh New Testament in 1567, actually had a Welsh mother and grandmother.[26]

As Linda Colley, William Ingram, and others have noted, identities are not like hats; individuals, immigrants especially, may wear more than one at a time, and they nearly always did.[27] It may have been possible to vanish into a sea of Englishness in London, but Welsh migrants who did not perceive the need to do so are easily found. Instead, they constructed lives for themselves that found room for new friends and old, both English and Welsh. The naming of witnesses, debtors, and beneficiaries in wills provides a rough notion of the testator's social network, and Welsh Londoners' wills usually mention both Welsh and English individuals in a range of roles. The detailed 1584 will of David ap John David ap John ap Edward alias David Jones, gentleman, is a good example. Jones, a tutor for some years to the upper-class Carey family, left personal legacies of weapons or jewelry to his master, mistress, and all the Carey children. But, widowed and childless, Jones gave his land in Denbigh to his sister's sons. His five London cousins, the Joneses (one a clothworker, one an apprentice), were remembered, as were several kin still using the Welsh patronymic and a mother who had had five more children with an English husband. His maid Katherine, clearly a protégé or personal friend, received household goods including Jones's "best Welche coverlett" and fifty pounds. His native Welsh parish and his current London one were left similar sums, a frequent division for affluent Welsh-born testators.[28]

What's in a name? For London Welsh like David Jones, it is evidence of their origins. London migrants would be ideal subjects for investigating the expression of self-identity through names. In England, their distinctive accents would have marked the Welsh, probably for life: John Williams, bishop of Lincoln under James I, was teased about his accent as a student at Cambridge.[29] But anglicizing their names swiftly was entirely possible, perhaps even desirable for the Welsh, as their native patronymic system was a great source of fun to English writers. The 1647 pamphlet "The Honest Welch Cobbler" is typical of satirical literature in that its purported narrator is a Welshman, his name greatly lengthened for readers' amusement:

Shinkin ap Shon ap Griffith ap Gerard ap Sniles ap Shoseph ap Lewis ap Laurence ap Richard ap Thomas ap Sheffre ap Shaemes ap Taffie ap Harie, all Shentleman in Wales. Printed by M. Shinkin, printer to S. taffie, to be sold at the sign of the goat on the Welch mountain.[30]

Equally typically, having a Welsh narrator gave the author an excuse to write the piece in "Wenglish," or an exaggeratedly mispronounced version of the accented English spoken by native Welsh speakers.[31]

However, instead of wholesale anglicization, we find a variety of adaptations which in context are more suggestive of nonconflictual dual identities than of simple assimilation. Some London Welsh of humbler ranks kept the patronymic, although it was easy to construct an anglicized version from one's first two names and one might use both forms. We have Londoners Jevan ap Rees, merchant tailor, and Lewis ap Jenkin, schoolmaster (were his pupils Welsh or English?), while tailor John ap Rytherch to his Welsh contacts was John Prytherch as a plaintiff in Chancery in 1615. Gwyn ap Llewelyn, a Flintshire yeoman who may have been visiting his married daughter when he died in the parish of St. Savior's Southwark in 1619, had three sons: John, Lewis, and Evan Gwyn. Simplifying Welsh practice in London was another sign of adaptation. One option was to freeze the patronymic at one generation and thus convert it to a kind of surname, hence tradesmen Rice ap Owen and his son William ap Owen.[32] The use of aliases by London Welsh such as David Jones was also not uncommon.

For women, streamlining meant some loss of individuation in names such as English women already experienced. In Wales, women used the patronymic "verch," or "daughter of," with their first names and retained it after marriage, but in the capital we find women instead using "ap," or "son of," even before marriage, the identical form men used, and adopting their husband's patronymic at marriage as if it were a surname.[33] Ambition as well as convenience was probably involved in name changes. In Wales, the patronymic was in steady decline among the gentry, so recent migrants may well have associated discarding it with plans to enhance their social standing. Anglicization was not a process confined to London.

Nor was it the only or necessarily most significant change in the lives of new Londoners. While economic factors shaped much of the experience of Protestant refugee migrants, so too might religious impulses weigh heavily in some individuals fleeing poverty toward London. The prophet Arise (born Rhys) Evans was one such mix of the mundane and the reverent. Evans left behind first his poor mountain parish in Merioneth (where he learned English from the curate) and then the life of a tailor's apprentice in Chester. Drawn to London by fiery visions of disasters afflicting it, in 1629 he settled as a tailor in Blackfriars and began seeking out famous men to hear his prophecies. In St. Botolph's Church, Bishopsgate, in 1647 he proclaimed himself Christ.[34]

In the capital, new arrivals were suddenly exposed to diverse faiths, intense forms of Protestantism, and a great variety of works in print. This environment represented a greater change for some migrants, such as the Welsh, than for others. Wales was very rural, with low literacy rates, its people Welsh-speaking or bilingual, its church extremely poor and staffed by few preachers even at the end of the sixteenth century. The Reformation was introduced late, hampered by a language barrier that the government was reluctant to acknowledge. The New Testament and Prayer Book were translated into Welsh in 1567, but no cheap Welsh Bibles were published until 1630, when they were sponsored by two Welsh Londoners, Rowland Heylin and Sir Thomas Myddelton.[35] Meanwhile Welsh such as Lewis Hughes might turn to London to satisfy their hunger to hear the word of God. In his family's commonplace book he kept careful records of the many sermons he attended there in the 1620's and 1630's. He heard at least thirteen preachers, most of them favorites whom he sought out repeatedly and whose preaching inspired him to copy out prayers and related bits of Scripture as well. The commonplace book itself, kept in English, Latin, and Welsh, displays the wide-ranging world of letters for educated Welsh.[36]

Religion in itself did not unite or identify the Welsh in London. Although we can assert with confidence that in the metropolis Welsh migrants encountered the early modern explosion of print culture and new opportunities for religious instruction, their individual responses to this exposure ranged widely: some became more Protestant than others. David Jones bequeathed two of Calvin's books to his London half brother. Edward ap John, a poor man who from the weapons he possessed may have been a soldier in the Civil War, left his little Bible to a friend. Yet the 1631 will of alderman Robert Geoffreys, a pillar of the St. Michael's Bassishaw parish community, suggests conservative religious views, and although he, like David Jones, left money to his native parish and to his London one, the Haberdashers' Company received far more than either.[37] Wills illustrate the various ways religion offered individuals to express identity. Faith and ethnicity might converge in testamentary bequests: a donation to one's native parish was simultaneously an act of piety that demonstrated remembrance, acknowledged origins, displayed status and success.

Faith might itself become a new source of identity and community. The brief records of William ap Owen/Bowen's life sketch his multiple identities as staunch Protestant, citizen, guildsman, household head, neighbor, and Welshman. William ap Owen (his preference, as it was the name he used in his will), a joiner, appears in the parish records of St. Antholin's as William Bowen. He was a ratepayer ten years before becoming church-warden in 1595, the year before he died and left the parish five pounds toward its lectureship plus six pounds a year to augment the stipend of its morning preacher. William decided to leave his property to a London hospital if his only son died before attaining his majority, a major departure from Welsh testamentary custom and one with which his father, Rice, was unenthusiastic; he also left his native parish in Wales unacknowledged. William ap Owen had a number of Welsh relatives living nearby in London, but he chose as overseers of his will three "loving friends," the Taylor brothers and Geoffrey Prescott, who probably knew him by both names and from their own could be no more than part Welsh.[38] His strong Protestantism (he may have been a Puritan) would have brought him English friends and membership in a London community with perhaps firmer, though different, boundaries than those between Welsh and English.[39]

I I

Anglicization, then, was not monolithic but left migrants a range of choices in their self-presentation, and went hand in hand with Welsh solidarities and attachments of all kinds. When we turn from London records to provincial ones, to the correspondence of Welsh gentry families, their friends, kin, and clients, the picture of the London Welsh is different and yet much the same. Different because from the provincial view looking east and south, the Welsh in London were not scarce but ubiquitous, and advantageously so; the same because the Welsh in Wales took for granted that one could wear two hats, be both Londoner and countryman. While it may have paid to become English in the capital, it also paid to stay Welsh. One did not have to choose between them. Moreover, this ready multiplicity of identities, of social selves, was itself a facilitator of migrants' success, particularly in their early years, for it expanded their social connections and hence their opportunities to prosper in the capital. Joan Thirsk has pointed to the movements of the gentry as one of three major influences knitting London and the provinces together in the sixteenth and seventeenth centuries.[40] Also appreciated should be their role in the lives of new Londoners.

The papers of the Wynns of Gwydir, a prominent north Welsh family, illustrate over a period of several decades the range of ways in which the education, consumption, litigation, and ambitions of the Welsh gentry eased migration for others besides themselves. The Wynns' varied experiences with their messengers, carriers, and upper servants in London, for example, show how these men familiarized themselves with the metropolis and developed their own contacts there at their employers' expense. Some messengers dropped off letters and then got so drunk at alehouses that the Wynns were reluctant to entrust them with the replies. In 1610 Moris Owen, a family agent, persuaded young Richard Wynn to write his father that Owen had given him his allowance in London, but then borrowed the money himself for some personal business in the city.[41]

We must cast our net more widely than historians of the French and Dutch communities, whose subjects had a convenient means of demonstrating continued attachment to their origins in bequests to their churches. Staying Welsh in the metropolis might take various forms, including having other Welsh friends there, remembering one's native parish in one's will, or keeping one's original name or language. But it could also entail remaining receptive to the provincial Welsh in need of goods, services, or assistance, a participant in the informal ethnic networks of kinship, fosterage, friendship, employment, and tenancy connections used and sometimes created by families like the Wynns. The Wynns displayed a sharp sense of the utility of these networks. Their efforts in assiduously seeking out fellow Welsh who might be useful London contacts helped foster metropolitan Welsh connections; indeed, they suggest the difficulty for new Londoners, their Welshness rendered obvious by their persons or their kin from home, of avoiding such attentions. Thomas Griffith's peaceful retirement in Westminster was interrupted by Richard Wynn's request for help in arranging his brothers' schooling in 1615. The search for a rich English bride for the Wynn heir in the early seventeenth century prompted Sir John Wynn's brother, Ellis Wynn, to cultivate distant kinsman Piers Morgan, apprentice to the fabulously wealthy merchant Sir Baptist Hicks.[42] Morgan later rediscovered his homeland in his appetite for the Welsh cheeses with which the Wynns provided him.

While introductions, advice, and consumption were essential for the provincial gentry, they should be seen as part of a pattern of reciprocal exchanges that benefited Londoners, too. In general, country gentry such as Sir John Wynn or his kinsman, Sir William Maurice of Clenennau, visiting the capital once or twice a year for a few weeks, were in the habit of patronizing Welsh-owned businesses, predisposed to draw upon even the most distant kin or personal connection. If they wished, they could conduct all their business in the capital using only the services of their fellow Welsh. London Welsh in the tavern and innkeeping trades could provide a convenient home base for country customers and expect steady business from them. The Wynns nearly always used Welsh mercers, haberdashers, goldsmiths, and even barbers for their many purchases: such establishments could further cement bonds with their clients by providing an address from which to post and receive mail from the country: for example, "Mr. Cadwalader the barber at the sign of the White Hart in Holborn."[43]

Connections with large gentry families like the Wynns were useful in part because elites deployed their London contacts in the service of client kin and friends at home, which generated more business for Londoners. Haberdasher Robert Geoffreys, the son of a Gwydir tenant, began lending Sir John Wynn money at interest only a few years after finishing his apprenticeship in the late 1590's, and after years of cordial business dealings, he eventually arranged apprenticeships for both Owen and Morus Wynn, the latter to his neighbor Rowland Backhouse in 1615. The prosperous Geoffreys was relatively well documented in the London sources, but his Welsh ties are nearly invisible.[44] We assume that personal connections are behind many metropolitan activities such as moneylending, tradesmen selection, and apprenticeship bindings, but provincial sources can allow us actually to trace them. They are also valuable in identifying Welsh migrants in the capital. John Powell, the migrant son of Sir John Wynn's foster brother, was a mercer and the Wynns' first stop for clothing purchases in London even before he went into business for himself; they bought from Piers Morgan as well. Powell's case also illustrates the limits of these networks. When he went bankrupt in 1620, the Wynns wrote off the money he owed them but abandoned him to the Fleet Prison.[45]

The gentry were, of course, themselves numbered among London migrants, gravitating particularly toward the law and the court. Wilfrid Prest has noted that lawyers typically depended on their provincial connections for a client base when launching London careers, so the Inns of Court were always a major nexus of metropolitan-provincial connections.[46] In the 1630's, the fee notebook of Henry Wynn illustrates this pattern, with fellow Welsh constituting between 20 and 50 percent of his clientele while he built a career as a barrister, doubtless assisted by his brother Richard's post at court. The notebook of Evan Lloyd, a lawyer who did some work for the Wynns, lists clients mostly of humbler status than Henry's but with a similar proportion of Welsh among them.[47] In earlier decades the Wynns, like Sir William Maurice and other leading gentry, mostly used other Welsh lawyers in their extensive lawsuits: lawyers who expected their business, were miffed when it went elsewhere, and kept close tabs on the vicissitudes of provincial faction struggles.[48] Like tradesmen and merchants, London lawyers advantaged themselves in a competitive environment by weaving close connections to their provincial clients with personal services. Staying identifiably Welsh was good business sense. Evan Lloyd and William Jones helped the Wynns with matchmaking, and Robert Lewis supervised several teenaged Wynns at Westminster School. Sir John Wynn reciprocated with small gratuities and, frequently, assistance with their own property affairs back in Wales. Even well-placed royal officials looked for provincial aid from their petitioners. John Panton, a Wynn kinsman in Chancery, charged them ten pounds and legal help for his brother in north Wales in exchange for getting two Wynns onto the commission of the peace in 1610.[49]

A commonsensical formula for success in London thus included using the potential assets of one's regional and personal background. We might expect the practice of chain migration among the Welsh in London, since even optimistic assessments of social mobility there conclude that migrants needed all the help they could get to do well.[50] One implication of migrants' multiple identities underlined by the perspective of gentry family papers is that their new lives brought them anglicization and assimilation and *also* an intensified consciousness of their Welshness.[51] These ethnic networks were not just acted upon in London, responsive to its demands, but were themselves among the constituents of metropolitan society. And in contrast with French and Dutch immigration, which diminished drastically in the seventeenth century, new Welsh members continued to replenish them.

Welshness itself, then, had more than one dimension. It supplied an identity and a basis for community, as well as a greater need for such community in London. But "community" meant that the Welsh felt connected with one another—not that their interactions were uniformly harmonious and mutually loyal, although such cases are available. Dean Gabriel Goodman of Westminster provided a hospitable base in the cloisters for Welsh scholars and translators, for example. The Wynns made no assumptions that their complex connections were always nurturing. In 1604 Sir John Wynn instructed his son to ingratiate himself with their cousin Rowland White, "whom you are to respect as the most sufficient man of our country belonging to the court, and a very true friend where he liketh and taketh."[52] But they normally sought to maximize their resources, and their ethnicity was a resource. Their caution that more might be both hoped and feared from other Welsh is echoed in the evidence of litigation, for some suits show Welsh preying upon one another in the capital. Trusting old friends was not always wise, as a naive William Lloyd, gentleman, learned in 1620 after he was swindled out of his only horse by John Powell, servant to the earl of Southampton. Powell took the animal but reneged on his promise to sell it for Lloyd at a handsome profit.[53]

While the Wynns made full use of their Welshness in London, only scattered comments suggest that they found it a liability as well. In the early seventeenth century, Sir John Wynn was unpleasantly surprised by the resistance of English parents to a Welsh match for their daughters. One explanation was offered by his servant, William Lloyd: "If you consider their precise humor in London, who think our countrymen to be far more irreligious than they are." However, distance was the largest obstacle. John Wynn junior may have been sensitive to stereotyping when he predicted that his teenaged brothers Owen and Robert would behave like rubes ("steal to the town & run among the carts or else go to the Thames to swim, or to any other dangerous place") and embarrass him on their first trip to London. Occasionally they stereotyped themselves. In the 1570's, John Wynn, then at Furnivall's Inn, denied his father's accusation that he had wasted time "gadding" about the city with the other Welsh students. But as a parent himself 30 years later, Sir John only once tried to find English roommates for a son at the Inns; usually they shared chambers with other Welsh. However, the Wynns were certainly aware that for all their internal divisions, the Welsh were perceived as a distinct group. When a rival of theirs, a client of the duke of Buckingham, gave an overly sycophantic speech in Parliament, Owen Wynn's concern was that the man had made "his countrymen in general ridiculous to such as heard him."[54]

I I I

Part of the adjustment process for London migrants must have involved coming to terms with their origins and with the identities with which they had been born, reconciling their Welsh pasts with their London present.[55] The transition was most likely different for each individual, bound up with notions of selfhood and belonging that were not static over the course of a lifetime. In the absence of diaries we can catch only glimpses of these experiences. Edward Meredith, an affluent military contractor who styled himself "gentleman," was abruptly pulled back by his brother's death and his own guardianship of three Welsh nieces. In 1608, 40 years after he was orphaned as a small child, Jevan ap Rees, a merchant tailor, was still suing the Welsh kin who held his father's Denbighshire leaseholds. He wanted back the land he felt he should have inherited, but why? What meanings did it hold for him besides the extra income?[56]

The experience of Sir John Wynn's younger brother, Ellis, a Chancery clerk who died in 1623, highlights the personal trajectory implicit even for successful London migrants. Ellis Wynn moved to London as a young man and was happy there, prone to declaring that he should have known not to expect any good out of the country: a favorite duty was helping his nephews make the transition to the city life he so heartily recommended.[57] Yet until the last decade of his life his links with north Wales remained frequent, complex, and conflicted: the countryside for Ellis was represented in his ego-threatening, emotionally draining, and financially risky relationship with his elder brother, Sir John, whom he helped for 20 years as his London business agent and chief broker of large loans. Especially in his first decades in London, such work for country kin brought in useful extra funds, along with more complications, such as when Ellis and an English moneylender friend were sued in Chancery in 1597 by Welsh kin involved in a feud with Sir John and anxious to damage him through Ellis.[58]

Struggling to establish control over his ties with Wales, to recast them on his own terms, was for Ellis the project of a lifetime. His experience of multiple identities was explicit in his quarrels with his older brother, in which he spoke as kinsman and countryman but also sometimes argued his point by noting what "we," meaning sensible Londoners, considered proper. By their old age, Ellis and Sir John had stopped speaking, and the childless Ellis had seemingly turned his back on north Wales and fashioned an independent metropolitan existence with a close circle of English friends. At his death he left them most of his property, with an interesting exception: a large cash bequest to his friend and distant kinsman, the lord keeper of the Great Seal, John Williams, in terms redolent of pride in Williams's great achievement as a Welshman.[59]

Surveying the behavior of the visible and mostly successful Welsh displays London as a social environment in which clearly, with hard work and one another's help, they could succeed, negative stereotypes and possible prejudice notwithstanding. Faith drew some people toward London, helped keep others there, and was not a particularly compelling issue for still others, which we might expect from so socially diverse a group. No evidence indicates that a Welsh background shunted migrants in a specific religious direction; rather, the Welsh shared with the French and Dutch that their foreignness and not their religion was what made them different, noticed. However, drastic anglicization was unnecessary, for London's common culture had room to accommodate some elements of native Welsh culture. The light 1642 pamphlet *The Welchmens Jubilee*, for example, offers jovial praise of the patriotic traditions of St. David's Day, which honored Wales's patron saint.[60] Yet other, more equivocal evidence is available to contextualize this optimistic picture, starting with the spate of pamphlets harshly satirizing Welsh gullibility, superstition, and cowardice that were also published in London in the first years of the Civil War.

Suggesting that identities as Welsh and Londoner could coexist successfully is not the same as understanding what it was like to live alongside your own stereotype. After his nearly half a century of residence in London, what might Ellis Wynn's bequest have meant to him? Perhaps that he felt that Welsh solidarity was still necessary and that Welsh achievement should be celebrated and supported: that ethnicity should be a basis for community as well as a source of identity. It reminds us that migrants' attainment of prosperity, which we can measure, still leaves much unsaid about cultural hierarchies, the daily social experience of ethnicity, and their street sense of what it meant to be Welsh in early modern London. That having a place may not have been the same as being equal is suggested in a rare instance in which a real Welshman and his caricature can be found in the same place at the same time. In February 1618, Prince Charles arranged for a masque to be performed before his father and the court. To invigorate its second showing, Nathaniel Brent reported to Sir Dudley Carleton, the prince added live goats and Welshmen making speeches "sufficient to make an Englishman laugh and a Welshman choleric."[61] Sir Richard Wynn of Gwydir, then a gentleman of the privy chamber to the prince, can be placed in London during this winter, and he is very likely to have attended a masque sponsored and designed by his young master. Was Richard embarrassed or angered by the show? Was he indifferent to such jokes—all in a day's work for the Welsh in London? Or did he perhaps laugh with his English friends? Would you?

ROBERT B. SHOEMAKER

Separate Spheres?

IDEOLOGY AND PRACTICE IN LONDON
GENDER RELATIONS, 1660–1740

The study of gender has tended to concentrate primarily on ideas about gender, on representations and ideologies, rather than on social practice, although this approach has recently been criticized.[1] Following an approach so successfully adopted by Paul Seaver in his work on Puritanism, this chapter examines the relationship between ideas and social practice, between the prescriptions found in printed literature and the ideas about appropriate gender roles that are *implicit* in the ways men and women acted in day-to-day life.

According to the standard history of English gender roles, the period 1650 to 1850, or more commonly the decades after 1780, witnessed the emergence of a separate spheres regime, articulated in evangelical ideology and other literature, in which women were increasingly confined to the home, and public life became male dominated. I have argued elsewhere, following Amanda Vickery, that there are two problems with this argument. First, these conceptions of gender difference were already present in the seventeenth century, despite the fact that the term *separate spheres* had not yet been introduced. Second, in many ways even in the nineteenth century men and women did not follow these prescriptions: in practice there was always a degree of overlap in the activities of the two sexes, and such differences as did exist occurred along fault lines very different from the public/private dichotomy implicit in the separate spheres metaphor.[2] This chapter will assess whether this metaphor is any more appropriate for characterizing gender roles in the late seventeenth and early eighteenth centuries. A significant part of the ideological framework of separate spheres was

already in place in this period. Was it echoed in men's and women's behavior?

Revisionist accounts of seventeenth-century gender roles are moving
toward a separate spheres model, as the influence of Alice Clark's now very
dated picture of women's work in the early modern period is finally beginning to wane. Clark argued that married couples tended to work together
in the same occupations and that this led to a significant sharing of responsibilities between men and women. Recent research has shown that Clark
underestimated the extent of the sexual division of labor and power in the
workplace: men and women may have both worked at home, but their
tasks and responsibilities were very different. Presenting an alternative
model of early modern gender roles, Bernard Capp has recently argued
that women inhabited "semi-separate domains"; despite areas of overlap,
there were aspects of life, including childbirth and gossiping, where they
acted separately from men and possessed distinctive authority.[3]

Capp's argument offers a helpful way of reconceptualizing gender relations in the early modern period. Whether it applies to the largest and most
rapidly changing city in Europe at the turn of the eighteenth century remains
to be seen. If overlapping activities and responsibilities are to be found in any
aspect of early modern gender relations, it is likely to be in post-Restoration
London. The Civil War and Interregnum had set new precedents for wom-
en's involvement in political and religious life, calling into question accepted
gender differences and definitions, and after 1660 traditional gender roles
were potentially undermined by demographic pressures, changing employment patterns, and new forms of leisure. There were more women than men
in London, primarily due to the large numbers of women who migrated in
order to take up domestic service. As a result of this "surplus" of women,
unmarried women (spinsters and widows) in the City of London outnum-
bered their male equivalents by almost a quarter.[4] The urban environment
contained many dangers for women as well as opportunities. Women on
their own were vulnerable to poverty and the frequent suspicion of, as well as
less commonly the reality of, prostitution. Yet urban women worked in a
wider range of jobs than in rural areas; they could socialize in a number of
new venues; and more of them were literate than their rural counterparts.
And when they ran into trouble, they more frequently availed themselves of
the judicial system, where they accounted for much higher proportions of
litigants than in the countryside.[5]

At the same time, as the center of the printing trade, London was the source of most of the literature that disseminated ideas about gender, ideas which, as we will see, were for the most part unchanging. In the decades after the Restoration, Londoners of both sexes were presented, in religious instruction, conduct books, and periodicals, with clearly differentiated prescriptions for gender roles that would not have seemed out of place 100 years later (or earlier). This contrast between traditional conceptions of gender difference and women's unprecedented opportunities in public life in late seventeenth- and early eighteenth-century London is the central issue addressed by this chapter. After outlining the ideas about gender that were in circulation at the time (confining the discussion, for reasons of space, to explicitly prescriptive literature), this chapter will compare them with conceptions of gender implicit in public social practice in the metropolis, assessing whether these should be conceptualized in terms of separate or "semi-separate" spheres and the extent to which gender behavior reflected the ideas of difference found in the prescriptive literature. We will then conclude with some suggestions for how we should explain differences between ideology and practice.

I

The Christian tradition allowed for a variety of interpretations of gender difference, but by the early seventeenth century the dominant view emphasized women's fundamental inferiority to, and difference from, men. Arguments for spiritual equality during the Civil War and Interregnum raised the potential for a radical reordering of gender relations, but the Restoration saw most Christian writers, both radical and conservative, once again stressing traditional gender differences, with some important exceptions, such as the Quaker Margaret Fell.[6] As N. H. Keeble has written, it is not surprising that conservative Anglicans like Richard Allestree condemned women's speaking in public, "but even in the Puritan tradition the old liberties were restrained." Even nonconformist writers such as Richard Baxter stressed the authority of husbands over their wives and instructed women to attend to their domestic duties: "As the primary provision of maintenance belongeth most to the husband, so the secondary provision within doors, belongeth specially to the wife. . . . Watching over the family at home, when your husbands are abroad, is your proper work."[7]

These ideas were echoed in sermons,[8] and they achieved even wider circulation through conduct books, where writers from various Protestant perspectives (including at least two Anglican clergymen) made similar arguments.

Books outlining the proper behavior of men and women were an established genre dating back to at least the Reformation, and they consistently provided clear-cut prescriptions of the different behavior expected of each sex. The Restoration saw the publication, or republication, mostly in London, of a number of conduct books, many of which were explicitly addressed to women. The most popular author was undoubtedly Richard Allestree, whose *Whole Duty of Man*, first published in 1659, went through 59 reprints or editions by 1740 (all published in London), with rarely any change to the text. He followed this up with *The Ladies Calling*, published in 1673 in Oxford and reprinted twelve times by 1727. Allestree, an Anglican divine, was based in Oxford, but his works were clearly in circulation in London. Other publishing successes include the republication of Gervase Markham's *The English House-Wife, containing the inward and outward vertues which ought to be in a compleat woman* (first published in 1614, this went through eleven editions during this period under various titles, and although originally published as Book Two of a book called *Country Contentments*, it was published in London); Robert Codrington's *The Second Part of Youth's Behavior, or Decency in Conversation Amongst Women* (London, 1664, 1672); Lord Halifax's *The Lady's New Year's Gift; or, Advice to a Daughter* (London, 1688; reprinted twelve times before 1740); and William Fleetwood's *The Relative Duties of Parents and Children, Husbands and Wives, Masters and Servants* (London, 1705; reprinted four times before 1740). Fleetwood was rector of St. Augustine's and lecturer at St. Dunstan-in-the-West, Fleet Street. Although no significant new books were published between 1705 and 1740, the books listed above were frequently reprinted (and occasionally plagiarized) for the remainder of our period.

Rejecting the spiritual egalitarianism found in some Interregnum sects, these books portrayed the two sexes as fundamentally different, both in terms of the virtues that men and women were expected to have and in terms of the activities in which they were advised to engage. While women were described as more modest, merciful, compassionate, pious, temperate, and gentle, men were represented as harder, stronger, bolder, and more intelligent, but with more violent tempers. But it is with the duties and responsibilities that were accorded to each sex that it becomes clear that these writers were thinking of gender in terms that would later be encapsulated in the metaphor of separate spheres. Allestree, for example, argued that while husbands were expected to support their families and provide instruction in matters concerning their "eternal welfare," their wives were expected to devote themselves to motherhood (a duty to which they were seen as naturally inclined) and other household duties: as he noted in *The Ladies Calling*, "there appear so many particulars [of family duties] that if they were all duly attended, Ladies need not be much at a loss how to entertain themselves, nor run abroad."[9]

The implicit public/private distinction noted here is more fully developed in Markham's book, where he noted that the "office and employments" of men "are for the most part abroad," while the woman, as mother and mistress of the family, "hath her most general employments within the house." Similarly, Halifax told his daughter that the "government of your house, family, and children . . . is the province alloted to your sex," while a husband's "province is without doors" since to him running "the economy of the house would be in some degree indecent." Some authors, however, recognized that men's work also often took place at home in this period: Fleetwood argued that "nature . . . has given [men] the greatest strength and abilities . . . to the carrying on business at home, and trade abroad." What was different for women was that they were not expected to go "abroad," although this was not a blanket prohibition: Codrington argued that, by setting a good example, a "virtuous and discreet gentlewoman, [may] by her resort into public places . . . confer no less benefit to such as see her behavior, than she doth profit to her family."[10] Yet it is important to note here that Codrington is referring to gentlewomen, who were accorded greater public responsibilities than their social inferiors.

The idea of separate spheres is thus clearly present in these conduct books: for the most part women are expected to stay at home, while men go "abroad." Nonetheless, the spheres are not watertight. It is recognized that men possessed ultimate authority in the household, particularly on spiritual issues, and that some men ran trades from their home. Similarly, women were expected occasionally to go out in public, not only for social purposes but also for work. Since, Allestree noted, it was "unreasonable the husband should toil to maintain the wife in idleness," wives were also expected to engage in "labour and industry."[11] Such allowances were also made 100 years later when the metaphor of separate spheres came into use, but what is missing from these earlier prescriptions is the contrast between the virtue of home life and the corruption of the wider world, which led in the later period to the use of the image of the husband returning home, after a hard day at work, to the virtuous protection of his household, where he could sit at the fireside surrounded by his loving family. The greater separation of home and work evident in these nineteenth-century scenes reflected in part the increasing amount of work performed outside the home. But this was a long process, and in any case it contributed in only a minor way to accentuating gender differences that were already common in late seventeenth-century prescriptions.

A more complex set of ideas about appropriate gender roles can be found in the influential new form of prescriptive literature that emerged in this period: the periodical. Early periodicals emerged in the 1690's and early 1700's out of the world of London coffeehouses, and they sought to instruct their readers, like conduct books. From the very start, periodicals sought explicitly to attract both female and male readers, and through their commentaries and articles they constructed ideals of masculinity and femininity for the upper middle class and gentry. It has been argued that in doing this they adopted a model of separate spheres, with men and women accorded distinctive, complementary virtues and "'separate but equal' area[s] of activity and authority."[12] It is true that some early periodicals addressed specifically to women, such as the *Ladies Mercury* (1693, a satirical response to the *Athenian Mercury*) and *The Visiter* (1723–24), concerned themselves solely with domestic issues, with *The Visiter* covering those subjects "which tend to the improvement of the mind and manners as they are relative to a domestic life."[13] But the most successful periodicals presented a rather more sophisticated understanding of gender difference to a mixed audience.

Support for Kathryn Shevelow's argument that the *Athenian Mercury* (1691–97) "conceived an explicit structural equation between the feminine and the private" can be found in the fact that the one issue a month devoted to "ladies topics" concentrated on questions concerning love, sex, and marriage. Yet there was no attempt to discourage women from reading the other issues, where a much wider range of issues were discussed, and a response to a question concerning gender difference argued that "men and women [are] in essence the same." Significantly, *The Ladies Diary*, an annual publication that ran from 1704, soon abandoned recipes in order to devote more space to enigmas and mathematical questions; space was also devoted to science, geography, history, religion, and philosophy, as well as instruction on love, marriage, and motherhood.[14]

The periodicals did seek to construct gender differences, but most did not draw these explicitly along public/private lines. Like the *Athenian Mercury*, the *Spectator* (1711–14) also printed special issues for women concerning love and marriage, and the *Tatler* (1709–11) at times promoted the distinction between public, masculine life and the private, feminine sphere of home and family. But at other times these journals sought to encourage the participation of elite women in public life. Female readers of the *Tatler* were told that it would keep them politically informed by providing "the exact characters of all the chief politicians who frequent any of the coffee-houses from St. James's to the Change." As Lawrence Klein has argued, these two periodicals sought to encourage educated, polite *public* discourse, and women were thought to play an important role in this as agents of politeness and civility: their vivacity would temper male gravity and vulgarity. As this suggests, men and women were thought to possess different virtues. Nonetheless, in seeking to reform upper-middle-class male behavior and adapt it to an urban setting, these prescriptions modified traditional gender distinctions, not only in public life but also at home. Men were expected to possess a capacity for feeling and softness, give up violence, be companionable and faithful husbands, and participate in domestic management.[15] In this sense these periodicals, like the conduct books, conceptualized men and women as fundamentally different in terms of the virtues they possessed, but the periodicals adapted to their urban context by diluting the public/private dichotomy. Both in companionate marriages at home and in the coffeehouses of London, men and women were expected to act together, but each sex contributed different qualities and skills.

II

Although the argument shifted somewhat in the periodical literature, there was no lack of ideas circulating around the turn of the eighteenth century to promote gender differentiation in ways that anticipate the nineteenth-century metaphor of separate spheres. But to what extent did these ideas mirror, or help shape, actual social practice in London at this time? To answer this question, we will examine a number of aspects of public life, defined as life outside the home: religious practice, paid employment, street life, popular protest, and leisure activities, focusing on middle- and lower-class Londoners.

The information available on the gendered dimensions of religious practice is limited, but it illustrates some of the main themes that we will encounter in examining other aspects of social life. Just as writers from most religious perspectives in the Restoration drew back from the radical ideas of the Interregnum, so the sects themselves closed down most opportunities for women after 1660. Even the Quakers discouraged female preaching and prophesying. In a climate of repression, nonconformist women were to a certain extent pushed into the vital but domestic role of facilitating family and household worship.[16] Yet women in London continued to play an important public role as well. Although they were largely excluded from the Anglican religious societies, founded in 1678 for the purpose of encouraging spiritual reflection (according to Margaret Hunt, these men feared that feminine sexuality would undermine their program of rational discipline), women accounted for a third of the dissenters who were arrested for worshiping at "conventicles" in London in the 1660's and 1680's and over two-thirds of the members of Baptist and Congregational churches in London between 1651 and 1750, a higher proportion than in the rest of the country.[17]

With the establishment of Quaker women's meetings in London in 1671, Quaker women acquired responsibility for charity, education, evaluating proposed marriages, and enforcing moral discipline. These were all issues where women were thought to speak with knowledge and moral authority. Nonetheless, men also discharged some of these responsibilities. And while women sat in a different part of the room in mixed-sex meetings, their essential unity with men was emphasized. Both sexes participated in the London Six Weeks Meeting, "the prime meeting of the city" according to George Fox, and the six meetings held monthly across London. In the eighteenth century, however, women appeared to have stopped attending many of these meetings.[18] By this time women found their greatest and least gender-limited opportunities in marginal sects such as the French Prophets and the Philadelphians, where more women than men became prophets and where inspired women could convoke assemblies, give blessings, and issue orders. Yet as Hillel Schwartz has argued, even in these sects men monopolized sacerdotal functions and the power to determine whether those claiming to be inspired were true prophets or not.[19] Unfortunately, much less is known about the gendered dimensions of Anglicanism, where women's public activities were largely confined to attendance at church (in separate seating) and participation in the ceremony of "churching" after childbirth. Yet both these activities confirm the impression that arises out of the available evidence concerning nonconformist religion. Women did not lose their public religious role after 1660, but, female prophets apart, they were more likely to participate in activities that were often, though not always, segregated by sex and that frequently arose out of the activities (such as motherhood, charity, and moral discipline) which were defined as essentially feminine by the conduct books.

III

In studying the more fully documented topic of gender roles at work, we are fortunate to be able to refer to the research of Peter Earle, whose study of the London Church Court depositions between 1695 and 1725 has unearthed valuable evidence of the employments of both lower- and middle-class men and women. Contrary to Alice Clark, Earle argues that there was "an extreme gender division of labour in London and . . . the work of women was almost entirely divorced from" that of men. Both men and women worked, but they worked in different occupations, with women's work concentrated in the occupations of domestic service, charring and laundry work, the needle trades, nursing, catering, and shopkeeping and hawking. Where both men and women worked in the same occupation, such as domestic service, Earle says they carried out very different tasks. Only 12 percent of wives worked in their husband's trades, and Earle suggests that "most wives, far from being in partnership with their husbands, probably rarely saw them in the hours of daylight." Thus he concludes, deliberately refuting Alice Clark, "the world of women's work was in fact a very female world in which women worked with women, talked to women, and amused themselves with women, and were even for the most part employed by women. This is a world of parallel spheres and not a world of economic partnership between the sexes." According to Earle, the nineteenth-century division of labor at work (as evident in the 1851 census) was already in place around 1700.[20]

There are, however, problems with this argument. Earle's own evidence shows some significant areas of overlap in the work of men and women: many couples did work together, for instance by jointly running a food and drink outlet. (In fact, he suggests that the labor in this sector of the economy was "probably" evenly divided between the sexes.) His evidence also shows that both men and women worked hawking and peddling goods in the streets, and in bakeries, the needle trades, and market gardening, though not, of course, always on the same tasks.[21] Among the street sellers of London, there was a division of labor between the women, who sold most of the food items (fresh fruits and vegetables, fish, meat, bread, prepared food) and bought up materials of small value (such as grease, old clothes, and rabbit skins) for resale, and men, who sold more consumer goods and offered services (as chimney sweeps, chair menders, knife and scissor grinders, and tinkers). Yet women also sold a wide range of consumer goods, and men sold fish and some fruits and vegetables. In some cases, husbands and wives worked together, and both sexes sold ballads.[22]

In her recent book on the middle class between 1680 and 1780, Margaret Hunt provides further evidence of overlap in the employments of the two sexes. From her study of a range of evidence, including litigation in debt cases, she found that many middle-class women did work in their husbands' businesses, especially if that business involved keeping a shop. (Hunt suggests such work would have been underreported, in the judicial records looked at by Earle, since status-conscious wives may have been unwilling to admit they worked in this way.) The worlds of men's and women's work were by no means entirely separate. Hunt also shows from an examination of insurance policies that many wives ran their own businesses, often with other women who pooled available capital resources. Nonetheless, possibly out of status concerns, they tended to identify themselves in legal records as the wives of, for example, surgeons or plaisterers, failing to identify their own trades. Hunt calls these women "the first substantial body of independent, literate, and self-supporting women in English history." As impressive as this evidence is, it is important to note that the occupations most such women engaged in were concentrated in the textile, catering, and shopkeeping trades, which Earle's evidence would suggest were commonly practiced by women, such as milliner, mantua maker, house chandler, pawnbroker, haberdasher, and tea dealer. Yet it was not only women who worked in these trades. Only in two trades did women dominate: 61 percent of the milliners, and 58 percent of the mantua makers. In other cases, women account for 18.5 percent or less of the insured in each trade (although Hunt suggests that the real proportion of women would have been higher, since women were less likely than men to insure their property).[23] This suggests that men and women occasionally did engage in the same trades, although most trades were dominated by one or the other sex: the overlap in the work activities of each sex was in this sense limited.

In sum, there was a division of labor in the types of work men and women engaged in, with occupations which had "domestic" connotations often dominated by women (domestic service, laundry work, the textile trades, food sales). Nonetheless, we should not ignore the considerable evidence of overlap: Earle's formulation that this was a "world of parallel spheres" seems exaggerated. Moreover, women were by no means kept out of the public sphere with regards to work. Much of their labor took place outside their homes, and although some occupations, such as domestic service, placed them inside the homes of other people, many trades (notably hawking goods) took place on the streets, where their street cries would have been very noticeable, and others involved considerable interaction with the "public," such as shopkeeping. On the basis of Earle's data, Hunt even argues that it was during the years when women had small children to take care of that they were most likely to work outside the home: economic rather than domestic considerations shaped their working lives.[24]

I V

Clearly women were present on the streets of London in significant numbers in this period. What we need to ascertain is whether in any sense spatial experiences of urban life were distinctive for each sex. Evidence of day-to-day street behavior is, of course, patchy, but it is clear that, probably more than in rural areas, women as well as men of all social classes were present on urban streets. Not only did both sexes frequently work the streets as hawkers and peddlers, but it is remarkable that respectable men and women who did not know each other traveled across town together in hackney coaches.[25] Middle-class women pedestrians were also present, although they may have been less likely to loiter than their social inferiors. This can be seen in William Hogarth's "Morning" print (1738), with an elite woman walking purposefully toward Covent Garden Church, passing stationary female beggars, one or two prostitutes, and some market-women. Reflecting the growth of consumerism, middle-class women spent a considerable amount of time shopping, a point which led Hunt to conclude that "many middling women consumers may have spent less time at home than their husbands did."[26]

There were, however, important differences in how each sex used the streets. Most important, it was best for women to avoid some streets and some types of behavior if they wished to avoid being suspected of prostitution. In districts (such as Covent Garden or parts of the East End) where prostitution was tolerated (within limits), unaccompanied women were liable to be considered fair game by lascivious men and reforming constables alike, particularly late at night. In *The London Spy*, Ned Ward describes an encounter with some sailors on an East End street, who "were so mercurial in their actions, and so rude in their behavior, that a woman could not pass by 'em but they fell to sucking her lips. . . . [They] could have committed a rape in public without a sense of shame, fear or danger."[27] When out in public, women unaccompanied by men, especially when young, needed to regulate their appearance, plan their routes, and pay attention to the time of day in ways that men rarely had to consider, although poorer men did need to dress and act in ways that prevented them from being labeled vagrants, and all men may have felt some need to avoid the contexts (certain types of dress, specific taverns) that might lead them to being labeled "sodomites."[28]

Another important difference in how men and women acted on the streets is that both middle- and lower-class women may have spent more time working and socializing in that liminal area between public and private spaces, around the doorstep. Much of this time was spent talking, or "gossiping" as it was called, and as several historians have pointed out, this activity served as a form of social control, since it often led to public accusations against friends and neighbors suspected of behaving improperly. As Bernard Capp has argued, this type of public censure gave women a form of informal public authority in which the activities of men, as well as women, could be criticized; this is part of the "semi-separate female domain" which, he argues, women possessed in this period. In her study of defamation in early seventeenth-century London, Laura Gowing has argued that the gendered language of insult played a major role in constructing gender differences.[29]

The evidence of defamation cases from this period, however, does not support the argument that the public insult was a distinctly female activity. In both the London Consistory Court and Middlesex Quarter Sessions, men accounted for around two-fifths of the defendants accused of defamation. Despite contemporary stereotypes that labeled women as the sex most inclined to loquaciousness, defamation was not a preserve of the female tongue, and in fact there is evidence of increasing concern in the early eighteenth century that it was becoming a particularly male vice.[30] As is evident from depositional evidence, men as well as women spent considerable amounts of time loitering in doorways and shops, conducting conversations which could lead to public accusations of misconduct. Fifty-nine percent of the audiences (those who heard the insult) in a sample of 71 London defamation cases between 1679 and 1740 included both men and women.[31]

If we look at the types of insults and the language used in defamation cases, however, we can see some important gender differences. Most, but not all, of the insults made by women or targeted at women were sexual (involving some use of the term *whore*), which reflects the importance that chastity played in establishing a woman's reputation. Even when Londoners wanted to criticize a woman for something else, they used the language of sexual promiscuity to make the insult. Thus one female butter vendor was called "bitch, whore, common whore" when she was accused of "cheating people in the weight of her butter."[32] When men made sexual insults against women, the language they used was somewhat different, in that they were more likely to make specific accusations of sexual misbehavior, which even occasionally involved bragging about having had sex with the woman they were insulting. Men, too, could be insulted for their sexual misdemeanors, although examples of this are fairly rare and typically involve accusations of something more than simple fornication, such as sodomy, or siring a bastard child, or running a brothel.[33] But men were the victims of a much wider range of insults than women, with other men questioning, for example, their courage or their financial credit. We have seen that women also ran businesses, however, and they appear to have publicly attacked the credit of tradesmen and women, though apparently not as often as did men.[34]

The defamation evidence thus suggests a number of areas of similarity in the public behavior of the two sexes: honor and reputation were clearly important to both, and both men and women were involved, as participants and victims, in the public voicing of scandalous words, not only in the public/private location of the doorstep and through windows, but also in streets and markets and in taverns. There *were* differences in how men and women behaved, but these are perhaps best construed as differences of degree rather than kind: women were the primary victims and propagators of sexual insults, and most recorded insults directed at women were of this kind. The insults directed by and against men, on the other hand, tended to be more specific and concerned a wider variety of alleged malfeasance than women. Yet women, too, could insult and be insulted on issues other than their sexual honor, such as their business reputation.

Not only did men and women sometimes make the same kinds of insults, but they often acted together. Many incidents of public insulting actually involved groups of people and thus were essentially small riots or mob actions. In contrast to Capp's evidence, these groups were frequently composed of both sexes. Thirteen out of twenty cases of defamation with more than one defendant prosecuted at the Middlesex Sessions involved men and women acting together. In five cases, married couples were charged, but in eight other cases, some of the participants were unrelated. In 1703, for example, Euan and Anne Evans of Wells Yard in the parish of St. Giles in the Fields assaulted Eleanor Price and called her "old bawd and common whore" and threatened revenge against her. It is not clear why they thought they needed to take revenge, but around about the same time Price, her husband, Richard, and Elizabeth Woodfield (also from Wells Yard) riotously assaulted Anne Evans, "calling her whore and other reproachful language [and] giving her a daily disturbance in her habitation."[35] The court records do not provide any further details of the cause of this dispute, but it clearly involved frequent public insults and included men and women acting together. Public insult was often a mixed-sex neighborhood activity. Nonetheless, it is notable that in most cases the insults were targeted at women.

With women and men both spending a significant amount of time in public, and with both engaging in defamation, it is not surprising that both sexes were active participants in the incidents of collective protest that so frequently erupted on the streets of London in this period. In my study of the London "mob," I found that women were involved in one-third of the cases of riots, mobs, and tumults that were reported to the Middlesex Sessions in this period. The large number of women in these protests, many of whom were unmarried, reflects the considerable social and economic independence that urban women enjoyed at this time.[36] But there was something of a sexual division of labor in rioting. The political protests of the period were male dominated, with very few women participating. Although large groups of women had lobbied Parliament during the Civil War, in the more stable environment after 1660 there is virtually no evidence of female participation in the political crowds of Restoration London, and few women participated in early eighteenth-century London political protests such as the Sacheverell riots or the rioting on the occasion of the accession of George I. This is not to say that women did not voice their political opinions in public. A small minority of the writers, printers, and sellers of political tracts were women, and some were arrested for individually speaking seditious words: 11 percent of the defendants prosecuted for seditious words during the reign of Charles II were women.[37] Other types of riots in which women were relatively inactive were protests involving disputes over property rights (all 34 defendants identified in my sample were men), riots involving the explicit use of violence (13 percent of defendants were women), and riots directly challenging officers of the law (women accounted for 24 percent of defendants in riots involving the rescue of prisoners and 30 percent of defendants involved in attacks on officers of the peace).[38] One could conclude, as I did somewhat hastily in 1987, that these issues were "outside [women's] traditional sphere of influence,"[39] but now I want to stress the fact that, property disputes aside, women did participate in a quarter or more of these attacks on legal authority.

Yet women, often alongside men, played a much more prominent role in riots concerning sexual morality and economic issues. This is hardly surprising, given the greater importance (evident in the defamation cases) accorded to the sexual reputation of women than men in this period, and the fact that so many women, as we have seen, engaged in paid labor, as well as performing much of the household shopping. Small-scale protests involving women frequently arose outside shops, caused by trade rivalries or customers who felt they had been cheated. For example, in 1727 a married woman from Holborn raised a mob attacking a husband-and-wife team of fishsellers, "driving them from the stand where they sell fish."[40] These protests can perhaps be seen as London's version of the food riot in this period.

The fact that most organizations of workers excluded women, and that women workers often worked in isolation from one another, helps explain why women played a minor role in most industrial disputes in this period, with some important exceptions. Intriguingly, the mixed-sex protests reveal apparently separate strategies adopted by each sex for organizing disorder. In 1675, both male and female weavers joined the riots that destroyed engine looms for the production of silk ribbons (the machines were accused of putting weavers out of work). The participation of both sexes reflects the fact that they worked together on the looms. Significantly, however, a woman identified as a weaver's wife was heard to say that "if the women would rise to pull down the engine looms, she would ... help and assist them,"[41] suggesting that she thought the female weavers might riot separately (all the available evidence suggests the contrary).[42] In 1697, women and men once again defended their jobs, this time by demonstrating in front of Parliament in favor of a bill to restrain the wearing of imported silks and calicos. In this case, women emphasized their role as mothers by bringing along their children, thereby highlighting the hardships that families experienced as a result of these imports. Although it was alleged that it was the male weavers who *sent* their wives and children, other evidence suggests that it was the women who organized the men. According to one observer, a group of poor women paid a bell woman "to go about to raise the weavers, and so go to Westminster, and petition Parliament." Once again it appears that it was both sexes who actually went to Parliament.[43] But this evidence points to the fact that even where men and women participated jointly in popular protests, they did not necessarily do so in the same ways or for the same reasons.

V

Similarly, women as well as men played an important public role in leisure pursuits, although the nature and significance of their activities differed in important ways. Both sexes attended and performed at Bartholomew Fair, Mayfair, and even the extraordinary Thames Frost Fair of 1684. As Ned Ward observed in his description of comedy booths and drolls at Bartholomew Fair, a "mixture of sexes . . . is customary at such sort of entertainments."[44] Popular sports involved women much less often, except as spectators, although there is some evidence of women playing cricket, engaging in running races, and fighting. Elizabeth Pepys went with Samuel to see bull-baiting and prize fights. But as César de Saussure commented, clearly shocked by the violation of traditional gender roles at staged fights between women, "fortunately, it is very rarely one hears of women gladiators."[45]

Women were also involved in day-to-day socializing at the alehouse, although not invariably, and, as at fairs, there was the distinct danger that they would be labeled prostitutes. Like street behavior more generally, context was the key. Some women ran alehouses, with or without the help of their husbands, and many others worked there as maidservants. But they were only occasionally present as clients, typically but not exclusively accompanied by men, as is evident in mid-eighteenth-century prints such as "The Wapping Landlady" and Hogarth's "Beer Street." Samuel Pepys normally drank publicly with his male colleagues, but he occasionally took female relations or his mistresses to alehouses. Because alehouses were associated with sexual promiscuity, women on their own were likely to be viewed as sexually available, and as a result some women were reluctant to visit alehouses. In a revealing episode, Pepys went to the Fleece Tavern in Covent Garden with a courting couple, Clement Sankey and Mary Archer, "but Mr Sanchy [sic] could not by any argument get his lady to trust herself with him into the tavern." Although diary evidence and the writings of contemporary observers suggest that, in terms of customers, the alehouse was commonly a male homosocial environment, there is some evidence of *groups* of women drinkers, including several women dancing to a fiddler, female traders conducting business, and a group of lower-class women attempting to resolve a defamation dispute.[46] Ned Ward's semifictional "London Spy" visited a down-market alehouse in Billingsgate, which he called a "dark-house," where he encountered, in separate rooms, groups of "fish-wives" ("engaged in a mess of tittle-tattle") and seamen. The gin shops that became so popular in the early eighteenth century were also, as contemporary commentators frequently complained, visited by great numbers of the poor of both sexes.[47]

The coffeehouses that flourished with a more elevated clientele from the start of our period were more male dominated. Evidence from diarists and commentators, including Samuel Pepys, Peter Briggens, Ned Ward, William Ryder, and César de Saussure, suggests that coffeehouses were primarily fraternized by men, despite Steve Pincus's claim that "there is every reason to believe that women frequently attended the newly fashionable coffeehouses" in the Restoration period. Women occasionally ran coffeehouses, but otherwise they seem only to be present as prostitutes.[48] Clubs and voluntary societies frequently met in coffeehouses and alehouses, and these too were largely restricted to men in this period.[49]

Elite women were much more numerous in outdoor social venues such as bowling greens, walks, and gardens and at organized social events such as assemblies, the theater, and the opera. Typically these were mixed-sex activities, and male contemporaries frequently commented on the significance of women's participation in terms of the display of their status and wealth and that of their husbands; the women may well have seen things differently. Saussure wrote that "English women walk fast and well, but in reality I think they do it more in order to show their clothes than for the pleasure of the exercise; and this is the case too with plays and concerts, in which they do not really seem to take much interest."[50] To men like Saussure, women's clothes and demeanor displayed wealth and status, but of course such display could also be interpreted as advertising women as sexually available, and there were frequent concerns about the presence of prostitutes in all these venues. Of course, the men who joined respectable women in these activities can also be interpreted as displaying their wealth and status, but men were conscious that too much attention to their appearance could lead to them being considered effeminate "fops."[51] Nonetheless, largely because of the meanings men attached to female behavior, it was women who faced the most restrictions on what they could do in public, despite their substantial involvement, in patterns somewhat different from those of men, in a range of leisure activities outside the home.

VI

It should be clear that there were significant differences in the activities and opportunities open to women and men in London at this time, but these differences were not in any way divided along public/private lines. Women as well as men were an important physical presence in the public spaces of early modern London, and they engaged in a variety of activities including paid employment, the public censuring of misbehaving neighbors, popular protests, and recreational pursuits. As Lawrence Klein has pointed out, eighteenth-century definitions of public and private were varied, and they often differed from the more modern characterization of the dichotomy as home/outside the home used in this chapter. Further research on early modern understandings of the "public" and the "private" is clearly necessary. Yet however the dichotomy is defined, the evidence presented here suggests that it is unlikely to correspond directly with differences between male and female behavior.[52]

One can, however, detect a rough "separation of spheres" in the *types of issues and activities* each sex engaged in, with women's public acts often extensions of their expected domestic functions as virtuous wives and mothers: hence the essentially domestic nature of most types of paid employment they performed (domestic service, laundry work, catering, nursing, textile work); the concern with the enforcement of sexual morality in defamation cases (with the defamers calling attention to their own sexual virtue by pointing out the misbehavior of others); their role as primary consumers, which is evident in their disputes with shopkeepers; the concern with the survival of the family economy in labor unrest; the emphasis on the display of their families' wealth and status in elite leisure pursuits; and the concerns about sexual promiscuity that constrained their involvement in virtually every aspect of public life, especially leisure (with any inappropriate activity likely to lead them to being labeled "whores"). Similarly, men's engagement in a much wider range of employments, their use of defamation to address a somewhat different and broader mix of issues, their participation in popular protests concerning property disputes and politics where women were largely absent, and their domination (with some exceptions) of some leisure venues such as the alehouse and the coffeehouse—all can be seen to constitute a distinctive male "sphere" of activities and concerns. Given that the behavior of the sexes overlapped in so

many ways, however, the term *sphere*, with its connotations of imperme-
able physical barriers, is not appropriate for characterizing these patterns
of activity. Capp's term *domain*, if stripped of its physical dimensions and
conceived instead in terms of activities and responsibilities, seems more
appropriate.

Why, then, was social practice so different from the clear separation of
gender roles, along the public/private dichotomy, outlined in the prescriptive literature? It is, of course, not surprising that social practice was
messier than ideological prescriptions, particularly in a rapidly changing
urban environment where so much of men's and women's lives took place
outside the home. Patterns of behavior did reflect some of the ideas of gender difference found in the literature, particularly the periodicals. Women
did focus on issues where they could exercise their expected virtues of
compassion and chastity and which could be perceived as domestic, while
men did participate in activities where their expected qualities of strength
and forwardness could be exercised. In an urban environment, perhaps
this was as close to the prescriptions that men and women could realisti-
cally achieve. But the conduct books continued to articulate a model of
public/private gender difference that contrasted markedly with social practice. What were these writers seeking to achieve?

Three possible explanations merit consideration. First, it is possible that
writers were seeking to impose order on socially diverse practices as part of
a broader agenda of attempting to promote religious and political stability,
possibly as a conservative reaction against the disorder (gender and otherwise) of the Civil War and Interregnum or, in the case of later publications, as an attempt to consolidate the position of the new post-1688 regime. In this sense, prescriptions of gender difference could be seen as part
of a broader strategy for imposing order, much as writings attacking assertive women in the early seventeenth century have been interpreted as a
product of wider concerns about social and political instability.[53] This
might explain Allestree's motivations: he was a royalist Anglican writing at
the time of the Restoration.[54] As an ardent Whig writing in the early
1700's, Fleetwood could be seen as seeking to prevent any disorder that
might undermine the Revolution settlement. Yet we have seen that writers
from a variety of religious and political points of view promoted similar
views about gender. Moreover, the ideas disseminated at this time in the
conduct books were not new. Some, like Markham's *English House-Wife,*

were first published earlier, in this case in 1614. Other conduct books published in the early 1600's, such as William Gouge's *Of Domesticall Duties* (1622), contain similar ideas about the separation of spheres found in the conduct books and periodicals discussed here. For example, Gouge discussed the relative duties of each partner in marriage: "To take order for the provision of things without doors, is more fit for the husband . . . to order the smaller things within doors is more fit for the wife."[55] Thus, these arguments about gender cannot be seen as specific responses to the religious or political instability of the 1660's or 1680's.

Second, it is possible that the authors of prescriptive literature were attempting to create a distinctive new code of behavior for the upper-middle and gentry classes in London, much as Davidoff and Hall argue that evangelical writers promoted separate spheres for the middle class in late eighteenth-century provincial England.[56] Certainly periodicals like the *Tatler* and *Spectator* can be interpreted as having this intention. Yet, as we have seen, these periodicals in some ways undermined, rather than reinforced, the model of separate spheres found in the conduct books. Moreover, the ideas in the conduct books were not directed solely at a middle-class or elite audience. This is clear from the full title of Allestree's *Whole Duty of Man, Laid Down in a Plain and Familiar Way for the Use of All, But Especially the Meanest Reader*. Given the large numbers of copies sold (the standard print run was about 1,000, and we have seen that Allestree's book went through 59 editions by 1740),[57] the conduct books must have reached a reasonably large and socially diverse audience.

Finally, it is possible that, in prescribing clearly delineated gender roles, writers were responding to a breakdown of gender differences in London, where women had unprecedented opportunities to act in public in ways not possible in the countryside. In redefining the public/private divide, the *Tatler* and *Spectator* do seem to have been written for a specifically London audience. Several of the conduct books were written explicitly for a female audience, taking advantage of the rapid increase in female literacy that occurred in the metropolis. Yet while some were written by Londoners (Halifax, Fleetwood, Codrington) and could possibly be construed as directly aimed at urban inhabitants, the others were not, and it is not possible to detect any differences in approach between the London and provincial authors. Moreover, the social world that the conduct books implicitly imagine does not seem distinctively urban.

Despite these objections, all three arguments do help us understand why these largely conventional ideas about gender difference were so commonly voiced after 1660. Although the content of the ideas was not apparently shaped by the religious and political uncertainty of those years, and only in a limited way by the values of newly prosperous elite social groups and the novel pattern of gender relations found in the rapidly changing metropolis, their repetition in such contexts can be interpreted in part as responses to the anxieties aroused by these changes. During times of uncertainty, conventional ideas about gender difference, rooted in the Judeo-Christian tradition, were given new prominence. Their influence on the day-to-day lives of the inhabitants of this bustling city, however, was limited.

REFERENCE MATTER

Notes

MCCLENDON AND WARD: INTRODUCTION

EPIGRAPHS: William Walwyn, *The Compassionate Samaritane: Liberty of Conscience Asserted and the Separatist Vindicated*, in *Divine Right and Democracy: An Anthology of Political Writing in Stuart England*, ed. David Wootton (Harmondsworth, Middlesex: Penguin Books, 1986), p. 260; Richard Hooker, *Of Lawes of Ecclesiasticall Politie: The Sixth and Eighth Books* (1648), in *Divine Right*, ed. Wootton, p. 228.

1. Christopher Haigh, *English Reformations: Religion, Politics, and Society Under the Tudors* (Oxford: Oxford University Press, 1993); Eamon Duffy, *The Stripping of the Altars: Traditional Religion in England, c. 1400–c. 1580* (New Haven: Yale University Press, 1992). The main object of revisionist criticism is A. G. Dickens, *The English Reformation* (New York: Schocken Books, 1964), and *The English Reformation*, 2d ed. (London: Batsford, 1989). Earlier revisionist works include Christopher Haigh, *Reformation and Resistance in Tudor Lancashire* (Cambridge: Cambridge University Press, 1975); J. J. Scarisbrick, *The Reformation and the English People* (Oxford: Blackwell, 1984); Christopher Haigh, ed., *The Reformation Revised* (Cambridge: Cambridge University Press, 1987); and Robert Whiting, *The Blind Devotion of the People: Popular Religion and the English Reformation* (Cambridge: Cambridge University Press, 1989).

2. Haigh, *English Reformations*, p. 295.

3. We recognize the importance of Marjorie McIntosh's recent call for historians to reconsider traditional chronologies, but in the area of religious change we are still of the opinion that something quite important occurred in the mid-sixteenth century; as Paul Seaver has noted in this context, within the current historiography of religious change, "the centrality of the 1530s was in a sense reaffirmed by church historians who saw the English Reformation as beginning with Henry VIII's removal of the English church from its Roman obedience, perhaps the one thing on which such different historians as A. G. Dickens and Eamon Duffy would agree." Paul Seaver, introduction to "Symposium: Controlling (Mis)behavior," *Journal of British Studies* 37 (1998): 232, which is part of a discussion of Marjorie McIntosh, *Controlling Misbehavior in England, 1370–1600* (Cambridge: Cambridge University Press, 1998). Two important postrevisionist books—Eric Carlson, ed., *Religion and the English People, 1500–1640: New Voices/New Perspectives*, Sixteenth-Century Essays and Studies, vol. 45 (Kirksville, Mo.: Thomas

Jefferson University Press, 1998), and Christopher Marsh, *Popular Religion in Six-teenth-Century England: Holding Their Peace* (New York: St. Martin's Press, 1998)—appeared too recently to be considered here.

4. "Cromwell's Injunctions, 1538," in Arthur J. Slavin, ed., *Humanism, Reform, and Reformation in England* (New York: Wiley, 1969), pp. 156–57.

5. "The Cruel Treatment of William Maldon," in John Gough Nichols, ed., *Narratives of the Days of the Reformation*, Camden Society, ser. 1, vol. 77 (1860), pp. 348–51; John Guy, *Tudor England* (Oxford: Oxford University Press, 1988), p. 194.

6. Elaine V. Beilin, ed., *The Examinations of Anne Askew* (Oxford: Oxford University Press, 1996); Haigh, *English Reformations*, p. 165; Susan Brigden, *London and the Reformation* (Oxford: Clarendon Press, 1989), pp. 305–6, 321–22.

7. "Autobiographical Narrative of Thomas Hancock, Minister of Poole," in *Narratives*, ed. Nichols, pp. 71–84.

8. Caroline Litzenberger, *The English Reformation and the Laity: Gloucestershire, 1540–1580* (Cambridge: Cambridge University Press, 1997), pp. 67–75.

9. Dickens, "The Early Expansion of Protestantism in England, 1520–1558," *Archiv für Reformationgeschichte* 78 (1987): 197; idem, *The English Reformation*, 2d ed., pp. 325–34; Brigden, *London and the Reformation*, ch. 10; Haigh, *English Reformations*, p. 197; Muriel C. McClendon, *The Quiet Reformation: Magistrates and the Emergence of Protestantism in Tudor Norwich* (Stanford: Stanford University Press, 1999), ch. 4.

10. A. G. Dickens, ed., "Robert Parkyn's Narrative of the Reformation," *English Historical Review* 62 (1947): 58–83.

11. See, e.g., "Autobiographical Narrative of Thomas Hancock," in Nichols, ed., *Narratives*, pp. 77–78.

12. For a good short summary and analysis of the rebellion, see Anthony Fletcher and Diarmaid MacCulloch, *Tudor Rebellions*, 4th ed. (London, 1997), pp. 50–63.

13. Haigh, *English Reformations*, pp. 206–7.

14. The classic work remains Patrick Collinson, *The Elizabethan Puritan Movement* (Berkeley: University of California Press, 1967). See also Peter Lake, *Moderate Puritans and the Elizabethan Church* (Cambridge: Cambridge University Press, 1982).

15. David Cressy and Lori Anne Ferrell, eds., *Religion and Society in Early Modern England: A Sourcebook* (London: Routledge, 1996), ch. 4.

16. The best introduction to the early seventeenth-century church and its historiography remains Kenneth Fincham, *The Early Stuart Church, 1603–1642* (Stanford: Stanford University Press, 1993). Useful studies of specific aspects of the evolution of church policy and the controversies it ignited include Nicholas Tyacke, *Anti-Calvinists: The Rise of English Arminianism, c. 1590–1640* (Oxford: Oxford University Press, 1987); Anthony Milton, *Catholic and Reformed: The Roman and Protestant Churches in English Protestant Thought, 1600–1640* (Cambridge: Cambridge University Press, 1995); and Tom Webster, *Godly Clergy in Early Stuart England: The Caroline Puritan Movement, c. 1620–1643* (Cambridge: Cambridge University Press, 1997).

17. David Underdown, *Fire from Heaven: Life in an English Town in the Seventeenth Century* (New Haven: Yale University Press, 1992); Keith Lindley, *Popular Politics and Religion in Civil War London* (Aldershot, Hants.: Scolar Press, 1997); Ann

Hughes, "The Frustrations of the Godly," in John Morrill, ed., *Revolution and Restoration: England in the 1650s* (London: Collins and Brown, 1992).

18. John Spurr, *The Restoration Church of England, 1646–1689* (New Haven: Yale University Press, 1991); J. A. I. Champion, *The Pillars of Priestcraft Shaken: The Church of England and Its Enemies, 1660–1730* (Cambridge: Cambridge University Press, 1992); W. M. Spellman, *The Latitudinarians and the Church of England, 1660–1700* (Athens: University of Georgia Press, 1993). The interplay of religious and political radicalism from the Restoration to the Glorious Revolution is chronicled in Richard Greaves's trilogy: *Deliver Us from Evil: The Radical Underground in Britain, 1660–1663* (Oxford: Oxford University Press, 1986), *Enemies Under His Feet: Radicals and Nonconformists in Britain, 1664–1677* (Stanford: Stanford University Press, 1990), and *Secrets of the Kingdom: British Radicals from the Popish Plot to the Revolution of 1688–1689* (Stanford: Stanford University Press, 1992).

19. Gordon Rupp, *Religion in England, 1688–1791* (Oxford: Clarendon Press, 1986); John Walsh, Colin Haydon, and Stephen Taylor, eds., *The Church of England, c. 1689–c. 1833: From Toleration to Tractarianism* (Cambridge: Cambridge University Press, 1993); W. M. Jacob, *Lay People and Religion in the Early Eighteenth Century* (Cambridge: Cambridge University Press, 1996).

20. Christopher Haigh, "Some Aspects of the Recent Historiography of the English Reformation," in *Stadtbürgertum und Adel in der Reformation: Studien zur Sozialgeschichte der Reformation in England und Deutschland*, ed. Wolfgang J. Mommsen (Stuttgart: Klett-Cotta, 1979), p. 88 and above, n. 1.

21. See above, n. 1.

22. Patrick Collinson, *The Religion of Protestants: The Church in English Society, 1559–1625* (Oxford: Oxford University Press, 1982); idem, *The Birthpangs of Protestant England: Religious and Cultural Change in the Sixteenth and Seventeenth Centuries* (Basingstoke, Hampshire: Macmillan, 1988); Nicholas Tyacke, ed., *England's Long Reformation, 1500–1800* (London: University College London Press, 1998).

23. Peter Marshall, ed., *The Impact of the English Reformation, 1500–1640* (London: Arnold, 1997), p. 4.

24. Collinson, *Birthpangs*, p. ix.

25. Judith Maltby, *Prayer Book and People in Elizabethan and Early Stuart England* (Cambridge: Cambridge University Press, 1998), p. 20.

26. Ibid., pp. 76–80, esp. the case concerning the curate John Maltby of Grainthorpe, Lincolnshire. See also pp. 83–98.

27. Tessa Watt, *Cheap Print and Popular Piety, 1550–1640* (Cambridge: Cambridge University Press, 1991), p. 325.

28. For an overview of this argument, see Litzenberger, *English Reformation*, pp. 13–20.

29. See also David Cressy, *Bonfires and Bells: National Memory and the Protestant Calendar in Elizabethan and Stuart England* (Berkeley: University of California Press, 1989); Christopher W. Marsh, *The Family of Love in English Society, 1550–1630* (Cambridge: Cambridge University Press, 1994); Margaret Spufford, ed., *The World of Rural Dissenters, 1520–1725* (Cambridge: Cambridge University Press, 1995).

30. Stephen Greenblatt, *Renaissance Self-Fashioning: From More to Shakespeare* (Chicago: University of Chicago Press, 1980), p. 2; Margo Todd, "Puritan Self-Fashioning: The Diary of Samuel Ward," *Journal of British Studies* 31 (1992): 236–64.

CRESSY: DIFFERENT KINDS OF SPEAKING

1. John Gother, *A Discourse of the Use of Images in Relation to the Church of England and the Church of Rome* (London, 1687), pp. 22, 27.

2. Martin Luther claimed in 1528 that, although pictures from the Scriptures could be useful, "they are nevertheless free and open to arbitrary interpretation"; quoted in Ernst Ullman, "Reformation and Iconoclasm," *Journal of Popular Culture* 18 (1984): 101.

3. S. A. Strong, ed., *A Catalogue of Letters and Other Historical Documents Exhibited in the Library at Welbeck* (London: John Murray, 1903), p. 189.

4. Moryson quoted in John Guy, *Tudor England* (Oxford: Oxford University Press, 1988), p. 425; James A. Muller, ed., *The Letters of Stephen Gardiner* (Cambridge: Cambridge University Press, 1933), p. 274. See also Diderot: "The people make better use of their sight than of their understanding. Images preach without ceasing"; quoted in William Cohen, "Symbols of Power: Statues in Nineteenth-Century Provincial France," *Comparative Studies in Society and History* 31 (1989): 492.

5. *Calendar of State Papers Domestic* (hereafter *CSPD*), Add. 1566–67, pp. 107, 110; *Depositions and Other Ecclesiastical Proceedings from the Courts of Durham* (Durham: Surtees Society, 1845), pp. 127–205.

6. Philip Caraman, ed., *John Gerard: The Autobiography of an Elizabethan* (London: Longmans, Green, 1951), p. 10; Paul Slack, "Religious Protest and Religious Authority: The Case of Henry Sherfield, Iconoclast, 1633," in Derek Baker, ed., *Schism, Heresy and Religious Protest,* Studies in Church History, 9 (Cambridge: Cambridge University Press, 1972), pp. 295–302.

7. David Cressy, *Bonfires and Bells: National Memory and the Protestant Calendar in Elizabethan and Stuart England* (Berkeley: University of California Press, 1989), esp. chs. 5, 9, and 11.

8. Martin Bucer, *Scripta Anglicana Fere Omnia* (Basel, 1577), pp. 915–35.

9. Nicholas Canny, *Kingdom and Colony: Ireland in the Atlantic World, 1560–1800* (Baltimore: Johns Hopkins University Press, 1988), p. 62; Nicholas Canny, "In Defence of the Constitution? The Nature of the Irish Revolt in the Seventeenth Century," in L. Bergeron and L. Cullen, eds., *Culture et Pratiques Politiques en France et en Irlande, XVI–XVIII⁰ Siècle: Acts due Colloque de Marseille* (Paris, 1991), p. 34; John Temple, *The Irish Rebellion* (1646); A. B. Worden, ed., *Edmund Ludlow: A Voyce from the Watch Tower,* pt. 5, *1660–1662* (Camden Society, 4 ser., 21, 1978), pp. 272, 283. Frenzied iconoclasts in Essex in 1642 allegedly exhumed and dismembered corpses from the Cavalier Lucas family tombs; see William Hunt, *The Puritan Moment: The Coming of Revolution in an English County* (Cambridge, Mass.: Harvard University Press, 1983), pp. 301–2.

10. Historians of the eighteenth century are more familiar with this vocabulary. See, e.g., E. P. Thompson, "Patrician Society, Plebian Culture," *Journal of Social History* 7 (1974): 400, on the early Hanoverian "language of ribbons, of bonfires, of oaths

and of the refusal of oaths, of toasts, of seditious riddles and ancient prophecies, of oak-leaves and of maypoles, of ballads with a political *double entendre,* even of airs whistled in the street."

11. Folger Shakespeare Library, Bagot Papers, Folger Ms. L. a. 97; William H. Hale, ed., *A Series of Precedents and Proceedings in Criminal Causes, Extending from the Year 1475 to 1640* (London, 1847), p. 229; Walter C. Renshaw, "Notes from the Act Books of the Archdeaconry Court of Lewes," *Sussex Archaeological Collections* 49 (1906): 64. See also the display of horns in later Stuart London reported in Henri Misson, *Misson's Memoirs and Observations in His Travels over England* (1719), p. 129.

12. British Library, Sloane Ms. 1447, f. 15v; *William Whiteway of Dorchester His Diary 1618 to 1635* (Dorchester: Dorset Record Society, 1991), p. 144; Henry Burton, *A Divine Tragedie Lately Acted* (London, 1636; STC 4140.7); John Phillips, *The Reformation of Images: Destruction of Art in England, 1535–1660* (Berkeley: University of California Press, 1973), pp. 88–97, 163–65; Ernest B. Gilman, *Iconoclasm and Poetry in the English Reformation: Down Went Dagon* (Chicago: University of Chicago Press, 1968), p. 10; Ann Kibbey, *The Interpretation of Material Shapes in Puritanism: A Study of Rhetoric, Prejudice, and Violence* (Cambridge: Cambridge University Press, 1986), pp. 43–48; Margaret Aston, "Iconoclasm in England: Official and Clandestine," in Clifford Davidson and Ann Eljenholm Nichols, eds., *Iconoclasm vs. Art and Drama* (Kalamazoo, Mich.: Medieval Institute Publications, 1989), pp. 47–91; Margaret Aston, "Iconoclasm in England: Rites of Destruction by Fire," in Bob Scribner and M. Warnke, eds., *Bilder und Bildersturm* (Wiesbaden: Wolfenbütteler, 1990). For Dagon see 1 Samuel 5.

13. Margaret Aston, *England's Iconoclasts,* vol. 1, *Laws Against Images* (Oxford: Oxford University Press, 1988), pp. 2–10; Patrick Collinson, *From Iconoclasm to Iconophobia: The Cultural Impact of the Second English Reformation* (Reading: University of Reading, 1986). See also Clifford Davidson, "The Anti-Visual Prejudice," in Davidson and Nichols, eds., *Iconoclasm vs. Art and Drama* (Kalamazoo, Mich.: Medieval Institute Publications, 1989), pp. 33–46; Lee Palmer Wandel, *Voracious Idols and Violent Hands: Iconoclasm in Reformation Zurich, Strasbourg, and Basel* (Cambridge: Cambridge University Press, 1995).

14. Phillips, *Reformation of Images,* pp. 184–86; Jacqueline Eales, *Puritans and Roundheads: The Harleys of Brampton Bryan and the Outbreak of the English Civil War* (Cambridge: Cambridge University Press, 1990), pp. 38, 47; John Morrill, "William Dowsing, the Bureaucratic Puritan," in John Morrill, Paul Slack and Daniel Woolf, eds., *Public Duty and Private Conscience in Seventeenth-Century England* (Oxford: Oxford University Press, 1993), pp. 173–203.

15. Cressy, *Bonfires and Bells,* chs. 9 and 11.

16. Tim Harris, *London Crowds in the Reign of Charles II* (Cambridge: Cambridge University Press, 1987).

17. Charles Ripley Gillett, *Burned Books: Neglected Chapters in British History and Literature* (New York: Columbia University Press, 1932); Donald Serrell Thomas, *A Long Time Burning: The History of Literary Censorship* (London: Routledge and Kegan Paul, 1969).

18. Gillett, *Burned Books,* p. 92.

19. In July 1600, after the Essex revolt, 1,500 copies of the second edition of John

Heywood's *Life and Raigne of King Henrie the IIII* were taken to the bishop of London's house and there destroyed. Other offensive books were subject to an "order of conflagration" and burned at Stationers Hall; see Gillett, *Burned Books*, pp. 88–89.

20. For Stubbe see *Dictionary of National Biography*; Gillett, *Burned Books*, pp. 62–65, 82–83.

21. Gillett, *Burned Books*, p. 112.

22. Daniel Featley, *Cygnea Cantio; or, Learned Decisions* (London, 1629: STC 10731), pp. 5–7; Aston, *England's Iconoclasts*, p. 388. In February 1625, the Arminian Richard Mountague remarked to Northumberland's chaplain that "Elton's books must be burnt," and he told John Cosin, "The next return I shall hear by you what a goodly fire our sabbatarians made at the cross." Earlier he had written, half-jestingly, about the "masked puritan," Abraham Darcie, that "his books should fire him at a stake; before God it will never be well till we have our inquisition." See George Ornsby, ed., *The Correspondence of John Cosin*, 2 vols. (Durham: Surtees Society, 1869), vol. 1, pp. 32, 53, 59; Thomas Birch, *The Court and Times of James I*, 2 vols. (London, 1849), vol. 2, p. 498.

23. Gillett, *Burned Books*, p. 148.

24. Thomas B. Howell, ed., *Cobbett's Complete Collection of State Trials*, vol. 3 (London, 1809), p. 576.

25. Ibid.

26. Gillett, *Burned Books*, pp. 190, 223, 245.

27. Thomas Fuller, *The Church History of Britain* (London, 1655), book 11, pp. 153–54; William Prynne, *A New Discovery of the Prelates Tyranny* (London, 1641), p. 65.

28. The Rev. Canon Blomfield, "On Puritanism in Chester in 1637: An Account of the Reception of William Prynne," *Journal of the Architectural, Archaeological, and Historic Society, for the County, City, and Neighbourhood of Chester* 3 (1885): 271–88. The story is also told in R. C. Richardson, *Puritanism in North-West England: A Regional Study of the Diocese of Chester to 1642* (Manchester: Manchester University Press, 1972), pp. 182–83.

29. Prynne, *Discovery*, p. 103.

30. Ibid., pp. 221, 104–6.

31. Ibid., pp. 107, 105.

32. Peter Lake, "The Laudian Style: Order, Uniformity, and the Pursuit of the Beauty of Holiness in the 1630s," in Kenneth Fincham, ed., *The Early Stuart Church, 1603–1642* (London: Macmillan, 1993), pp. 161–85; Peter Smart, *A Catalogue of Superstitious Innovations in the Change of Services and Ceremonies* (London, 1642), p. 26.

33. George Hakewill, *The Vanitie of the Eie* (Oxford, 1608; STC 12621), pp. 1, 2, 17, 124.

34. Edmund Gurnay, *Toward the Vindication of the Second Commandment* (Cambridge, 1639; STC 12531), pp. 82, 147, 150; Gurnay, *An Appendix Unto the Homily Against Images in Churches* (London, 1641); Gurnay, *Gurnay Redivivus; or, An Appendix Unto the Homily Against Images in Churches* (1660), pp. 2, 9–10, 40, 59.

35. Thomas Warmstry, *A Convocation Speech . . . Against Images, Altars, Crosses, the new Canons, and the Oath, etc.* (London, 1641), pp. 3, 6, 8, 9, 10–11.

36. George Salteren, *A Treatise against Images and Pictures in Churches* (London, 1641), pp. 1–6, 13–14, 23, 41.

37. John Vicars, *The Sinfulness and Unlawfullness, of having or Making the Picture of Christs Humanity* (London, 1641), "to the reader" and pp. 36, 38. See also the call to take away "the very monuments of idolatry . . . as Hezekiah did the brazen serpent," in John Cotton, *A Brief Exposition of the Whole Book of Canticles* (London, 1642), pp. 46–47.

38. 1 Samuel 5; Joshua 7, 1–26.

39. Roy C. Strong, *Portraits of Queen Elizabeth I* (Oxford: Oxford University Press, 1963), p. 40.

40. *CSPD Ireland, 1588–92*, pp. 142–3, 273, 336, 408, 432, 439, 440.

41. C. L'Estrange Ewen, *Witchcraft and Demonianism* (London: Heath Cranton, 1933), pp. 79–80, 143–44; Keith Thomas, *Religion and the Decline of Magic* (New York: Scribner, 1971), pp. 437–48; Samuel Y. Edgerton, Jr., *Pictures and Punishment: Art and Criminal Prosecution during the Florentine Renaissance* (Ithaca: Cornell University Press, 1985), pp. 15, 69–70; David Freedberg, *The Power of Images: Studies in the History and Theory of Response* (Chicago: University of Chicago Press, 1989), pp. 246–8, 257–63.

42. Robert Ashton, ed., *James I by His Contemporaries* (London: Hutchinson, 1969), pp. 125–26; Edgerton, *Pictures and Punishment*, pp. 47–58, 69; Mikhail Bakhtin, *Rabelais and His World* (Cambridge, Mass.: MIT Press, 1968), p. 147; Morris Palmer Tilley, *A Dictionary of the Proverbs in England in the Sixteenth and Seventeenth Centuries* (Ann Arbor: University of Michigan Press, 1950), p. 688; Freedberg, *Power of Images*, pp. 263–67.

43. William Quelch, *Church-Customes Vindicated* (London, 1636; STC 20555), pp. 20, 32.

44. William Prynne, *A New Discovery of the Prelates Tyranny* (London, 1641), p. 215; British Library, Add. Ms. 22,084, f. 55. Servants in aristocratic households learned to bow toward their master's seat, even if the hall was empty, Sibbald David Scott, ed., "A Booke of Orders and Rules of Anthony Viscount Mountague in 1595," *Sussex Archaeological Collections* 7 (1854). See also John Day, *Day's Festivals; or, Twelve of His Sermons* (Oxford, 1615; STC 6426), p. 229, on the behavior of reverent children toward their parents, "be it capping, or bowing the leg, or kneeling, or whatsoever gesture else is to be performed by the body."

45. *CSPD 1635*, p. 443.

46. Bruno Ryves, *Mercurius Rusticus; or, The Countries Complaint of the Barbarous Out-rages Committed by the Sectaries of this Late Flourishing Kingdome* (London, 1646), p. 212; William Dugdale, *A Short View of the Late Troubles in England* (London, 1681), p. 558.

47. Andrew Clark, ed., *The Life and Times of Anthony Wood, Antiquary of Oxford, 1632–1695, Described by Himself*, vol. 1, *1632–1663* (Oxford: Oxford Historical Society, 1891), p. 64.

48. Ryves, *Mercurius Rusticus*, pp. 32, 212–13.

49. Ibid., p. 112.

50. E. S. de Beer, ed., *The Diary of John Evelyn* (Oxford: Oxford University Press, 1955), vol. 1, p. 555; *CSPD 1650*, pp. 261, 286.

51. Matthew Storey, ed., *Two East Anglian Diaries, 1641–1729*; Isaac Archer and William Coe (Woodbridge, Suffolk: Boydell Press, 1994), p. 49.

52. Aston, *England's Iconoclasts*, pp. 76, 249, 311.

53. Ryves, *Mercurius Rusticus*, pp. 203–4; Aston, *England's Iconoclasts*, p. 94.

54. 2 Kings 25:7, Jeremiah 39 and 52. Responding to the call, "Let all the traitor's titles be defaced, His images and statues be pulled down," an angry mob dismantled all statues of Sejanus and destroyed Sejanus himself, rending his body "limb from limb" and cruelly "digging out his eyes," in Ben Jonson, *Seianus His Fall* (London, 1605), Act 5.

55. Edgerton, *Pictures and Punishment*, p. 152, Freedberg, *Power of Images*, pp. 415–17.

56. John Vicars, *Jehovah-Jireh. God in the Mount; or, Englands Parliamentarie Chronicle* (London, 1644), p. 327; Aston, "Iconoclasm in England," pp. 76–80.

57. *The Downe-fall of Dagon, or the taking downe of Cheap-side Crosse* (London, 1643); *A Dialogue between the Crosse in Cheap, and Charing Crosse, Comforting each other, as fearing their fall in these uncertain times* (London, 1641).

HOLIEN: A CONVERSION AND ITS CONSEQUENCES

I gratefully acknowledge the "cyber" assistance and encouragement I received from D. Andrew Penny while writing this chapter. His quick and concise e-mail responses to my many queries were a godsend. Any errors of judgment are of course mine alone.

1. John Foxe, *Acts and Monuments* (hereafter *A&M*), 8 vols., ed. G. Townsend (1839–1843), vol. 7, pp. 168–71. In the words of Foxe, John Bradford was "called . . . to the understanding and partaking of the gospel" early in the reign of Edward VI while a student in the Inner Temple (ibid., p. 143). According to at least one source, the agent of his conversion was his fellow student and friend Thomas Sampson. In his 1574 preface to Bradford's sermons on Repentance (1553) and the Lord's Supper, Sampson does not claim such a role for himself, but he does describe Bradford's conversion in detail. For both the source of Sampson's agency and this description, see *The Writings of John Bradford*, edited for the Parker Society by Aubrey Townsend (Cambridge: Cambridge University Press, 1848), vol. 1, pp. 29–37. For a brief sketch of Bradford's life and a lucid discussion of his soteriology, see Carl R. Trueman, *Luther's Legacy: Salvation and the English Reformers, 1525–1556* (Oxford: Clarendon Press, 1994), pp. 27–30, 243–88.

2. The terms of this debate appear in their fullest form in A. G. Dickens's *English Reformation* (London: B. T. Batsford, 1989) and in Christopher Haigh's *English Reformations: Religion, Politics, and Society Under the Tudors* (Oxford: Oxford University Press, 1993). For present purposes, a sentence will suffice: Whereas Dickens regards the protestantization of England as an inexorable process of popular conversion, well under way by the accession of Elizabeth I, Haigh sees it as a disjointed affair, largely effected by coercion and far from complete late in her reign. For a recent study of conversion in the late sixteenth and early seventeenth centuries, see Michael C. Questier, *Conversion, Politics and Religion in England, 1580–1625* (Cambridge: Cambridge University Press, 1996).

3. Not only does the text of Bilney's famous letter to Bishop Tunstal (*A&M*, vol. 4, pp. 633–36) need line-by-line scrutiny—something it has never received—but Bilney's motives for writing it need reevaluation, at least according to Greg Walker, who sug-

gests at the end of his provocative article "Saint or Schemer? The 1527 Heresy Trial of Thomas Bilney Reconsidered" that Bilney deliberately attempted to manipulate Tunstal, his main judge, by citing and praising in his letter a work—Erasmus's *Novum Testamentum* (1519)—to which Tunstal had contributed. Walker's article appeared in the *Journal of Ecclesiastical History* 40, no. 2 (Apr. 1989): 219–38.

4. John Fines, *A Biographical Register of Early English Protestants and Others Opposed to the Roman Catholic Church, 1525–1558, Part 1, A–C* (Abingdon: Sutton Courtenay Press, c. 1981). In his laudatory preface to the *Register*, A. G. Dickens observes that "the process of examining the popular grass roots must continue to form an essential Reformation studies feature." After praising Fines's work as a "valuable tool" in this process, he listed what could be learned from it, concluding, "Above all we can learn how the less privileged men and women of the . . . [sixteenth century] reacted, when they found themselves swept by their own convictions into a great and complex series of movements, the perils of which were more apparent than the advantages, the future of which remained hidden except to the eye of faith." I note these last eloquent words of Dickens because it was precisely Nicholas Sheterden's reaction to these circumstances that first drew me to him and then convinced me that he deserved more attention that he had received.

5. For the most recent work on Foxe and his *Acts and Monuments*, see David M. Loades, ed., *John Foxe and the English Reformation* (Aldershot, Hants., U.K.; Brookfield, Vt., U.S.A: Scolar Press, 1997). Loades's brief introduction (pp. 1–11) is especially recommended for those unfamiliar with the publishing history of the *Acts and Monuments* and the pressing need for a modern scholarly edition.

6. Young's age, status as a mother, and number of children come out in the course of her nine examinations (*A&M*, vol. 8, pp. 536–48), all of which make for fascinating reading as she endures with equanimity and poise intermittent badgering about her beliefs and, at one point, even wagering about her womanhood. See pp. 539–40.

7. *A&M*, vol. 8, pp. 541–42. The obvious difference is the assurance with which Young speaks of the Holy Spirit and the lack of the same in the chancellor's statements. Foxe generalizes about this difference in a footnote, claiming, "The papists dare not assure themselves to have the Holy Ghost" (p. 542). Both a similar and more a substantive exchange can be found in the First Examination of the Marian martyr Richard Woodman (pp. 339–40). It is also worth noting—if only to show how the issue of the Holy Spirit was raised by the opponents of reform—that later in the same "talk" between Bradford and Harpsfield excerpted above, Harpsfield responded to Bradford's appropriation of St. Stephen's speech to "prove" his faith by saying, "Yea sire, if we did know that you had the Holy Ghost then could we believe you" (*A&M*, vol. 7, pp. 170–71). Finally, to put all of this in some perspective, a couple of observations from Geoffrey F. Nuttall's *The Holy Spirit in Puritan Faith and Experience*, with a new introduction by Peter Lake (Chicago: University of Chicago Press, 1992; 1st ed. Basil Blackwell, 1946), pp. 4–6. First, "in the doctrine of the Holy Spirit lay the fundamental difference between Protestantism and Roman Catholicism, a difference deeper than that over Scripture, for which in fact it was the basis." Second, "as a rule, however, neither martyrs nor leaders had the mental powers or the leisure of spirit to perceive the importance of this, and to examine its implications for faith and experience." Taken together, these

points suggest that it is a difference well worth pursuing, but one that will reveal mostly new understanding—like the foregoing examples—rather than new thinking.

8. "The Troubles of Thomas Mowntayne" appears in the *Acts and Monuments* only as a footnote in the fifth volume. Added by Foxe's modern editor, the note reads in part, "A very interesting narrative of the trouble of Thomas Mountain . . . which has not found a place in Foxe's volumes might here be introduced" (vol. 5, p. 394). A "complete and literal" printed copy of the MS (British Library, Harleain 425, f. 106) is included in John Gough Nichols, ed., *Narratives of the Days of the Reformation* (Camden Society, 1st ser., no. 77, 1859), pp. 177–217. The passage that appears above was taken from this copy and the spelling was modernized.

9. Ibid., p. 179. The person being addressed here is Sir Anthony St. Leger, lord deputy of Ireland under Henry VIII, Edward VI, and Mary I. For the facts of his life and career, see *Dictionary of National Biography*, s.v. "St. Leger, Sir Anthony (1496?–1559)," by David James O'Donoghue.

10. *Narratives of the Days of the Reformation*, pp. 179–80. J. A. Muller excerpted this passage and a couple of adjoining ones in his very old but still valuable study *Stephen Gardiner and the Tudor Reaction* (New York: Macmillan, 1926), pp. 230–32. Since then Mowntayne's narrative has certainly received attention from historians—Susan Brigden, for example, cites it some seven times in her *London and the Reformation* (Oxford: Clarendon Press, 1989)—but it still has not received the sustained attention it deserves, at least to my knowledge.

11. William James, *The Varieties of Religious Experiences: A Study in Human Nature* (New York: Random House, 1929), p. 193.

12. How large a part is, of course, one of the questions at the center of the debate briefly outlined above in n. 2. That it is largely an unanswerable question is readily admitted by both sides.

13. One of the latest and best of these local studies is Caroline Litzenberger's *The English Reformation and the Laity Gloucestershire, 1540–1580* (Cambridge: Cambridge University Press, 1997). In terms of historiography, the most noteworthy aspect of Litzenberger's study is her decision to concentrate on the diversity of religious belief in Gloucestershire rather than the dynamics of religious change. Historically, she has demonstrated that in this western county, 40 years of Reformation or Reformations produced a "broad spectrum of religious beliefs, albeit one with an increasingly Protestant accent" (167). My use here and in the text of Reformation in both the singular and plural is meant to draw attention to Christopher Haigh's persuasive argument, set out in his *English Reformations* (12–21), that England did not have one Reformation but a series of them.

14. *A&M*, vol. 7, pp. 306–18.

15. By way of background and explanation, Dewey D. Wallace Jr. writes, "There emerged and developed among England's Protestant leadership from the beginnings of the English Reformation through the end of the reign of Queen Mary, a Swiss or Reformed theology of grace emphasizing Predestination. This doctrine of predestination was rooted in the more basic Protestant belief in justification by faith alone and was used to defend that latter doctrine." *Puritans and Predestination: Grace in English Protestant Theol-*

ogy, 1525–1695 (Chapel Hill: University of North Carolina Press, 1982), 27. About the Freewillers, D. Andrew Penny explains, "[They] do not *a priori* oppose Predestination. They oppose a particular interpretation of predestination. They accept the doctrine of justification alone. . . . They do not believe that the sovereignty of God must preclude what they consider to be genuine human responsibility—the capacity to respond to or reject overtures of divine grace. They accept that salvific grace is available to all men equally, and those who perish do so willfully, not as a result of an inscrutable eternal decree." *Freewill or Predestination: The Battle over Saving Grace in Mid-Tudor England,* Royal Historical Society Studies in History 61 (1990): 24. Burned with Sheterden were John Bland, John Frankesh, and Humphrey Middleton. *A&M,* vol. 7, p. 312.

16. For discussion of this region's religious radicalism, see Peter Clark, *English Provincial Society from the Reformation to the Revolution: Religion, Politics, and Society in Kent, 1500–1640* (Cranbury, N.J.: Associated University Presses, 1977), pp. 1–69.

17. For Henry Harte and Freewill Radicalism I have relied on Penny, *Freewill or Predestination;* J. W. Martin, *Religious Radicals in Tudor England* (London: Hambledon Press, 1989); M. T. Pearse, *Between Known Men and Visible Saints: A Study in Sixteenth-Century English Dissent* (Cranbury, N.J.: Associated University Presses, 1994).

18. Thomas Cranmer, *Works,* ed. John Cox (Cambridge, 1844, 1846), 2: 367. Compare interpretations of this letter in Pearse, 63, and Diarmaid MacCulloch, *Thomas Cranmer: A Life* (New Haven: Yale University Press, 1996), p. 205.

19. Penny, p. 44.

20. Champlin Burrage, *The Early English Dissenters in the Light of Recent Research, 1550–1641* (Cambridge: Cambridge University Press, 1912), vol. 2, pp. 1–6. Penny, pp. 52ff.

21. Penny, pp. 106–15.

22. John Bradford, *Writings,* ed. A. Townsend (Cambridge: Cambridge University Press, 1848–53), vol. 2, pp. 133–35.

23. Ibid., p. 133.

24. Ibid., pp. 134–35.

25. Ibid., pp. 194–98.

26. Ibid., p. 194; Penny, p. 143; Pearse, p. 48. Martin characterizes the recipients as "13 persons who had been on all sides of the dispute" (p. 52).

27. Bradford, *Writings,* vol. 2, p. 195.

28. Ibid., p. 196.

29. Ibid., p. 197. Beyond the fact that Bradford leaves open the possibility that some could "think with her therein," it hardly seems plausible that he would have entrusted such a seemingly vulnerable convert into the hands of only those who could not.

30. Patrick Collinson, "Truth and Legend: The Veracity of John Foxe's Book of Martyrs," in A. C. Duke and C. A. Tamse, eds., *Clio's Mirror Historiography in Britain and the Netherlands* (Zutphen, Netherlands: De Walburg Pers, 1985), p. 43.

31. Ibid., p. 41; J. W. Martin, p. 61; Penny, p. 144; Pearse, p. 236.

32. *A&M,* vol. 7, pp. 306–8. Harpsfield, the archdeacon of Canterbury, along with Richard Thornden, the bishop of Dover, directed the Marian reaction in the diocese. Harpsfield was also the first in print to attack John Foxe and his martyrology. Clark, p. 99; Collinson, p. 42.

33. *A&M*, vol. 8, p. 306.

34. "No one has ascended into heaven except the one who descended from heaven, the son of man" (NRSV).

35. *A&M*, vol. 7, pp. 307–8.

36. Ibid., pp. 308–9. The last several lines of this examination appear to have been written by Foxe.

37. The unidentified suffragan is Richard Thornden. With regard to the commission in question, royal commissions were issued by Mary I throughout her reign as instruments for initiating local heresy investigations. As Gina Alexander writes in her article, "Bonner and the Marian Persecutions," "She [Mary] saw no ambiguity in renouncing the Royal Supremacy while maintaining the prerogative Henry had established in issuing royal commissions to deal with religious matters": Christopher Haigh, ed., *The English Reformation Revised* (Cambridge: Cambridge University Press, 1987), p. 162.

38. *A&M*, vol. 7, p. 308.

39. Ibid.; Haigh, *English Reformations*, p. 230.

40. In a passage detailing the restoration of the Mass after Mary's August proclamation encouraging it, Haigh writes, "At Canterbury the suffragan bishop, Richard Thornden (called 'Dick of Dover' by his many critics) sought to disown his Protestant past and in September celebrated solemn high mass in full pontificals": ibid., p. 207. For the priest's criticism of Thornden, see *A&M*, vol. 7, pp. 297–98. It makes for fascinating reading.

41. *A&M*, vol. 7, p. 308.

42. Ibid., p. 309. In making this statement Sheterden raises the issue of the motivation of the Marian examiners. For an insightful article about the chief of them, Edmund Bonner, bishop of London, see Alexander's "Bonner and the Marian Persecutions," pp. 157–75.

43. *A&M*, vol. 7, pp. 310–12.

44. Muller, *Stephen Gardiner*, p. 283; *A&M*, vol. 7, p. 311.

45. *A&M*, vol. 7, p. 310. The English Bible was never officially taken away during the reign of Mary I. Derek Wilson, *The People and the Book: The Revolutionary Impact of the English Bible, 1380–1611* (London: Barrie and Jenkins, 1976), pp. 104–5.

46. *A&M*, vol. 7, p. 310.

47. *A&M*, vol. 7, p. 312; Muller, p. 129.

48. *A&M*, vol. 7, pp. 306, 312.

49. For the letters of another son attempting to convert his mother to the reformed faith, see *The Plumpton Correspondence*, ed. Thomas Stapleton, Camden Society 4 (1839), pp. 231–34. A. G. Dickens provides background and commentary on these letters in his *Lollards and Protestants in the Diocese of York, 1509–1558* (Oxford: University of Hull, 1959; rev. ed. Hambledon Press, 1982), pp. 131–37.

50. *A&M*, vol. 7, p. 313.

51. He had written to his mother earlier. Ibid., p. 308.

52. Ibid., p. 314.

53. Ibid.

54. Ibid.

55. Pearse, p. 45.

56. *A&M*, vol. 7, p. 315.

57. Philip Hughes, *The Reformation in England* (New York: Macmillan, 1954), vol. 2, p. 275.

58. *A&M*, vol. 7, pp. 316–17.

59. Katherine Parr, *The Lamentation of a Sinner, bewailing the ignorance of her blind life* (London: Edward Whitechurch, Nov. 5, 1547), STC 4827, Ai^{r-v}.

60. "In the presence of God and of Christ Jesus, who is to judge the living and the dead, and in view of his appearing and his kingdom, I solemnly urge you: proclaim the message; be persistent whether the time is favorable or unfavorable": 2 Timothy 4:1–2 (NRSV). For a discussion of the obligation to witness with reference to the sermons of Hugh Latimer, see Patricia Cricco, "Hugh Latimer and Witness," *Sixteenth-Century Journal* 10 (1979): 21–34.

61. Parr makes a similar declaration; see *The Lamentation*, Bviii^v–Ci^r.

COMO: THE KINGDOM OF TRASKE

The author would like to thank the participants in the Institute of Historical Research's seminar on the Religious History of Britain from the Fifteenth to the Eighteenth Century for their very useful comments on an earlier draft of this paper. In addition, the essay has profited immensely from the suggestions offered by T. D. Bozeman, Severa Keith, Peter Lake, John Reichmuth, Michael Winship, and most especially Paul Seaver.

1. C. Hill, *The World Turned Upside Down: Radical Ideas During the English Revolution* (New York: Viking Press, 1972); see also A. L. Morton, *The World of the Ranters: Religious Radicalism in the English Revolution* (London: Lawrence and Wishart, 1970); J. F. McGregor and B. Reay, eds., *Radical Religion in the English Revolution* (New York: Oxford University Press, 1984).

2. C. Hill, *Society and Puritanism in Pre-Revolutionary England* (New York: Schoken Books, 1964); D. Levine and K. Wrightson, *Poverty and Piety in an English Village* (New York: Academic Press, 1979); W. Hunt, *The Puritan Moment: The Coming of Revolution in an English County* (Cambridge, Mass.: Harvard University Press, 1983); P. Collinson, *The Religion of Protestants* (Oxford: Clarendon Press, 1982). For a discussion of this ambiguity in the historiography of Puritanism, see P. Lake, introduction to G. F. Nuttall, *The Holy Spirit in Puritan Faith and Experience* (Chicago: University of Chicago Press, 1992).

3. C. Hill, "From Lollards to Levellers," in M. Cornforth, ed., *Rebels and Their Causes: Essays in Honour of A. L. Morton* (London: Lawrence and Wishart, 1978), pp. 49–68.

4. C. Marsh, *The Family of Love in English Society, 1550–1630* (Cambridge: Cambridge University Press, 1994).

5. For his sentence see "Trask in the Star-Chamber, 1619," in *Transactions of the Baptist Historical Society* 5 (1916–17): 8–14 (the date was later corrected to 1618), which shows that Traske was in prison by November 1617. The sentence was carried out sometime between June 23 and June 30, for which see T. Birch, ed., *The Court and Times of James the First* (London, 1849), vol. 2, p. 77. The two indispensable modern

studies of Traske's career are B. R. White, "John Traske (1585–1636) and London Puritanism," *Transactions of the Congregational Historical Society* 20 (1968): 223–33, and D. S. Katz, *Philo-Semitism and the Re-admission of the Jews to London, 1603–1655* (Oxford: Clarendon Press, 1982), pp. 18–34. See also B. Ball, *The Seventh-Day Men, Sabbatarians and Sabbatarianism in England and Wales, 1600–1800* (Oxford: Clarendon Press, 1994), which includes additional details. The diocesan researches of Margaret Stieg and Kenneth Fincham have also greatly increased our knowledge of Traske's career.

6. For Traske's involvement in this underground, see S. Foster, "New England and the Challenge of Heresy, 1630 to 1660: The Puritan Crisis in Transatlantic Perspective," *William and Mary Quarterly* 38 (1981): 624–60.

7. Our best contemporary evidence concerning the Traskite movement (including information regarding Jackson, Traske's "conversion," the claim that Traske was the second Elijah of the book of Malachi, and a discussion of Traskite "Judaizing") is provided by the anonymous London Puritan "T.S.," who wrote a letter and an extensive biographical "relation" concerning his acquaintance Traske in the mid-1630's. The former was published in Edward Norice, *The New Gospel, Not the True Gospel* (1638), pp. 6–8, while the latter was included in Ephraim Pagitt, *Heresiography; or, A description of the Hereticks and Sectaries of these latter times* (1661), pp. 184–97. For proof that this second "relation" was written by T.S., compare his comments on Dorothy Traske (ibid., p. 197) against those contained in a letter by the same man, which was unpublished until transcribed by B. R. White in his "Samuel Eaton (d. 1639) Particular Baptist Pioneer," *Baptist Quarterly* 24 (1971): 18–19. T.S.'s claim that Traske was converted to Seventh-Day observance by Jackson (which has been questioned by B. W. Ball) may likewise be confirmed by comparison with a manuscript examination of Traske from 1627, in which he admitted that "he . . . and his wyfe were both drawen into these Opinions by one Jackson nowe a professed Jewe dwelling at Amsterdam." See PRO, SP Dom. 16/73/64, fol. 96r.

8. He may, as is often assumed, have been John, son of Lionell, born in East Coker in 1585, although a close examination of the published records of this family suggests that this John Traske died in 1634, when the minister was still very much alive. See extracts published in *New England Historical and Genealogical Register* 54 (1900): 279–81; Traske described his parents as "godly" in the prefatory epistle of his *Treatise of Libertie From Judaisme* (1620); for his (lack of) education and his schoolmastership, see John Falconer, *A Briefe Refutation of John Traskes Judaical and Novel Fancyes* (St. Omer, 1618), pp. 8–9, and Norice, *New Gospel*, p. 7. He may possibly have been the unidentified "Mr. Traske" suspended from the curacy of Brimpton in 1605 for failure to wear the square cap and for being unlicensed, although he would have been little more than twenty years old at the time. See Somerset Record Office [hereafter SRO], D/D/CA 140, p. 379.

9. The image of clouted shoes or "cloutshoes" had long been used to symbolize England's "lower orders," apparently carrying a connotation of popular political action. Thus, in Henry VIII's reign, Elizabeth Wood, a sympathizer with the Norfolk "Walsingham conspirators," had been executed for claiming that "it was a pity that these Walsingham men were discovered, for we shall have never good world till we fall

together by the ears, and with clubs and clouted shone/shall the deeds be done, for we had never good world since this king reigned." In 1589, the term would again be invoked, this time disparagingly, by Thomas Nashe, who sneered that Martin Marprelate and his presbyterian co-conspirators had made headway in England only because they had "closde with the clouted shoe," that is, pandered to the lower orders. Half a century later, John Lilburne would likewise deploy the image, appealing to "Hobnayles and clouted Shoes" during the early stages of the Leveller agitation. See S. L. Jansen, *Dangerous Talk and Strange Behavior* (New York: St. Martin's Press, 1996), pp. 81–82; A. Grossart, ed., *The Complete Works of Thomas Nashe* (London and Aylesbury: The Huth Library, 1883–84), vol. 1, p. 126; I. Roots, *The Great Rebellion, 1642–1660* (London: B. T. Batsford, 1966), p. 117. I would like to thank Ethan Shagan and Peter Lake, respectively, for turning my attention to the first two sources.

10. PRO STAC 8/61/27. Punctuation has been added to the libel. That this John Traske of Frome Selwood was the John Traske of later fame is inherently unprovable but extremely likely. Transcripts of the parish registers of Frome (SRO, DD/SOG/1208, 1211, 1214) contain only a single reference to Traske (for 1610, when his son was baptized), demonstrating that he was not a native of the town, and that he moved on shortly thereafter, all of which is consonant with our knowledge of the minister Traske's career and whereabouts.

11. John Falconer, *A Briefe Refutation*, p. 10 for Drake; Thomas Fuller, *The Church-History of Britain* (London, 1655), p. 76 for Ward; SRO D/D/CA 177, Oct. 15, 1612, unfoliated, where Traske was suspended from the cure of Chilton Cantelo for unlicensed preaching.

12. Cambridge University Library, Ely Diocesan Records B/2/35, fols. 31, 621, 76–77, 821, 113–14, 1901. Most of those brought before the court stood accused of attending a sermon preached by Traske in Littleport. In addition, however, two laymen admitted that they had allowed Traske to pray in their homes in Ely and Chettisham.

13. SRO D/D/CA 189 (Consistory Court Act Book), fol. 150v, Nov. 22, 1614. Traske was excommunicated on Nov. 29 (ibid., fol. 158v). It was alleged that Traske had shared Richard Bernard's pulpit at Batcombe, in addition to preaching at Mearston Magna, Stratton, Broadmeareton, Doulting, and in the homes of two laymen of Shepton Mallet (ibid., fols. 183–84, Dec. 20, 1614).

14. William Le Hardy, ed., *Calendar to the Sessions Records*, Middlesex Sessions Records, n.s., vol. 3, 1615–1616 (London: Sir Ernest Hart, 1935), p. 107.

15. PRO SP 14/96/15, fol. 35, in which John Chamberlain claimed Traske had been a separatist. See also *Heresiography*, pp. 165–66.

16. H.M.C., *Report on the Records of the City of Exeter*, pp. 95–96. From the conference between the bishop of Exeter and John Hazard, Apr. 5, 1616.

17. See P. Lake, *Moderate Puritans and the Elizabethan Church* (Cambridge, 1982), pp. 77–92.

18. *Heresiography*, pp. 184–85; for hints of sexual abstinence and sleep deprivation, see Traske, *Christs Kingdom Discovered; or, that the true Church of God is in England, clearly made manifest against all Sectaries whatever* (1615), pp. 54–55.

19. *Heresiography*, p. 187.

20. The Catholic priest Falconer, in his *A Briefe Refutation*, p. 7, contended that

Traske "is infallibly assured, that he himselfe hath truly repented, and is made sure of his eternall election in Christ: and that he can in this life neither sinne, nor repent any more." William Sclater claimed in 1619 that Traske had violently appropriated Sclater's manuscript notes on I Thessalonians to bolster his claim that the elect could recognize one another. See W. Sclater, *An Exposition with Notes upon the first Epistle to the Thessalonians* (1619), pp. 14–31.

21. Nuttall, *The Holy Spirit.*

22. *A Pearl for a Prince, or a Princely Pearl. As it was delivered in two sermons* (1615), Sig. A3v.

23. Ibid., pp. 10–11.

24. Ibid., pp. 13–15.

25. His most extreme statement of the wonders of faith may be found in the last pages of Traske's *Heavens Joy, or Heaven Begun on Earth* (1616), pp. 139–59, which amounts to a personal testimonial concerning the overwhelming joys of grace, incidentally confirming beyond all doubt that Traske believed that he, and all the faithful, had finished the period of repentance (p. 157).

26. *A Pearl*, pp. 6–7. 27. Ibid., p. 4.

28. Ibid., p. 5. 29. Ibid., pp. 5–6.

30. *Christs Kingdom Discovered* (1615) was initially published anonymously, but was reissued in 1616 under Traske's name; *Heavens Joy* (1616), was also published anonymously, but an examination of internal evidence has led the editors of the STC to ascribe it tentatively to Traske (see A. W. Pollard et al., *Short-Title Catalogue of Books Printed in England . . . 1475–1640* [London: Bibliographical Society, 1976–1991], vol. 1, p. 569; vol. 3, p. 313), a judgment with which I wholly concur.

31. *Christs Kingdom*, p. 42.

32. Ibid., pp. 18–19.

33. Ibid., pp. 6–8. Traske argued that the scriptural phrases "Kingdome of Heaven," "Kingdome of Christ," and "Sonne of Mans Kingdome" "concerne the Church, here in this life," and were interchangeable. Only the "Kingdom of God" referred to the afterlife, although he claimed that even this term "doeth concerne moste the estate of the Church in this life."

34. *Christs Kingdom*, p. 28.

35. Ibid., p. 41. Traske's comment verifies, beyond all doubt, the claims made by T.S. and William Sclater that Traske claimed that believers could infallibly recognize one another. See above, n. 20.

36. Ibid., pp. 15–16.

37. Ibid., p. 11.

38. Ibid., pp. 64–66. Traske closed with a discussion of the duties of believers to one another, ending his treatise by reproducing—unequivocally and without comment—those passages from the New Testament that show believers holding goods in common.

39. *Heresiography*, p. 185.

40. W. Sclater, *An Exposition*, p. 31.

41. Returne Hebdon, *Guide to the Godly* (1648), pp. 32–33. In keeping with the Traskite aversion to external compulsion, Hebdon added that this communion was to

be "left free to the will of the possessor, and not in bondage under the feare of carnall compulsion; for this is contrary to the nature and holy spirit of love."

42. This is all the more remarkable since Traske had probably been forced to alter the pamphlet to get it into print. *Heavens Joy* began with this cryptic statement: "This small Treatise of Hell being fitted for the presse, it was thought fit by the learned examiner, that it should not passe alone, but that as much at least of *Heaven* should be added to it: that as the reader should be driven by *Judgements*, so he might also be drawne by *Mercies*, to turne unto God by true & unfeigned *Repentance*." This comment seems bizarre, since there is little or no reference to hell throughout the treatise. There may have been a companion treatise "of hell," which was subsequently suppressed. It is more likely, however, that this was a coded message, suggesting that the contents of the treatise had been altered because of difficulties in licensing the original, perhaps less acceptable version of the treatise. This reading is supported by the fact that on the "errata" page, which would have been inserted after licensing, this suspicious note has been inserted: "There is a little Booke called Christs Kingdome discovered, which is worth thy reading." *Christs Kingdom* had been more straightforward in its claim that the "Kingdom of Heaven" referred to this life alone. Traske may have been forced by the censor to dilute this message and may thus have been directing his readers to the earlier, more authoritative text. *Heavens Joy*, sig. A4r, p. 1.

43. *Heavens Joy*, p. 11.

44. Ibid., p. 12.

45. See, e.g., ibid., p. 34, in which Traske argued that believers were overcome with a "*Love* wherewith the soules of the children of God are ravished, with a desire to see God face, to face." Although he refrained from claiming that believers already participated in this heavenly vision, the priest Falconer (*A Brief Refutation*, p. 33) claimed that Traske went further, defining the church as "a small number of such little ones as have truly repented, and are made sure of their election in Christ, hated and persecuted by men, but beloved by God & guarded by Angells, seeing the face of their Heavenly Father." Falconer's charge that Traske held that the elect were guarded by angels was entirely accurate (*Heavens Joy*, pp. 85–86), but it remains a question as to whether he actually believed that they saw the face of God in this life, a privilege that Moses himself had been denied.

46. *Heavens Joy*, p. 30.

47. Ibid., pp. 37–38.

48. Ibid., pp. 59–60.

49. *Christ's Kingdom*, p. 13.

50. *Heavens Joy*, p. 22; also pp. 69–70, which repeats the claim that believers "have the mind of *Christ*," citing 1 Cor. 2 to show "the wonderful *Wisdome* of a Child of God, in whom *Christ dwelleth*."

51. Hebdon, *Guide*, pp. 30–31. See also p. 54 for further examples of "perfectionist" language.

52. For an important recent study of early Stuart antinomianism, detecting a similar impulse in the thought of John Eaton, see T. D. Bozeman, "The Glory of the 'Third Time': John Eaton as Contra-Puritan," *Journal of Ecclesiastical History* 47 (1996): 638–54.

53. Hebdon, *Guide*, pp. 88–89

54. *Christs Kingdom*, p. 34.

55. *Heavens Joy*, p. 136.

56. John Traske, *The True Gospel Vindicated, From the Reproach of a New Gospel* (n.p., 1636), sigs. A6v-A8r, claims that twelve letters were sent to the king. For Traske's rumored offer to cure James's gout, see Norice, *New Gospel*, pp. 7–8.

57. Quoted from the National Library of Scotland, Advocates' MS 33.1.6 (Denmilne state papers), vol. 20, fol. 60. This document, dated Sept. 11, 1616, is an examination of John Pecke, a student at the Inner Temple, who had delivered a manuscript and letter written by Traske to the king. Traske was imprisoned in Newgate at the time. I would like to thank Arnold Hunt for alerting me to the existence of this important document and for graciously providing a transcript of relevant passages.

58. J. Spedding, ed., *The Letters and the Life of Sir Francis Bacon* (London, 1872), vol. 6, p. 315. This document was first noted by D. S. Katz.

59. The notion that perfection was to be preceded by a period of penitent, legal mortification is ubiquitous in the works of H.N. See also J. Etherington, *The Defence of John Etherington against Stephen Denison* (1641), pp. 9–11; Niclaes persistently criticized those who claimed that their own ecclesiastical organization constituted the true church, attacking those who claimed "We have it, we are the Congregation of Christ, we are Israel, lo here it is, lo there it is, this is truth, here is Christ, there is Christ" (quoted by William Haller, *The Rise of Puritanism* [New York: Harper and Row, 1957], p. 206); for the claim that (some) Familists held goods in common as late as 1638 and for the allegorization of heaven and hell, see the deposition of the ex-sectary Giles Creech in PRO SP 16/520/85. The most convincing specific textual support for the hypothesis that Traske had been exposed to H.N.'s teachings lies in their respective doctrines of baptism. Compare H.N.'s doctrine of "double baptism" with that of the sometime Familist John Etherington, and then compare both against John Traske's comments on the subject. See H.N., *Evangelium Regni* (Cologne?, 1574?), fols. 45v-46v; Etherington, *Defence*, pp. 11, 52–56; Traske, *Heavens Joy*, pp. 54–55.

60. Marsh, *Family of Love*, pp. 214–18.

61. Ely Diocesan Records B/2/35, fols. 76v, 190v, 76v, 62r for the respective references to Traske's auditors. The two Ely residents, both described as gentlemen, were Nicholas Massy and J. Orwell. Massy had allowed Traske to pray in his house, with Orwell present. For their participation with Saunders on the committee to audit the churchwardens' accounts of St. Mary's, Ely, see ibid., fol. 82r. For evidence of Saunders's Familism, the Gunton clan, David Thickpenny and Downham, see Marsh, *Family of Love*, pp. 46, 103–4, 107, 147–48, 194, 214–15, 259, 274, 279, 282. Another accused auditor of Traske, one Sidrach Cave of St. Trinity, Ely (EDR B/2/35, fols. 113v-141), would find his name immortalized by John Taylor "the water-poet" 25 years later. Taylor's *A Swarme of Sectaries, and Schismatiques* (1641), which lampooned puritan hypocrisy and presumption, included a verse entitled "*Another sweet youth in a Basket*":

> One *Sidrach Cave* made Baskets late in Elie,
> A constant brother, rais'd up his maids belly:
> But 'twas in Gandermonth, his wife lay in,
> His flesh rebell'd, and tempted him to sin;
> And *Cave's* wife tooke the wrong most patiently,
> For which the Brethren prais'd her sanctity. (p. 5)

62. For apparently literal references to a future Judgment, see *Heaven's Joy*, pp. 152–55.

63. The phrase "the Love of Christ," which appears on several occasions in *Heavens Joy*, was a favorite catchphrase of H.N. See, e.g., H[enry] A[insworth], *An Epistle Sent unto two daughters of Warwick from H.N.* (Amsterdam, 1608), pp. 9, 12, 62, 63, 64. Nevertheless, the larger part of Traske's works do not resemble H.N.'s writings in style and rhetoric.

64. For the pervasiveness of biblical primitivism in early Stuart puritanism, see T. D. Bozeman, *To Live Ancient Lives: The Primitivist Dimension in Puritanism* (Chapel Hill: University of North Carolina Press, 1988).

65. For Traske's later career, see White, "John Traske"; for Traske's later opinions see his *The True Gospel Vindicated.*.

66. J. C. Davis, "Cromwell's Religion," in J. Morrill, ed., *Oliver Cromwell and the English Revolution* (London: Longman, 1990).

MCGEE: THE MENTAL WORLD OF

SIR RICHARD BERKELEY

1. Rev. Beaver H. Blacker, ed., *Gloucestershire Notes and Queries* 2 (1884): 379–80. I am grateful to His Grace the Duke of Beaufort for permitting me to study the papers of this branch of the Berkeley family and to the expert counsel of his archivist, Mrs. Margaret E. Richards. Versions of this essay were presented at the Western Conference on British Studies, the Arizona Center for Medieval and Renaissance Studies, and the annual meeting of the Pacific Coast Branch of the American Historical Association. I appreciate many suggestions from colleagues who attended those sessions. I also take pleasure in thanking Michael MacDonald and Raymond B. Waddington for invaluable help.

2. Sig. *4r. All references are to the 1603 edition—to be cited as *Discourse*. The 1603 edition (STC 1382—University Microfilms, reel 651), described as "newly corrected and augmented" on the title page, has a small amount of additional material inserted but is otherwise identical with the original. On the same page of the dedication, Berkeley explains that he began writing the book "some four yeares past . . . for my exercise onely, without meaning to publish it." However, he explains, some of his friends read it and, unbeknownst to him, it came "to the Printers hands." He then decided to allow it to proceed, "unperfect and unpolished" though it might be. Sigs. *4r, *4v. I find this show of false modesty unconvincing. For examples of praise of Elizabeth, see pp. 261–62, 555. A surviving manuscript offers insights into late-Elizabethan printing practices. See Michael Brennan, "The Badminton Manuscript of Sir Richard Barckley's *A Discourse of the Felicitie of Man* (1598)," in *English Manuscript Studies, 1100–1700* (British Library, 1997), vol. 6, pp. 70–92. Brennan notes that Berkeley's book was printed by Richard Field for William Ponsonby, "two of the most prestigious names in the stationers' trade." The former printed works by Shakespeare and Puttenham, and the latter published "most of Sidney's and Spenser's major works" (p. 70).

3. *CBEL* vol. 1, pp. 2027, 2331. In the *MLA Index* for the period from 1980–90, the only item concerning Berkeley is a paragraph in *Notes and Queries* 31 (Mar. 1984), p. 156, in which Richard F. Kennedy mentions the one Chaucer allusion in the book. At

least one person read Berkeley in the nineteenth century—see the examples for the word *corzie* in the OED—it appears on p. 276 in Berkeley's book. C. A. Patrides took brief notice of Berkeley in two places: *Milton and the Christian Tradition* (Oxford, 1966), pp. 62, 110; *Premises and Motifs in Renaissance Thought and Literature* (Princeton, 1982), p. 35. Two recent studies also give some attention to Berkeley. See Giles D. Monsarrat, *Light from the Porch: Stoicism and English Renaissance Literature* (Paris, 1984), pp. 95–98; and Stephen L. Collins, *From Divine Cosmos to Sovereign State* (Oxford, 1989), pp. 83–86.

4. W. R. Williams, *The Parliamentary History of the County of Gloucester* (Hereford, 1898), p. 49; F. D. Price, "The Commission for Ecclesiastical Causes for the Diocese of Bristol and Gloucester, 1574," *Transactions of the Bristol and Gloucestershire Archeological Society* 59 (1938): 61–184. Hereafter cited as *TBGAS*. According to Price, Berkeley, Sir John Tracy, Sir Nicholas Poyntz, and other magnates sat rather rarely (usually when the weight "of the chiefs of the ecclesiastical and civil administration of the shire" was needed).

5. *TBGAS* 56 (1934): 214; John Smyth of Nibley, *The Berkeley Manuscripts* (Gloucester, 1885), vol. 1, p. 264. Smyth's report that Berkeley had the Lieutenancy cannot be confirmed in the PRO records and may be an erroneous conflation of his appointment to have charge of a particular prisoner.

6. HMC De L'Isle and Dudley, vol. 2 (1934): 220, 434, 448, 487; 9 Salisbury vol. 13, p. 457. Berkeley greatly admired the writings of Mornay, also a favorite with the Sidney circle. The many studies of Sir Philip Sidney turn up no indication that Berkeley had any sort of connection with the Sidneys except for an odd report of Berkeley's signature on a letter concerning a proposed marriage (which never occurred) of the then eleven-year-old Philip Sidney to Lord Berkeley's daughter and heir in 1565. Percy Addleshaw, *Sir Philip Sidney* (London, 1909), pp. 237–38.

7. Samuel Rudder, *A New History of Gloucestershire* (Cirencester, 1779), p. 698.; VCH Gloucestershire, vol. 7 (1981), pp. 221–22. He died on Apr. 26, 1604, the date being noted on the inscription below his effigy in the Lord Mayor's Chapel in Bristol Cathedral. *TBGAS* 26 (1903): 267. This article is the source of the 1531 birthdate. The epitaph describes him as "full of years" when he died. His son Henry was born in 1559 (Rudder, p. 699); thus 1531 is a plausible year for Sir Richard's birth.

8. HMC Salisbury, pt. 2, p. 84. It is difficult to know how far to credit this report. See, on p. 87, an indication that the same informant, Thomas Graves, may have had a quarrel with Berkeley. The matter is obscure—but Graves may have been currying favor with Burghley by informing, perhaps inventively, on Berkeley and others. As I note below, Berkeley read Italian and may well have been fluent in it. Also, a "Sir Richard Bartley" was under consideration for the office of Controller of the Household in 1596 (HMC Hatfield 6:287–88). Since the office was highly coveted by some of the queen's own kinsmen, that Berkeley was even in the hunt suggests that she had held him in some esteem (or that she found it useful to feign that she did in order to hold importunate men at bay). I am grateful to my former student Dr. Robert Mueller for this reference, the one below about gentlemen of "good consideration," and many informative conversations about Elizabethan officeholding.

9. *TBGAS* 26 (1903): 266.

10. B. L. Lansdowne MSS 104:42, f. 103. On the surveys see John Guy, *Tudor England* (Oxford, 1990), p. 386.

11. For his use of Italian, see *Discourse*, pp. 19, 64, 104. Although his son Sir Henry did not matriculate, his grandson Richard and stepson, Sir Thomas Roe, did at Magdalen, Oxford in 1592 and 1593, respectively. C. W. Boase and Andrew Clark, eds., *Register of the University of Oxford* (Oxford, 1885–89), vol. 2, pp. 188, 197. Berkeley's method of writing reminds one of some of Bacon's essays, such as "Of Vain-Glory," which cites Aesop, a French proverb, Livy and the younger Pliny in close proximity, in that a commodious commonplace book must have been near to hand.

12. John Wallace argued impressively for the pervasiveness of a Plutarchian approach to reading in seventeenth-century England, one in which "true reading, as opposed to fanciful allegorical reading, extracted the moral philosophy that good authors mixed with their fictions, or imported it from the outside." "'Examples Are Best Precepts': Readers and Meanings in Seventeenth-Century Poetry," *Critical Inquiry* 1 (Dec. 1974): 278.

13. Rather surprisingly, he seems not to have read Castiglione's *Courtier*. He did, however, make frequent use of Antonio de Guevarra's *The Dial of Princes* (1529; English translation, 1447). According to Quentin Skinner, Guevarra's work was patterned on Castiglione. *The Foundations of Modern Political Thought* (Cambridge, 1978), p. 214. Nor does Berkeley cite such Neostoic writers as Lipsius.

14. Quoted in Glenn Burgess, *The Politics of the Ancient Constitution* (University Park, Penn., 1992), p. 9. See pp. 8–10 for Burgess's demonstration that this was one of the "platitudes" of the era."

15. *Discourse*, pp. 13–17. Cf. his account of Nero, pp. 18–19, who "put his own mother to death, & caused her to be be opened, that he might see the place where he lay. . . . He was in all things given to please his senses and above all the rest of his abhominable vices, extremely addicted to the pleasure of women, and to lecherie, which because it will abhorre all modest eares, I will forbeare to recite."

16. Ibid., p. 23.

17. Ibid., pp. 165–66.

18. Ibid., sig A1 (verso). "I desire rather to bee taken for a Relator of other mens sayings and opinions, then to arrogate such sufficiency, as to be author of any thing my self."

19. Ibid., p. 438. However gruesome they might seem to us, it is quite possible that Berkeley's readers found genuine humor in the punishment of sinners in graphic and appropriate ways.

20. Ibid., pp. 44, 305 (*Fumo punitur qui fumum vendidit*).

21. Sir Keith Thomas, "The Place of Laughter in Tudor and Stuart England," *TLS* (Jan. 21, 1977): 78. Barbara Bowen has shown that in the sixteenth century, both emblem books and joke collections were "intended to provide moral instruction as well as amusement." She states that joke books had "no formal organization," a characteristic that does not apply to Berkeley's work. See Bowen, "Two Literary Genres: The Emblem and the Joke," *Journal of Medieval and Renaissance Studies* 15 (1985): 31, 33. See also her listing of joke collections (1344–1528) in *Renaissance Quarterly* 39 (1986): 1–15, 263–75.

22. *Discourse*, pp. 183–84. Charles, cardinal of Lorraine, was the duke of Guise's

brother and is therefore depicted in a menage that included his sister-in-law and his niece. For other material from the French civil wars, see pp. 232–38, 307–10. Castiglione was quite fond of anticlerical jokes, especially when the target was a cardinal. See *The Courtier*, book 2 (62, 72, 76, 78, 82), and Robert Grudin, "Renaissance Laughter: The Jests in Castiglione's *Il Cortegiano*," *Neophilologus* 58 (1974): 199–204. On the flood of books and pamphlets coming out of France in the 1570's and 1580's, see Lisa Ferraro Parmelee, *Good Newes from Fraunce: French Anti-League Propaganda in Late Elizabethan England* (Rochester, N.Y., 1996). According to Parmelee, prominent in its content were "riveting stories of ambition and betrayal featuring the villainous Guises, the hated Jesuits, the Pope" (p. 50).

23. Robert M. Kingdon, *Myths About the St. Bartholomew's Day Massacres, 1572–1576* (Cambridge, Mass., 1988), p. 70. Its authorship remains uncertain, and there were several versions and numerous editions in various languages beginning in 1573. See pp. 74–75 for Kingdon's account of the story about the cardinal of Lorraine and his painting.

24. Thomas, "Place of Laughter." A story that Thomas mentions from Poggio Bracciolini is in the *Discourse* on pp. 180–81. A priest told his parishioners that Christ fed 400 rather than 4,000 people at Cana. "The clarke that stood under the pulpit, hearing him say foure hundred, stepped up to him; Ye mistake the matter Sir (quoth he) it was not foure hundred, it was foure thousand. Peace foole (quoth the Priest) let them beleeve this first." For lecherous clergy, see pp. 28, 38, 49, 52, 54–56. See Charles Speroni, *Wit and Wisdom of the Italian Renaissance* (Berkeley, 1964), p. 52, for this particular joke, and many others Berkeley used appear in this anthology.

25. *Discourse*, pp. 555–56. Further, ibid., "We condemne Papists for their superstition and confidence in their good works: and wee blame Puritans for their affected singularitie and formall precisenesse."

26. See, e.g., ibid., p. 184: "But how soever these wilde Buls that are sent from Rome by the Popes, to terrifie the world, are obeyed of the Angels and Divels, they are not so daungerous (thankes be to God) among men as they have bin, nor so much regarded." For references to "these latter daies," see ibid., pp. 227, 273, 315.

27. See ibid., pp. 190–95, 241–50; Burton, *The Anatomy of Melancholy* (New York, 1941), pp. 886, 895–96.

28. *Discourse*, pp. 49, 195–97, 115. Similarly, pp. 38, 52–56, 111–12, 174, 308. Clarendon was still retailing such stuff seven decades later. He described Pope John XII's adultery and murder by the offended husband "admitted by Catholic writers" in his *Animadversions* (1673), p. 209. My thanks to Viviana Marsano for this reference. On the sources for Pope Joan, see C. A. Patrides, *Premises and Motifs in Renaissance Thought*, ch. 10. Florimond de Raemond, a Frenchman who was nearly Berkeley's exact contemporary, wrote a book refuting the story of Pope Joan. For a discussion see Barbara Sher Tinsley, *History and Polemics in the French Reformation* (Selinsgrove, 1992), ch. 4.

29. *Discourse*, pp. 185–89. Cf. pp. 50, 206ff., 228. Cf. Burton's references to "Hildebrand the Magician" and "necromantical" popes.

30. Ibid., pp. 190–95.

31. Ibid., pp. 247–49.

32. Ibid., p. 550. Cf. p. 315: "If we runne over all the vertues and vices in this sort,

we shall see such a metamorphosis or transformation, that it were sufficient to per-
swade us, that the ages past have discharged all their mallice into the age we live in, as
into a gowt or sinke."

33. Ibid., pp. 317–18. The spider/bee analogy is from Plutarch and was very popular
in the seventeenth century (see the article by John Wallace cited in n. 12 above, p. 277).
Berkeley could not resist repeating it to another purpose on p. 628. For other denunciations of the latest sartorial fashions, see pp. 267ff., 324–30, 404–5, 524, 532–33. Berkeley also disliked the adornment of buildings (see pp. 342–43). For denunciations of
Machiavelli: pp. 79, 315, 545, 554–55. The Jacobean preacher Thomas Adams had much
in common with Berkeley in these and other matters. See my "On Misidentifying Puritans: the Case of Thomas Adams," in *Albion* (forthcoming).

34. *Discourse*, pp. 345–48. Cf. pp. 267–68, 325–26. In 1598, the earl of Essex similarly denounced the way that Englishmen, rather than display the "ancient virtue" of
paying taxes for the nation's defense, instead spent on luxuries: "our sumptuous
buildings, our surfeiting diet, our prodigality in garments, our infinite plate and our
costly furniture of houses." Quoted in Malcolm Smuts, "Court-Centered Politics and
the Uses of Roman Historians, c. 1590–1630," in Kevin Sharpe and Peter Lake, eds.,
Culture and Politics in Early Stuart England (Stanford, 1993), p. 37.

35. *Discourse*, p. 545.

36. Ibid., pp. 269–70. For similar concerns expressed by Ben Jonson, William
Camden, John Selden and others, see Blair Worden, "Ben Jonson Among the Historians," in Sharpe and Lake, eds., pp. 69, 71, 83–87.

37. *Discourse*, pp. 554–55.

38. Ibid., p. 631.

39. Ibid., p. 578. Cf. pp. 354, 542. If he was finishing the writing of the *Discourse* in
1596 or 1597, he was writing at the same time that the storm kicked up at Cambridge by
the proto-Arminian Peter Baro was at full strength. But there is no clear evidence that
he was aware of it. Berkeley's admiring references to Philippe de Mornay suggest that
he considered himself a good "reformed Protestant," but he may not have understood
the finer points of double predestinarian theology well enough to realize how fraught
with difficulty the problem was.

40. Ibid., pp. 206–8, 227–28, 229–32.

41. Ibid., pp. 200–204. For oracles see pp. 70, 81, 89f., 97, 197, 604.

42. Ibid., p. 6.

43. I am grateful to Jeffrey Burton Russell for advice on this point.

44. One of the censors in 1598 and 1604 was Samuel Harsnet, then a chaplain to the
bishop of London, Richard Bancroft. He had preached a well-known anti-Calvinist
sermon in 1584. On the sermon see Nicholas Tyacke, *Anti-Calvinists: The Rise of English Arminianism, c. 1590–1640* (Oxford, 1987), pp. 164–65.

45. Peter Lake, "Deeds Against Nature: Cheap Print, Protestantism and Murder in
Early Seventeenth Century England," in Sharpe and Lake, eds., p. 277.

46. Keith Thomas, *Religion and the Decline of Magic* (New York, 1971), pp. 93–96.
See also Willard Farnham, *The Medieval Heritage of Elizabethan Tragedy* (Oxford,
1963).

47. For an excellent discussion of these and similar works, see David D. Hall,

Worlds of Wonder, Days of Judgment (New York, 1989), ch. 2. On Beard see John Morrill, *Oliver Cromwell and the English Revolution* (London, 1990), pp. 27–28. The vision of God as an "interventionist" rather than a clockmaker remained powerful into the eighteenth century, as J. Paul Hunter shows in *Before Novels: the Cultural Context of Eighteenth-Century English Fiction* (New York, 1990), pp. 217–22.

48. I have used the 1631 edition of Beard's *Theatre.* It is in two "books," one on sins against the "First Table" (the first four commandments concerning the worship of God) and the other on the "Second Table" (commandments five through ten concerning relations with people). Broadly speaking, the first concerns worship, the second morals. On this distinction see J. Sears McGee, *The Godly Man in Stuart England: Anglicans, Puritans, and the Two Tables* (New Haven, 1976). Nehemiah Wallington's providentialism is that of Clarke and Beard, not Berkeley. See Paul S. Seaver, *Wallington's World: A Puritan Artisan in Seventeenth-Century London* (Stanford, 1985), pp. 47–66.

49. Perhaps he had them in mind when he related the comparison of the rich man and the peacock. Like the latter, the former wears "faire feathers, and so delighteth to bee seene and to behold his taile, that he discovereth his filthie parts behind" (*Discourse*, p. 119).

50. *Oxford Classical Dictionary,* 2d ed. (Oxford, 1970), p. 530.

51. The 1631 edition, sig A2v. For a summary of the Stationers' *Register* entries, see A. M. Clark, "A Bibliography of Thomas Heywood," *Oxford Bibliographical Society Proceedings and Papers,* vol. 1, pt. 2 (1924): 143.

52. Kevin Sharpe, *Criticism and Compliment* (Cambridge, 1987), pp. 275, 62, 240.

53. *Discourse,* p. 344.

HEAL AND HOLMES: "PRUDENTIA ULTRA SEXUM"

1. Hertfordshire Record Office, Hertford (hereafter HRO), Gorhambury, IX D 55. Printed in Royal Commission on Historical Manuscripts, ser. 64, earl of Verulam, p. 54. For Stanton see M. Whinney, *Sculpture in Britain, 1530 to 1830* (Harmondsworth, 1964), p. 35; M. Whinney and O. Millar, *English Art, 1625–1714* (Oxford, 1957), pp. 114, 235, n. 3. K. A. Esdaile first suggested the relationship between the Culford and St. Alban's monuments: see *English Church Monuments, 1510–1840* (Oxford, 1947), p. 89. The authors would like to thank Dr. Nigel Llewellyn for most helpful discussion of the monument.

2. Cambridge University Library (hereafter CUL) Hengrave Mss. 22.4*. Blomefield's description also provides the date of Nicholas Bacon's death, from a memorial inscription in the church, now lost. Davy, visiting the church in 1829, also misread the monument: British Library (hereafter BL) Additional Mss 19079 fol. 96v. This arrangement of the figures has also confused several generations of art historians commenting on the tomb. Following Mrs. Esdaile, it has been usual to describe the recumbent figure as Lady Jane's first husband, Sir William Cornwallis, although he is clearly buried at Oakley Church, with a tomb paid for by Jane in her will: Esdaile, p. 86; Whinney and Millar, p. 113; N. Pevsner (revised E. Radcliffe), *The Buildings of England: Suffolk,* 2d ed. (Harmondsworth, 1974), p. 181. One of the few commentators

who has described the tomb accurately is G. Storey, "Culford Hall," in *People and Places: An East Anglian Miscellany* (Lavenham, 1973), p. 139.

3. The Cornwallis-Bacon correspondence was partially edited by Lord Braybrooke when it came into the hands of the owners of Audley End in the early nineteenth century. This text, *The Private Correspondence of Lady Jane Cornwallis, 1613–1644* (London, 1842) (hereafter *Correspondence*) contains examples of letters from all Lady Jane's major correspondents, except William Greenhill, and gives in full her own few surviving letters, those of Lucy, countess of Bedford, and those of her husband, Sir Nathaniel. The original letters are now deposited in the Essex Record Office at Chelmsford (hereafter ERO), filed under Acc. D/Dby/C12–26. There are large files of correspondence from Jane's brother, Thomas Meautys, her sister-in-law, Anna, her younger son, Nicholas, her London-based cousin, Dorothy Randolph, and her cousin, Thomas Meautys, all of which are only sampled in the printed text. An important series of letters from Greenhill, Lady Jane's chaplain, have been transcribed in K. W. Shipps, "Lay Patronage of East Anglian Puritan Clerics in Pre-revolutionary England" (Ph.D. diss., Yale University, 1971), app. xii.

4. On Sir Nathaniel Bacon and his art, see the brief comments in Whinney and Millar, pp. 82–83: they cite Henry Peacham, himself an artist, who described Bacon in *The Compleat Gentleman* as "not inferiour in my judgement to our skilfullest Masters."

5. For discussions of the conduct literature, see K. Davies, "Continuity and Change in Literary Advice on Marriage," in R. B. Outhwaite, ed., *Marriage and Society: Studies in the Social History of Marriage* (London, 1981); S. Hull, *Chaste, Silent, and Obedient: English Books for Women, 1475–1640* (San Marino, Calif., 1982); L. Woodbridge, *Women and the English Renaissance: Literature and the Nature of Womankind, 1540–1620* (Urbana, Ill., 1984). One of the most popular forms in which the ideal was disseminated was the funeral sermon, notably Philip Stubbes's encomium on his wife, Katherine, that ran through 24 editions by 1637: Philip Stubbes, *A Christal Glasse for Christian Women* (London, 1591). An excellent example of women who circumvented the formal expectations of gentlewomen's behavior is in A. Wall, "Elizabethan Precept and Feminine Practice: The Thynne Family of Longleat," *History* 75 (1991): 23–38. On women and the Civil War, see C. Durston, *The Family in the English Revolution* (Oxford, 1989); J. Eales, *Puritans and Roundheads: The Harleys of Brampton Bryan and the Outbreak of the English Civil War* (Cambridge, 1990); D. J. H. Clifford, ed., *The Diaries of Lady Anne Clifford* (London, 1990), p. 97–99.

6. *Correspondence*, p. xlviii; M. K. McIntosh, "The Cooke Family of Gidea Hall, Essex, 1460–1661" (Ph.D. diss., Harvard University, 1967), pp. 116–20; Public Record Office (hereafter PRO), PROB 11/73/9; Thomas's wife Anna recalled this story when discussing with Jane the future of her eldest son, ERO, D/DBy/C23/2, fol. 106; C. L'E. Ewen, "Robert Radcliffe, Fifth Earl of Sussex: Witchcraft Accusations," *Transactions of the Essex Archaeological Society*, n.s., 22 (1938–40): 232–38; *Calendar of State Papers: Domestic Series* (hereafter *CSPD*), 1603–10, pp. 602.

7. E. McClure, ed., *The Letters of John Chamberlain* (hereafter *Chamberlain*), Memoirs of the American Philosophical Society, vol. 12 (1939), pp. 285, 288, 315, 341.

8. Royal Commission on Historical Manuscripts, ser. 9, Salisbury (Cecil) Mss. at

Hatfield [hereafter HMC Salisbury], vol. 3, pp. 3, 376–78; vol. 4, pp. 181, 578; vol. 5, pp. 4, 30, 40, 136, 497; vol. 6, p. 498; vol. 7, pp. 86, 297; vol. 15, pp. 147, 176; PRO SP 12/263/75; CUL Hengrave Mss., 88/2 nos. 78, 85. For biographical material on Sir William, see P. W. Hasler, ed., *The History of Parliament: The House of Commons, 1558–1603* (London, 1981), vol. 1, pp. 659–60; Alan Simpson, *The Wealth of the Gentry, 1540–1660: East Anglian Studies* (Cambridge, 1961), pp. 148–72; P. McGrath and J. Rowe, "The Recusancy of Sir Thomas Cornwallis," *Proceedings of the Suffolk Institute of Archaeology* 28 (1961): 226–71.

9. CUL Hengrave Mss., 88/2 nos. 78, 85. Something of the character of Charles emerges in the sententious tone of his correspondence: see Bodleian Library Tanner MSS (hereafter Bodl. Tanner) 285 fols. 6, 15, 20, 33, 39, 43, 45, 51, 54; *Chamberlain*, p. 547.

10. HMC Salisbury, vol. 20, pp. 119–20; Edmund Sawyer, ed., *Memorials of Affairs of State . . . from the Original Papers of Sir Ralph Winwood* (1725), vol. 2, p. 94.

11. *Chamberlain*, pp. 288, 315, 341; PRO, C142/329/185; PRO, PROB 11/118/93.

12. *Correspondence*, pp. 1, 97, 103, 181; Bodl. Tanner, 115, fol. 199; 283, fol. 71; *Chamberlain*, p. 3.

13. Translated from the memorial inscription to Sir William Cornwallis in Oakley Church; the "remarkable" character of this tomb is noted by Pevsner, p. 382.

14. *Chamberlain*, p. 341.   15. *Correspondence*, pp. 1, 2.

16. *Correspondence*, pp. 2, 3–9.   17. *Correspondence*, pp. 15, 22.

18. PRO, C142/329/185, I.P.M. of Sir William Cornwallis; Correspondence, pp. 2–3, 5–11, 15–16, 100–107; W. A. Copinger, *The Manors of Suffolk*, 7 vols. (Woodbridge, 1905–11), vol. 1, pp. 282–85; ERO, D/DBy/C26, fol. 57; D/DBy/A382.

19. *Correspondence*, pp. 33–53, 56–63, 71–79, 84–91, 125–31, 145–48.

20. *Correspondence*, pp. 79–80.

21. On the religious views of the Cookes of Essex, see McIntosh, pp. 116–23. Among the key influences on Jane at court, Lucy, countess of Bedford, and Princess Elizabeth were both firm Protestants; Essex RO, D/DBy/C24, fol. 1; Elnathan Parr, *The Grounds of Divinitie* (London, 1614), sig. A3–4, *Abba Father; or, A Plaine and Short Direction concerning Private Prayer* (London, 1618), sig. A3–4, *The Workes of that faithfull and powerfull preacher Elnathan Parr*, 3d ed. (London, 1632), pp. 1–2; PRO, PROB 11/1660/172; HRO, Gorhambury, IX. D.54.

22. ERO, D/DBy/C26, fols. 55, 60–63. On Greenhill and his relationship with Lady Jane, see Shipps, pp. 151–62 and app. xii; for Burroughs, see Shipps, pp. 176–78, 314–15, and app. xiii.

23. *Correspondence*, pp. 98–99, 108.

24. *Correspondence*, pp. 50–52; HRO, Gorhambury, IX D 54; ERO, D/DBy/C25, fol. 42.

25. ERO, D/DBy/C25, fol. 42.

26. ERO D/DBy/C24, fols. 3, 4, 29; for a later example of Greenhill's championship of Fred, see ibid., fol. 17.

27. ERO, D/DBy/C16, fols. 17–39; *Correspondence*, pp. 273–74, 278–79. Lord Braybrooke chose to print only four of an extensive series of Nicholas's letters, wisely deciding that the repetitiveness of the notes made further quotation unnecessary.

28. *Correspondence*, pp. 205–10, 213–14, 220–27, 230ff.

29. *Correspondence*, pp. 230–39; ERO, D/DBy/C24, fol. 17; one of the least pleasing aspects of Frederick's apologies for his marriage was his attempt to claim that it had been engineered at the command of the king and queen.

30. *Correspondence*, pp. 280–84, 287–89; ERO, D/DBy/C26, fol. 65; HRO, Gorhambury IX D 38; PRO SP 23/204/591–99, /207/121, 133. For Sir Frederick's money-raising schemes as a courtier, see *CSPD, 1635–36*, p. 433 and *1636–37*, p. 303. If Frederick failed to meet her conditions, Jane's executors were instructed to provide him with only an annuity of £500.

31. PRO, SP 23/65/85–96; HRO, Gorhambury IX D 38, 39.

32. For Nicholas Bacon see PRO SP 23/65/85–96: his wife, Elizabeth, first appears in November 1645; for Sir Frederick see M. F. Keeler, *The Long Parliament, 1640–41: A Biographical Study of Its Members*, Memoirs of the American Philosophical Society, vol. 36 (Philadelphia, 1954), p. 143; G. J. Warner, ed., *Correspondence of Sir Edward Nicholas*, vol. 3, 1655–56, Camden Society, 2d ser., vol. 57 (1897), pp. 5, 286; David Lloyd, *Memoires of the Lives, Actions, Sufferings, and Deaths* (1668), pp. 662–63; R. Latham and W. Matthews, eds., *The Diary of Samuel Pepys*, 12 vols. (1971–83), vol. 3, p. 10.

33. A. E. Green, ed., *Calendar of the Proceedings of the Committee for the Advance of Money* (1888), pp. 480–81.

34. ERO, D/DBy/C24, fols. 1, 6–8, 16; O. Airey, ed., *Burnet's History of My Own Times: part 1, The Reign of Charles II*, 2 vols. (Oxford, 1900), vol. 2, pp. 77–78; HRO, Gorhambury, IX D 54.

35. ERO, D/DBy/C25, fols. 38ff.

36. ERO, D/DBy/C25. Anne's aunt living in the Low Countries thought that she was married in 1635 and sent congratulations, but she was not married until the end of 1640 or beyond, *Correspondence*, pp. 276, 295.

37. *Correspondence*, pp. 212, 228. The best account of Meautys is provided by L. Jardine and A. Shearer, *Hostage to Fortune: The Troubled Life of Francis Bacon* (London, 1998), pp. 418, 465, 468, 475, 483–85, 489, 511–14. See also G. E. Aylmer, *The King's Servants*, 2d ed. (London, 1974), pp. 78, 133–34, 156–58, 164, 204, 290–94, and A. C. Bunten, *Sir Thomas Meautys, Secretary to Lord Bacon and His Friends* (London, 1918). For Meautys's dealings with the Gorhambury estate, see Jardine and Shearer, pp. 515–18, and Rev. C. Moor, "The Bacon Deeds at Gorhambury," *Genealogists' Magazine* 7 (1937): 561–74.

38. HRO, Gorhambury I A 37; II A 9, 16–17, 19, 23–24; IX D 39.

39. PRO PROB 11/1660/172.

40. Airey, ed., vol. 2, pp. 77–78.

BEN-AMOS: "GOOD WORKS" AND SOCIAL TIES

1. C. Hill, *Society and Puritanism in Pre-Revolutionary England* (London: Secker and Warburg, 1964), pp. 259–97, 483–87; P. Slack, *Poverty and Policy in Tudor and Stuart England* (London: Longman, 1988), pp. 17–36; M. Todd, *Christian Humanism and the Puritan Social Order* (Cambridge: Cambridge University Press, 1987), pp. 118–75; F. Heal, *Hospitality in Early Modern England* (Oxford: Oxford University Press, 1990), pp. 122–24; R. Jutte, *Poverty and Deviance in Early Modern Europe* (Cambridge:

Cambridge University Press, 1994), pp. 100–142, esp. 108–9. For Puritan attitudes to poverty, see also P. Lake, "Serving God and the Times: The Calvinist Conformity of Robert Sanderson," *Journal of British Studies* 27 (1988): 90; D. Underdown, *Fire from Heaven: Life in an English Town in the Seventeenth Century* (London: Fontana, 1993), pp. 90–129; S. Hindle, "Exclusion Crises: Poverty, Migration and Parochial Responsibility in English Rural Communities, c. 1560–1660," *Rural History* 7 (1996): 137–38. For a recent account that appeared after this article had been completed and that effectively demonstrates a gradual rise in public concerns with the problem of vagrancy over the whole period between 1370 and 1600, see M. K. McIntosh, *Controlling Misbehavior in England, 1370–1600* (Cambridge: Cambridge University Press, 1998), pp. 81–96.

2. Among the many studies pointing to the mobility of the population and its chronological contours, see P. Clark, "Migration in England During the Late Seventeenth and Early Eighteenth Centuries," *Past and Present* 83 (1979): 56–90; P. Clark and D. Souden, eds., *Migration and Society in Early Modern England* (London: Hutchinson, 1987); A. Kussmaul, *Servants in Husbandry in Early Modern England* (Cambridge: Cambridge University Press, 1981); J. Landers, *Death and the Metropolis: Studies in the Demographic History of London, 1670–1830* (Cambridge: Cambridge University Press, 1993), pp. 40–47.

3. P. Seaver, "The Puritan Work Ethic Revisited," *Journal of British Studies* 19 (1980): 35–53, esp. 37–39.

4. R. Chartier, "Culture as Appropriation: Popular Cultural Uses in Early Modern France," in *Understanding Popular Culture: Europe from the Middle Ages to the Nineteenth Century*, ed. S. L. Kaplan (New York: Mouton, 1984), pp. 229–53, esp. pp. 234–36.

5. *The Book of Examinations and Depositions, 1622–1644*, vol. 1: *1622–1627* (Southampton Record Society, vol. 29, 1929), p. 42.

6. I. Krausman Ben-Amos, *Adolescence and Youth in Early Modern England* (New Haven: Yale University Press, 1994), pp. 69–83; A. H. Smith, "Labourers in Late Sixteenth-Century England: A Case Study from North Norfolk [Part I]," *Continuity and Change* 4 (1989): 370.

7. Ben-Amos, *Adolescence and Youth*, p. 108.

8. Ibid., pp. 162–65, 228; Adam Martindale, *The Life of Adam Martindale* (Chetham Society, vol. 4, 1845, born 1623), p. 213; Edward Coxere, *Adventures by Sea* (1945, born 1633), p. 51; Benjamin Bangs, *Memoirs of the Life* (1757, born 1652), p. 324; George Trosse, *The Life of the Late Reverend Mr George Trosse* (1974, born 1631), p. 106.

9. A. Kussmaul, ed., *The Autobiography of Joseph Mayett of Quainton, 1783–1839* (Buckinghamshire Record Society, 1986), vol. 23, pp. 11–12.

10. *The Ordinary of Newgate, His Account of the Behaviour, Confessions and dying Words of the Malefactors . . . executed at Tyborn* (1720–1734), account of Joseph Powis, Oct. 9, 1732, pp. 21–22.

11. Ibid., account of Thomas Tavernor, July 9, 1734, p. 10; account of Daniel Malden, Nov. 2, 1736, p. 12.

12. A. L. Beier, "Vagrants and the Social Order in Elizabethan England," *Past and Present* 64 (1974): 16–17.

13. *Books of Examinations and Depositions 1570–1594* (Southampton Record Society, vol. 16, 1914), p. 28; *Southampton Examinations 1622–27*, vol. 29, pp. 3, 57.

14. Heal, *Hospitality*, chs. 2, 4; pp. 390–91.

15. *Southampton Examinations, 1570–94*, vol. 16, p. 39.

16. Heal, *Hospitality*, p. 293.

17. *Southampton Examinations, 1622–27*, vol. 29, pp. 57–58. See also Heal, *Hospitality*, ch. 7.

18. *Ordinary of Newgate*, Oct. 9, 1732, p. 27.

19. P. Collinson, "Puritanism as Popular Religious Culture," in C. Durston and J. Eales, ed., *The Culture of English Puritanism* (London: Macmillan Press, 1996), p. 53.

20. Heal, *Hospitality*, ch. 9.

21. Ibid., pp. 360–65; R. W. Malcolmson, *Popular Recreations in English Society, 1700–1850* (Cambridge: Cambridge University Press, 1973), pp. 18–19; R. Hutton, *The Rise and Fall of Merry England* (Oxford: Oxford University Press, 1994), p. 243; R. Houlbrooke, "Death, Church, and Family in England Between the Late Fifteenth and Early Eighteenth Centuries," in R. Houlbrooke, ed., *Death, Ritual, and Bereavement* (London: Routledge, 1989), pp. 35–36.

22. For an estimate of the growing number of fairs in the period 1660–1740, see J. A. Chartres, *Internal Trade in England, 1500–1700* (London and Basingstoke: Macmillan Press, 1977), p. 48.

23. *Ordinary of Newgate*, account of Joseph Powis, Oct. 9, 1732, p. 23.

24. A. L. Beier, *Masterless Men: The Vagrancy Problem in England, 1560–1640* (London: Methuen, 1985), p. 82.

25. Ibid., pp. 83–84.

26. *Ordinary of Newgate*, Oct. 9, 1732, pp. 26–27.

27. Ibid., account of James White, Nov. 6, 1723, p. 3; Joseph Powis, Oct. 9, 1732, p. 23; George Price, Mar. 8, 1738, pp. 11–12.

28. Ibid., account of Edward Bonner, Sept. 27, 1736, pp. 14–15.

29. *British Parliamentary Papers 1852–53*, vol. 88, pt. 1, pp. ccxx, ccxxv, ccxxvii.

30. P. Clark, "Migrants in the City: The Process of Social Adaptation in English Towns, 1500–1800," in Clark and Souden, eds., *Migration and Society*, pp. 280–81.

31. *Southampton Examinations, 1601–1602*, vol. 26, p. 29.

32. Clark, "Migrants in the City," p. 272.

33. Ben-Amos, *Adolescence and Youth*, p. 168.

34. *Ordinary of Newgate*, Sept. 12, 1726, pp. 1–2, and see also the account of John Lineham, Feb. 13, 1739, p. 8.

35. *The Proceedings of the King's Commission . . . Held in the City of London and County of Middlesex at Justice Hall in the Old Bailey* (hereafter *Proceedings*), Dec. 6–11, 1732, p. 2; June 2–4, 1731, p. 12.

36. Ibid., Dec. 6–11, 1732, p. 15.

37. P. Seleski, "Women, Work, and Cultural Change in Eighteenth- and Early Nineteenth-Century London," in Tim Harris, ed., *Popular Culture in England, c. 1500–1850* (London: Macmillan Press, 1995), pp. 150–51. For kin and migration to towns in the nineteenth century, see M. Anderson, *Family Structure in Nineteenth-Century Lancashire* (Cambridge: Cambridge University Press, 1971), pp. 152–56; A. Janssens, *Family and Social Change: The Household as a Process in an Industrializing Community* (Cambridge: Cambridge University Press, 1993), pp. 160–62.

38. Thomas Hardy, *Memoirs of Thomas Hardy* (1832, born 1752), p. 4.

39. *Southampton Examinations 1622–1627*, vol. 29, p. 56.

40. Ben-Amos, *Adolescence and Youth*, p. 177; Clark, "Migrants in the City," pp. 269–76, 282–85.

41. N. E. Key, "The Political Culture and Political Rhetoric of County Feasts and Feast Sermons, 1654–1714," *Journal of British Studies* 33 (1994): 226–47.

42. *Ordinary of Newgate*, Feb. 13, 1739.

43. Landers, *Death and the Metropolis*, pp. 41, 44–47, 50–51.

44. For evidence of company on the road mentioned in testimonies in the early seventeenth century, see *Southampton Examinations, 1570–1594*, vol. 16, pp. 39, 40 ("he came to Farnham whereupon he fell acquainted with a strange man . . . whereupon this said strange man sayed that he would be verie glad of his companye for that he had occasion to goe thither also); ibid., 1622–27, vol. 29, p. 3. For a similar account in early eighteenth-century London, see *Proceedings*, Dec. 6–11, 1732, pp. 9–10.

45. *Proceedings*, July 6–8, 1732.

46. *Proceedings*, Jan. 6–7, 1720; Sept. 7–11, 1732, p. 219; June 2–4, 1731, p. 4. For overcrowding in early eighteenth-century London, see Landers, *Death and the Metropolis*, pp. 68–70.

47. *Proceedings*, Dec. 7–8, 1733, p. 20; Dec. 6–8, 1733, p. 7.

48. Landers, *Death and the Metropolis*, p. 49.

49. *Proceedings*, Dec. 6–11, 1732, p. 41.

50. *Proceedings*, Dec. 6–11, 1732, p. 4.

51. *Proceedings*, Sept. 3–5, 1690; Aug. 28–31, 1700, p. 1; Jan. 13–16, 1720, pp. 1–2.

52. *Proceedings*, Jan. 17–19, 1732, pp. 33, 49; Jan. 1730, p. 73; Apr. 1732, p. 121; Jan. 25–26, 1730/1, pp. 25–26; Dec. 7–8, 1733, p. 21.

53. *Southampton Examinations, 1570–1594*, vol. 16, p. 40; *Proceedings*, Jan. 6–7, 1720; Jan. 17–19, 1732, p. 32; Dec. 7–8, 1733, p. 21.

54. *Southampton Examinations, 1639–1644*, vol. 36, pp. 77–78; *Proceedings*, Jan. 14–17, 1694/5; Jan. 13–16, 1720, p. 1; Jan. 13–16, 1720, p. 2; Aug. 28–31, 1700, p. 1; Feb. 1732, p. 85; Dec. 5–8, 1733, pp. 17–18; Dec. 6–8, 1733, p. 9.

55. *Proceedings*, Jan. 13–16, 1720, p. 2; Dec. 10–13, 1730/31, pp. 8–9; 6–8 May 1732, p. 128; 6–8 May 1732, p. 130; Dec. 7–8, 1733, p. 20.

56. *Proceedings*, 6–8 May 1732, p. 128; Dec. 10–13, 1730/31, p. 8; Feb. 21–24, 1733, p. 75; Sept. 7–11, 1732, p. 219.

57. *Proceedings*, 6–8 May 1732, p. 130.

58. For the force of "weak" ties among the poor, see M. H. D. van Leeuwen, "Logic of Charity: Poor Relief in Preindustrial Europe," *Journal of Interdisciplinary History* 24 (1994): 589–613, esp. 603–4.

59. M. K. McIntosh, "Local Responses to the Poor in Late Medieval and Tudor England," *Continuity and Change* 3 (1988): 210–11; M. Rubin, *Charity and Community in Medieval Cambridge* (Cambridge: Cambridge University Press, 1987), ch. 3; Todd, *Christian Humanism*, pp. 118–58; Slack, *Poverty and Policy*, pp. 22–27.

60. Slack, *Poverty and Policy*, pp. 20–21; Todd, *Christian Humanism*, pp. 163–65; Heal, *Hospitality*, pp. 131–34.

61. Slack, *Poverty and Policy*, pp. 20–21; Heal, *Hospitality*, pp. 136–37; Underdown,

Fire from Heaven, pp. 92, 120–26; J. S. McGee, *The Godly Man in Stuart England: Anglicans, Puritans, and the Two Tables, 1620–1670* (New Haven: Yale University Press, 1976), pp. 93–94. For the greater interest of the godly in duties to God than in those to man, see also Heal, *Hospitality*, p. 137

62. Slack, *Poverty and Policy*, pp. 26, 148–52; Heal, *Hospitality*, pp. 130–34; Todd, *Christian Humanism*, pp. 163–65; Hindle, "Exclusion Crises," pp. 131–38; Underdown, *Fire from Heaven*, pp. 102–3.

63. For the increase in bequests and endowments for institutions, see W. K. Jordan, *Philanthropy in England, 1480–1660: A Study of the Changing Pattern of English Social Aspirations* (London: Allen and Unwin, 1959). For a summary of the critique of Jordan's findings and a modified assessment, see Slack, *Poverty and Policy*, pp. 162–65; I. Archer, *The Pursuit of Stability: Social Relations in Elizabethan London* (Cambridge: Cambridge University Press, 1991), pp. 163–82.

64. Heal, *Hospitality*, p. 137; Hindle, "Exclusion Crises," pp. 131–38

65. R. L. Greaves, *Society and Religion in Elizabethan England* (Minneapolis: University of Minnesota Press, 1981), pp. 557–62; Todd, *Christian Humanism*, pp. 158–62; Heal, *Hospitality*, pp. 124–26.

66. Heal, *Hospitality*, p. 134; Archer, *The Pursuit of Stability*, p. 179.

67. Underdown, *Fire from Heaven*, pp. 91–92.

68. Thomas Cranmer, *Catechismus . . . A short instruction into Christian Religion* (1548), p. lxii.

69. Alexander Nowell, *A Catechism; or, First Instruction and Learning of Christian Religion* (1571), sig. Biii.

70. Edward Dering, *A Short Catechisme for Householdres* (1583), "the ladder of thrife," fol. 32.

71. For the principles of interpretation of the Ten Commandments in catechistic literature, based on a large sample of catechisms written in the period from the mid-sixteenth century through the early eighteenth, see I. Green, *The Christian ABC: Catechisms and Catechising in England, c. 1530–1740* (Oxford: Clarendon Press, 1996), pp. 427–30.

72. John Craig, *A Short Summe of the Whole Catechisme, wherein the Question is propounded, and Answere in few Words* (1581), eighth commandment, no fol.; Dering, *A Short Catechisme*, sig. B3; *A Catechism or Institution of Christian Religion . . . after the Little Catechism Appointed in the Book of Common Prayer* (1583), sig. Bii. For interpretations of the eighth commandment in other catechisms, see also Green, *The Christian's ABC*, pp. 462–63.

73. Nowell, *A Catechism*, sig. Fiii. See also *A Catechism or Institution of Christian Religion*, sig. Bii (on the duty to relieve the poor, widows, fatherless, "and strangers"). For similar pronouncements in catechisms in the seventeenth century, see Green, *The Christian's ABC*, pp. 463–64.

74. T. Bezza, *A Little Catechism* (1578), no fols. See also Nowell, *A Catechism*, sig. G1; Dering, *A Short Catechisme*, sig. B3; Christopher Shutte, *A Compendious forme and Summe of Christian Doctrine Called the Testimonie of a True Faith* (1581), sigs. D2–D3, D9; *A Catechism of Christian Religion Allowed to Be Taught in the Churches and Schooles* (1617), sig. D1; William Whitaker, *A Short Summe of Christianity Delivered by Way of Catechisme* (1630), no fol.

75. Cranmer, *Catechismus*, sig. G1; Nowell, *A Catechism*, sig. G1; Thomas Pearston, *A Short Instruction unto Christian Religion, Briefly Noting our Profession, Exercise, and Obedience* (1590), sig. A1; Whitaker, *A Short Summe* (1630), no fol. See also Green, *The Christian's ABC*, pp. 469–70.

76. Dering, *A Shorte Catechisme*, sig. B3.

77. *A Catechism, or Institution of Christian Religion*, sig. B1.

78. Green, *The Christian's ABC*, p. 475.

79. Ibid., pp. 469–75.

80. Slack, *Poverty and Policy*, p. 21.

81. Quoted in M. Todd, "Puritan Self-Fashioning: The Diary of Samuel Ward," *Journal of British Studies* 31 (1992): 236.

82. Edward Terrill, *The Records of a Church of Christ Meeting in Broadmead, Bristol, 1640–1678* (1847), p. 58.

83. Richard Davies, *An Account of the Convincement* (1794; born 1635), p. 145.

84. "Some Account of the Forepart of the Life of Elizabeth Ashbridge," in "A Commonplace Book Containing an Account of the Early Life of Elizabeth Ashbridge" (1755), Oxfordshire Record Office, BMM viii/1, fol. 2.

85. James Fretwell, *A Family History*, in *Yorkshire Diaries and Autobiographies in the Seventeenth and Eighteenth Centuries* (Surtees Society, vol. 65, 1877), p. 217. For other eulogies in autobiographies, see Simonds D'Ewes, *The Autobiography and Correspondence of Sir Simonds D'Ewes* (1845), p. 116; William Stout, *The Autobiography of William Stout, 1665–1752* (Chetham Society, 3d ser., vol. 14, 1967), p. 175.

86. J.D., *A Sermon Preached at the Funeral of Mary Armyne* (1676), "to the reader."

87. Richard Werge, *A Sermon Preach'd at the funeral of George Johnson* (1683), p. 30; John Goodwin, *A Sermon Preached at the Funeral of Daniel Taylor, esq.* (1655), "dedication"; William Sclatter, *Crowne of Righteousness: Solemn Funeral of Mr. Abraham Wheelock* (1654), "dedication"; F. Moore, *A Sermon Preached at the Funeral of the Vertuous and Godly Mrs Mary Forbes* (1656), sig. A2; Josiah Hunter, *A Sermon Preached at the funeral of Mrs Anne Mickle-Thwait* (1658), sig. B; William Alchorne, *A Sermon Preached at the funeral . . . of Mrs Elizabeth Atwood* (1674), "dedication"; John Lake, *The True Christian's Character and Crown: A Sermon . . . at the Funeral of Mr. William Cade* (1671), "dedication" ("He was noble and generous with frugality . . . with mercy and clemency. . . . He fed the Hungry and cloth'd the naked.") See also Heal, *Hospitality*, pp. 114–15, 176–80.

88. D. Andrew, *Philanthropy and Police: London Charity in the Eighteenth Century* (Princeton: Princeton University Press, 1989), pp. 12–22, quotations on pp. 16 and 19; W. M. Jacob, *Lay People and Religion in the Early Eighteenth Century* (Cambridge, 1996), pp. 155–56. For charity in county feast sermons in late seventeenth-century London, see Key, "The Political Culture," pp. 243–47.

89. For the continuity of begging in the large towns, see Slack, *Poverty and Policy*, pp. 166–69; Archer, *The Pursuit of Stability*, pp. 178–80; van Leeuwen, "Logic of Charity," pp. 601–2; Andrew, *Philanthropy and Police*, pp. 20–21; M. J. D. Roberts, "Reshaping the Gift Relationship: The London Medicity Society and the Suppression of Begging in England, 1818–1869," *International Review of Social History* 37 (1991–92): 201–31, esp. 202.

90. McIntosh, "Local Responses to the Poor," pp. 211–12.

WARD: GODLINESS, COMMEMORATION, AND COMMUNITY

Earlier versions of this paper were presented at Michigan State University, Harvard University, the North American Conference on British Studies, the Northeast Conference on British Studies, and the International Medieval Congress. I would like to thank the participants in these discussions, as well as Caroline Barron, David Cressy, Sue Grayzel, Newton Key, Muriel McClendon, Michael MacDonald, Catherine Patterson, Paul Seaver, and Robert Tittler for their useful suggestions.

1. Eamon Duffy, *The Stripping of the Altars: Traditional Religion in England, 1400–1580* (New Haven: Yale University Press, 1992), pp. 327–37, quotations on pp. 335–36.

2. George Unwin, *The Gilds and Companies of London*, 4th ed. (London: Frank Cass, 1963); Pamela Nightingale, *A Medieval Mercantile Community: The Grocers' Company and the Politics and Trade of London, 1000–1485* (New Haven: Yale University Press, 1995); Ian W. Archer, *The History of the Haberdashers' Company* (Chichester, Sussex: Phillimore, 1991), pp. 43–45; Susan Brigden, *London and the Reformation* (Oxford: Clarendon, 1989), esp. pp. 335–36, 411–13; C. John Sommerville, *The Secularization of Early Modern England: From Religious Culture to Religious Faith* (Oxford: Oxford University Press, 1992), pp. 76–78; Joseph P. Ward, *Metropolitan Communities: Trade Guilds, Identity, and Change in Early Modern London* (Stanford: Stanford University Press, 1997), pp. 110–15. C. J. Kitching, ed., *London and Middlesex Chantry Certificate, 1548*, London Record Society (1980), vol. 16, pp. 81–95, details the seized spiritual endowments of 34 companies.

3. C[lothworkers'] H[all] A[rchive], Orders of Courts (1605–1623), fol. 79v; Sk[inners'] H[all] A[rchive] Court Book 3 (1617–51), fols. 44r, 181r; Ward, p. 114; D[rapers'] H[all] A[rchive] Minutes and Records (1603–40), fol. 138r, and Minutes and Records (1640–67), fols. 13v, 41r. For the refashioning of civic traditions in the wake of the Reformation in provincial towns, see Robert Tittler, "Reformation, Civic Culture and Collective Memory in English Provincial Towns," *Urban History* 24, no. 3 (1997): 283–300; Tittler, "Civic Portraiture and Political Culture in English Provincial Towns, ca. 1560–1640," *Journal of British Studies* 37 (July 1998): 306–29; and Tittler, "The Cookes and the Brookes: Uses of Portraiture in Town and Country Before the Civil War," in Gerald MacLean, Donna Landry, and Joseph P. Ward, eds., *The Country and the City Revisited: England and the Politics of Culture, 1550–1850* (Cambridge: Cambridge University Press, 1999), pp. 58–73.

4. M[ercers'] H[all] A[rchive], Acts of Court (1560–1595), fols. 99r, 105r, 151r-v, 246v, 253v, 284r, 385r, 394v, 471r; (1595–1629), 132v, 162v, 174v. Of course, the officers of other companies were not necessarily as well informed as the mercers. In 1664, the master of the Brewers' Company ordered that the coat of arms of the person who had, among other things, originally built the company's hall be displayed in a stained glass window so that his memory would be preserved; this was despite the embarrassing revelation that no company member knew their great benefactor's name; G[uildhall] L[ibrary] MS 5445/19, p. 368.

5. CHA Orders of Courts (1665–83), pp. 204–6; GL MS 5445/21, pp. 138, 149; DHA

Minutes and Records (1667–1705), fols. 124v, 245v, 265r, and Wardens Accounts (1700–1701), p. 40.

6. Ian Doolittle, *The Mercers' Company, 1579–1959* (London: Mercers' Company, 1994), p. 16. For similar examples in other companies, see CHA, Orders of Courts (1581–1605), fol. 209v (Roger Hanor's cup to be used at the company's elections), and SkHA Court Book 1 (1551–1617), fols. 79r–80r, Court Book 3 (1617–51), fol. 114r (the cock-shaped cups of William Cockayne to be used at the company's elections).

7. GL MS 15842/1, fols. 223v, 224r. When the company had to liquidate additional pieces in 1643, a note in the wardens' accounts listed the weights and detailed descriptions of items that were sold so that in the future the "arms, markes, letters and words" engraved on them by their donors could be copied onto replacement pieces "for the perpetual memory of the donors," GL MS 15866/1, pp. 431–33. See also Archer, *Haberdashers*, p. 260.

8. The Skinners' master and wardens set an example by paying the company for the five cock cups donated by William Cockayne with the expectation that each successive set of company officers would repay their predecessors for the pieces until the company could afford to reclaim them, which it did three years later; SkHA Court Book 3 (1617–1651), fols. 114r, 125r. When the company needed to raise money to contribute to a City loan in 1643, the records reveal only that the officers were to "survey the plate and to sell such part thereof as they in their discretions shall think may be spared": ibid., fol. 205v. For similar action that year by the Clothworkers' officers, see CHA Orders of Courts (1639–49), fol. 83r.

9. G[oldsmiths'] H[all] A[rchive] Court Minute Books T (1637–39), fols. 29v–30r, 32r–33v; 3 (1660–63), fols. 282v, 287v, 293v; 4 (1663–65), fols. 93r, 94v, 114r, 214v, 230v; 5 (1665–69), fol. 153v.

10. DHA Minutes and Records (1667–1705), fols. 246r-v, 257ar, 264r-v. See also M. A. Greenwood, *The Ancient Plate of the Drapers' Company with Some Account of Its Origin, History, and Vicissitudes* (London: Humphrey Milford, 1930).

11. W. K. Jordan, *The Charities of London, 1480–1660: The Aspirations and Achievements of the Urban Society* (New York: Russell Sage Foundation, 1960); J. E. C. Hill, "Puritans and 'The Dark Corners of the Land,'" *Transactions of the Royal Historical Society*, 5th ser., 13 (1963): 77–102; Paul S. Seaver, *The Puritan Lectureships: The Politics of Religious Dissent, 1560–1662* (Stanford: Stanford University Press, 1970); Archer, *Haberdashers*, pp. 71–88. The standard work on the Puritan interest in education remains Richard L. Greaves, *The Puritan Revolution and Educational Thought: Background for Reform* (New Brunswick, N.J.: Rutgers University Press, 1969). While the later Tudor and Stuart benefactions of provincial charities have been seen as evidence of the Puritan desire for godly reform, there were several important fifteenth-century examples of this process; see Caroline M. Barron, "The Expansion of Education in Fifteenth-Century London," in John Blair and Brian Golding, eds., *The Cloister and the World: Essays in Medieval History in Honour of Barbara Harvey* (Oxford: Clarendon, 1996), pp. 236–37. I would like to thank Dr. Barron for sending me a copy of this important essay.

12. GHA Court Minute Book P part 2 (1617–24), fol. 181v; GL MS 15842/1, fol. 361r.

13. GL MS 11588/5, p. 508.

14. For the purposes of this chapter, "provincial" refers to schools that were in the

seventeenth century at least several hours' ride from the City of London; most were several days away. The schools and companies considered for this study are Aldenham, Hertfordshire (Brewers); Ashwell, Hertfordshire (Merchant Taylors); Barton, Staffordshire (Drapers); Bromyard, Herefordshire (Goldsmiths); Bunbury, Cheshire (Haberdashers); Colwall, Herefordshire (Grocers); Cromer, Norfolk (Goldsmiths); Deane, Cumberland (Goldsmiths); Farthingoe, Northamptonshire (Mercers); Goosnargh, Lancashire (Drapers); Great Crosby, Lancashire (Merchant Taylors); Holt, Norfolk (Fishmongers); Horsham, Sussex (Mercers); Kirkham, Lancashire (Drapers); Macclesfield, Cheshire (Merchant Taylors); Monmouth, Monmouthshire (Haberdashers); Newport, Shropshire (Haberdashers); Oundle, Northamptonshire (Grocers); Stockport, Cheshire (Goldsmiths); Sutton Valence, Kent (Clothworkers); Tonbridge, Kent (Skinners); Topcliffe, Yorkshire (Grocers); Wallingford, Berkshire (Merchant Taylors); West Lavington, Wiltshire (Mercers); Wolverhampton, Staffordshire (Merchant Taylors). This is a provisional list, and it includes only those schools over which a company maintained some supervisory interest beyond merely serving as the disbursing agent for the teachers' stipends.

15. DHA Minutes and Records (1584–94), pp. 695, 710; GL MS 15842/1, fol. 192r. On the appointment of schoolmasters generally, see David Cressy, "A Drudgery of Schoolmasters: The Teaching Profession in Elizabethan and Stuart England," in Wilfred Prest, ed., *The Professions in Early Modern England* (London: Croom Helm, 1987), pp. 129–53, and Michael Van Cleave Alexander, *The Growth of English Education, 1348–1648: A Social and Cultural History* (University Park: Penn State University Press, 1990), pp. 195–97.

16. GHA Court Minute Book X (1645–48), fol. 6v; GL MS 5570/1, pp. 418–19; SkHA Court Minute Book 1 (1551–1617), fols. 146v–47r. Judd was a kinsman of the founder of All Souls; Septimus Rivington, *The History of the Tonbridge School* (London: Rivingtons, 1925), pp. 18–20.

17. GL MS 15842/1, fols. 288r, 292r, 326r; SkHA Court Book 1 (1551–1617), fol. 147v.

18. DHA Minutes and Records (1584–94), p. 695; CHA Orders of Courts (1605–23), fols. 56v, 74v, 263v, (1623–36), fol. 45v, (1639–40), fol. 32r.

19. GL MSS 11588/1, fols. 262r, 272r, 275r, 339r, 350r; 5570/1, pp. 432, 449; 15842/1, fol. 299v, /2, fols. 110v, 165r. I would like to thanks Newton Key for sharing his expertise on Monmouth with me.

20. GHA Court Minute Books Q/1 (1624–29), fol. 85r; Q/2 (1629–30), fols. 132r, 138v, 143v, 145r; R/1 (1630–31), fols. 2r, 3v, 15r; R/2 (1631–34), fols. 174r, 196r-v; S/1 (1634–35), pp. 13–14; X (1645–48), fol. 165r; Y (1648–51), fols. 167r, 236v–38r.

21. DHA Minutes and Records (1667–1705), fols. 134r, 135v.

22. GL MS 15842/2, fols 431r-v; Ward, p. 113.

23. CHA Orders of Courts (1581–1605), fol. 97v; SkHA Court Book 1 (1551–1617), fol. 45v.

24. GL MS 15842/1, fols. 202v, 203r, 204v, 206v, 207r-v.

25. Rosemary O'Day, "The Anatomy of a Profession: The Clergy of the Church of England," in Prest, ed., p. 47; Alexander, pp. 191–96.

26. A. N. Wilson, *A History of Collyer's School* (London: Edward Arnold, 1965), p. 195; DHA K.90/1; Court Minutes (1667–1705), fols. 70r–73r.

27. CHA Orders of Courts (1605–23), fol. 263v, (1639–1649), fols. 22r, 93r; GL MSS 5570/4, p. 929 and 15842/1, fols. 351r, 353v.

28. SkHA Court Books 1 (1551–1617), fols. 45r, 128r; 4 (1651–67), fols. 163v–164r; 5 (1667–87), pp. 111, 329, 347; and 7 (1697–1716), pp. 350–51; GL MSS 5570/4, p. 625 and 15842/2, fol. 51r.

29. GL MS 11588/4, pp. 241–44, 247.

30. P[ublic] R[ecord] O[ffice], P[rerogative] C[ourt] of C[anterbury] PROB 11/8, fol. 98v and /14, fol. 322r. As a Goldsmiths' officer, Reade was well aware of Shaa's endowment. For the requirement that schoolmasters be university graduates, see the will of Richard Collyer (PRO, PCC PROB 11/14, fols. 182v–183v) and the statutes of Tonbridge School in Rivington, pp. 63–70; for this development more generally, see Alexander, p. 195.

31. Rivington, pp. 63–70; Alexander, p. 195; Michael L. Zell, "Economic Problems of the Parochial Clergy in the Sixteenth Century," in Rosemary O'Day and Felicity Heal, eds., *Princes and Paupers in the English Church, 1500–1800* (Totowa, N.J.: Barnes and Noble Books, 1981), pp. 19–43.

32. SkHA Court Book 1 (1551–1617), fol. 137bv; GL MS 11588/4, p. 634.

33. MHA Acts of Court (1595–1629), fol. 3r; GL MSS 15842/2, fols. 52v, 54r, 63v, 107v, 122v, 136r, and /3, pp. 147–48, 380, 415.

34. GL MS 5570/3, pp. 326, 451–52, and /5, pp. 607, 613, 697; Cressy, p. 146. The records are unclear about the final disposition of the advowson.

35. GHA Court Minutes K, part 1 (1557–1566), p. 111; W (1642–1645), fol. 60v; and 6 (1669–1673), fol. 158v.

36. MHA Acts of Court (1595–1629), fols. 354v–55r, 358r; (1625–1631), fols. 237r–38r, 305v, 314v; and (1631–1637), fol. 9v.

37. GL MS 15842/2, fols. 81v, 83r, 84v, 88v, 89v, 98v, 122v.

38. GL MS 15842/3, pp. 148, 152, 158, 161, 183–84, 188–89, 198–99, 223, 229, 245, 284, 296.

39. DHA Court Minutes (1667–1705), fols. 264v, 269v, 271r, 276r; Rc. 15/2–/11; the quotation is at /4.

40. CHA Orders of Courts (1605–23), fol. 233r, (1639–1649), fols. 112r, 149r, (1683–1712), pp. 42–43, 45, 63.

41. GHA Court Minute Book Z (1651–54), fols. 65r, 113v; 2 (1657–60), fol. 154r. The Cromer curriculum was returned to its classical basis in 1670; GHA Court Minute Book 6 (1669–73), fols. 158v–159r.

42. SkHA Court Book 6 (1687–97), p. 156. The low enrollment continued until Roots's death in 1714. See G. P. Hoole, *A Tonbridge Miscellany* (privately printed), pp. 2–32. I would like to thank Mrs J. M. Cook, Tonbridge School Librarian, for bringing Hoole's research to my attention.

43. David Rollinson, *The Local Origins of Modern Society: Gloucestershire, 1500–1800* (London: Routledge, 1992); Peter Borsay, "The London Connection: Cultural Diffusion and the Eighteenth-Century Provincial Town," *London Journal* 19, no. 1 (1994): 21–35; David Underdown, "Regional Cultures? Local Variations in Popular Culture During the Early Modern Period," in Tim Harris, ed., *Popular Culture in England, c. 1500–1850* (New York: St. Martin's Press), pp. 28–47.

GRIGGS: REMEMBERING THE PURITAN PAST

I thank the editors for their many helpful comments on earlier drafts of this essay. I would also like to thank David Underdown for his continued guidance and Paul Seaver for his example.

1. Michael Finlayson, *Historians, Puritanism, and the English Revolution: The Religious Factor in English Politics Before and After the Interregnum* (Toronto: University of Toronto Press, 1983); Jonathan Scott, "England's Troubles, 1603–1702," in Donna B. Hamilton and Richard Strier, eds., *Religion, Literature, and Politics in Post-Reformation England, 1540–1688* (New York: Cambridge University Press, 1996); J. G. A. Pocock, "The Significance of 1688: Some Reflections on Whig History," in Robert Beddard, ed., *The Revolutions of 1688* (Oxford: Clarendon Press, 1991), p. 273; J. C. D. Clark, *The Language of Liberty, 1660–1832* (Cambridge: Cambridge University Press, 1994), pp. 225–40.

2. Tim Harris, Paul Seaward, and Mark Goldie, eds., *The Politics of Religion in Restoration England* (Oxford: Basil Blackwell, 1990).

3. Jonathan Scott, "Restoration Process; or, If This Isn't a Party, We're Not Having a Good Time," *Albion* 25 (1993): 622; Gary de Krey, "Rethinking the Restoration: Dissenting Cases for Conscience, 1667–72," *Historical Journal* 38 (1995): 53–83; Richard Greaves, "Great Scott! The Restoration in Turmoil, or Restoration Crises and the Emergence of Party," *Albion* 25 (1993): 618.

4. De Krey, "Reformation in the Restoration Crisis, 1679–82," in Hamilton and Strier, eds. The most recent book on the Exclusion Crisis is hostile to the term or at least its definite article: Mark Knights, *Politics and Opinion in Crisis, 1678–1681* (Cambridge: Cambridge University Press, 1994).

5. Geoffrey Holmes, *British Politics in the Age of Anne*, 2d ed. (London: Hambledon Press, 1987); J. P. Kenyon, *Revolution Principles* (Cambridge: Cambridge University Press, 1977), p. 17; G. V. Bennett, *The Tory Crisis in Church and State, 1688–1730: The Career of Francis Atterbury, Bishop of Rochester* (Oxford: Clarendon Press, 1975); J. C. D. Clark, *English Society, 1688–1832* (Cambridge: Cambridge University Press, 1985).

6. Because most of the people cited from manuscripts in this article referred to the war in the singular—as "the Great Rebellion," "the time of usurpation"—or in an indeterminate plural, such as "the late times," I have referred to it in the singular.

7. Mark Goldie, "Danby, the Bishops, and the Whigs," in Harris, Seaward, and Goldie, eds., pp. 79, 77; Tim Harris, *London Crowds in the Reign of Charles II: Propaganda and Politics from the Restoration Until the Exclusion Crisis* (Cambridge: Cambridge University Press, 1987), esp. chs. 4–6.

8. Pocock, p. 272; quotation from Kenyon, p. 69. Despite Kenyon's belief in the relevance of the Civil War to later Stuart political argument, he is the principal target of Scott, in Harris, Seaward, and Goldie, eds., p. 108.

9. Clark, *Language of Liberty*, esp. ch. 4.

10. Keith Feiling, *A History of the Tory Party* (Oxford: Clarendon Press, 1924), p. 484.

11. Steven C. A. Pincus has pointed out how analyses of Restoration political conflict become insufficient when they stress religious or denominational motives to the

exclusion of other ideological ones. See Pincus, *Protestantism and Patriotism: Ideologies and the Making of English Foreign Policy, 1650–1668* (Cambridge: Cambridge University Press, 1996).

12. G. R. Cragg, *From Puritanism to the Age of Reason: A Study of Changes in Religious Thought Within the Church of England* (Cambridge: Cambridge University Press, 1966); John Spurr, *The Restoration Church of England* (New Haven: Yale University Press, 1991), pp. 272–73.

13. Mark Goldie, "The Theory of Religious Intolerance in Restoration England," in Ole Peter Grell, Jonathan Israel, and Nicholas Tyacke, eds., *From Persecution to Toleration: The Glorious Revolution and Religion in England* (Oxford: Clarendon Press, 1991).

14. Cragg, p. 182.

15. Justin Champion, *The Pillars of Priestcraft Shaken: The Church of England and Her Enemies, 1660–1730* (Cambridge: Cambridge University Press, 1992), p. 16; Goldie, "The Political Thought of the Anglican Revolution," in Beddard, ed., p. 134.

16. John R. Knott, *Discourses of Martyrdom in English Literature, 1563–1694* (Cambridge: Cambridge University Press, 1993), ch. 7; N. H. Keeble, *The Literary Culture of Nonconformity in Later Seventeenth-Century England* (Avon: Leicester University Press, 1987).

17. Gilbert Burnet, *History of the Reformation* (1679–1714), Edmund Stillingfleet, *Origines Brittanicae* (1685), and Peter Heylyn, *Aerius Redivivus; or, The History of the Presbyterians* (1670), represent their authors' respective ecclesiological principles.

18. David Cressy, *Bonfires and Bells: National Memory and the Protestant Calendar in Elizabethan and Stuart England* (Berkeley: University of California Press, 1989).

19. Henry Care, *The Weekly Pacquet of Advice from Rome; or, The History of Popery* (1678–83); *The Weekly Discovery of the Mystery of Iniquity; In the Rise, Growth, Methods, and Ends of the Late Unnatural Rebellion in England, Anno 1641* (London, 1681).

20. Bodleian Library, MS. Eng. Hist. c. 237 fol. 64.

21. Edmund Calamy, *An Abridgment of Mr Baxter's History of his Life and Times. With an Account of the Ministers &c. who were Ejected after the Restauration of King Charles II,* 2d ed. (London, 1713), vol. 1, p. vi. Because Walker's notes in the MSS. J. Walker correspond to the pagination of the second edition, it has been cited here.

22. Ibid., 2:iv, 2:v.

23. Ibid., 2:227, 2:293, 2:133.

24. Ibid., 2:53–56, 2:87, 2:109, 2:4. Calamy's proud praise for Presbyterians well versed in scholasticism illustrates Hobbes's attack upon both; Hobbes, *Leviathan,* ed. Richard Tuck (Cambridge: Cambridge University Press, 1991) 472, 475–76; Hobbes, *Behemoth,* ed. Ferdinand Tonnies (Chicago: University of Chicago Press, 1990), 21–24.

25. Calamy, 2:iv, 2:148, 2:86; Steven Shapin, *A Social History of Truth: Civility and Science in Seventeenth-Century England* (Chicago: University of Chicago Press, 1994), pp. 74–86.

26. Calamy, 2: 213, 2:214, 2:217.

27. Ibid., 2:17, 2:120, 2:221–22.

28. Ibid., 2:273. Compare her plight with the travails of Mrs. John Fetty, in John

Foxe, *Acts and Monuments* (1563; rev. ed. 1843–49; reprint, New York: AMS Press, 1965), 8:510–11. Mrs. Fetty recovered.

29. Calamy, 1:vi.

30. Paul S. Seaver, *Wallington's World: A Puritan Artisan in Seventeenth-Century London* (Stanford: Stanford University Press, 1985), 155.

31. Bodleian Library, MS. J. Walker, c. 1 fol. 392.

32. Spurr, "'Virtue, Religion, and Government': The Anglican Uses of Providence," in Harris, Seaward, and Goldie, eds., p. 33.

33. Goldie, "Theory of Religious Intolerance," in Grell, Israel, and Tyacke, eds., pp. 343–45.

34. Thomas Long, *A Review of Mr. Baxter's Life* (London, 1697); *A Rebuke to Mr. Edmund Calamy* (London, 1704), p. 31.

35. MSS. J. Walker, e. 11 fol. 3; c. 1 fol. 8.

36. *London Gazette*, Mar. 13–16, 1703; MSS. J. Walker, c. 1 fols. 21, 6.

37. MSS. J. Walker, c. 2 fol. 52; c. 1 fols. 335, 359; c. 6 fol. 2. For a full account of the genesis of Walker's work, see G. B. Tatham, *Dr. John Walker and the Sufferings of the Clergy* (Cambridge: Cambridge University Press, 1911), pp. 1–37. Bruno Ryves, *Mercurius Rusticus* (London, 1647); George Bate, *Elenchus Motuum Nuperorum in Anglia* (London, 1650); *Persecutio Undecima* (London, 1648); and *Querela Cantabrigiensis* (London, 1648) are representative of royalist pamphlets in Goodall's collection.

38. MSS. J. Walker, c. 10 fol. 26; c. 2 fol. 393.

39. MS. J. Walker, c. 2 fols. 393v, 394.   40. Shapin, pp. 225–26.

41. MS. J. Walker, c. 1 fol. 95.   42. MS. J. Walker, c. 2 fol. 129.

43. MSS. J. Walker, c. 1 fols. 76–77; c. 2 fol. 452.

44. MSS. J. Walker, c. 2 fol. 150; c. 3 fols. 125–26.

45. MS. J. Walker, c. 1 fol. 9.

46. Tatham, 27.

47. *Dictionary of National Biography*, Newte; MSS. J. Walker, c. 2 fols. 445, 447; c. 3 fols. 195, 238; c 4. fols. 82, 108; c. 5 fol. 177.

48. MS. J. Walker, c. 2 fol. 394.

49. MS. J. Walker, c. 1 fol. 400.

50. Goldie, "Theory of Religious Intolerance," in Grell, Israel, and Tyacke, eds., pp. 332–34.

51. MS. J. Walker, c. 1 fols. 356–357v.

52. Walter Raleigh, *Reliquiae Raleighanae, being discourses and sermons on several subjects*, ed. Simon Patrick (London, 1679).

53. MS. J. Walker, c. 1 fol. 94.

54. MS. J. Walker, c. 1 fols. 1–1v. This letter is not calendared in Tatham.

55. MS. J. Walker, c. 3 fols. 321–321v.

56. John Walker, *An Attempt Towards Recovering an Account of the Numbers and Sufferings of the Clergy of the Church of England, Heads of Colleges, Fellows, Scholars, &c. who were Sequester'd. Harass'd, &c. in the late Times of the Grand Rebellion: Occasion'd by the Ninth Chapter (now the second volume) of Dr. Calamy's abridgment of the Life of Mr. Baxter* (London, 1714), 2:71; Patrick's preface in Raleigh, pp. iv–vii; MS. J. Walker, e. 6 fols. 103v–104.

57. A. G. Matthews, *Walker Revised, Being a Revision of John Walker's Sufferings of the Clergy During the Grand Rebellion, 1642–60* (Oxford: Clarendon Press, 1948, reissued 1988), p. 318. (Hereafter *WR*.) Matthews states that Raleigh died six weeks after the stabbing.

58. Walker, 2:71–72; While Patrick cites *Mercurius Rusticus*, it contains no account of Raleigh's murder.

59. MS. J. Walker c. 4 fol. 27; Walker, 2:238.

60. Goldie, "Theory of Religious Intolerance," in Grell, Israel, and Tyacke, eds., p. 337.

61. MS. J. Walker, c. 3 fol. 182.

62. *WR*, 189.

63. MS. J. Walker, c. 1 fols. 42–43v. Although Cooper held the benefice of Little Barningham, Walker included him in his *Attempt* as rector of Edgefield. *WR*, 266. See MSS. J. Walker, c. 2 fols. 286, 311–12 for other cases of Dissenters bringing false evidence. Joe Ward kindly kept me from mistaking Cooper for Francis Wright, the schoolmaster at Holt at the time of Cooper's execution.

64. Walker, 2:223.

65. MS. J. Walker, c. 2 fols. 133–34.

66. MS. J. Walker, c. 1 fols. 44–45v.

67. "I thank God, whom I serve from my forefathers with pure conscience, that without ceasing I have remembrance of thee in my prayers night and day."

68. MS. J. Walker, c. 2 fol. 206.

69. Calamy, 2:133.

70. MS. J. Walker, c. 2 fols. 384–86.

71. MSS. J. Walker, c. 2 fol. 213v; e. 6 fol. 90v.

72. MS. J. Walker, c. 3 fols. 119–20; *WR*, p. 179.

73. MS. J. Walker, c. 1 fols. 309–309v.   74. MS. J. Walker, c. 1 fol. 123.

75. MS. J. Walker, c. 2 fols. 131–32.   76. MS. J. Walker, c. 1 fols. 220–21.

77. MS. J. Walker, c. 2 fols. 393–94.

78. MS. J. Walker, c. 2 fols. 352, 384–86.

79. MS. J. Walker, c. 2 fols. 246–47.

80. *WR*, 195; MS. J. Walker, c. 1 fol. 326.

81. MS. J. Walker, c. 3 fol. 171; *WR*, p. 289.

82. MS. J. Walker, c. 3 fols. 304–5. Like the rest of the correspondents who related such stories, John Brayne, Sharpe's grandson, resisted making explicit analogies with Foxe. The soldiers only threaten a bonfire, and they do not abuse the fetus. Compare Foxe, 8:251–53.

83. MS. J. Walker, c. 3 fol. 11.

84. MS. J. Walker, c. 1 fol. 283; *WR*, 177.

85. MS. J. Walker, c. 1. fols. 218–19. For other examples of pregnant women, see MSS. J. Walker, c. 1 fols. 175–76, 184–184v, 229, 397–98; c. 3 fol. 56; c. 4 fol. 25.

86. MS. J. Walker, c. 2 fols. 337, 340–41.

87. The stories that seem too similar to the clichés of contemporary atrocity literature to receive much credence are conspicuously few. Richard Clark remembered how a soldier tried to roast him and his brother in a drippings-pan, and how soldiers at Sturminster Castle in Dorset tortured his father, burning his fingers and binding him

so tightly that his eyes bled. Clark's example encouraged his son to enter the ministry. MS. J. Walker, c. 1 fol. 194.

88. MS. J. Walker, c. 3 fols. 64–65.

89. MS. J. Walker, c. 1 fols. 37–37v.

90. MS. J. Walker, c. 2 fol. 200.

91. I owe the term "pathology of error" to Frank M. Turner.

92. MS J. Walker, c. 1 fol. 207; *WR*, p. 174; MS. J. Walker, c. 1 fol. 112.

93. MS. J. Walker, c. 3 fols. 368–69.   94. MS. J. Walker, c. 1 fol. 149.

95. MS. J. Walker, c. 1 fol. 263.   96. MS. J. Walker, c. 1 fol. 31.

97. MS. J. Walker, c. 1 fol. 249.

98. Calamy, *Abridgment of Mr Baxter's History*, 2:17, 2:120, 2:221–22.

99. MS. J. Walker, c. 2 fols. 422v–423.   100. MS. J. Walker, c. 2 fol. 208.

101. MS. J. Walker, e. 5 fol. 218.   102. MS. J. Walker, c. 8 fols. 50–51.

103. MS. J. Walker, e. 6 fol. 73.   104. Shapin, pp. 91–93.

105. Ibid., p. 96.

106. Walker noted that Devon was fit to be a standard for the country as a whole, since the greatest number of Calamy's ministers were from that county, "and yet farthest from London, the seat of their roguery." MS. J. Walker, e. 6 fol. 48v. Walker also printed a separate list of queries for Devon clergy, MS. J. Walker, e. 8 fol. 7v.

107. MS. J. Walker, c. 2 fols. 443–443v.

108. MS. J. Walker, c. 8 fols. 25–28v.

109. MS. J. Walker, c. 2 fol. 278.

110. Quentin Skinner, *Reason and Rhetoric in the Philosophy of Hobbes* (Cambridge: Cambridge University Press, 1996), pp. 434–35.

111. MS. J. Walker, c. 3 fol. 156.

112. MS. J. Walker, c. 4 fol. 143.

113. MS. J. Walker, c. 3 fol. 117.

114. MS. J. Walker, c. 1 fol. 163; *WR*, p. 216.

115. MS. J. Walker, c. 1 fol. 250.

116. MS. J. Walker, c. 1 fol. 255; *WR*, p. 278.

117. MS. J. Walker, c. 3 fol. 220.

118. MSS. J. Walker, c. 4 fols. 108–9, 54–55; *WR*, p. 287.

119. MS. J. Walker, c. 1 fols. 211–12.

120. MS. J. Walker, c. 1 fols. 39–39v.

121. MS. J. Walker, c. 1 fols. 51–53v; Thomas Babington Macaulay, *The History of England, from the Accession of James II* (London, 1849–65), 3:54.

122. MSS. J. Walker, e. 6 fol. 2; e. 5, front cover.

123. MS. J. Walker, c. 1 fol. 181.

124. MS. J. Walker, e. 6 fols. 211–211v.

125. MS. J. Walker, e. 6 fols. 32–33. Walker would most likely not have been surprised to find that Ludlow was an apocalyptic Puritan. Blair Worden, introduction to *A Voyce from the Watch Tower* by Edmund Ludlow (London: Royal Historical Society, 1978).

126. Walker, 1:xi.   127. MS. J. Walker, e. 6 fol. 212.

128. MS. J. Walker, c. 6.   129. MS. J. Walker, e. 6 fol. 63.

130. MS. J. Walker, e. 6 fol. 11.   131. Shapin, ch. 5.

132. Benjamin Hoadly, *The Reasonableness of Conformity to the Church of England* (London, 1703); John Ollyffe, *A Defence of Ministerial Conformity to the Church of England* (London, 1702), 2, 14.

133. Champion, ch. 1.

134. MS. J. Walker, e. 5 fols. 7–225.

135. MS. J. Walker, e. 6 fols. 225–225v.

136. MS. J. Walker, e. 5 fol. 82v.

137. MS. J. Walker, e. 6 fols. 235–235v.

138. MS. J. Walker, e. 6 fol. 65v.

139. MS. J. Walker, e. 6 fol. 173.

140. MS. J. Walker, c. 2 fols. 211–15, 441, 200.

141. MS. J. Walker, e. 6 fol. 70.

142. MS. J. Walker, e. 6 fols. 84, 19–23v.

143. Champion; Shapin, chs. 1, 2, 5.

144. I. M. Green, "The Persecution of 'Scandalous' and 'Malignant' Parish Clergy During the English Civil War," *English Historical Review* 194 (1979): 507. Green argued that many of the sequestrators divorced their charges of malignancy from doctrinal conflict; 60 years after the sequestrations, Walker did not (520).

145. MS. J. Walker, c. 7 fol. 119; *Examiner*, Feb. 23–27, 1715.

146. Walker, 1:xvi.

147. Feiling, 493.

MCCLENDON: RECONSIDERING THE
MARIAN PERSECUTION

1. G. R. Elton, "Persecution and Toleration in the English Reformation," in W. J. Sheils, ed., *Persecution and Toleration* (Oxford: Basil Blackwell, 1984), p. 163.

2. Ole Peter Grell and Bob Scribner, eds., *Tolerance and Intolerance in the European Reformation* (Cambridge: Cambridge University Press, 1996).

3. Bob Scribner, "Preconditions of Tolerance and Intolerance in Sixteenth-Century Germany," in Grell and Scribner, eds., *Tolerance and Intolerance*, pp. 32–47, esp. pp. 34–38. See also "Civic Unity and the Reformation in Erfurt," in Bob Scribner, *Popular Culture and Popular Movements in Reformation Germany* (London and Ronceverte, W.Va.: Hambledon Press, 1987), pp. 185–216, where Scribner found that in 1530 local magistrates sanctioned a treaty of state that permitted both Catholic and Protestant worship in the city.

4. Lorna Jane Abray, "Confession, Conscience, and Honour: The Limits of Magisterial in Sixteenth-Century Strassburg," in Grell and Scribner, eds., *Tolerance and Intolerance*, pp. 94–107; Lorna Jane Abray, *The People's Reformation: Magistrates, Clergy, and Commons in Strasbourg, 1500–1598* (Ithaca: Cornell University Press, 1985), pp. 85–87, 104–41.

5. Muriel C. McClendon, "Religious Toleration and the Reformation: Norwich Magistrates in the Sixteenth Century," in Nicholas Tyacke, ed., *England's Long Reformation, 1500–1800* (London: University College London Press, 1998), pp. 87–116; McClendon, *The Quiet Reformation: Magistrates and the Emergence of Protestantism in Tudor Norwich* (Stanford: Stanford University Press, 1999).

6. Scribner, "Preconditions," pp. 43–44.

7. Protestantism was chiefly an urban phenomenon at this time, although the city

of York was a notable exception. A. G. Dickens, "The Early Expansion of Protestantism in England, 1520–1558," *Archiv für Reformationgeschichte* 78 (1987): 197; Christopher Haigh, *English Reformations: Religion, Politics, and Society Under the Tudors* (Oxford: Oxford University Press, 1993), p. 197.

8. Haigh, *English Reformations*, p. 232.

9. "Queen Mary's First Proclamation About Religion, A.D. 1553," in Henry Gee and William John Hardy, comps., *Documents Illustrative of English Church History* (London: Macmillan, 1921), pp. 373–76.

10. Gee and Hardy, comps., *Documents*, p. 382.

11. 1&2 P&M c. 8. Gee and Hardy, comps., *Documents*, pp. 385–415.

12. 1&2 P&M c. 6. Gee and Hardy, comps., *Documents*, p. 384. For a more extensive treatment of the restoration of Catholicism, see, e.g., David M. Loades, *The Reign of Mary Tudor: Politics, Government, and Religion in England, 1553–58*, 2d ed. (London: Longman, 1991), chs. 3 and 8.

13. Haigh, *English Reformations*, pp. 230–31; Susan Brigden, *London and the Reformation* (Oxford: Clarendon Press, 1989), pp. 606–14.

14. In Norwich diocese, Bishop William Alnwick's investigations uncovered about 60 Lollards in 1428–29. Three were burnt in 1428, and the rest were permitted to abjure and do penance. This was sufficient, apparently, to cripple heresy in the diocese until the early sixteenth century. In Kent in 1511, the archbishop of Canterbury, William Warham, presided over the burning of 5 Lollards and the recantations of about 30 more, which also seems to have curtailed heresy there for over a decade. Haigh, *English Reformations*, p. 53.

15. Loades, *Reign of Mary Tudor*, p. 272; Haigh, *English Reformations*, p. 230.

16. Haigh, *English Reformations*, p. 231; Brigden, *London and the Reformation*, pp. 607–13.

17. On Bilney's life and views, see J. A. Guy, *The Public Career of Sir Thomas More* (London: Harvester Press, 1980), pp. 167–71; John F. Davis, "The Trials of Thomas Bylney and the English Reformation," *Historical Journal* 24 (1981): 775–90; Richard Marius, *Thomas More: A Biography* (New York: Knopf, 1984), p. 346; Haigh, *English Reformations*, pp. 67–68.

18. McClendon, *The Quiet Reformation*, ch. 2; Leslie P. Fairfield, *John Bale: Mythmaker for the English Reformation* (West Lafayette, Ind.: Purdue University Press, 1976), pp. 39–40; Ralph Houlbrooke, "Refoundation and Reformation, 1538–1628," in Ian Atherton, Eric Fernie, Christopher Harper-Bill, and Hassell Smith, eds., *Norwich Cathedral: Church, City, and Diocese, 1096–1996* (London: Hambledon Press, 1996), pp. 510–12.

19. McClendon, *The Quiet Reformation*, ch. 2.

20. Ibid., ch. 4.

21. See ibid., ch. 5, on the cases of John Hallybred, Robert Watson, Robert Gold, and William Mason.

22. Rev. Josiah Pratt, ed., *The Acts and Monuments of John Foxe*, vol. 8 (London: Religious Tract Society, n.d.), pp. 380–81.

23. Dunning was actually the cochancellor of the diocese, sharing the post with Miles Spenser, who had been appointed by Richard Nix in 1531. Spenser was the sole

occupant of that post under Nix and his successor, William Rugge, and appears to have held it jointly after Rugge's 1550 resignation.

24. Pratt, ed., *Acts and Monuments*, vol. 8, pp. 427–29.

25. Wolman's recantation can be found among Foxe's papers: British Library Harleian 421, fol. 154. On Richard Crashfield and Thomas Carman, see Pratt, ed. *Acts and Monuments*, vol. 8, pp. 398–400, 462–66, 781. For Wolman's will (Norwich Consistory Court 160 Colman), see M. A. Farrow, ed., *Index of Wills Proved in the Consistory Court of Norwich . . . 1550–1603*, Norfolk Record Society 21 (1950), p. 185.

26. Pratt, ed., *Acts and Monuments*, vol. 8, p. 381.

27. Philip Hughes, *The Reformation in England* (London: Hollis and Carter 1953), vol. 2, p. 274. According to Hughes, Foxe identified 273 Marian martyrs. Of those narratives, 102 described the apprehension of the victims. Sixty (58.82%) were captured by lay justices and constables, while thirteen (12.74%) were turned over by friends or family. Twelve (11.76%) had already been in prison before the revival of the heresy laws, eight (7.84%) were seized through their own public actions, and seven (6.86%) detentions were a result of clerical initiative. One (.98%) person had been turned in by someone hoping for a reward, and another's (.98%) arrest had been directly ordered by the Privy Council.

28. Loades, *Reign of Mary Tudor*, pp. 274–75.

29. Ralph Houlbrooke, *Church Courts and the People During the English Reformation, 1520–1570* (Oxford: Oxford University Press, 1979), p. 237.

30. Houlbrooke, *Church Courts*, pp. 232–37.

31. On the general problems of interpreting wills, see: Eamon Duffy, *The Stripping of the Altars: Traditional Religion in England, c. 1400–c. 1580* (New Haven: Yale University Press, 1992), ch. 15; Michael Zell, "The Use of Religious Preambles as a Measure of Religious Belief in the Sixteenth Century," *Bulletin of the Institute of Historical Research* 50 (1977): 241–53, and J. D. Alsop, "Religious Preambles in Early Modern English Wills as Formulae," *Journal of Ecclesiastical History* 40 (1989): 19–27. For a discussion of religious divisions among the magistrates before Mary's reign, see McClendon, *The Quiet Reformation*, chs. 2 and 4.

32. For a fuller discussion and analysis of these wills, see McClendon, *The Quiet Reformation*, ch. 5 and app. 4. On Barret see Houlbrooke, "Refoundation and Reformation," pp. 521–22.

33. The only person from Norwich known certainly to have gone into exile was the lay Protestant preacher Robert Watson. On Watson see *Dictionary of National Biography*; McClendon, *The Quiet Reformation*, chs. 4, 5; Christina Hallowell Garrett, *The Marian Exiles: A Study in the Origins of Elizabethan Puritanism* (Cambridge: Cambridge University Press, 1938), pp. 322–23.

34. Martha C. Skeeters, *Community and Clergy: Bristol and the Reformation, c. 1530–c. 1570* (Oxford: Oxford University Press, 1993), pp. 132–33.

35. Brigden, *London and the Reformation*, pp. 602–3, 606, 624. A few of London's martyrs were put to death elsewhere; see table 6, pp. 608–12.

36. Pound's figures suggest that Norwich's population dipped from about 8,500 in 1525 to about 8,000 in 1570. London's population, on the other hand, climbed from about 50,000 in 1500 to about 70,000 in 1550. John Pound, *Tudor and Stuart Norwich*

(Chicester, Eng.: Phillimore, 1988), pp. 28, 125; Steve Rappaport, *Worlds Within Worlds: Structures of Life in Sixteenth-Century London* (Cambridge: Cambridge University Press, 1989), p. 61 n. 1.

37. See Joseph P. Ward, *Metropolitan Communities: Trade Guilds, Identity, and Change in Early Modern London* (Stanford: Stanford University Press, 1997).

38. A. G. Dickens, *The English Reformation*, 2d ed. (London: Batsford, 1989), p. 293.

39. Brigden, *London and the Reformation*, pp. 613–14.

40. Ibid., pp. 321, 626.

41. Ibid., p. 626.

42. Ibid., pp. 626–27.

43. Ibid., p. 627.

44. Ibid., p. 628.

GREAVES: THE "GREAT PERSECUTION" RECONSIDERED

1. Gerald R. Cragg, *Puritanism in the Period of the Great Persecution, 1660–1688* (Cambridge: Cambridge University Press, 1957); Geoffrey Holmes, *The Making of a Great Power: Late Stuart and Early Georgian Britain, 1660–1722* (New York: Longman, 1993), pp. 12–13, 351; B. R. White, "The Twilight of Puritanism in the Years Before and After 1688," in Ole Peter Grell, Jonathan I. Israel, and Nicholas Tyacke, eds., *From Persecution to Toleration: The Glorious Revolution and Religion in England* (Oxford: Clarendon Press, 1991), pp. 307–15. All of the above focus on England. For the view from the top, see Tyacke, "The 'Rise of Puritanism' and the Legalizing of Dissent, 1571–1719," in *From Persecution to Toleration*, pp. 32–39.

2. See, e.g., Ole Peter Grell and Bob Scribner, eds., *Tolerance and Intolerance in the European Reformation* (Cambridge: Cambridge University Press, 1996).

3. Scribner, "Preconditions of Tolerance and Intolerance in Sixteenth-Century Germany," ibid., p. 39.

4. James Nayler, *The Lambes Warre Against the Man of Sinne* (London, 1658), pp. 1–4, 14–15; Edward Burrough, *A Discovery of Some Part of the War Between the Kingdom of the Lamb, and the Kingdom of Anti-Christ* (London, 1659).

5. Library of the Society of Friends, London (henceforth LF), Swarthmore MSS 5/20 (Perrot); Swarthmore MSS, vol. 6, fol. 67r (Penn); Nayler, *Milk for Babes: and Meat for Strong Men* (London, 1661), p. 10.

6. Richard L. Greaves, *John Bunyan and English Nonconformity* (London: Hambledon Press, 1992), pp. 13–14, 177–83.

7. Isaac Penington, *Concerning Persecution* (London, 1661), pp. 14–15; William Penn, *No Cross, No Crown* (n.p., 1669), pp. 38–39.

8. John Audland, *The Suffering Condition of the Servants of the Lord at This Day Vindicated* (London, 1662), p. 19; LF, Swarthmore MSS 5/54 (Howgill and Burrough).

9. E[dward] B[urrough], *A General Epistle to All the Saints, Being a Visitation of the Fathers Love* (London, 1660), p. 11.

10. Sharon Achinstein, "*Samson Agonistes* and the Drama of Dissent," *Milton Studies* 33 (1996): 149.

11. Barry Reay, *The Quakers and the English Revolution* (London: Temple Smith, 1985), pp. 81–100 (esp. 98).

12. Thomas Wight, *A History of the Rise and Progress of the People Called Quakers, in Ireland, from the Year 1653 to 1700*, ed. John Rutty, 4th ed. (London: William Phillips, 1811), p. 77. Quaker activity in Ireland was part of a sustained campaign that took the Friends throughout Europe, to the Americas, and to the Ottoman Empire.

13. Ibid., pp. 73–77, 78 (quoted), 81–82, 84–86, 104–5, 126–28, 131–32; Kenneth L. Carroll, "Quakerism in the Cromwellian Army in Ireland," *Journal of the Friends' Historical Society* (henceforth *JFHS*) 54 (1978): 147; William C. Braithwaite, *The Beginnings of Quakerism*, 2d ed., rev. Henry J. Cadbury (York: William Sessions, 1981), p. 214.

14. Wight, *History*, pp. 77, 80, 82.

15. British Library (henceforth BL), Lansdowne MSS 821, fol. 68r.

16. LF, Swarthmore MSS 6/30; 5/55 (quoted).

17. LF, Swarthmore MSS 5/2; cf. 6/4.

18. Carroll, "Quakerism in the Cromwellian Army," pp. 142–47; John Thurloe, *A Collection of the State Papers of John Thurloe, Esq.*, ed. Thomas Birch, 7 vols. (London, 1742), vol. 4, p. 508; BL, Lansdowne MSS 822, fol. 17r.

19. LF, Swarthmore MSS 5/8 (Howgill and Burrough); 5/7 (Burrough).

20. Samuel Fuller and Thomas Holme, *A Compendious View of Some Extraordinary Sufferings of the People Call'd Quakers* (Dublin, 1731), p. 123.

21. For Quaker reaction to the Restoration in England, see Greaves, "Shattered Expectations? George Fox, the Quakers, and the Restoration State, 1660–1685," *Albion* 24 (1992): 237–40.

22. S. J. Connolly, *Religion, Law, and Power: The Making of Protestant Ireland, 1660–1700* (Oxford: Clarendon Press, 1992), pp. 5–6, 8–10; J. I. McGuire, "The Dublin Convention, the Protestant Community, and the Emergence of an Ecclesiastical Settlement in 1660," in *Parliament and Community*, ed. Art Cosgrove and J. I. McGuire, *Historical Studies* (Dublin: Appletree Press, 1981), vol. 14, pp. 127–29; Carroll, "Quakerism in Connaught, 1656–1978," *JFHS* 54 (1979): 188; S. Fuller and Holme, *Compendious View*, p. 126.

23. William Edmundson, *A Journal of the Life, Travels, Sufferings, and Labour of Love*, 2d ed. (London, 1774), p. 45.

24. LF, Swarthmore MSS 4/238.

25. [Edward Burrough], *A Visitation and Presentation of Love unto the King, and Those Call'd Royallists* (London, 1660), pp. 6, 13, 24–25. Cf. Richard Crane, *A Fore-Warning, and a Word of Expostulation* (London, 1660), p. 5; Margaret Fell, *A Declaration and an Information from Us the People of God Called Quakers* (London, 1660), p. 6; George Fox the Younger, *A Noble Salutation and a Faithful Greeting to Thee Charles Stuart* (London, 1660), p. 8.

26. [Burrough], *Visitation*, pp. 7, 10–11, 22–23. The Quakers, he told the magistrates of Ireland, "are not of a principle of Rebellion, but of a principall of patient suffering." LF, Swarthmore MSS 5/5.

27. LF, Swarthmore MSS 5/39. For Perrot in Ireland, see BL, Lansdowne MSS 821, fol. 127r-v; LF, Swarthmore MSS 5/14, 5/19, 5/22. While he was imprisoned in Rome Perrot touched off a schism among Friends by attacking all formalism in public worship, including the removal of hats during prayer. See Carroll, *John Perrot: Early*

Quaker Schismatic, JFHS, Supplement no. 33 (London, 1971); Stefano Villani, *Tremolanti e Papisti: Missioni Quacchere nell'Italia del Seicento* (Roma: Edizioni di Storia e Letteratura, 1996), pp. 69–77.

28. The argument briefly sketched for background purposes in this section is developed at length in Richard L. Greaves, *God's Other Children: Protestant Nonconformists and the Emergence of Denominational Churches in Ireland, 1660–1700* (Stanford: Stanford University Press, 1997), chs. 1–3.

29. Jeremy Taylor, *A Sermon Preached at the Opening of the Parliament of Ireland, May 8, 1661* (London, 1661), sigs. A4v–a1r.

30. John Bramhall, *A Fair Warning* [1661], pp. 1, 34; Bramhall, *A Sermon Preached at Dublin, upon the 23. of Aprill, 1661* (Dublin, 1661), p. 35.

31. Bodl., Carte MSS 45, fol. 113v; Huntington Library, MS HA 15,556 (quoted).

32. Bodl., Carte MSS 49, fol. 20r-v.

33. Samuel Cox, *Two Sermons Preached at Christ-Church in the City of Dublin, Before the Honourable Convention of Ireland* (Dublin, 1660), p. 21; PRO, SP 63/306/20. Cf. Orrery to Clarendon, Jan. 23, 1661, Bodl., Clarendon MSS 74, fol. 98r-v.

34. Bodl., Carte MSS 49, fol. 92r.

35. Maurice Ashley, *John Wildman, Plotter and Postmaster: A Study of the English Republican Movement in the Seventeenth Century* (New Haven: Yale University Press, 1947), p. 192. For security precautions see Bodl., Carte MSS 32, fol. 538r; Carte MSS 33, fols. 216r, 303r.

36. Bodl., Carte MSS 33, fols. 225r (Thompson), 148r (George Clapham). Cf. ibid., fols. 146r and 269r for more of Thompson's remarks.

37. Bodl., Carte MSS 33, fol. 332r.

38. *A Collection of the State Letters of the Right Honourable Roger Boyle, the First Earl of Orrery*, ed. Thomas Morrice, 2 vols. (Dublin, 1743), 2, pp. 132–33; Huntington Library, MSS HA 14,448, HA 14,452; Bodl., Rawlinson MSS, A255, fol. 244; *CSP, Ireland, 1669–70*, p. 22.

39. Bodl., Rawlinson MSS, A255, fol. 292; Bodl., Carte MSS 37, fol. 707v; BL, Stowe MSS 213, fols. 11v–12r, 57v; ibid., 200, fol. 287r.

40. BL, Add. MSS 32,095, fols. 32r–33v; *HMC, Reports*, 36, *Ormonde*, new ser., 4, p. 85; PRO, SP 63/342/25, 35, 44; Bodl., Carte MSS 45, fol. 531r-v (quoted).

41. Bodl., Carte MSS 168, fols. 146–47, 151, 155, 159; ibid., 219, fols. 488r-v, 490r, 506r; Nottingham University Library, MSS PwV95, fol. 306; Historical Library of the Society of Friends in Ireland (henceforth DF), Sufferings, Dublin Monthly Meeting, 1660–1780, fols. 24r–25r; *HMC, Reports*, 36, *Ormonde*, new ser., 7, p. 124; *Collections of the Massachusetts Historical Society*, 8, pp. 62–64.

42. For the contemporary debate over the possible Catholic threat, see Connolly, *Religion, Law, and Power*, pp. 27–32.

43. E[dward] B[urrough], *To the Beloved and Chosen of God in the Seed Elected* (London, 1660), p. 8.

44. Joseph Besse, *A Collection of the Sufferings of the People Called Quakers*, 2 vols. (London, 1753), vol. 1, pp. 491–518; John Miller, *Popery and Politics in England, 1660–1688* (Cambridge: Cambridge University Press, 1973), p. 267.

45. Greaves, *God's Other Children*, p. 360.

46. Michael Watts, *The Dissenters: From the Reformation to the French Revolution* (Oxford: Clarendon Press, 1978), pp. 270, 507, 509; Greaves, *God's Other Children*, p. 270.

47. Thomas Jenner, *Quakerism Anatomiz'd and Confuted* (n.p., 1670), pp. 172–73.

48. *A Short Relation of Some Part of the Sad Sufferings, and Cruel Havock and Spoil, Inflicted on the Persons and Estates of the People of God, in Scorn Called Quakers* (n.p., 1670), p. 74; *Letters, &c., of Early Friends; Illustrative of the History of the Society*, ed. A. R. Barclay (London: Harvey and Darton, 1841), pp. 346–53.

49. John Whiting, *Persecution Expos'd, in Some Memoirs Relating to the Sufferings of John Whiting* (London, 1715), pp. 33–34.

50. Miller, *Popery and Politics*, p. 267.

51. Greaves, *Deliver Us from Evil: The Radical Underground in Britain, 1660–1663* (New York: Oxford University Press, 1986), pp. 57–59.

52. Cf. Whiting, *Persecution Expos'd*, pp. 123–27.

53. PRO, SP 29/32/69.

54. LF, Swarthmore MSS 4/78.

55. Besse, *Collection*, vol. 2, p. 471; Thomas Holme and Abraham Fuller, *A Brief Relation of Some Part of the Sufferings of the True Christians, the People of God (in Scorn Called Quakers) in Ireland* (n.p., 1672), pp. 9–16, 18, 23.

56. S. Fuller and Holme, *Compendious View*, p. 126.

57. PRO, SP 29/67/155, 155.1.

58. S. Fuller and Holme, *Compendious View*, p. 126.

59. Whiting, *Persecution Expos'd*, pp. 33–34; S. Fuller and Holme, *Compendious View*, p. 126.

60. Craig W. Horle, *The Quakers and the English Legal System, 1660–1688* (Philadelphia: University of Pennsylvania Press, 1988), p. 284; S. Fuller and Holme, *Compendious View*, pp. 126, 130.

61. Besse, *Collection*, vol. 2, p. 472; LF, Great Book of Sufferings, vol. 2, Leinster Province, co. Kildare, 1670; ibid., Leinster Province, King's Co., 1662.

62. S. Fuller and Holme, *Compendious View*, p. 135.

63. Greaves, *God's Other Children*, pp. 360–61.

64. National Archives, Dublin, MSS T6899; D18500; D18501; Audrey Lockhart, "The Quakers and Emigration from Ireland to the North American Colonies," *Quaker History* 77 (Fall 1988): 76. Although I have found no figures for Clarridge's wealth, he was rich enough to make substantial loans, such as those owed by a merchant (£700) and a gentleman (£300) in 1677. Dublin City Archives, Registers of Statute Staple, 1664–1678, fols. 181v, 182v.

65. DF, Sufferings, Leinster Quarterly Meeting, 1656–1701, fols. 14–15, 27; DF, Sufferings, Dublin Monthly Meeting, fols. 3v–31r passim.

66. DF, Testimonies Against Tithes, fols. 119 (quoted), 125.

67. DF, Sharp MSS, S2, fol. 6; S3, fol. 90 (marked 22).

68. LF, Great Book of Sufferings, vol. 2, Ulster Province, co. Armagh, 1665; ibid., vol. 2, Munster Province, Limerick, 1663; ibid., vol. 2, Ulster Province, co. Armagh, 1666.

69. DF, Sharp MSS, S5, fol. 74v; DF, Minutes of the Dublin Men's Meeting (henceforth DMM), 2, fols. 17–20, 189, 243–44; 3, fol. 7.

70. LF, Great Book of Sufferings, vol. 2, Leinster Province, co. Wexford, 1662;

ibid., vol. 2, Ulster Province, co. Armagh, 1670; Holme and A. Fuller, *Brief Relation*, pp. 32–33.

71. LF, Great Book of Sufferings, vol. 2, Ulster Province, co. Cavan, 1660; ibid., vol. 2, Leinster Province, co. Kildare, c. 1670.

72. Ibid., vol. 2, Ulster Province, co. Armagh, 1670; ibid., vol. 2, Munster Province, Cork, 1670.

73. Ibid., vol. 2, Leinster Province, Queen's Co., 1669; ibid., vol. 2, Ulster Province, co. Antrim, 1663.

74. Lockhart, "Quakers and Emigration," p. 75; Richard T. Vann, "Quakerism: Made in America?" in Richard S. Dunn and Mary Maples Dunn, eds., *The World of William Penn* (Philadelphia: University of Pennsylvania Press, 1986), p. 163.

75. *The Papers of William Penn*, vol. 2, ed. Mary Maples Dunn and Richard S. Dunn (Philadelphia: University of Pennsylvania Press, 1982), pp. 630–64.

76. Albert Cook Myers, ed., *Quaker Arrivals at Philadelphia, 1682–1750* (Philadelphia: Ferris and Leach, 1902).

77. Sharon V. Salinger, *"To Serve Well and Faithfully": Labor and Indentured Servants in Pennsylvania, 1682–1800* (Cambridge: Cambridge University Press, 1987), p. 118.

78. Lockhart, "Quakers and Emigration," p. 77.

79. Kerby A. Miller, *Emigrants and Exiles: Ireland and the Irish Exodus to North America* (New York: Oxford University Press, 1985), pp. 151–52.

80. Richard S. Harrison, *Cork City Quakers: A Brief History, 1655–1939* (n.p.: by the author, 1991), p. 4; DF, Minutes of the Leinster Provincial Meeting (henceforth LPM), fols. 26, 34, 90; Public Record Office of Northern Ireland (henceforth PRONI), MSS LGM 1/1 (Minutes of the Lurgan Men's Meeting), fol. 49; John Banks, *A Journal of the Life, Labours, Travels, and Sufferings* (London, 1712), p. 135.

81. DF, Minutes of the Half-Yearly National Meeting (henceforth HYNM), 2, fol. 305.

82. DF, HYNM, 1, fols. 24–25, 30, 84, 91, 95–96; DF, DMM, 1, fols. 17, 91, 95, 113, 157; 2, fols. 104, 219–20; 3, fols. 11, 13, 17–18, 26v–27r, 32v; DF, LPM, fols. 173–74.

83. DF, DMM, 3, fols. 168v, 170v, 172v–73r, 184v–85r.

84. DF, DMM, 1, fol. 51; 3, fols. 77v–78r.

85. DF, LPM, fols. 53–54.

86. DF, HYNM, 1, fols. 54, 71; DF, DMM, 1, fol. 83.

87. DF, HYNM, 1, fol. 104.

88. DF, HYNM, 1, fols. 63–64.

89. Benjamin Bangs, "Memoirs of the Life and Convincement of Benjamin Bangs," *The Friends' Library* (Philadelphia: Joseph Rakestraw, 1840), vol. 4, pp. 228–29.

90. "Record of Friends Travelling in Ireland, 1656–1765," *JFHS* 10 (July 1913), pp. 158–61; John Burnyeat, *The Truth Exalted in the Writings of That Eminent and Faithful Servant of Christ John Burnyeat* (London, 1691), pp. 26–29, 32–33, 37–38, 61–62, 82, 88–89, 96, 99, 160; Banks, *Journal*, pp. 34–90 passim, 95, 133, 135–37, 173; *The Short Journal and Itinerary Journals of George Fox*, ed. Norman Penney (Cambridge: Cambridge University Press; New York: Macmillan, 1925), pp. 325n, 352n. Among the public Friends whose travels in Ireland are omitted in the list noted above are Humphrey Norton, James Adamson, David Palmer, Elizabeth Smith, Elizabeth Fletcher, Sarah Childers, Katherine Evans, Si-

mon Harrison, Anthony Sharp, Christopher Story, Thomas Lorimer, and John Browne. LF, Swarthmore MSS 6/22; LF, Portfolio 16, no. 75, and 17, nos. 16, 21, 22, 24; DF, Sharp MSS, S5, fols. 4–5, 71r-v; ibid., S8, fol. 13r-v; Christopher Story, "A Brief Account of the Life of Christopher Story," *The Friends' Library* (Philadelphia: Joseph Rakestraw, 1837), vol. 1, p. 154; Penney, ed., "*The First Publishers of Truth*": *Being Early Records (Now First Printed) of the Introduction of Quakerism into the Counties of England and Wales*, supplements 1–5, *JFHS* (1907): 338; Carroll, *John Perrot*, pp. 49–50.

91. Burnyeat, *Truth Exalted*, p. 99; LF, Portfolio 16, no. 58.

92. "A Memoir of the Life and Religious Labours of . . . Edward Burrough," *The Friends' Library* (Philadelphia: Joseph Rakestraw, 1850), vol. 14, p. 483.

93. George Fox, *The Journal of George Fox*, ed. Penney, 2 vols. (Cambridge: Cambridge University Press, 1911), vol. 2, pp. 136–39; *Narrative Papers of George Fox*, ed. Cadbury (Richmond, Ind.: Friends United Press, 1972), pp. 144–45, 181.

94. Somerset Record Office, MSS DD/SFR 10/2, fol. 24r.

95. *Letters*, ed. Barclay, pp. 195–96.

96. DF, Sharp MSS, S9, fols. 23r–25v.

97. Ibid., S2, fols. 83–84.

98. DF, HYNM, 1, fol. 100. For efforts in England to seek redress of grievances, see Greaves, "Shattered Expectations?" pp. 242–48; Horle, *The Quakers and the English Legal System*, chs. 4–5.

99. PRONI, Minutes of the Ulster Provincial Meeting, fol. 57.

100. DF, Sharp MSS, S1, fols. 22–25; ibid., S2, fols. 6, 8 (mismarked 9), 119–20.

101. Huntington Library, MS HA 14,471. For Lady Conway see ibid., MSS HA 14,549; HA 14,558; *The Rawdon Papers*, ed. Edward Berwick (London: John Nichols and Son, 1819), p. 254; Fox, *Short Journal*, pp. 267, 377–78n.

102. *Historical Manuscripts Commission, Reports*, 36, *Ormonde*, new ser., 7, p. 121.

103. DF, Sufferings, Dublin Monthly Meeting, 1660–1780, fols. 24r–25r.

104. On this practice see Carroll, "Early Quakers and 'Going Naked as a Sign,'" *Quaker History* 67 (1978): 69–87.

105. For the suffering of Clarridge and Turner, see LF, Great Book of Sufferings, vol. 2, Leinster Province, Dublin, 1663 and 1669; Holme and A. Fuller, *Brief Relation*, pp. 12–13.

106. LF, Barclay MSS, 1, fol. 103; Royal Society of Antiquaries of Ireland, A Book Generall from 1676 to 1702 for the Corporation of Weavers, fols. 147v, 166v.

107. The development of an institutional structure was no less important for English Quakerism, where it provided a crucial check on the radical individualism present in the movement's early years. See H. Larry Ingle, *First Among Friends: George Fox and the Creation of Quakerism* (New York: Oxford University Press, 1994), pp. 150–52.

108. Michael Walzer, *Obligations: Essays on Disobedience, War, and Citizenship* (Cambridge, Mass.: Harvard University Press, 1970), pp. 51–52.

109. Greaves, *God's Other Children*, pp. 357–58.

110. Jim Smyth, "The Communities of Ireland and the British State, 1660–1707," in Brendan Bradshaw and John Morrill, eds., *The British Problem, c. 1534–1707: State Formation in the Atlantic Archipelago* (New York: St. Martin's, 1996), p. 247.

111. DF, Sharp MSS, S12, fols. 3r-v, 16r (quoted).

SMAIL: LOCAL POLITICS IN
RESTORATION ENGLAND

I would like to thank Michael MacDonald for his helpful comments on an earlier version of this essay.

1. Bill Stevenson, "The Social Integration of Post-Restoration Dissenters, 1660–1725," in Margaret Spufford, ed., *The World of Rural Dissenters, 1520–1725* (Cambridge: Cambridge University Press, 1995), pp. 360–87. See also Margaret Spufford, "The Importance of Religion in the Sixteenth and Seventeenth Centuries," ibid., pp. 19–21. For a particular instance see Jonathan Barry, "The Politics of Religion in Restoration Bristol," in Tim Harris, Paul Seward, and Mark Goldie, eds., *The Politics of Religion in Restoration England* (Oxford: Basil Blackwell, 1990), pp. 163–90.

2. For some recent examples, see Tim Harris, Paul Seward, and Mark Goldie, eds. *The Politics of Religion in Restoration England* (Oxford: Basil Blackwell, 1990); Mark Knights, *Politics and Opinion in Crisis, 1678–81* (Cambridge: Cambridge University Press, 1994); Gary S. De Krey, "The First Restoration Crisis: Conscience and Coercion in London, 1667–73," *Albion* 25 (1993): 565–80; Tim Harris, "Party Turns? or, Whigs and Tories Get Off Scott Free," *Albion* 25 (1993): 581–90; Richard L. Greaves, "Great Scott! The Restoration in Turmoil, or Restoration Crises and the Emergence of Party," *Albion* 25 (1993): 605–18; Andrew Coleby, *Central Government and the Localities: Hampshire, 1649–1689* (Cambridge: Cambridge University Press, 1987); C. Lee, "Fanatic Magistrates: Religion and Political Conflict in Three Kent Boroughs, 1680–84," *Historical Journal* 35 (1992): 43–61; Perry Gauci, *Politics and Society in Great Yarmouth, 1660–1722* (Oxford: Clarendon Press, 1996).

3. The text of the Heywood's "diary" has been published: J. Horsfall Turner, ed., *The Diary of Rev. Oliver Heywood*, 4 vols. (Brighouse, 1882). It is not, of course, a diary in anything like the traditional sense of the word. Some of the surviving notebooks that Turner transcribed do contain sections in which Heywood recorded his day-to-day activities, but there are also many pages of reflections, notes on "returns of prayer," and even an informal "register" with information about the members of his congregation and the community at large. Some of Heywood's published and unpublished sermons have been gathered in Richard Slate, *Select Nonconformist Remains* (London, 1814); and John Vint, ed., *The Whole Works of Oliver Heywood*, 5 vols. (Idle: West Yorkshire, 1825).

4. J. Fawcett, *The Life of the Rev. Oliver Heywood* (Halifax, 1797); J. Hunter, *The Rise of the Old Dissent, Exemplified in the Life of Oliver Heywood* (London, 1842); W. J. Sheils, "Oliver Heywood and His Congregation," in W. J. Sheils and Diana Wood, eds., *Voluntary Religion*, Studies in Church History (Oxford: Basil Blackwell, 1986), vol. 23, pp. 261–77. The first volume of Vint's edition of Heywood's works contains his narrative of Heywood's life with many references to his connections among the Nonconformist community throughout England. These ties are illustrated by the lists he kept of those people to whom he had presented copies of his published sermons: Turner, *Heywood's Diary*, vol. 2, pp. 211–16, and vol. 4, pp. 259–63.

5. The impulse to record God's providences and the theology behind it is most clearly explicated in Paul Seaver's study of the diaries of Nehemiah Wallington: *Wal-*

lington's World: A Puritan Artisan in Seventeenth-Century London (Stanford: Stanford University Press, 1985). See also N. H. Keeble, The Literary Culture of Nonconformity in Later Seventeenth-Century England (Athens: University of Georgia Press, 1987), pp. 207–8.

6. Dissenters, of course, were not themselves a unified group. For a useful survey of both the divisions within Dissent and their main criticisms of the Anglican Church, see John Spurr, "From Puritanism to Dissent, 1660–1700," in Christopher Durston and Jacqueline Eales, eds., The Culture of English Puritanism (New York: St. Martin's Press, 1996), pp. 234–65, and John Spurr, "Schism and the Restoration Church," Journal of Ecclesiastical History 41 (1990): 408–24.

7. Turner, Heywood's Diary, vol. 2, pp. 257, 260.

8. Ibid., vol. 2, p. 295.

9. Ibid., vol. 2, p. 268; vol. 3, p. 208.

10. Ibid., vol. 2, pp. 267, 250–51.

11. Ibid., vol. 3, pp. 78–79; vol. 2, p. 267.

12. These include the passage of the key acts of the Clarendon code, the Declaration of Indulgence, the failure of Parliament to sanction Dissent in 1673, the Test Act, the meetings of the various exclusion parliaments, and, of course, the deliverance brought by William in 1688: ibid., vol. 1, p. 190; vol. 2, p. 278; vol. 3, pp. 134, 153–54; vol. 4, pp. 133–34, 136–39.

13. Ibid., vol. 2, p. 224.

14. Ibid., vol. 3, p. 19.

15. Ibid., vol. 3, pp. 153–54.

16. Most obvious among these was the annual remembrance of "Black Bartholomew Day," doubly blighted for the massacre of French Protestants and the ejection of Nonconformist ministers: ibid., vol. 1, p. 90; vol. 3, p. 123.

17. Ibid., vol. 3, p. 19.

18. There is, for example, a chapter entitled "The Sins of Menasseh" in William Hunt's wonderful study of pre–Civil War Essex: The Puritan Moment (Cambridge, Mass.: Harvard University Press, 1983), pp. 235–78.

19. Turner, Heywood's Diary, vol. 4, p. 49.

20. Ibid., vol. 4, p. 50.

21. Ibid., vol. 2, p. 279.

22. Ibid., vol. 4, p. 50.

23. Ibid., vol. 3, p. 154; vol. 2, p. 280.

24. Ibid., vol. 3, p. 154; vol. 2, p. 288.

25. Ibid., vol. 3, p. 355.

26. Ibid., vol. 4, p. 95.

27. Ibid., vol. 3, pp. 323, 154. In 1681, a minister in nearby Birstall ordered that the church bells be rung on hearing news of the dissolution of the last Exclusion parliament, vol. 2, p. 278.

28. Ibid., vol. 2, p. 266.

29. Ibid., vol. 3, p. 339.

30. Ibid., vol. 2, p. 224.

31. Ibid., vol. 2, pp. 264, 271–72, 279; vol. 3, p. 98. The mention of stoolball brings to mind the not inappropriate comparison between Halifax and the upland regions in the West Country studied by David Underdown: Revel, Riot, and Rebellion (New York: Oxford University Press, 1985).

32. Turner, *Heywood's Diary*, vol. 1, p. 189; vol. 2, p. 244, vol. 4, p. 93.

33. Ibid., vol. 1, p. 133.

34. Ibid., vol. 2, pp. 244–46.

35. Ibid.

36. Ibid., vol. 2, pp. 250–51, 295; vol. 3, pp. 116–17.

37. Ibid., vol. 3, p. 349; vol. 2, p. 260.

38. Ibid., vol. 2, p. 255.

39. Harley makes extensive use, among other sources, of Heywood's diaries: David Harley, "Mental Illness, Magical Medicine, and the Devil in Northern England, 1650–1700," in Roger French and Andrew Wear, eds., *The Medical Revolution of the Seventeenth Century* (Cambridge: Cambridge University Press, 1989), pp. 114–44.

40. For an explication of the term "practical divinity," see Michael MacDonald, "Psychological Healing in England, 1600–1800," in W. J. Sheils, ed., *The Church and Healing*, Studies in Church History, vol. 19 (Oxford: Basil Blackwell, 1986), pp. 101–26 and the sources cited there. Richard Baxter's works reveal this emphasis on the practical side of Puritan and Nonconformist divinity: *The Practical Works of Richard Baxter*, 4 vols. (reprint, Ligonier, Penn: Soli Deo Gloria, 1990–91). The necessity of the Nonconformists' attentiveness to the practical aspects of pastoral care is evident in Harley's work: "Mental Illness," p. 124.

41. Turner, *Heywood's Diary*, vol. 2, p. 289.

42. Ibid., vol. 2, p. 294; vol. 4, p. 15. Heywood's ambiguous feelings toward Anglican clergymen are matched by the ambiguity of his perceptions of other Dissenting groups. Although generally supportive of the Independents as a group, Heywood took the occasional swipe at individuals, comparing the persecution received at their hands to that of the "prelatists" and the "papists": ibid., vol. 3, pp. 181, 201, 315. Quite the reverse was true of Heywood's feelings toward the more radical Dissenting groups such as the Quakers and Baptists. While generally taking pains to distance respectable nonconformity from these extremists, many entries show Heywood's sympathy for the heavy persecutions that the Quakers in particular suffered: ibid., vol. 3, pp. 116–17, 123, 326; vol. 2, p. 192; vol. 1, pp. 341, 356; vol. 4, pp. 90–91.

43. Ibid., vol. 3, pp. 104–5. On another occasion, Heywood noted the presence of two gentlemen who had been great adversaries of his at one of his sermons: vol. 3, p. 121.

44. Ibid., vol. 4, p. 26.

45. Ibid., vol. 1, pp. 183, 186, 196, 200, 359; vol. 4, pp. 87–88, 94, 103.

46. Ibid., vol. 1, p. 359.

47. John Vint, ed., *The Whole Works of the Rev. Oliver Heywood* (1827), p. 148.

48. One sermon used the story of Daniel to explicitly compare Nonconformists to the persecuted Israelites in Babylon: Richard Slate, *Select Nonconformist Remains* (London, 1814), pp. 90–96.

49. Turner, *Heywood's Diary*, vol. 3, p. 140.

50. Ibid., vol. 2, p. 228. A similar attempt was also made in 1676, and in this instance Heywood explicitly mentions the fact that many of those who petitioned the vicar "have neither heard nor owned me for almost two seven years [*sic*]" vol. 3, p. 170.

51. Ibid., vol. 1, pp. 350–51.

52. Ibid., vol. 2, p. 281.

53. Ibid., vol. 4, pp. 110–11; vol. 3, p. 185.

54. Ibid., vol. 2, p. 287; vol. 3, pp. 119–20; vol. 4, p. 50.

55. James Raine, ed., *Depositions from the Castle of York*, Surtees Society Publications (1861), vol. 40, pp. 164–65.

56. John Smail, *The Origins of Middle-Class Culture* (Ithaca, N.Y.: Cornell University Press, 1994), pp. 19–26.

57. Raine, *Depositions from the Castle of York*, pp. 164–65; Turner, *Heywood's Diary*, vol. 2, pp. 122–23, 199–203; vol. 3, p. 201; vol. 4, p. 52. For another example of attitudes to wealth in Halifax in the period, see the notes on members of the Priestly family, some of whom were members of Heywood's congregation: "Some Memoirs Concerning the Family of the Priestlys, Written by Jonathan Priestly, 1696," *Surtees Society Publications*, vol. 77 (1883).

58. Joan Thirsk, "The Farming Regions of England," and Alan Everitt, "Farm Laborers," in Joan Thirsk, ed., *The Agrarian History of England and Wales*, vol. 4 (Cambridge: Cambridge University Press, 1967); Underdown, *Revel, Riot, and Rebellion*. For details on Halifax as an upland parish, see Smail, *Origins of Middle-Class Culture*, pp. 21–22.

59. Will and inventory of Stephen Ellis of Hipperholme, Borthwick Institute of Historical Research, York, Original Wills, Pontefract Deanery, May 1689. Ellis died owning goods and debts valued at over £400 and made bequests of £1,300 in cash as well as several messuages in his will.

60. Turner, *Heywood's Diary*, vol. 2, pp. 271–72; for a discussion of the event, see Smail, *Origins of Middle-Class Culture*, pp. 33–34.

61. There was a burst of persecution in 1672 and 1673, apparently in reaction to Charles's declaration of indulgence: Turner, *Heywood's Diary*, vol. 3, pp. 153–55. In contrast, in 1683 and 1684, in a period when Charles was putting pressure on Dissent in the aftermath of the Exclusion Crisis and amidst the fear of plots, there seems to have been some attempts by those in the West Riding to ease the pressure: ibid., vol. 3, p. 218; vol. 4, pp. 95, 100–102.

62. Ibid., vol. 2, p. 285.

63. Ibid., vol. 2, pp. 261, 264, 271–72, 277, 280, 283; vol. 3, p. 101.

64. Ibid., vol. 2, p. 274, vol. 3, pp. 88, 138.

65. Ibid., vol. 2, p. 285. Horrified that Tories should appropriate the name for Irish rebels, Heywood was not pleased at the Whigs' willingness to take their name from a Scots word for "fanatics or Dissenters," no doubt because it magnified a feature of his own beliefs that he would rather have masked.

66. Ibid., vol. 2, p. 294.

67. The approach I am suggesting attempts to build on David Underdown's pioneering analysis of popular allegiance in the West Country during the Civil War by incorporating a greater awareness of the interplay between national and local, a greater awareness of the range of different opinions with a community, and a greater awareness of the fact that people might hold apparently similar opinions for quite different reasons: Underdown, *Revel, Riot, and Rebellion*. For other suggestions along these same lines, see Ann Hughes, "Local History and the Origins of the English Civil War," in

Richard Cust and Ann Hughes, eds., *Conflict in Early Stuart England: Studies in Religion and Politics, 1603–1642* (London: Longman, 1989), pp. 224–53.

68. Barry, "Politics of Religion," pp. 171–72.

69. Mark Goldie and John Spurr, "Politics in the Restoration Parish: Edward Fowler and the Struggle for St. Giles Cripplegate," *English Historical Review* 109 (1994): 572–96. In other parishes the vicar, the vestry, and the congregation as a whole might all line up together as in the case of Heywood's father-in-law, who maintained his Lancashire living throughout the Restoration despite his refusal to wear a surplice or comply with other Anglican dictates.

70. P. J. Norrey, "The Restoration Regime in Action: The Relationship between Central and Local Government in Dorset, Somerset, and Wiltshire, 1660–1678," *Historical Journal* 31 (1988): 789–812.

71. I am adapting here a theoretical model proposed by Roger Chartier, *The Cultural Origins of the French Revolution*, trans. Lydia Cochrane (Durham, N.C.: Duke University Press, 1991). For a more extensively argued example which argues for the necessity of local history on these grounds, see Smail, *Origins of Middle-Class Culture*, pp. 14–17, 191–221.

SWETT: "BORN ON MY LAND"

1. National Library of Wales (hereafter NLW) MS 9053E f. 78, Dec. 1, 1605. Sir Thomas Mostyn at Mostyn, Flintshire, to John Wynn at Gwydir, Caernarfonshire.

2. Peter Clark, "Migrants in the City: The Process of Social Adaptation in English Towns, 1500–1800," in Peter Clark and David Souden, eds., *Migration and Society in Early Modern England* (London: Hutchinson, 1988), pp. 267–91; see pp. 274, 282–83. Clark notes briefly that ethnicity was surely influential in adaptation, but he has little specific information on the subject. But see Kathleen M. Noonan, "'The Cruell Pressure of an Enraged, Barbarous People': Irish and English Identity in Seventeenth-Century Policy and Propaganda," *Historical Journal* 41, no. 1 (1998): 151–78. Also see Paul S. Seaver, "Declining Status in an Aspiring Age: The Problem of the Gentle Apprentice in Seventeenth-Century London," in Bonnelyn Young Kunze and Dwight D. Brautigam, eds., *Court, Country, and Culture: Essays on Early Modern British History in Honor of Perez Zagorin* (Rochester, N.Y.: University of Rochester Press, 1992), pp. 129–48; Seaver, "A Social Contract? Master Against Servant in the Court of Requests," *History Today* 39 (Sept. 1989): 50–56; Seaver, "Thomas Dekker's *Shoemaker's Holiday* and the World of London Artisans and Apprentices," in David L. Smith, Richard Strier, and David Bevington, eds., *The Theatrical City: London's Culture, Theatre, and Literature, 1576–1649* (Cambridge: Cambridge University Press, 1995), pp. 87–100.

3. Donald Lupton, *London and the Country Carbonadoed* (London, 1632), reprinted in facsimile by Theatrum Orbis Terrarum, The English Experience, no. 879 (Amsterdam and Norwood, N.J.: Walter J. Johnson, 1977), p. 1. Lupton, a translator and writer on many subjects, supposedly wrote this piece in ten days. He served as vicar of Sunbury, Middlesex, in his old age and died in 1676.

4. Ole Peter Grell, *Dutch Calvinists in Early Stuart London: The Dutch Church in Austin Friars, 1603–1642* (Leiden: E. J. Brill, 1989), pp. 1–26; Andrew Spicer, "'A Fayth-

ful Pastor in the Churches': Ministers in the French and Walloon Communities in England, 1560–1620," in Andrew Pettegree, ed., *The Reformation of the Parishes: The Ministry and the Reformation in Town and Country* (Manchester: Manchester University Press, 1993), pp. 195–214; Charles Littleton, "Competing Communities? The French Church of London, Its Congregation, and the London Parishes, 1560–1625," paper presented Oct. 5, 1995, at the North American Conference on British Studies, Washington, D.C. See also Andrew Pettegree, *Foreign Protestant Communities in Sixteenth-Century London* (New York: Oxford University Press, 1986), and "'Thirty Years On': Progress Towards Integration Amongst the Immigrant Population of Elizabethan London," in John Chartres and David Hey, eds., *English Rural Society, 1500–1800: Essays in Honour of Joan Thirsk* (Cambridge: Cambridge University Press, 1990), pp. 297–312; Kathleen M. Noonan, "'Brethren Only to a Degree': Irish Immigration to London in the Mid-Seventeenth Century" (Ph.D. diss., University of California, Santa Barbara, 1989). There is no published history of the Welsh in early modern England, but for a brief overview, see David Mathew, "Wales and England in the Early Seventeenth Century," *Transactions of the Honourable Society of Cymmrodorion*, 1955, pp. 36–49.

5. For an interesting discussion of occupational solidarity among London seamen and their families, see Cheryl Fury, "The Lot of Seamen's Wives and Widows During the Anglo-Spanish War, 1585–1603," paper given 15 May 1997 at the Third Carleton Conference on the History of the Family, Carleton University, Ottawa. The Society of Ancient Britons was not set up in London until 1715. For the apparent lack of Welsh neighborhoods or residential concentrations in London, see Emrys Jones, "The Welsh in London in the Seventeenth and Eighteenth Centuries," *Welsh History Review* 10 (1981): 461–79.

6. Vivien Brodsky Elliott, "Mobility and Marriage in Pre-Industrial England" (Ph.D. diss., Cambridge University, 1979), pp. 158–60, 166–68. This formidable piece of research has a wealth of valuable data for the study of London migration. Brodsky Elliott charted the origins of apprentices from fifteen London companies of all ranks between 1574 and 1640. The Welsh were in every company, between 3 and 5 percent of the total apprentice intake. To my knowledge, no one has yet calculated whether they took up their freedom in the same proportions. W. K. Jordan found 32 London Welsh philanthropists. Cited in Glanmor Williams, *Renewal and Reformation: Wales, c. 1415–1642* (Oxford: Oxford University Press, 1993), p. 468. Williams also supplies a good short survey of the achievements of Welsh migrants to England, pp. 462–70. See also Alfred Beaven, *The Aldermen of the City of London, Temp. Henry III–1908* (London: Eden Fisher, 1908), 2 vols. See also *The Members of the City Companies in 1641 as Set Forth in the Return for the Poll Tax*, typescript, transcribed by Rev. T. C. C. Dale (London: Society of Genealogists, 1935); *A Dictionary of Printers and Booksellers in England, Scotland, Ireland . . . 1557–1640*, comp. H. G. Aldis et al. (London: Bibliographical Society, 1910).

7. W. P. Griffith, "Welsh Students at Oxford, Cambridge, and the Inns of Court During the Sixteenth and Early Seventeenth Centuries" (Ph.D. diss., University of Wales, 1981). See also Public Record Office (hereafter PRO) LC2/4 (4), Queen Elizabeth's Funeral List, 1603; LC2/6, King James I's List, 1625. Sir Richard Wynn is listed on p. 69 among the gentlemen of the privy chamber in Prince Charles's household.

8. J. O. Bartley, *Teague, Shenkin, and Sawney, Being an Historical Study of the Earliest Irish, Welsh, and Scottish Characters in English Plays* (Cork, Eire: Cork University Press, 1954), p. 48. The shiring of Wales left Welsh-speaking areas in Shropshire, Herefordshire, and Gloucestershire.

9. On the comic figure of the impoverished Welsh gentleman, see Christie Davies, "Ethnic Jokes and Social Change: The Case of the Welsh," *Immigrants and Minorities* 4 (1985): 46–63.

10. Bartley, *Teague, Shenkin, and Sawney*, pp. 48–77; Davies, "Ethnic Jokes"; E. J. Miller, "Wales and the Tudor Drama," *Transactions of the Honourable Society of Cymmrodorion*, 1948, pp. 170–83; W. R. Jones, "England Against the Celtic Fringe: A Study in Cultural Stereotypes," *Cahiers d'Histoire Mondiale* 13 (1971): 155–71. On the popular influence of playgoing in London and on the subjects of satire (including, to quote Sir Philip Sidney, "strangers, because they speak not English so well as we do") in general, see also Brian Gibbons, *Jacobean City Comedy* (London: Methuen, 1968), p. 46. Also Andrew Gurr, *Playgoing in Shakespeare's London* (Cambridge: Cambridge University Press, 1987).

11. Thomas Middleton, *A Chaste Maid in Cheapside*, in Russell A. Fraser and Norman Rabkin, eds., *Drama of the English Renaissance II: The Stuart Period* (New York: Macmillan, 1976), pp. 369–98. Edward F. Rimbault, ed., *The Miscellaneous Works in Prose and Verse of Sir Thomas Overbury* (London: Reeves and Turner, 1890), pp. 68–69. For a darker view of portrayals of the Welsh in chapbook literature, see Margaret Spufford, *Small Books and Pleasant Histories: Popular Fiction and Its Readership in Seventeenth-Century England* (London: Methuen, 1981), pp. 5, 182–84, 191–92. She attributes the rise in satire to increased migration levels and poorer migrants: mockery was one way to cope with the social menace that the poorest migrants posed.

12. By contrast, Keith Lindley argues that it was his scornful repudiation of traditional elite social values that made parvenu Sir Giles Overreach in Philip Massinger's *A New Way to Pay Old Debts* so threatening a character. "Noble Scarlet vs. London Blue," in Smith, *Theatrical City*, pp. 183–93.

13. For an intriguing ethnographic study of perceptions of Welshness in contemporary Wales, see Carol Trosset, *Welshness Performed: Welsh Concepts of Person and Society* (Phoenix: University of Arizona Press, 1993).

14. George Williams to Sir William Maurice of Clenennau, Caernarfonshire, Nov. 18, 1620, from John Prudderch's house in Chancery Lane. Maurice owed Price £100, and Williams was trying to arrange payment. *The Clenennau Letters and Papers in the Brogyntyn Collection*, calendared and ed. T. Jones Pierce. National Library of Wales Journal suppl., 4th ser., pt. 1. 1947, pp. 113–15.

15. John Earle, *Micro-cosmographie*. Number 61, "Acquaintance." 1st ed., 1628, with additional characters from 1629 and 1633 eds. Edward Arber, ed., for English Reprints (London: Alexander Murray and Son, 1868).

16. Brodsky Elliott, "Mobility and Marriage," pp. 158, 167.

17. Guildhall Library MS 15857/1. Haberdashers' Register of Freedom Admissions, 1526–1642. I compiled the sample from the register.

18. Prerogative Court of Canterbury (hereafter PCC) 83 Wood 1611. Will of Humfrey Lloyd, late of London, apprentice. PCC 99 Dorset 1609. Will of Gilbert Lloyd,

citizen and merchant tailor. PCC 118 St. John 1631. Will of Robert Geoffreys, citizen and haberdasher. PCC 23 Lyon 1569. Will of Sir Richard Clough, mercer. His master was Sir Thomas Gresham.

19. Richard Grassby, *The English Gentleman in Trade: The Life and Works of Sir Dudley North, 1641–1691* (Oxford: Clarendon Press, 1994), p. 187. Brodsky Elliott, "Mobility and Marriage," p. 221, citing Davis's deposition.

20. Jeremy Boulton, "Neighborhood Migration in Early Modern London," in Clark, *Migration and Society*, pp. 107–49, see 134–37.

21. Guildhall Library MS 3016/1. Vestry minutes, St. Dunstan's in the West. MS 2968/2, Churchwarden's accounts. MS 2601/1, Churchwarden's accounts, St. Michael's Bassishaw. MS 3505, Record and Assessment Book. MS 1046/1, Churchwarden's accounts, St. Antholin's. MS 642 vol.1, Vestry minutes, St. Peter's Westcheap.

22. For some Jacobean examples from the Court of Requests, see PRO REQ2/410/38 about Rowland Wynn's disputed guardianship-for-profit of lunatic Edward Mompesson, REQ2/388/38 about widow Elizabeth Powell's attempt to collect on a debt owed her late husband, Robert, a cook, by victuallers Jarvis and Agnes Smith, REQ2/389/40 in which Morrice Llewelin defends himself and partner Silvanus Payne from charges of swindling John Snelling in the purchase of a ship from a Scottish merchant in 1606, and REQ2/302/35, a particularly complex case in which Ellis Lloyd, citizen and draper, sues for the return of a cancelled bond from Richard Griffith, the husband of an Elizabeth Hampton, deceased, who had lent Lloyd £50 at interest twenty years earlier. Lloyd charged that his dealings with Elizabeth before her death had been mutually satisfactory and that Griffith was now conspiring with a Mr. Gwynn of the Inner Temple, who owed Lloyd £8, to have him arrested and thrown in prison.

23. PCC Will of Sir Thomas Myddelton, Nov. 20, 1630. A rich source is NLW Chirk MSS F12540, Myddelton's account book from 1583, right after he became free of the city, until 1603. See also A. H. Dodd, "Mr. Myddelton the Merchant of Tower Street," in S. T. Bindoff, J. Hurstfield, and C. H. Williams, eds., *Elizabethan Government and Society: Essays Presented to Sir John Neale* (London: Athlone Press, 1961), pp. 249–81.

24. Vivien Brodsky Elliott, "Single Women and the London Marriage Market," in R. B. Outhwaite, *Marriage and Society: Studies in the Social History of Marriage* (London: Europa, 1981); Jean Howard, "The Domestic and the Foreign: Category Crisis in the Material London of Jacobean City Comedy," paper presented Mar. 18, 1995, at the conference "Material London, ca. 1600," Folger Library, Washington D.C.

25. PCC 96 Pell. 1659. Will of Edward ap John of St. Martins in the Fields, Middlesex. 191 Pell. 1659. Will of Anne ap John, widow, of St. Margaret's Westminster.

26. Toy's mother had formerly run the business herself. John Roland Phillips, *Memoirs of the Civil War in Wales and the Marches, 1642–9*, 2 vols. (London: Longman, 1874), vol. 1, p. 18.

27. Linda Colley, *Britons: Forging the Nation, 1707–1837* (New Haven: Yale University Press, 1992), p. 6. William Ingram, "Both Inside and Outside in Tudor London: How Useful a Category Is 'Stage Player'?" paper presented Nov. 4, 1995, at the Midwest Conference on British Studies, Ann Arbor, Mich.

28. PCC 8 Watson. 1584 Will of David ap John David ap John ap Edward alias

David Jones, gent., of St. Nicholas Coleabbey, London. See also the wills of Robert Geoffreys and Sir Thomas Myddelton.

29. Williams's protégé and English biographer, John Hacket, says that "such as had giggling spleens would laugh at him for his Welsh tone." Quoted in B. Dew Roberts, *Mitre and Musket: John Williams, Lord Keeper, Archbishop of York, 1582–1650* (Oxford: Oxford University Press, 1938.), p. 11.

30. British Library 102.b.63.

31. For instance, from this pamphlet, p. 1: "Though her have not so much Creek, which her holds to be heathenish; nor Hebrew which her holds to be Shewish language, nor Latin which is the language of Rome, yet her shall endeavor herself to teliver herself in as cood Tialect as her can for her hart plood, for the petter understanding of all her friends and kindred." On "Wenglish" and its relation to the English spoken by Welsh migrants, see the two articles by Thomas Gwynn Jones, "Tudor Welshmen's English," *Y Cymmrodor* 29 (1919): 56–69. Idem, "Welsh Consonants and English Ears," *Journal of the Welsh Bibliographical Society* 1 (1910): 20–22. On satire see also M. Dorothy George, "Some Caricatures of Wales and Welshmen," *National Library of Wales Journal* 5, no. 1 (1947): 1–12, plus plates. Many of these pamphlets are listed in vols. 1–2 of Frederick George Stephens, *Catalogue of Political and Personal Satires Preserved in the Department of Prints and Drawings in the British Museum*, 11 vols. (British Museum Publications, 1978).

32. Prytherch helped the Wynn of Gwydir family in London with advice, arrangements, and small loans for the sons around the time of this Chancery suit, in which he and his wife, Joan, the widow of the keeper of a victualling house, John Wynsor, were suing to recover Wynsor's debts. PRO C2/JAS1/P7/7. *Exchequer Proceedings Concerning Wales in tempore James I*, comp. T. I. Jeffreys Jones (Board of Celtic Studies, University of Wales). History and Law Series no. 14. Pp. 155, 163. PCC 77 Dorset, 1609. Will of Lewis ap Jenkin of St. Sepulchers without Newgate. PCC 41 Lawe, 1619. Will of Gwyn ap Llewelyn, yeoman, late of the parish of Nacquyse, Flintshire, and now of the parish of St. Savior's Southwark. At his death he was staying with his daughter Katheryn and her husband, Michael Rawlyns. PCC 81 Drake, 1596. Will of William ap Owen, citizen and joiner.

33. For example, PCC 78 Dixy, 1594. Will of Margaret ap Robert, spinster and servant to William Starkey, feltmaker. She bequeaths to her uncle John Griffin the £10 due to her in her father Robert ap Harry's will, and asks Griffin to look after her sister, Margery ap Robert.

34. Henry Thomas, "Arise Evans, the Welsh Conjurer," *Journal of the Merioneth Historical and Record Society* 3 (1960): 280–85. Geraint H. Jenkins, *The Foundations of Modern Wales, 1642–1780* (Oxford: Oxford University Press, 1993), pp. 67–68, 111.

35. Phillips, *Memoirs of the Civil War*, p. 60. On religious practice in early modern Wales, see Williams, *Reformation and Renewal*.

36. Hughes lists dates and preachers, often also place and subject: for instance, "Dr. Peters 7 November on Romans 6:23 the wages of sin is death . . . 2 December Mr. Shute St. Dunstans." His descendant in the late seventeenth century used the book to write down poetry and political prophecies. Both men were fond of genealogies—their

own, especially. *Llyer Byrr Llangadwaladr.* British Library Additional MSS 14900. Sermon notes run from pages 1 to 75. Carla Pestana alerted me to this document.

37. The will's opening explicitly mentions the Virgin St. Mary, and he bequeaths a ring with a picture of Jesus on it. For so wealthy and literate a Londoner, in 1631, with a lengthy, detailed will that donates no money for sermons, I take these phrases to suggest Geoffreys's own conservative religious views rather than those of the scribe.

38. PCC 81 Drake 1596. Will of William ap Owen, citizen and joiner of London. Guildhall MS 1046/1. The property to the hospital is to descend instead to William's rightful heirs if the city does not follow the terms of the bequest: "I am urged to this by my father and by the parish churchwardens." Churchwarden's accounts for St. Antholin's, 1574–1708, pp. 20, 50, 54, 58. The parish records show that William's bequest was received.

39. On London Puritans' relations with their parishes and neighborhoods, see Paul S. Seaver, *Wallington's World: A Puritan Artisan in Seventeenth-Century London* (Stanford: Stanford University Press, 1985).

40. Joan Thirsk, "England's Provinces: Did They Serve or Drive Material London?" paper presented Mar. 17, 1995, at the conference "Material London, ca. 1600." The other two named are the indigenous skills and specialties of the provinces, ripe for development, and the rapid proliferation of new fashions, trends, and styles.

41. NLW 9054E f. 8.

42. NLW Wynnstay MS C2. NLW 9052E ff. 51, 53, 54. 9054E f. 25.

43. NLW 9054E f. 46.

44. His will leaves money to both his native parish and his London parish. NLW 9052E f. 11. NLW Additional MS 465E f. 95. 9053E ff. 170–72, 176. 9055E f. 76, 108. In 1615 Sir John Wynn described Geoffreys as "my friend Mr. Robert Geffrey a merchant adventurer born on my land."

45. When he was first sent up to London in 1614, young Morus Wynn lodged in Cheapside next door to Powell. Powell and John Williams the goldsmith helped Geoffreys arrange his apprenticeship. On Powell, NLW 9054E f. 54, 9055E ff. 76, 108, 168, 171, 9056E f. 142, 152. 9061E f. 11.

46. Wilfrid R. Prest, *The Rise of the Barristers: A Social History of the English Bar, 1590–1640* (Oxford: Clarendon Press, 1986).

47. NLW Wynnstay MSS 160. Henry Wynn's Fee Book. His Welsh clients were from both London and Wales. Wynnstay MSS 84 probably belonged to Evan Lloyd and dates from the 1620's. MSS 85 may have been kept by Henry Wynn's clerk. For more on Welsh lawyers, see Rees L. Lloyd, "Welsh Masters of the Bench of the Inner Temple from Early Times Until the End of the Eighteenth Century," *Transactions of the Honourable Society of Cymmrodorion* (1937–38), in 2 parts.

48. NLW 9057E ff. 54, 14 are good examples.

49. NLW Add. MS 465E ff. 100, 102. NLW 9053E ff. 151, 186, 9054E ff. 216, 218.

50. Steve Rappaport, *Worlds Within Worlds: Structures of Life in Sixteenth-Century London* (Cambridge: Cambridge University Press, 1989), ch. 8, "Patterns of Mobility," pp. 285–376. Vivien Brodsky Elliott also notes the importance of regional connections for migrants and the difficulty of tracing them: "Mobility and Marriage," pp. 207–13.

51. I owe this point to Newton Key. "Identity . . . is fundamentally relational and

frequently oppositional." Cynthia Herrup, "Introduction," *Journal of British Studies* 31 (1992): 307–8.

52. NLW 9052E f. 71.

53. Powell pawned the horse and then died without paying Lloyd. His executors, John Owen and Robert ap Thomas ap Hoell, concealed his goods and refused to prove his will. Jones, *Exchequer Proceedings*, p. 190.

54. NLW 9052E f. 51, 9053E f. 136, 9051E f.40, 9061E f. 20.

55. This is a theme of J. A. Jackson's useful short survey, *Migration* (London: Longman, 1986).

56. Jones, *Exchequer Proceedings*, pp. 155, 163, 168.

57. Of Richard Wynn's desire to do anything rather than return to Wales, Ellis said, "In which I must needs commend him, as there is nothing to be had there for preferment." NLW 9053E f. 154.

58. PRO C2/Elizabeth/W16/57. Robert Wynn of Conway vs. Ellis Wynn and Hugh Beeston.

59. "Beseeching almighty God to bless him with long life, health and much increase of honor to be an ornament to his country, a comfort to his friends and for the general good of the commonwealth." PCC Will of Ellis Wynne, esquire, clerk of the Petty Bag in Chancery, Sept. 25, 1623.

60. *The Welchmens Jubilee to the honour of St. David, shewing the manner of that solemn celebration which the Welshmen annually hold in honour of St. David, describing likewise the true and real cause, why they wear that day a leek on their hats.* Composed by T. Morgan. Printed for J. Harrison. British Library E.136. (16) 83. T. Morgan was probably of Welsh descent.

61. William Ralph Douthwaite, *Gray's Inn: Its History and Associations* (London: Reeves and Turner, 1886), pp. 234–37. Douthwaite takes his quotations from the State Papers Domestic.

SHOEMAKER: SEPARATE SPHERES?

I would like to thank Laura Gowing, Jeremy Gregory, Paul Griffiths, Tim Hitchcock, Margaret Hunt, Lawrence Klein, and the editors of this volume for many helpful comments and suggestions.

1. Jane Rendell, "Uneven Developments: Women's History, Feminist History, and Gender History in Britain," in K. Offen et al., eds., *Writing Women's History: International Perspectives* (Bloomington, Ind., 1991), p. 52; Amanda Vickery, "Golden Age to Separate Spheres? A Review of the Categories and Chronology of English Women's History," *Historical Journal* 36 (1993): 383–414.

2. Robert B. Shoemaker, *Gender in English Society, 1650–1850: The Emergence of Separate Spheres?* (London, 1998); Vickery, "Golden Age to Separate Spheres?"

3. Alice Clark, *Working Life of Women in the Seventeenth Century* (London, 1919). In her introduction to the latest edition of Clark (London: Routledge, 1992), Amy Louise Erickson asserts that Clark's arguments are confirmed by recent research as often as they are contradicted. See also Bernard Capp, "Separate Domains? Women and Authority in Early Modern England," in P. Griffiths, A. Fox, and S. Hindle, eds., *The*

Experience of Authority in Early Modern England (Basingstoke and London, 1996), pp. 117–45.

4. D. V. Glass, "Notes on the Demography of London at the End of the Seventeenth Century," *Daedalus* 97 (1968): 584–86. Glass calculated that there were 87 men for every 100 women in the City of London in 1695.

5. David Cressy, *Literacy and the Social Order: Reading and Writing in Tudor and Stuart England* (Cambridge, 1980), pp. 145–49; Robert B. Shoemaker, *Prosecution and Punishment: Petty Crime and the Law in London and Rural Middlesex, c. 1660–1725* (Cambridge, 1991), pp. 179–82, 185–87, 207–12.

6. [Margaret Fell], *Women's Speaking Justified* (London, 1666).

7. N. H. Keeble, *The Cultural Identity of Seventeenth-Century Woman* (London, 1994); Richard Baxter, *A Christian Directory* (London, 1673), p. 532.

8. *Husbands Love Your Wives. A Sermon Preached: Proving the Duty of Husbands to Their Wives* (London, 1698); John Shuttlewood, *Marriages Made in Heaven: A Wedding Sermon Preach'd July 22, 1711*, 2d ed. (London, 1712).

9. [Richard Allestree], *The Whole Duty of Man* (London, 1703), p. 304; [Richard Allestree], *The Ladies Calling* (Oxford, 1693), p. 230.

10. G. M. [Gervase Markham], *The English Housewife, Containing the Inward and Outward Virtues Which Ought to be in a Compleat Woman* (London, 1664), pp. 1–2; [George Savile, Lord Halifax], *The Lady's New Year's Gift; or, Advice to a Daughter* (London, 1688), pp. 68, 74; W. Fleetwood, *The Relative Duties of Parents and Children, Husbands and Wives, Masters and Servants* (London, 1705), p. 168; R. Codrington, *The Second Part of Youth's Behavior, or Decency in Conversation Amongst Women* (London, 1664), p. 38.

11. [Allestree], *Whole Duty of Man*, p. 304.

12. Kathryn Shevelow, *Women and Print Culture: The Construction of Femininity in the Early Periodical* (New York, 1989), p. 3.

13. Cynthia L. White, *Women's Magazines, 1693–1968* (London, 1970), p. 26.

14. Shevelow, *Women and Print Culture*, p. 69; *Athenian Mercury* 3, no. 13, question 2 (1691) (see also vol. 5, no. 3, question 2 [1691]); White, *Women's Magazines*, p. 25.

15. Shevelow, *Women and Print Culture*, pp. 130–31; *Tatler* 10 and 172 (May 3, 1709, and May 13–16, 1710); Lawrence E. Klein, "Gender, Conversation, and the Public Sphere in Early Eighteenth-Century England," in J. Still and M. Worton, eds., *Textuality and Sexuality: Reading Theories and Practices* (Manchester, 1993), pp. 109–12; *Spectator* 81 and 128 (June 2, 1711, and July 27, 1711).

16. Phyllis Mack, *Visionary Women: Ecstatic Prophecy in Seventeenth-Century England* (Berkeley, 1992), ch. 8; Patricia Crawford, *Women and Religion in England, 1500–1720* (London, 1993), pp. 190–91, 205–6.

17. Margaret Hunt, *The Middling Sort: Commerce, Gender, and the Family in England, 1680–1780* (Berkeley, 1996), pp. 104, 111–14; T. J. G. Harris, "The Politics of the London Crowd in the Reign of Charles II" (Ph.D. diss., Emmanuel College, Cambridge, 1984), p. 279; Clive D. Field, "Adam and Eve: Gender in the English Free Church Constituency," *Journal of Ecclesiastical History* 44 (1993): 67.

18. Mack, *Visionary People*, ch. 9, esp. pp. 327, 344, 349; William Beck and T. Frederick Ball, *The London Friends' Meeting* (London, 1869), pp. 125–26, 352–54.

19. Hillel Schwartz, *The French Prophets: The History of a Millenarian Group in Eighteenth-Century England* (Berkeley, 1980), pp. 136, 142, 231.

20. Peter Earle, *A City Full of People: Men and Women of London, 1650–1750* (London, 1994), chs. 3 and 4, quotes at pp. 120, 122.

21. Ibid.

22. Sean Shesgreen, *The Criers and Hawkers of London: Engravings and Drawings by Marcellus Latroon* (Aldershot, Hants., 1990); Earle, *City Full of People*, pp. 144–45.

23. Hunt, *Middling Sort*, pp. 128, 132, 133. It should be noted that Hunt's statistical evidence is from the period 1775–87.

24. Peter Earle, "The Female Labour Market in London in the Late Seventeenth and Early Eighteenth Centuries," *Economic History Review*, 2d ser., 42 (1989): 338; Hunt, *Middling Sort*, pp. 136–37.

25. William Matthews, ed., *The Diary of Dudley Ryder* (London, 1939), pp. 37, 46. For some suggestions concerning the differences between urban and rural street behavior, see Shoemaker, *Gender in English Society*, pp. 270–71.

26. Margaret Hunt, "Wife Beating, Domesticity, and Women's Independence in Eighteenth-Century London," *Gender and History* 4 (1992): 12.

27. Ned Ward, *The London Spy* (4th ed., 1709; reprint, ed. Paul Hyland, Colleagues Press, East Lansing, 1993), pt. 14, pp. 245–46.

28. Shoemaker, *Gender in English Society*, pp. 271–73. For the different meanings ascribed to behavior depending on the time of day, see Paul Griffiths, "Meanings of Nightwalking in Early Modern England," *The Seventeenth Century* (forthcoming). For the distinctive haunts and dress of "sodomites," see R. Trumbach, "London's Sodomites: Homosexual Behavior and Western Culture in the Eighteenth Century," *Journal of Social History* 11 (1977): 1–33; Rictor Norton, *Mother Clap's Molly House: The Gay Subculture in England, 1700–1830* (London, 1992).

29. Capp, "Separate Domains?" pp. 128–36; Laura Gowing, *Domestic Dangers: Women, Words, and Sex in Early Modern London* (Oxford, 1996).

30. Robert B. Shoemaker, "Reforming Male Manners: Public Insult and the Decline of Violence in London," in T. Hitchcock and M. Cohen, eds., *English Masculinities, 1660–1800* (London, 1999); Tim Meldrum, "A Women's Court in London: Defamation at the Bishop of London's Consistory Court," *London Journal* 19 (1994): 6.

31. London Metropolitan Archives, Consistory Court Deposition Books, DL/C/240, 243, 255, 262, 272.

32. London Metropolitan Archives, MJ/SR/2409, R. 251 (Aug. 1723).

33. See, e.g., MJ/SR/1651, R. 175 (Sept. 1684); 1820, R. 20 (Sept. 1693); 2488, R. 113 (Aug. 1727).

34. Shoemaker, "Reforming Male Manners," p. 141; Daniel Defoe, *The Complete English Tradesman* (1726; Gloucester, 1987), p. 138.

35. MJ/SR/2016, R. 107,110 (Sept. 1703).

36. Robert B. Shoemaker, "The London 'Mob' in the Early Eighteenth Century," *Journal of British Studies* 26 (1987): 285–86.

37. Harris, "The Politics of the London Crowd," p. 301; Lois G. Schwoerer, "Women and the Glorious Revolution," *Albion* 18 (1986): 202–8. On the different language of political speech used by women, see Dagmar Friest, "The King's Crown Is the

Whore of Babylon: Politics, Gender, and Communication in Mid-Seventeenth-Century England," *Gender and History* 7 (1995): 457–81.

38. Shoemaker, "London 'Mob,'" table 2, p. 283.

39. Ibid., p. 285.

40. MJ/SR/2488, R. 165 (Aug. 1727); see also MJ/SR/2600, R. 332 (Aug./Sept. 1733).

41. Public Record Office, Assi 35, 116/9, information of Ratcliffe, cited by Harris, "Politics of the London Crowd," p. 232.

42. Although the majority of those prosecuted for these riots were male, in one incident three married women were charged along with six unrelated men. In another case, a journeyman went to observe a disturbance with his mother and sister. Although the journeyman was arrested, no one from this group was charged. It is likely that where family groups rioted, only the male head of household was liable to be arrested and/or indicted, and thus the number of female participants was probably higher than the records suggest. J. C. Jeaffreson, ed., *Middlesex County Records*, 4 vols. (London, 1886–92), vol. 4, pp. 60–65; Corporation of London Record Office, Sessions Rolls, Sept. 1675; Sessions Papers, Sept. 1675, no. 6.

43. *Commons Journals* 11 (Jan. 29, 1696/97): 683; Narcissus Luttrell, *A Brief Historical Relation of State Affairs*, 6 vols. (1678–1714; reprint, Farnborough, Hants, 1969), vol. 4, pp. 172, 174–75. William Fleming, however, reported that it was the weavers' *wives* who marched to Parliament: *Historical Manuscripts Commission*, 12th report, appendix, pt. 7 (London, 1890), p. 346.

44. Ward, *London Spy*, quote at 186; E. S. de Beer, ed., *The Diary of John Evelyn*, 6 vols. (Oxford, 1955), vol. 4, p. 362.

45. R. Latham and W. Matthews, eds., *The Diary of Samuel Pepys*, 11 vols. (1970–83), vol. 3, p. 93 (May 26, 1662), vol. 5, p. 133 (Apr. 25, 1664), vol. 7, pp. 245–46 (Aug. 14, 1666), vol. 9, pp. 516–17 (Apr. 12, 1669); Madame van Muyden, ed., *A Foreign View of England in 1725–1729: The Letters of Monsieur César de Saussure to His Family* (1902; London, 1995), p. 174. For female boxing see also *London Journal*, June 23, 1722; Zacharias von Uffenbach, *London in 1710*, trans. W. H. Quarrell and M. Mare (London, 1934), pp. 88–91 (July 2, 1710).

46. Peter Clark, *The English Alehouse: A Social History, 1200–1830* (Harlow, Essex, 1983), pp. 206, 236; Matthews, ed., *Diary of Dudley Ryder*; Latham and Matthews, eds., *Diary of Samuel Pepys*, vol. 2, p. 220 (Nov. 25, 1661); van Muyden, ed., *A Foreign View of England*, p. 119; Hunt, *Middling Sort*, p. 127; London Metropolitan Archives, Accession 1268, depositions re death of Elizabeth Williams on Nov. 22, 1775, and DL/C/262, fol. 77 (Cowley vs. Bacon).

47. Ward, *The London Spy*, pt. 10, p. 39; London Metropolitan Archives, MJ/OC/III, fols. 41–43 (Jan. 1725/26); van Muyden, ed., *A Foreign View of England*, p. 119.

48. Latham and Matthews, eds., *Diary of Samuel Pepys*; Eliot Howard, *The Eliot Papers* (Gloucester, 1894), vol. 2, pp. 29–70; Ward, *London Spy*, pt. 2 (p. 30), pt. 4 (p. 154), pt. 10 (p. 171), pt. 12 (p. 209); Matthews, ed., *Diary of Dudley Ryder*; van Muyden, ed., *A Foreign View of England*, p. 10; *A Trip Through London: Containing Observations on Men and Things*, 8th ed. (London, 1728), p. 4; Steve Pincus, "'Coffee Politicians

Does Create': Coffeehouses and Restoration Political Culture," *Journal of Modern History* 67 (1995): 815–16.

49. Shoemaker, *Gender in English Society*, pp. 241–42.

50. Van Muyden, ed., *A Foreign View of England*, p. 129.

51. Shoemaker, *Gender in English Society*, p. 279; Matthews, ed., *Diary of Dudley Ryder*, p. 57; *Hell upon Earth; or, The Town in an Uproar* (London, 1729), p. 35; Philip Carter, "Men About Town: Representations of Foppery and Masculinity in Early Eighteenth-Century Urban Society," in H. Barker and E. Chalus, eds., *Gender in Eighteenth-Century England* (London, 1997), pp. 31–57. See also Laura Gowing, "Gender, Sex, and the 'Freedom of the Streets,'" in Paul Griffiths and Mark Jenner, eds., *Londinopolis: Essays in the Cultural and Social History of Early Modern London* (Manchester, forthcoming), for the argument that urban women's spaces were constantly colored by suspicions of female sexual immorality.

52. Lawrence E. Klein, "Gender and the Public/Private Distinction in the Eighteenth Century: Some Questions About Evidence and Analytic Procedure," *Eighteenth-Century Studies* 29 (1995): 97–109.

53. D. E. Underdown, "The Taming of the Scold: The Enforcement of Patriarchal Authority in Early Modern England," in A. Fletcher and J. Stevenson, eds., *Order and Disorder in Early Modern England* (Cambridge, 1985), pp. 116–36. This argument has been criticized in Martin Ingram, "'Scolding Women Cucked and Washed': A Crisis of Gender Relations in Early Modern England?" in J. Kermode and G. Walker, eds., *Women, Crime, and the Courts in Early Modern England* (London, 1994), pp. 48–80.

54. R. Martenson. "The Transformation of Eve: Women's Bodies, Medicine, and Culture in Early-Modern England," in R. Porter and M. Teich, eds., *Sexual Knowledge, Sexual Science: The History of Attitudes to Sexuality* (Cambridge, 1994), pp. 120–22.

55. William Gouge, *Of Domesticall Duties* (London, 1634), p. 265.

56. Leonore Davidoff and Catherine Hall, *Family Fortunes: Men and Women of the English Middle Class, 1780–1850* (London, 1987).

57. Fenela Childs, "Prescriptions for Manners in English Courtesy Literature, 1690–1760, and Their Social Implications" (Ph.D. diss., Oxford University, 1984), pp. 29–31.

Index

In this index an "f" after a number indicates a separate reference on the next page, and an "ff" indicates separate references on the next two pages. A continuous discussion over two or more pages is indicated by a span of page numbers, e.g., "57–59." *Passim* is used for a cluster of references in close but not consecutive sequence. Non-English names are treated as if they were anglicized; thus, Rice ap Owen is listed under "Owen, Rice ap."

Library of Congress Cataloging-in-Publication Data

Protestant identities : religion, society, and self-fashioning in post-
Reformation England / edited by Muriel C. McClendon, Joseph P.
Ward, Michael Macdonald.
    p.   cm.
    ISBN 0-8047-3611-1 (alk. paper)
    1. Reformation—England.   2. England—Social life and
customs—16th century.   3. England—Church history—16th century.
4. England—Social life and customs—17th century.   5. England—
Church history—17th century.   I. McClendon, Muriel C.   II. Ward,
Joseph P.   III. Macdonald, Michael

BR375.P76   1999
274.2'06—dc21   99-37228
                                                                  CIP

This book is printed on acid-free, archival-quality paper.

Original printing 1999
Last figure below indicates year of this printing:
08   07   06   05   04   03   02   01   00   99